Islam and *the* Cultural Accommodation *of* Social Change

Islam *and* *the* Cultural Accommodation *of* Social Change

Bassam Tibi

TRANSLATED BY CLARE KROJZL

Westview Press
BOULDER, SAN FRANCISCO, & OXFORD

To my beloved wife, Ulla,
my life companion and true friend

English-language edition copyright © 1990 by Westview Press, Inc. This translation has been revised and updated from the German original.

Published in 1990 in the United States of America by Westview Press, Inc., 5500 Central Avenue, Boulder, Colorado 80301, and in the United Kingdom by Westview Press, Inc., 36 Lonsdale Road, Summertown, Oxford OX2 7EW

First published in 1985 in the Federal Republic of Germany as *Der Islam und das Problem der kulturellen Bewältigung sozialen Wandels* by Suhrkamp Verlag Frankfurt am Main

Library of Congress Cataloging-in-Publication Data
Tibi, Bassam.
   [Islam und das Problem der kulturellen Bewältigung sozialen Wandels. English]
   Islam and the cultural accommodation of social change / Bassam Tibi : translated by Clare Krojzl.
      p. cm.
   Translation of: Der Islam und das Problem der kulturellen Bewältigung sozialen Wandels.
   "This translation has been revised and updated from the German original"—T.p. verso.
   Includes bibliographical references.
   ISBN 0-8133-0917-4
   1. Sociology, Islamic. 2. Islamic countries—Social conditions.
3. Islam—20th century. 4. Civilization, Islamic. I. Title.
BP173.25.T528 1990
306.6'97—dc20   90-34410
                                                      CIP

Printed and bound in the United States of America

The paper used in this publication meets the requirements of the American National Standard for Permanence of Paper for Printed Library Materials Z39.48-1984.

10   9   8   7   6   5   4   3   2   1

Contents

Preface to the U.S. Edition   vii
Acknowledgments   xi

Introduction   1

PART ONE
*What Does the Notion of Cultural Accommodation
of Social Change in Islam Mean? On the Relationship
Between Religion and Culture*   7

1   Religion as a Model for Reality and the Interaction
    Between the Two: Islam as a Cultural System   8

2   What Is Islam? Islam in the Past and Present   16

PART TWO
*Culture—A Catalyst of Change, a Reflection of Change,
or a Stumbling Block? Ascertaining the Position of Islam*   31

3   Basic Cultural Patterns for the Perception of
    Change in Islam: The Islamic Model for Reality   32

4   Culture and Social Change: Is Underdevelopment
    a Given of Cultural Tradition? The Problem of
    Cultural Innovation in Sociology   45

PART THREE
*Social Change and the Resistance of the Islamic
Sociocultural System: Law, Language, and the
Educational System*   57

5   Social Change and the Potential for Flexibility
    in the Islamic Notion of Law: The *Shari'a* as an
    "Open Texture," Legal Hermeneutics, and the
    Topics Thesis   59

6   'Arabiyya as a Sacred Language: Arabic as
    a Language Between Koranic and Historical
    Designations   76

7   Institutions of Learning and Education in Islam:
    Their Historical Contribution to the Cultural
    Accommodation of Change and Their Current State
    of Crisis   102

PART FOUR
*The Politicization of Islam as a Cultural System and
the Topicality of Islamic Revivalism: Islam Today*   119

8   A Religiosociological Interpretation of the
    Politicization of the Islamic Cultural System:
    Political Islam as a Defensive Cultural Reaction
    to Rapid Social Change   122

9   Oppositional Religiopolitical Underground
    Organizations and the Islam-legitimated
    Establishment in Egypt: The Roots of the
    Political Resurgence of Militant Islam   135

10 The Iranian Shi'ite Variant of Religiopolitical
    Revivalism: The Mullah Revolution in Iran   147

11 Islam as Legitimation for "Royal Authority":
    On the Relationship Between State, Religion, and
    Politics in the Islam-legitimated Monarchies of
    Morocco and Saudi Arabia   160

PART FIVE
*Conclusions and Future Prospects: Asymmetries in
the International Society, "Demonstration Effects,"
and Globalized Intercultural Communication as the
Structural Framework for Rapid Social Change in the
Islamic Middle East*   179

Notes   197
Selected Bibliography   243
Name Index   263
Subject Index   267

Preface to the U.S. Edition

This book was initially planned as an English translation of my
German book *Der Islam und das Problem der kulturellen Bewältigung
sozialen Wandels*. Thanks to the Harvard Center for Middle East Studies
and its director, Professor Roy Mottahedeh, who jointly with the Harvard
Center for International Affairs provided me in the academic year 1988/
89 with an affiliation as a research associate, the translation acquired
through reworking a new form and improved quality. At Harvard I had
the necessary time and research facilities to do this job in addition to
working on my chapter for *Tribes and State Formation in the Middle
East* (Philip Khoury and Joseph Kostiner, eds., 1990). I not only
thoroughly checked the translation by Dr. Clare Krojzl but also revised
the text and updated it together with the notes. In addition, I ventured
into largely rewriting and reformulating the earlier text, originally
completed in 1984 and published in German in 1985. While I was
carrying out this difficult job, Dr. Krojzl assisted me cooperatively by
integrating all my revisions and changes to the manuscript into her
translation.

The basic framework of this inquiry into Islam is the concept of
religion as a cultural system in the Geertzian sense. Religion, thus
conceptualized as a source of cultural patterns, has an intrinsically
dual aspect. The cultural patterns related to it "give meaning, that is,
objective conceptual form, to social and psychological reality both by
shaping themselves to it and by shaping it to themselves" (Clifford
Geertz, *The Interpretation of Cultures,* New York: Basic Books, 1973,
p. 93). The interplay between social and cultural change lies at the
heart of this book. This interplay cannot be grasped adequately if one
pattern of change, be it the social or the cultural, is reduced to the
other. A deeper insight into the complexity of this interplay calls for
wariness of reductionism. This book represents an effort toward that
end.

The methodological requirement for the proposed analysis having
been outlined, the focal question formulated and dealt with in Part 1
is: How do Muslims culturally accommodate the rapid and often

disruptive social change taking place in the "abode of Islam" under the present conditions of being integrated into the global society?

Part 2 is devoted to an inquiry into the interplay between social and cultural change. The extensive third part, which explores Islam as a cultural system, uses language, law, and education as examples and forms the principal part of the book. The subject of Part 4 is the politicization of the Islamic cultural system that we are witnessing today in various Islamic countries. In Part 5 I conclude with reflections on intercultural communication structures in today's world—which constitutes a global society at the level of socioeconomics, transport, and communication but not, however, at the level of its culture. There is a simultaneity of unified political and socioeconomic structures and of cultural fragmentation. I deal with the question of which models of interaction dominate current intercultural communication structures and in which direction they could develop in the future, in view of non-Western peoples' current cultural dissociation from the present global society.

This book reflects an integral part of the many years I have spent researching and studying the Islamic culture in which my own primary education took place and in relation to which, thanks to my Western academic education, I have by now acquired a discernible distance. The manuscript of the original German version took shape between spring 1983 and autumn 1984 and reached completion in October 1984. The rewriting of the book was pursued at Harvard in the spring term of 1989. In the rewritten Introduction I outline, in addition to the structural content of the book, the basic development of ideas leading from what was, seen from my present perspective, my first, "immature" book, *Die arabische Linke* (The Arab Left, 1969), through three other monographs to the present work.

Since the publication of the first U.S. and British edition of my book *Arab Nationalism* (2d ed., forthcoming, 1990), as well as *Krise des modernen Islams* (Crisis of Modern Islam, U.S. ed., 1988), both in 1981, I have had the good fortune to free myself from the confines of German scholarship and become integrated into a rather international communication network, from which this book has benefited greatly. The list of people to whom I am indebted is very long, and I have been obliged to restrict the Acknowledgments solely to those who have contributed to the book directly. Of course, any errors contained in it are my responsibility alone.

As always, my deepest gratitude goes to my beloved wife, Ulla, to whom this book is dedicated. She has had to put up with my absences during frequent research trips abroad (1980–1985) in connection with my work for this book, and she at various stages has read the manuscript critically and made helpful comments during the period when I was still working out the findings of my research in Göttingen. Fortunately Ulla was able to obtain leave and join me at Harvard during the spring term of 1989 while I was preparing this edition. It is likewise to her that I owe the profound realization that one can be an active scholar and still enjoy life.

Bassam Tibi
Harvard University
Center for Middle East Studies
Cambridge, Massachusetts

Acknowledgments

Heading the list of people to whom I owe a debt of gratitude with regard to both the German and U.S. editions of this book, aside of course from my own very dear wife, are two editors and a publisher. Friedhelm Herborth, editor of Suhrkamp Press in Frankfurt, was tireless in his encouragement of my idea to continue with the type of social theory–oriented research on Islam that is documented in my 1981 book *Krise des modernen Islams*. He also made possible the publication of the results of my work by Suhrkamp in his prestigious book series. The other editor is Barbara Ellington of Westview Press, whom I first met during the annual meeting of the Middle East Studies Association (MESA) of North America in Boston in 1986 and who later became a friend. She arranged a meeting with Fred Praeger in Washington, D.C., in January 1987 at which Fred promised to consider a U.S. edition of the book. He went on to make a commitment, during the 1988 MESA meeting in Los Angeles, for Westview Press to publish it.

The scholarly background of this book comprises three culturally different worlds: Its scope extends from Europe, in particular Germany, to the Middle East, the hub of the so-called World of Islam, as well as to North America, where I have been fortunate enough to establish most beneficial scholarly networks. Since the early 1980s my life has embraced all three worlds.

I am greatly indebted to two colleagues in Göttingen from whom I have learned a great deal: Professor Gustav Ineichen, a linguist, read the chapter on the relationship between language and social change and enriched my analysis with numerous suggestions. Professor Ralf Dreier from the law school of Göttingen read the chapter on Islamic law, urged me to undertake a further revision of the text, and enhanced my thinking with his valuable jurisprudential comments.

Among the very few German colleagues to whom I am indebted are Professor Gerhard Grohs of Mainz University and Professor Theodor Hanf of Freiburg University. Both read chapters of the book and made invaluable suggestions. After completing the revised manuscript I traveled to San Francisco to take part in the eighteenth annual MESA meeting. My mentor, colleague, and friend Reinhard Bendix arranged for me on that occasion a guest lecture on "Islam and Monarchy" at his nearby University of California at Berkeley, where I lectured on and led a discussion on the interpretation given in Chapter 11 of this book. Reinhard Bendix's monograph on Max Weber had formed part of my reading as a freshman, and his pioneering work *Kings or People* ranks among the intellectual fountainheads of this book. Before my arrival he had read the manuscript of Part 5 of this book, which contains the conclusions, and he was generous with his time in discussing my central theses with me. I am therefore grateful to him, both for his critical reading and for the conversations we had together, as these subsequently led me—after submission of the book to my publisher— at several points either to revise my ideas or to reformulate them more distinctly and precisely. In the course of Chapter 11 (Part 4) as well as in Part 5, the reader will see the extent to which I have been influenced intellectually by the work of Reinhard Bendix.

Since my first research affiliation in the United States (Harvard, 1982), I have, regrettably, grown out of the "high walls" of the German university, in which I now generally feel out of place. In the United States, I particularly and indeed enviably benefited from the customs of intercollegiate communication that are cultivated there and that are sadly lacking within German political science in its present form. I am therefore grateful to my colleagues at Harvard University (Professors S. P. Huntington and Herbert C. Kelman), at the University of Michigan, Ann Arbor (Professors Ernest McCarus, G. Windfuhr, and the late Richard Mitchell), and at Georgetown University in Washington, D.C. (Professors Barbara Stowasser and Michael C. Hudson), for the affiliations provided to me at these universities while working on this book during my 1982 sabbatical. A research grant from the Deutsche Forschungs-gemeinschaft (German Research Council) made it possible to take on these affiliations.

As acknowledged in the Preface, a further affiliation at Harvard in the academic year 1988/89 smoothed the way for the rewriting of the English translation of this book, which was first published in German in 1985. I should like to reiterate my gratitude to Professor Roy Mottahedeh for sponsoring me at Harvard. It goes without saying that my earlier terms as a research fellow at Princeton (1986/87) and as a Rockefeller Fellow at the University of Michigan, Ann Arbor (1988), contributed to widening the scope of my expertise on Islam. For this reason I am indebted to Professors Abraham Udovitch, Bernard Lewis, Charles Issawi, Carl Brown, and especially John Waterbury and Clifford Geertz of Princeton, and again to Professors Ernest McCarus and Gernot Windfuhr of Ann Arbor. Research grants from the German Research

Council and the Rockefeller Foundation are likewise gratefully acknowledged.

Although my origins lie in the Islamic Middle East and I regularly spend time there, my involvement in European and U.S. institutions of learning harbors the danger of my viewing my research topic as an outsider. Therefore the discussion and communication forum offered by the Euro-Arab Social Research Group (EASRG), an institutionalized association of European and Arab social scientists active from 1979 to 1983, was of inestimable help in keeping my perceptions in perspective. Arab social scientists working in Rabat, Tunis, or Cairo experience intercultural conflict more intensely than a friend living in an advanced industrial society. I should like to mention in particular the debates we conducted at our EASRG conferences in Marrakesh ("Patrimoine culturel et memoire collective," 1982) and in Cairo ("Cultural Identity in Time," 1983), which contributed to sharpening my views while working on this book.

Many of my research trips to the Middle East and sub-Saharan Africa were supported as lecture trips by the Goethe Institute (known in almost all parts of the world as the German Cultural Institute). Although the institute is not involved in research in terms of expertise pertaining to international cultural relations—a widely neglected field of the international relations discipline—intercultural dialogue, which is the major concern of the Goethe Institute, is undoubtedly the fieldwork of the scholar. Both in Africa and Asia, branches of the Goethe Institute have offered me invaluable lecture and discussion forums, enabling me to debate many of the theses contained in this book with people actually involved and to share my expertise with them. I am especially indebted to the respective heads of these institutes, who as a result of their work abroad are often more open-minded than their own exclusive German society.

I am grateful to Inter Nationes in Bonn for funding this translation and to my translator, Dr. Clare Krojzl, who was prepared to accept a modest, albeit augmented, grant for doing her best with the translation. Her work included the arduous task of integrating my revisions into the already-translated text. My research assistant, Dietmar Lück, assisted Dr. Krojzl by providing her with all the passages quoted from English sources in the original and by checking the translated notes section. He also assisted me in recompiling the bibliography to the book (a task that went far beyond updating the original German one insofar as it now has an entirely new form) and in preparing the index.

I cannot conclude these acknowledgments without expressing my deeply felt gratitude to my copy editor, Alice Colwell. She not only edited the manuscript in the most professional manner, but she also checked the revised translation while ably comparing the English with the German original. I am extremely grateful for her meticulous work. I am also grateful for the care my project editor, Martha Leggett, displayed during her supervision of the book's production.

B. T.

Introduction

At the center of this study lies the interpretation, developed from Clifford Geertz's anthropology of religion, that religions represent cultural systems, which are both influenced by processes of social change and are themselves able to affect them. I will proceed from this frame of reference, which will be developed in Chapter 1, and examine the concept of the cultural system in terms of its usefulness for understanding Islam and its relationship to social change. In order to clarify the methodological and conceptual framework of this study, I shall first outline the general course of my hitherto twenty years of involvement both with Islam and with the development of this work.

In my early works, my perspective in the study of Islam was solely that of a critic of ideology. Thus in my first work, *Die arabische Linke,*[1] I restricted myself to tracing historically the resistance to sociocritical, or more precisely socialist, thinking in Islam. Of course there have been social movements in Islam, as in Christianity (e.g., the Karmathians, active from the ninth century until 1030), but these were vigorously opposed by official Islam. When I published my first work, there still existed no major propensities towards a politically effective, modern social critique based on Islam, such as is being evolved by oppositional Islam-oriented movements today.

In the revised published version of my Ph.D. dissertation, "Nationalismus in der Dritten Welt am arabischen Beispiel,"[2] which has since been discovered by the Anglo-Saxon academic world and been published in an English translation,[3] I examined what has since the nineteenth century been the acute tension between Islamic universalism and modern nationalism, the latter having originated in Europe and then been taken up in the Islamic Orient, where it has become a political force to be reckoned with. The central classical Islamic category, the *umma* concept, which divides the world into the House of Islam (*dar al-Islam*) and the House of War (*dar al-harb*) has thus been partly abandoned, and partly merely opened to question. Taking up the cause of nationalism, the Young Turks began this process by providing Turanism with alleged antecedents in the spirit of the new ideology;

1

they were followed by the Arabs with the concept of *'uruba* (Arabism), which now conceded only the concept of the *umma 'arabiyya* (the Arab nation) and abandoned the *umma islamiyya* (the community of Islam). Important as that piece of research still seems to me even today, and pleased as I am at the Anglo-Saxon reception of that earlier work, it is nonetheless clear to me today that my earlier approach, based on the concept of the critique of ideology[4] and focused on the political level, needs to be amended. Islam is not only a political ideology, but also and above all a cultural system, and as such should form the focal point of analysis. Insight into this dimension of Islam compelled me to draw on cultural analysis in the chapter completed for the second edition of my book on Arab nationalism.

A similar focus, which has validity even today, on a single dimension of Islam, is apparent in my habilitation thesis, "Militär und Sozialismus in der Dritten Welt,"[5] the empirical part of which consists of case studies on the intervention of the Arab military in politics. This work was not primarily concerned with examining Islam; nevertheless because Islam, in the form of a modernist interpretation, was invoked at all by the supporters of a military regime (in the first instance by Gamal Nasser himself),[6] in order to legitimate its social policy, indeed its very right to power, forced me to undertake an analysis of Islam as an instrument for the legitimation of power.[7]

A significant turning point in the development of my ideas, which is documented in my book *Crisis of Modern Islam*,[8] was brought about by my study of Norbert Elias's magnificent work *The Civilizing Process*[9] during the second half of the 1970s. Elias enthrallingly reconstructs the European civilizing process, showing the unique character that *may* lie behind Europe's ability to conquer the whole world, and thereby unintentionally to universalize its own process of civilization.

Likewise, after the foundation of Islam as a religion, a specifically Islamic process of civilization was initiated from the seventh century onward that has to this day left traces in Asia, Africa, and parts of Europe. The European process of civilization, however, has reached a degree of universalization and globalization not yet achieved by any other civilization—not even Islam. It is no longer possible to study Islam, or any other non-Western culture, without taking into account the international society that has emerged out of that civilization process.[10] For this phenomenon I have devised the term *globalization of the civilizing process*. Elias's works, which I have studied in order better to grasp some of these connections, were and are fundamental to the development of my ideas. Just how little the fascination of Norbert Elias can be attributed merely to individual writings became clear to me with the enthusiasm of students in my graduate class on "International Politics and the Globalization of the Civilizing Process; Readings from Norbert Elias" in the summer term of 1981. At this time, as a result of the downgrading of academic training in the Federal Republic, most students were difficult to motivate and inspire. On the one hand this fascination was inspired by the reconstruction of the European civilizing process, enriched by a comparative review of the Islamic civilizing process—which Elias had unfortunately not undertaken and which we therefore took up in the graduate class. On the other hand my students and I were prompted to discussion by Elias's hypothesis that the standardization of civilization in the upper social strata of Europe has its parallel today throughout the whole world, as Europeans now constitute an "upper stratum" in relation to the non-Western peoples, in spite of the latter's own internal strata structure, which no longer corresponds to the now standardized civilization. This parallel is both interesting and at the same time problematical, although partly accurate. In Asia and Africa, for example, eating with a knife and fork and even dressing in a suit and tie at temperatures of 40°C or more are no longer considered European, but simply civilized!

In *Crisis of Modern Islam,* I established the existence of a scientific and technological age, which has been imbued by Europeans with its own specific character. The global structure, known in my discipline, international relations, as the *international system,* has been decisively affected by this. I was unable, however, to establish the existence of a corresponding global culture alongside this global entity linked together by a world order.[11] There is indeed a dominant, Western, technological- and scientific-oriented culture on which the globalization of the European process of civilization is based, but there are also many non-Western, and at the same time nonindustrial cultures that are incompatible with it. In other words, there is a simultaneity of structural unity and cultural diversity. I avoid here the term "preindustrial," which is correct in terms of content, so as to shield my line of argument from the accusation of evolutionism, a thesis to which I do not subscribe. In *Crisis of Modern Islam,* I focused on external conditioning factors, without omitting internal ones, for the crisis of this religious system was triggered by the European conquest of the world.

The focal point of this book is the Islamic cultural system in its own right, although I was not able to keep other factors from the international environment entirely out of my analysis: The researcher cannot escape reality. I have nevertheless attempted, both on the basis of my familiarity with this cultural system from the inside and with the aid of more recent social scientific theories and methods, to understand Islam as a system of cultural symbols with which Muslims

perceive reality and evolve their world view. My acknowledgment of
Clifford Geertz's anthropology of religion, which has been of great
conceptual help to me, falls within this context. Although my concern
with the elements of the Islamic cultural system (law, language,
education) considerably precedes this acknowledgment, Geertz's interpretation of religion as a cultural system (see Chapter 1) enabled
me to develop an interpretative framework into which I could integrate
the individual components of my work in a manner appropriate to the
subject.

In Part 1 of this book I develop the two central concepts of this
study, the "cultural system" and "the cultural accommodation of change"
(Chapter 1), and in a brief survey of Islam attempt to convey the extent
to which this religion does in fact represent a cultural system (Chapter
2). Part 2 is concerned with the cultural patterns (basic components),
by means of which Muslims perceive change (Chapter 3). Because I
am a social scientist and not an Orientalist in the sense defined by
the "hothouse disciplines," in this book interest in Islam is substantiated
conceptually. For this reason, a sociological discussion of "culture"
(Chapter 4) is taken up in order to ascertain whether culture is a
phenomenon that shapes a society, as is argued in cultural analysis—
or, as is asserted by some Marxists—whether it is merely a superstructure
reducible to a particular basis. At both the conceptual and the empirical
(with reference to Islam) levels, it becomes apparent that cultural
systems are created in conjunction with a process of social reproduction,
but that they themselves exert a decisive influence on the reality out
of which they emerge. It is therefore preferable for research on cultural
systems to dispense with reductionist methodology.[12] This awareness
is central to the subsequent analysis, taken up in Part 3, of the elements
of the Islamic cultural system: law (*shari'a*) (Chapter 5), language
(Chapter 6), and education (Chapter 7).

Part 4 departs from the general analytical level of the study of
Islam, offering instead case studies along the lines of the U.S. social
scientific understanding of area studies.[13] The formulation of problems
in these studies relates to the politicization of the Islamic cultural
system. Because I am unable to accept the narrow confines of purely
empirical area studies, the fourth, quasi-empirical part is introduced
by a general, both crossregional and conceptually structured interpretation based on the sociology of religion pertaining to the repoliticization
of the Islamic religiocultural system (Chapter 8). The case studies deal
with four countries: Egypt, Iran, Morocco, and Saudi Arabia—a choice
that can be justified in terms of both methodology and subject matter.
The politicization of the sacred in the Islamic Middle East began in
Egypt—not in Iran (Chapter 9). Nevertheless, it was in Iran and not

in Egypt that it developed into an Islamically legitimated revolution (Chapter 10). These circumstances—and because Egypt, with its al-Azhar University, forms the intellectual heart of Sunni Islam, whereas Iran is the stronghold of Twelver Shi'a Islam (not only on account of the university at Qum)—are the grounds for pairing Egypt and Iran. The choice of Morocco and Saudi Arabia was made not because they are both monarchies but because of the forty Islamic countries, these two are monarchies that were legitimated in the classic Islamic way. This does not mean that Islam is not invoked as a legitimating ideology by the governments of other Islamic states. But in contrast to those politicians who misuse Islam solely as an ideology to justify their own rule—for example, Muammar Qadhafi—the monarchs of Morocco and Saudi Arabia, as will be shown in the final chapter, are in keeping with tradition, both religious and political leaders, the political system hence documenting a congruence between the sacred and the political.

In making the earlier remark that Islam as a cultural system forms the focal point of this book, while at the same time asserting that a total abstraction from the global social environment of this religious system is scarcely possible, I have indicated that this study will not remain within the framework of Geertz's anthropology of religion but will attempt to go beyond it.[14] The reader will see that this applies throughout the whole of the book, although it is not brought to the point of systematic examination until the conclusions. In Part 5 I focus on the asymmetries of the current world as an international society and on the "demonstration effects" (Bendix) arising out of the "developed" models of industrial society, which find access to non-European societies in the context of globalized intercultural communication. This is the actual context in which processes of rapid social change, triggered externally and consequently disruptive, take place in today's Third World countries. The Arab Islamic concept of *mihna* has various meanings in the sense of test, crisis, or period of suffering, and it is the best expression for the situation that the Islamic cultural system has to cope with today. Is Islam enabling its faithful to accommodate culturally a *mihna* on a scale that it has never known in its history so far? What are the prospects for the future, and are they promising for Muslims, who rank among the underprivileged and deprived peoples of the world?

PART ONE

What Does the Notion of Cultural Accommodation of Social Change in Islam Mean? On the Relationship Between Religion and Culture

In this introductory part, the two central themes of this book will each be outlined in one chapter. In Chapter 1, the formulation of the question contained in the title of this study will be developed, both conceptually and with reference to Islam. Following Clifford Geertz's thesis, all religions, including Islam, are understood to be cultural systems. The categories of "religion" and "culture" will also be examined in more detail; at this point, however, we shall go beyond the social and cultural anthropological classifications of Geertz's approach, because, as we have already stated in a previous work,[1] since the time of the European penetration of the world through its colonial incursion into non-Western regions, the phenomenon of the religious as a cultural pattern can be adequately understood only in the context of the international society.

In the present period of the repoliticization of Islam, which began in the 1970s,[2] Islamic neofundamentalists, though unaware of the German theory of *Kulturganzheit* (cultural entirety), have been raising—in a similar vein—the claim that there is only *one* all-embracing culture, Islam, valid for all times, places, and peoples. In contrast to this monolithic understanding of Islam, even the uninformed traveler to some of the forty Muslim countries will have no difficulty observing just how diverse the cultures of those countries that call themselves Islamic actually are. In Chapter 2, therefore, we ask what Islam really is, if, in the Geertzian sense, we are to speak of the Islamic religion as a single cultural system.

1

Religion as a Model for Reality and the Interaction Between the Two: Islam as a Cultural System

The central hypothesis of this study is that religion consists of sociocultural symbols that convey a conception of reality and construe a plan for it. These symbols are concerned with reality but do not correspond to it, as is the case, for example, with symbols of nature. In this sense religion is understood here as a "cultural system"[1] as defined by Geertz.

There is of course an important distinction to be made between "models *of* reality" and "models *for* reality."[2] The former relate to the representation of objects, such as those in nature, whereas the latter apply to concepts of things, such as human activity. Models of reality are concrete, displaying structural congruence with the depicted object, whereas models for reality are abstract, that is, they are theories, dogmas, or doctrines for a reality with which they are not in structural congruence. On the contrary, they relate, either metaphysically or rationally, to human perceptions of reality and their character; they cannot be penetrated experimentally, only interpretatively. This is similarly the starting point of Geertz's anthropology.[3] Religions are cultural, and therefore also symbolic, systems; as models for reality, they are likewise not penetrable experimentally but only interpretatively.

In religion, human conceptions of reality are not based on knowledge but on belief in an authority, which varies from one religion to another. In the monotheistic religions this authority is God and every revelation that proceeds from Him. In the "primitive" religions,[4] it is represented by spirits and magic. Yet a process of becoming underlies every form of reality. The concepts for reality, then, undergo a parallel change: The adaptation of religiocultural concepts to changing reality thus forms a central component of the cultural assimilation of change, and of the way in which change is directed, inasmuch as people do not simply react to this process of change but also themselves direct it by means of cultural innovation. According to the orthodox Islamic conception, the revelation of the Koran, to the Prophet Muhammed, is the ultimate truth, valid for all times, all religions, and the whole of humanity.[5] Within this interpretation, the Islamic religion is unalterable and cannot be adapted to any reality, for it is itself the ultimate religion, revealed by the Seal of the Prophets (Koran: *"Khatam an-nabiyin,"* sura 33, verse 40); Muhammed is said to have proclaimed the final revelation of God. It is here that the question arises of how Muslims react to change, how they understand development and progress, or whether such concepts even existed before Islam's encounter with the West. In Islam, there is only one absolute truth, valid for all time and not at all conditioned by history. The tendency of every religion toward the Absolute is of course a universally observable phenomenon, but in Islamic theology it is manifest more intensely than in any other religion.

I have proposed the thesis that religions, as cultural systems, are in fact symbolic systems offering a way to perceive reality. If these conceptions are unalterable per se, as in the case of Islam, even though reality is changing continually, then we are bound to ask whether Islam represents an obstacle to change, as it would seem, in light of the above interpretation, to obstruct rather than facilitate the cultural reception of change. We cannot answer this question yet; some informative exploration will first be necessary. Only on the basis of this solid ground do we wish to venture an answer.[6] I may point out here, however, on the basis of comparative religious research, that the Reformation in Christianity was a process that at once both assimilated and made possible the rise of modern society. A similar substantively renewed understanding of Islam has so far not been forthcoming.

Some sociology-oriented religious researchers tend toward a reductionism that denies the partial autonomy of religions by unhesitatingly placing them as cultural systems in a virtually causal relationship with the level of development of the respective society. Religious content, always equated with cultural patterns, has, according to Geertz, a dual aspect: It conveys for its adherents meaning to current social and psychological realities, thereby acquiring "an objective conceptual form"; they are both shaped by reality and at the same time shape reality to themselves.[7] Within this preliminary interpretation, religiocultural symbols form part of reality but are not mere reflections of it, as they also affect it. It follows from this that the reduction of the position of a religion to the stage of development of a society is inadequate. Geertz calls attention to societies with comparable levels of development in which the "degree of religious articulateness"[8] is nonetheless very different. This is of course not intended to refute the notion that religious ideas can be correlated with social evolution; it is simply their reduction to a social structure that is criticized here. Every idea both "belongs to the continuity of a society and is at the same time autonomous."[9] This is especially true of religious ideas, which correlate with reality but at the same time are able to make themselves independent of it.[10] The history of Islam and Islamic ideologies offers ample material to support this statement, which reduces to absurdity the conventional superstructure-basis mode of thought.[11]

After these general remarks and the definition of a religion as a "cultural system," the categories of "culture" and "religion," which are central to this study, should now be more precisely delineated.

Both in the now more independent field of cultural science, as well as in cultural sociology and anthropology or the study of literature, the reader is faced with a veritable plethora of studies in these categories. An evaluation of this literature has become virtually a task in itself.[12] After a preliminary look through most of the available cultural analyses, however, I have no difficulty stating along with Geertz that there are ways to escape the difficulty of defining culture in "turning culture into folklore and collecting it, turning it into traits and counting it, turning it into structures and toying with it. But there are escapes." The only defense against this kind of cultural analysis, Geertz continues, is "to train such analysis on such realities and such necessities in the first place . . . to place these things in some sort of comprehensive meaningful framework"[13]—by which Geertz means the symbolic dimensions of social behavior. In those countries where there is not yet an existing sociostructural equivalent of secularization, these dimensions are articulated in a religiocultural way. In Muslim countries in particular, the "production of meaning"[14] out of which these religiocultural symbols spring is still to a large degree based on the Islamic world view. Even the world view of the secular- and Western-educated social strata of these forty countries, distributed between Asia and Africa and having a population of roughly 800 million, still has its roots in the Islamic world view.[15] Existing Western approaches to the sociology of religion contribute little to an understanding of this phenomenon. Apart from a few exceptions (for example, Niklas Luhmann), it consists of a repertoire of already somewhat hackneyed conceptual forms, borrowed from Max Weber and Emile Durkheim among others, which are of only limited use in trying to penetrate the subject at hand.[16]

Geertz's attempt, in the context of his interpretative anthropology, to conceive of religion as a system consisting of symbols that convey meaning, would seem to be of use here. According to Geertz, a religion is "[1] a system of symbols which acts to [2] establish powerful, pervasive and long-lasting moods and motivations in men [3] by formulating concepts of a general order of being and [4] clothing these concepts with such an aura of factuality that [5] the moods and motivations seem uniquely realistic."[17] Let us now unravel this comprehensive definition into its individual components and attempt in the process to ascertain the validity of the statements made in it for our analysis of Islam as a cultural system.

First, religion is described as a system of symbols, the prevailing symbols interfusing to form cultural patterns, which in turn constitute models. It is important here to call to mind the difference between "models of reality" and "models for reality." The former relate to objects they depict, making it important to distinguish between symbols and objects. "Models of reality" thus consist of symbols that correspond to real objects, whereas "models for reality" convey concepts or doctrines for reality. In this sense, a religion is a model *for* reality and not a model *of* it; religion has a dual character. It is now easier to understand, but for this reason it can only be comprehended adequately in an interpretative way.

If I take this suggested procedural method as my starting point, adequate for the study of my theme, I should point out, with regard to German Islamic studies in particular, that by "interpretative method" I mean one representing the social facts of reality—the *fait social* in the Durkheimian sense—and not the relevant text. German Islamic studies, in contrast to anthropological Islamic studies in the United States, as represented by Geertz[18] and Dale Eickelman[19] consist mainly of researching sources, that is, the quotation and interpretation of texts as a means of comprehending reality. Reality as such does not form the focus of interest. "Critical text analysis" thus does not differ in method from the procedure of Islamic fundamentalists, differing at most only in its intention to comprehend reality in a scholarly way, whereas fundamentalists perceive the concept of reality contained in the texts and reality itself as one and the same thing. Reality is measured by the model *for* it that is documented in the text. Religious symbols thus, for example, shape the conception of the unified Islamic community (*umma*), which has never had an objective equivalent, the objective reality always having been the cultural diversity within Islam. Even the open-minded Islamic scholar Gerhard Endress (University of Bochum) falls prey to this error, stating that this albeit symbolically characterized but nonexistent entity, the *umma,* was not destroyed until the impact of Western influences, the manifold changes brought about by "industrialization, the division of labor and mobility" *no longer permitting* an *all-embracing* definition of "Muslim society."[20] Endress insists on retaining this method of "textual deduction and source criticism" as an instrument for the study of Islam, responding to the call for more attention to social science methods with the polemic, "And anyone who cannot read the sources will often have to make do with half-measures and half-truths."[21] Of course it is important to read religious scripture—not in order to stop at source criticism, however, but rather to observe how people perceive these texts and how they create their religiocultural symbols in this context, so as better to understand the Islam of today as a social reality and a cultural system. As is widely known, the majority of Muslims are illiterate, which means that they are acquainted with the content of these texts (in the first instance the Koran and Hadith, the sayings of the Prophet) only in the form of oral tradition—which changes with history and cultural development.

According to Geertz, the symbols for reality that are offered by a religion as a cultural system produce pervasive and long-lasting motivations that cause people to act. These actions should be in harmony with religious scripture, but in reality they are not so. With regard to Islam, I can cite here the example of the strict proscription on interest charges Muslims accepted subjectively in the Middle Ages, although their actions objectively contravened this proscription. At that time, what were known as *hiyal* (legal dodges and tricks) were developed to enable people to circumvent the proscription on interest and at the same time to spare the consciences of the pious Muslims.[22] Geertz's interpretation of the motivations and moods evoked by a particular symbolic system is able to explain this circumstance fully: "To be pious is not to be performing something we would call an act of piety, but to be liable to perform such acts."[23] It thus becomes clear that interpretative anthropologists will not be able to find piety in the form of motivation and mood by looking for their literary sources in religious texts, although they must be acquainted with these; their task consists rather in understanding the perception and practice of religious scripture—which are considered Islamic by those concerned, although they vary to a great extent in practice—in the prevailing historically and culturally diverse situations.

The third part of Geertz's interpretation rests on the assumption that religion as a cultural system contains concepts of a general order of existence that are essential to the believers of a particular religious community. Geertz regards the existence of concepts of order in religious symbols as their life force. In this respect, "man depends upon symbols and symbol systems with a dependence so great as to be decisive for his creatural viability."[24] The "disquieting sense that one's moral insight is unequal to one's moral experience"[25] is present in all religions and can bring about a crisis. The crossregional resurgence of orthodox or neofundamentalist Islam is very closely linked to a growing consciousness of the discrepancy between moral insight (internalized symbol) and moral experience.[26]

Taking Egypt as an example, I shall show in Chapter 9, on the basis both of my own observations and research and that of Egyptian colleagues working on this problem, that militant neofundamentalists in Cairo are of rural origin and have been living in urban centers only for a short time. Unable to reconcile their symbols with experienced reality,[27] they rebel, in the belief that they can reshape that disturbing reality through the medium of their political militancy, so as to make it compatible with their religious symbols. Like all developing countries, Egypt is one in which indigenous structures are disintegrating as a result of exogenously induced influences (integration into the international society and its structures). The unorganic and rapid urbanization process is only one example of this. Only in this sense—that is, not in the sense of the evolutionist argumentation of modernization theory (from traditionality to modernity) can these societies be defined as transitional. The meaning and role of religious symbols increases in just such transitional social conditions. Luhmann has provided an approach that follows from this: According to his interpretation, those involved are unable to determine this "transitional situation." The recourse to religious symbols, which in this case are also politicized, is intended to assist in this process: "That which is to form the transition is 'both-and' or 'either-or'—moreover both at the same time! Its identity becomes unclear and indeterminable. This situation renders the problem of determining the indeterminable one of some urgency."[28] To use Geertz's terms, it is a question of understanding the conditions in which the need arises for bridging the gap between moral insight (symbol) and moral experience. This leads us to the fourth part of Geertz's line of argument.

According to Geertz's thesis, religious symbolic systems are aimed at clothing reality with "an aura of factuality." A religious person who senses a gulf between reality and concept experiences this as chaos. There is an internal struggle to restore the order of being of the religious symbolic system, now felt to be under threat. He does not attempt to understand the causes of this "chaos"; to return to the title of this study, he is not able to accommodate culturally the change that has taken place. Geertz emphasizes here "that religious belief involves not a Baconian induction from everyday experience—for then we should all be agnostics—but rather a prior acceptance of authority which transforms that experience."[29] For the religious person, the watchword is "commitment, rather than analysis, encounter."[30] The religious perspective in the perception of reality thus differs both from common sense and from the scientific perspective. It differs from the former in that it "moves beyond the realities of everyday life to wider ones which correct and complete them"; and it differs from the latter in that "it moves beyond the realities of everyday life . . . not out of an institutionalized scepticism . . . , but in terms of what it takes to be wider, nonhypothetical truths."[31]

This part of Geertz's line of argument, more than virtually any other approach, has the capacity of explaining the contemporary situation in Islam. It is written in the Koran that Muslims are the best *umma* (community) ever created by God on earth. The discrepancy between the religiocultural symbol of the *umma* and reality creates unease; the environment is perceived as chaos. The symbol is clothed in an aura of factuality, which is at the same time perceived by those involved as a call to political militancy.

In the final link in his chain of definition, however, Geertz recognizes that the feeling of "chaos" is not the general rule. The moods and motivations produced by symbols appear to correspond to existing reality by being adapted to it.

These symbols are not only of a general nature in the sense of ideals (for example, the ideal of the Islamic *umma*), but are also specific. It is precisely here that the significance of religion lies—"in its capacity to serve, for an individual or for a group, as a source of general, yet distinctive, conceptions of the world, the self, and the relations between them. . . . Religious concepts spread beyond their specifically metaphysical contexts to provide a framework of general ideas in terms of which a wide range of experience—intellectual, emotional, moral—can be given meaningful form."[32]

The metaphysical doctrines of Islam do not form the focus of attention in this analysis, which is where I diverge from the scholar of religion. Derivation from sources in the sphere of religious scripture is not the aim of this study either; I am familiar with these scriptures but am more interested in the perception of reality than in exegesis. This explains the point of divergence with the traditional Islamic scholar and the Orientalist. Similarly, it is not the aim of this book to provide an ethnographic description of contemporary Muslim societies. This is the point of divergence with the ethnologist. The focus of attention in this study is rather what Geertz calls "systems of meaning" and the way in which these are socially produced. My interest therefore centers on the social contingency of the production of meaning in Muslim societies. The theme of the following chapters, the conflict between believed symbols and experienced reality in contemporary Muslim societies, will be dealt with both at the *general level,* by means of a discussion of how Muslims understand change and how they seek to come to terms with it or cope with it, and at the specific level, in the context of examples and case studies.

A recurring question throughout the study will be that raised in the introduction, whether Islam as a cultural system demands absoluteness and nontemporality, and is therefore hostile to history and an impediment to change, or whether Muslims have developed their own ways of circumventing this absoluteness in their daily practice, without ceasing to believe in it. We have learned from Geertz that the moods and motivations produced by the religious symbolic system "appear to correspond fully with reality." This question must be asked in the interest of scholarly integrity. The thesis very open-mindedly developed so far by critics of Orientalism, such as Maxime Rodinson[33] and Edward Said,[34] which denounces the cliché of *homo islamicus* as the alleged cause of the backwardness of the Orient, asserting instead that sociohistorical and socioeconomic factors, not Islam itself, have characterized change so far, no longer seems adequate today. This study rests on the assumption that religious symbols—as ingredients of religion in its capacity as a cultural system—are influenced by reality, but that these symbols are themselves able, by means of appropriate human actions, to shape reality. The assertion that Islam is a reflex, a reflection, or merely a form of articulation, was once important in the Orientalism debate[35] but is now no longer in keeping with the current state of social scientific research into the role of religion in the process of social change. For this reason, an ethically committed scholar in search of truth cannot omit the question of the part played by Islam—as a cultural system—in existing structures.

This introductory chapter, however, also calls for an explanation of what Islam in fact is. On the one hand there is in reality the religious, political, cultural, and other diversity in this religion perceived by journalists who lack the necessary specialist knowledge as the "Muslim world," thus reducing it to a coherent entity and a world of its own. On the other hand, we can observe parallel to this real diversity repeated ideological attempts on the part of contemporary exponents of militant Islam to lay claim to the *Kulturganzheit* of Islam, the political and cultural entirety of this religion, and to take action to achieve this. This creates confusion and brings about a need to know what Islam in fact is. An attempt to meet this need is made in Chapter 2.

2

What Is Islam? Islam in the Past and Present

During a discussion with Senegalese writers and Arab diplomats in summer 1982 in Dakar, a heated argument arose as to whether drumming could be recognized as an Islamic ritual and whether belief in magic was at all admissible in Islam. For the Senegalese neither of these questions is controversial because drumming and magic both form part of their culture; Arab participants, however, rejected both these phenomena on the grounds that they were "un-Islamic."[1] On another occasion, at an international philosophical conference in November 1979, an Indonesian scholar of religion, Mukti Ali, lectured on the Indonesian conception of Islam; his remarks provoked discord among professors of al-Azhar University (the oldest Islamic university) because for them there is only one monolithic Islam, based on their own Arabocentric preconception.[2]

An orthodox Muslim would answer the question of what Islam is by saying simply that Islam consists of the commandments set forth in the Koran and the Hadith traditions of the Prophet Muhammed, as well as of the five pillars; the *shahada* (acknowledgment of the oneness of God and the prophecy of Muhammed); prayer, or *salat* (five times a day); fasting, or *siyam* (in the month of Ramadan); the payment of *zakat* (alms or gifts to the poor); and finally the *Hadj* (the pilgrimage to Mecca). Clearly, this simple interpretation of Islam is shared by all Muslims and forms the Islamic consensus.[3]

Religion, however, is also a social reality, consisting of a symbolic system that is culturally variable and which changes historically. The Koran does in fact recognize the existence of different peoples, as indicated in sura 49, verse 13: "And we have created you in peoples and tribes, so that you may come to know one another."[4] In other verses of the Koran, however, a special position, arising out of the revelation of the Koran in Arabic, may be derived for the Arabs,[5] which explains the dominant Arabocentric notion of Islam. Even a non-Arabic-speaking Turk, Indonesian, or other Muslim may practice religious rituals only in Arabic, for according to the Koran *'arabiyya* is the language of the Koran. Similarly, non-Arabs must Arabize their names when they convert to Islam, as only Arab names are recognized as Islamic. We shall be dealing with Koranic Arabic in a separate section of this study. There are two important questions. What is Islam? How can the affirmation that there is only one Islam be understood in view of the diversity that exists in reality? The assertion of a monolithic Islam appears to be contradicted not only by cultural diversity, but also by the variety of political structures (monarchy in Saudi Arabia and Morocco, republic in Algeria, autocracy in Libya, the populist government in Iran, and even the ethnic ideology of Muslim Malayans against Hindus and Chinese in Malaysia, among others).

Like other monotheistic religions, Islam is universalist. In the course of its dissemination it has been professed by many non-Arab and non-Arabized peoples of Africa and Asia. The study of Islamic religious history shows, however, that Islam developed out of a historical imperative according to an Arab ideology, and that it fulfilled that imperative historically.[6] In its Sunni form, Islam remains an Arab ideology to this day. The Iranian variant of this religion, Shi'a Islam, deviates substantially from the original form; Shi'a Islam, in the Persian form it has acquired in the course of history, is a variety of its own and is no longer equitable with orthodox, Sunni Arab Islam.

During the historical epoch in which Islam came into existence, the civilized world consisted of two empires: the one of Persian Sassanids and the other of Roman Byzantines. The Arabs of the sixth century were not among the civilized peoples; they were bedouin and camelherds who made a living by raiding merchant caravans and, to some extent, by trade. The bedouin would have been unable to produce a materially developed culture. The mercantile Quraish tribe, which dominated the merchant city of Mecca where Muhammed also began his activities and from where Islam was first proclaimed, belonged to a tradition that may be termed mercantile-urban; prior to the foundation of the Islamic religion, that tradition did not exert a decisive influence on the dominant Arab cultural patterns, which were bedouin. Islam transformed a hitherto predominantly bedouin Arab culture into an urban phenomenon. The pre-Islamic Arabs were likewise familiar neither with a state tradition nor, therefore, with central power structures of their own. Wherever they created states the people became vassals. Byzantium had its vassaldom of the Ghassanids, and the Persian Sassanids had in the Lachmid dynasty their own Arab satellite state. The Byzantines and Sassanids fought each other using Ghassanid and Lachmid Arab soldiers.

The pre-Islamic Arabs were polytheists. They could observe that Jewish and Christian monotheists had their own omnipotent deity. Jews and Christians, moreover, despised the Arabs and regarded them as heathens, an attitude that was to persist into the period after the founding of the Islamic religion and which was to play a special role in the Christian anti-Islam polemics of the Middle Ages.[7]

This then was the historical context in which a small religious sect emerged, founded by Muhammed, and soon developed into a worldwide movement. Muhammed's small religious sect formed the core of an empire and of a major world culture, as I have shown in my book *Crisis of Modern Islam*. It follows from this that the formation of a central power structure in Arabia is to be interpreted in the context of the foundation of Islam as a religion, and within the conceptual framework used by Elias as the Islamic variant in the *process of civilization*.[8]

Muhammed,[9] who called himself the Prophet of Allah, thus conceiving himself as God's messenger, was an Arab of the Quraish tribe. In 610 he proclaimed the Islamic revelation in Mecca, founding a small sect with whom he fled to Medina in 622 (the *Hijra*, or exodus, which marks the beginning of the Muslim era). In Medina he founded the first Islamic city-state, out of which an empire developed in the same century. In 630 he conquered Mecca, and in 632 he died. The period from 610 to 632 marks the foundation of Islam as a religion. After Muhammed's death, his successors (the caliphs) ruled; they were also Quraishi, of the tribe of the Prophet. After the murder of 'Uthman the Quraishi, the third successor of Muhammed, opponents of the Quraish tribe disputed the tenets that the caliph had to be of that tribe and that blood relationship with the Prophet, whose many wives had not all been Quraishi, should be the criterion for the succession. The murderers of the third caliph proclaimed the Prophet's son-in-law Ali as successor. Ali, who in fact was of the Quraish, was himself later murdered by a member of the Kharijite (seceders) sect for having entered into a compromise with the Quraishis. The latter were victorious in this conflict, their leaders founding the Umayyad dynasty (661–750), of which Damascus became the capital. This set the seal on the schism between Sunna and Shi'a in Islam.[10]

The establishment of the dynastic principle had the effect of anchoring orthodox Islam in the form of Sunni legitimacy and the religion of the urban Quraishi Arabs, usurping it from Arabs in their capacity simply as representatives of the dynasty. Opponents of Arab hegemony, the supporters of Ali, adopted the imam principle in opposition to the caliph principle. Shi'a Islam emerged out of this conflict;[11] understandably, Shi'a Islam was to find its greatest response among non-Arabs in the later course of the religion's development. Iran is the home of sectarian, Shi'a Islam, which is implicitly in conflict with Arab, Sunni Islam, however much rhetoric there may be about the indivisible unity of the Islamic *umma*. The murdered Caliph Ali, who was the fourth and last nondynastic caliph, is regarded in Shi'a Islam as the father of the imams; his two sons, Hassan and Hussain, were the two main imams in the Shi'a tradition. Hassan died young and Hussain was killed by the 'Umayyads during an armed uprising against them. Shi'ites have mourned the death of the martyr Hussain, killed by the Arab-Sunni 'Umayyads, since that year. "Annually, at the festival of Ashura, this classical Islamic festival of the dead, which takes on a special character with them, he is commemorated. Traditional Persian theater venues stage the drama and inspire an astonishing paroxysm of popular emotion."[12] It is interesting to point out here the topicality of this "popular emotion." In December 1978 the then Persian military government wanted to ban these religious mourning ceremonies, fearing that they could develop into protest demonstrations against the shah. But these processions have been taking place for centuries, and public pressure forced the military government to lift its ban. This marked the beginning of the collapse of the shah's regime.

Shi'ite means partisan; Shi'ites are partisans of Ali, in revolt against the Sunni, the orthodox Islam of Quraish (even though Ali himself was a Quraishi). In the course of Islamic history, Shi'a Islam became Iranian Islam despite the existence of Arab Shi'ites, among other places, in Lebanon and Iraq. The annual processions to commemorate the death of Imam Hussain perpetuate the tradition of pre-Islamic Persian theater. It is important to note that the ethnic conflict between the Arabs and the *mawalis* (non-Arab Muslims) was not itself the origin of the Islamic schism between Sunna and Shi'a. Rather, this ethnic conflict deepened the schism in the course of history.

In the middle of the eighth century, the Umayyad dynasty came to a bloody end with the founding in 750 of the second Arab dynasty, the capital of which was this time not Damascus but Baghdad. The Abbasid empire marked the zenith of Islam's development,[13] disintegrating into particularism and finally coming to an end in 1258. The particularism persisted until the fourteenth century, when the Ottoman Turks began their military conquests, at first restricted to Asia Minor, but by the sixteenth century covering the entire Arab-speaking world (excluding Morocco) in the Ottoman Empire they founded. The Ottoman Empire was Islamic, but no longer Arab. The Arab Middle East stagnated under Ottoman rule, relegated to the status of an Ottoman province. Iran did not belong to the Ottoman Empire: The Iranians established their own empires—the Safavid (1501–1722) and the Qajar (1796–1925).

The Ottoman Turks likewise invoked Sunni Islam as a legitimating ideology for their empire, even though they were not Arabs. They had court historians contrive a genealogy dating back to the Prophet Muhammed; they similarly asserted that the last surviving Arab caliph of the Abbasids, al-Mutawakkil, who had governed a "false caliphate" in Egypt, had passed on the caliphate to the Ottoman sultan Selim I when the latter conquered Egypt in 1517.

During its Ottoman phase, Islamic history in Europe became identified with the Turks, as Maxime Rodinson documents in his periodic division of this history of the East-West encounter.[14] This encounter is a very old one; with the foundation of the Islamic religion it was to develop into a centuries-long conflict that still continues.[15] The latest form of this "encounter" is the European colonial conquest of the Muslim world. Since this time Islam can no longer be adequately understood without reference to the existential challenge posed by Europe. This challenge is the common denominator of all modern tendencies in Islam but does nothing to resolve its historically evolved cultural and political diversity. This historical development was initiated by Napoleon's Egyptian campaign in 1798; Islam once again became a political ideology of the Arabs.[16]

Even before Napoleon's Egyptian campaign and the ensuing monumental reforms of Muhammed Ali produced an Arab, European bourgeois–educated generation of intellectuals on the Arabian peninsula (where Ottoman rule had never managed to gain a firm foothold), there had already been systematic tendencies toward a revival of the "original" form of Islam of the Arabs. These potentially nationalistic aspirations were directed against Ottoman foreign rule, and found politicoreligious expression in the Wahhabi movement, which dates back to the orthodox-educated Muslim Muhammed Ibn Abd al-Wahhab (1703–1791). On his travels in Ottoman-ruled regions of Asia, he believed that he had observed a deviation from the original Islam, and he regarded it as his mission to lead Muslims back to genuine, orthodox Islam.

Ibn Abd al-Wahhab did not question the autocratic, despotic style of Ottoman rule; he criticized only their debauched governance. According to Wahhab, the puritanical "original" Islam could only be revitalized by the Arabs, and he took it upon himself to mobilize Muslims for this backward-looking utopia. For him, true Islam was the original Islam of the Prophet Muhammed's generation; he thereby designated the Arabs as the legitimate guardians of Islam, disputing the lawfulness of Ottoman rule. The Orientalist R. Hartmann emphasizes that the "Wahhabi movement as a religious movement is nothing more than a natural reaction to the adaptation of Islam to complex cultural circumstances, which had clearly also led to a weakening of the core ideas of the religion's founder and which denoted a process of Westernization—a reaction, based on the most conservative of the four Sunni rites, that of Ahmad b. Hanbal, that is to be understood in terms of the social conditions prevailing in Arabia, which had hardly altered in any substantial way since the time of the Prophet."[17]

Islamic modernism was a revitalizing movement of a different tendency from that of the Wahhabis. Although both movements aimed at a revival of Islam, their concepts of the form that this revival should take were radically different. Islamic modernism, in its initial stages, was a primarily intellectual movement, for which civilization was not so much a target for attack as an element of the postulated renaissance. Islamic modernists, therefore, did not try to turn Islam toward an archaic doctrine; they tried instead to adapt it to the modern age by enriching it with those findings of the rational European sciences that did not open its substance to question.

The modern variety of Islamic revivalism, which sprang up in the nineteenth century, was the brainchild of Jemaladdin Afghani (1839–1897) and his pupil and friend Muhammed Abduh (1849–1905). Confronted with Europe as a colonial power, they adopted a tough position toward it. In their writings, Islam acquires the character of an anti-colonial ideology calling for political action against Europe.[18] This dimension of their thought is frequently, and with justification, referred to in the literature, although with very crude emphasis. In fact, neither Afghani nor Abduh had closed minds as far as Europe was concerned; they were nevertheless only prepared to adopt elements of bourgeois civilization and culture insofar as these would be able to strengthen Islam against Europe.

Roughly expressed, contemporary tendencies in Islam can still be traced back to these two components: the archaic, static interpretation of Islam that sees every innovation as a threat to its own existential frame of reference, and the modern-tinged concept of Islam, which interprets innovations, not always intentionally adopted from industrial societies, as authentically Islamic, adoption being understood as an act of retrieval. At a seminar on "Modern Management" I led in Cairo, Islamic modernists argued in all seriousness that the first concept of management is to be found in the Koran, and that the United States adopted it from there.[19] The Islamic fundamentalism of today differs from Islamic modernism of the nineteenth century not only in its fanaticized religiocultural exclusivity, but chiefly in that it no longer

seeks to achieve a conscious synthesis of Islam with the modern, as
Muhammed Abduh once tried to do.[20]

Over and above the archaic and modernist concepts of Islam,
since the turn of the century there have also been movements toward
a secularization of Islam. These are currently taboo, however; it arouses
great agitation if a Muslim so much as mentions secularization in
public.[21]

Nevertheless, taken as a whole, all these religiointellectual tendencies in modern Islam—archaic fundamentalism (Wahhabism), modernism (Afghani and Abduh, or later the integrist Muslim Brothers),
and secularism—are largely the preoccupation of the educated classes,
who form only a tiny minority of the Muslims living today, albeit
representing the "opinion leaders." If we depart from the level of
analysis concerned with religio-intellectual concepts and turn instead
to the question of how the majority of Muslims perceive the world
around them, that is, phrasing the question of the Islamic world view
in this way, it then becomes necessary to proceed to the matter of
popular Islam. We shall be seeing in this part of the study how the
daily language of Muslims is pervaded by popular religious concepts,
before undertaking later in a separate section a general examination
of the question of language in the Islamic Middle East. It is nevertheless
important before moving on to explain the concept of cultural diversity
in Islam, after having acquainted ourselves with an outline of the
historical development of Islam during the last thirteen centuries.

Using the example of the Sunni-Shi'a schism in Islam, which was
at first of a religiopolitical although not yet of an ethnic or cultural
nature, we have seen how out of this schism in the course of Islamic
history two culturally distinct interpretations of Islam, an Arab and a
Persian, took shape. Although there are Arab Shi'ites, *Shi'a Islam is
regarded by Arabs as a Persian religion.*[22] This division of Islam along
Arab and Persian lines was not the last of its kind, however, as Islam
was also adopted by many other peoples in Asia and Africa. We can
thus observe, among others, the many variants of Indo-Islam, to which
the Harvard scholar Annemarie Schimmel[23] is devoting her life's work,
as well as the equally numerous variants of African Islam, of which
the Senegalese variety has already been offered above as an example.
Islam as a cultural system has been adopted by non-Arabs and integrated
into non-Islamic, indigenous, previously existing symbolic systems. It
goes without saying that the resulting religiocultural synthesis is different
in each case, which totally contradicts the fundamentalist orthodox
concept of the timeless cultural entirety of Islam.[24] This tension between
the sacred concept of reality and reality itself is reflected in the tension
between legal and popular Islam. The former is the source of the legal

provisions, of the model for reality; the latter is Islam in practice.[25] In the mind of the average Muslim, however, this tension does not exist, and most Muslims believe that they live in accordance with Islamic law. A U.S. colleague, John Waterbury, who conducted fieldwork in Morocco, learned in the course of his stay to focus his observations on what Moroccans *really* did, and not on what they thought or said they did.[26] This observation, which I have also made repeatedly in my own research in various regions, moves us toward the hypothesis that Muslims do not consciously face the question of coping with social change, and indeed that they do not ask the question at all, although it directly affects their everyday life.

The tension between model and reality in Islam is made substantially clearer with the example of the tension between the Islamic *shari'a* (divine law), with which we shall be more closely concerned in Chapter 5, and Islamic mysticism (Sufi Islam). In Islamic history, Islamic mysticism represents a not always conscious attempt to undermine the dogmatic edifice of legal Islam (*shari'a* Islam). It achieves this on the one hand by seeking to expand the room for maneuver in the relationship between God and man, and on the other by incorporating spiritualizing elements into Islam. The late British scholar of Islam, R. A. Nicholson, was one of the few leading internationally-recognized experts on Sufi Islam. His working method is philological and narrative-historical, a method that is very important for the study of texts but that can nevertheless only produce work of a preliminary nature. Nicholson's work does not contribute to a comprehensive understanding of Sufi Islam as a historical religious phenomenon. This, to reiterate, is the central weakness of an Islamic scholarship devoid of conceptual content, unable to go beyond the study of sources and text analysis. Because we are concerned here with the contribution of Sufi Islam toward a redefinition of Islam, I shall only cite a few results of Nicholson's research, from which it is possible to derive some general observations. First of all, the distinction between *shari'a* and *tariqa* (literally, the way, the method) is a substantial one. Nicholson translates *tariqa* as "the Path of Sufism,"[27] thereby expressing the basic theological position of the Muslim mystic, according to which there are many different ways (hence the word, *tariqa*) to God. The Islam of the *shari'a*, on the other hand, recognizes only one way; the Koran is the sole authoritative source describing that way. Against this, the Muslim mystic Abu Sa'd, whose life and work are the focal point of Nicholson's research, argues, "Innumerable are the ways to God."[28] Abu Sa'd furthermore teaches, in contrast to the Islamic jurists, that God cannot be experienced intellectually but only spiritually. God is everywhere, says another mystic, Jili, and can therefore be experienced everywhere by the believer.

This doctrine drifted, as Nicholson shows, "far away from Koranic monotheism into pantheistic and monistic philosophies. The Sufi reciting the Koran in ecstatic prayer and seeming to hear, in the words which he intoned, not his own voice but the voice of God speaking through him, could no longer acquiesce in the orthodox conception of Allah as a Being utterly different from all other beings."[29] Not only does this position lead to pantheism, it also increases the human room for maneuver in the relationship between God and man, since man can take the initiative in the relationship to God. In the view of Muslim orthodoxy, this is *kufr,* heresy. The most important Muslim mystic, Hallaj, who declared consistently: "I saw my Lord with my heart's eye and said: Who art Thou? He said 'Thou,'"[30] met his end at the gallows.

We know from scholarly research into Sufi Islam as a mystical tradition that Sufism represents the religious philosophy of popular religion in Islam.[31] This Islamic tradition is invoked today by Islamic authors who are strictly rational and anything but mystics, on the one hand to point out ways toward a possible diversity in Islam itself (*tariqa*), and on the other to call to mind the Sufi concept of *batiniyya* (inwardness) in a discussion of the secularization of Islam.[32] Within this tradition, Islam could be construed as an over-spiritualizing religiosity or ethic and no longer as the ideology of a theocratic order.

In its popular form, Islam is a modified version of *tariqa* Islam, and was initially disseminated in this form outside the Arab region. There are numerous variants (African, Persian, Malaysian, and so on), each of which documents a fusion between Islam and a non-Islamic, indigenous culture. Legal Islam calls for the unified validity of the *shari'a,* whereas *tariqa* Islam permits numerous different ways to God, in other words, diversity.

This distinction explains the adoption of *tariqa* Islam by non-Arab cultures. This does not mean, of course, that the *shari'a* is rejected; it is also adopted, but remains on the surface as a formal, although *not formalized* sacral law, whereas *tariqa* Islam, based on the Sufi tradition, is fully integrated.

The Islamization of Africa is one of the best examples for illustrating the internal cultural differentiation of Islam. A central question here is whether Islam only found access to Africa as a popular religious form of worship. Islamic civilization remained outside the boundaries of black Africa; Africa did not adopt Islamic culture *in toto.* Islamic culture was based on an urban civilization; at that time, however, there were few urban centers in Africa. There are seven Islamic cultural zones in Africa, of which two are Arab or Arabized (Egypt and the Maghreb). The remainder comprise West, Central, and East Africa, as well as Nilotic Sudan and northeast Ethiopia.[33] The cradle of the popular religious forms of Islam in Africa was the Maghreb, where the Islamization and even more extensive Arabization of the Berbers took place. (Egypt already had an urban culture by the time the Arabs came.) Islam "came to be seen as a cultural element which could be assumed as additional to Berber custom, without displacing it."[34] It was in the Maghreb that religious brotherhoods[35] flourished, arising partly out of the Arab East (the *qadiriyya*), or else founded in North Africa itself (the *tijaniyya*). Of the four Islamic legal schools, the legal and religious internal differentiation of Sunni Islam into the Maliki school was adopted in the Maghreb, from where it spread throughout Africa. It was Sufi Islam as a popular religion, however, that "introduced into the rigid formalism of Maliki Islam aspirations towards personal spiritual growth and union with God through mystical ecstasy"[36] and that enabled Islam to become rooted there. As regards black Africa, this meant the emergence of an Afro-Islamic version of Islam. The spread of Islam in Africa was based primarily on "a fusion in life but not a true synthesis, the unyielding nature of the Islamic institutions precluding this. . . . There is, therefore, an ultimate dualism in life, since this rests upon a double foundation."[37] The separation of the sexes during rituals may be cited as an example. Because women are not permitted to pray beside men, African women remain bound up in animism, their Muslim menfolk carrying out the collective Friday prayer at the mosque. This explains why the cultivation and retention of non- or pre-Islamic cultural forms is predominantly the preserve of women, even in the most profoundly Muslim societies, and therefore not only in black Africa (for example, the pilgrimages to the "saints" in Morocco). According to the findings of J. Spencer Trimingham's research, African Islam simultaneously embraces three spheres of belief: (1) Islam in the strict sense, or the *shari'a;* (2) the African forms of animism; and (3) soothsaying and magic.[38] The African *marabouts,* who in the absence of a priesthood in Islamic doctrine represent a functional equivalent in African Islam, are not only priests, but also magicians and soothsayers, thereby retaining numerous magical forms of pre-Islamic African cultures. According to the Maghreb tradition, the Muslim priest or chief has the authority to bestow divine blessing (*baraka*). Islamic ideology admits of no priests; therefore there can be no clergy in Islam. In reality, however, there are functional equivalents for them. In Africa, *marabouts* are Muslim priests.[39] In addition to the *marabout* order, in African Islam there is also the position of the *wali* (saint), who is said at one time to have worked miracles and whose grave pilgrims visit to ask for his blessing. *Shari'a* Islam rejects this as superstition, recognizing only the pilgrimage to Mecca. In North Africa there is an abundance of such graves, to which predominantly women make pilgrimages.[40]

In practice, *shari'a* Islam in Africa can only be observed in the urban centers of Islamic regions, although formally it applies everywhere. In practical terms, the *shari'a* in Africa has permitted the indigenous culture to persist, so long as it does not threaten conflict. The dominant form of law is consequently what Africanists call the Islamic variant of customary law, in which elements of Islamic law, though not taken literally, are fused with pre-Islamic, animist habits and customs.[41] The oil-producing Arab countries, above all Saudi Arabia, are trying today, through their development aid to Africa, to strengthen the position of *shari'a* Islam; even the awarding of student grants to Africans (at Medina University, for example) serves to suppress *tariqa* Islam, in its specifically African form, through the medium of orthodox Islam.

In the debate on African Islam, the thesis has admittedly been put forward that legal Islam (*shari'a* Islam) takes a primarily Arab form, whereas popular Islam (*tariqa* Islam) has adopted non-Arab forms. This thesis cannot be held as absolute, however, for even in the Arab cultural sphere there are an incalculable number of variants of popular Islam. The Islam of everyday life differs in some respects from that of the *ulema,* who see themselves as the guardians of legal Islam.

Everyday language constitutes the medium of popular Islam. We know, not only from the philological research of M. Piamenta on the forms Islam takes in daily life, that the most common and central expressions in Arab everyday life are "largely inspired by religion, and in most instances include the name of Allah either explicitly or implicitly. They are habits established and performed as a result of learning and training in socio-emotional situations."[42] The fear of God is manifest in all these expressions; the dread of His punishment of deviant behavior governs their actions. The terms "socio-emotional content" and "socio-emotional situation" are key categories here, since emotions articulated in an Islamic, religious way cannot be understood as individual attitudes but as the patterns of a religiously dominated culture. We are only concerned here with the Islamic content of everyday language, in order to show the great extent to which it is pervaded by sacred concepts. To anticipate the analysis later in this work of the conflict between the two definitions of the Arabic language in Arab Islamic history, namely between Koranic and scientific Arabic, the following brief remark may be made here: During the epoch of High Islam (750–1258), in the context of the reception of the Ancient Greek heritage, a substantial Hellenization of the Arab Islamic culture was initiated, an important product of which was Islamic rationalism. I could mention in this context the theory of the dual nature of truth of the Arab philosopher Averroës (Ibn Rushd), which distinguished between religious and philosophical truth. As a result of this hellenization and the emergence of an Arab Islamic rationalism, Arabic also became a language of science. Conflict with the sacral language, characterized by Koranic expressions, was bound to occur, as I will show in detail in Chapter 6. The accusation of heresy was of course likewise inevitable. To this day, Muslim fundamentalists refer to the great Islamic philosophers, Averroës and Avicenna among them, as "heretics."[43]

Whence does this rigidity in the Muslim world view derive, and what are the underlying factors? According to orthodox Muslim teaching, the world is governed theocentrically in a nonfinite way. In a world of this kind, in which the human being is merely a receiver of commands and an obedient servant in relation to God, the room for human maneuver is necessarily very small. To this may be added that Islam perceives itself primarily as *fiqh* (jurisprudence) and only secondarily as *kalam* (theology). I shall be taking this up again at some length in Chapter 5. In other words, the relationship between God and man in Islam is defined more in legal terms, with the aid of the Islamic *shari'a,* than in terms of theology.

According to Islamic doctrine, the Koran constitutes both in form and in content the final, definitive word of God. Johan Bouman, the Marburg scholar of religion and Islam, attempts in an interesting examination of the text of the Koran to deduce the structural form of Islamic anthropology, in order to discern what room for maneuver remains for the individual in the theocentric Islamic interpretation of the world. Bouman correctly discerns that the "unique and incomparable nature of God" may be regarded as the fundamental principle of Islam, which comprehends itself as "uncompromising monotheism." In this respect, Islam is "above all the successor to the heritage of Judaism. . . . Acknowledgment of the absolute uniqueness of God [is] the fundamental principle of faith."[44] At the time of the foundation of the Islamic religion, there were of course two other monotheisms, Judaism and Christianity. Islam recognizes both, interpreting the history of humanity as a history of the prophets, in which the Islamic religious revelation is made by the final, definitive Prophet, the Messenger of God (*rasul Allah*), Muhammed, the "Seal of the Prophets" who will reunite humanity. Seen from the viewpoint of the doctrine of divine unity (*tauhid*), the monotheistic faiths constitute a single community that can only be divided by a lapse in monotheistic faith. It follows from this that according to Islamic doctrine "Muhammed assumes both a corrective and an authoritative position in this history of the prophets,"[45] which designates him as "the final seal" and defines him as the mediator of the final, ultimate word of God: Muhammed and his scripture thus have the same corrective and culminative task with regard to the history of divine communication and teaching as Muhammed had in relation to the history of the prophets. This fundamental position of classical Islamic doctrine forms the core of the doctrine behind the Islamic claim to dominance: "On the one hand the Koran appeared as a corrective and culminative manifestation, and everything good contained in the earlier scriptures conforms with the content of the Koran; on the other hand the homogeneous character of monotheistic revelation prohibited the existence of differences over major issues."[46] The Islamic community (*umma*) thus denies all forms of plurality and comprehends itself as the core of that proportion of mankind united by monotheistic faith. This Islamic claim to dominance is based on the assertion that Muhammed appeared as the "Seal of the Prophets" and that the Koran brought the "definitive, final, essential truth."[47] The Pax Islamica Muhammed set up within the city-state of Medina after 622 is regarded as the nucleus of the Islamic *umma,* which recognizes no boundaries; Muhammed appeared "as the final arbitrator for all cases in which disputes arise."[48] The tradition of the Prophet, the Sunna, is therefore regarded as the second source after and is legitimated by the Koran. "But Muhammed is not only an example, he is also the criterion by which the fate of man is worked out. The answer brought by a human being to this apostle decides the final judgment of Allah."

Bouman's discussion of the text of the Koran, of which he has full command, emphasizes that the relationship between God and man is defined, in view of strict monotheism, by a distance between man and God so unbridgeable "that the very nature of man makes it impossible for him to establish a relationship with God on his own initiative."[49] God acts in a sovereign manner with regard to man, on his own initiative; the world is formed and defined according to His will, for which reason Islam is based on a strictly theocentric interpretation of the world. It is here, according to Bouman, that both the potential and the limitations of Islamic anthropology lie;

> it stands in constant danger of being suffocated by the numinous omnipotence of God, although this omnipotence still leaves sufficient room for human decisionmaking . . . a possibility opens up for mutual relationship, in which Allah, however, remains the one who commands and decides, the human being, the believer, remaining the obedient servant. Within this structural form, the human being is perpetually subordinate.[50]

This explanation may serve to elucidate why the real tension which exists between legal and popular Islam is not manifest at the cultural level. The human being has to live according to Koranic commandments, but must at the same time adapt in his practical life to his ever-changing environment. Popular Islam facilitates such an adaptation; the discrepancy that has emerged between religious dogma and practical ritual is not permitted to exist, since all actions must be in accordance with the commandments (*ta'alim*).

This complex relationship requires further exploration; I therefore turn in the following chapter to the basic patterns existing in Islam for the perception of change and development.

PART TWO

Culture—A Catalyst of Change, a Reflection of Change, or a Stumbling Block? Ascertaining the Position of Islam

Having indicated the difficulties involved in conveying a general definition of culture, as well as pointing out, with Clifford Geertz, that cultural analysis needs to be focused on current realities, I highlighted the "symbolic dimensions of social conduct" as the focus of my theme. Starting with this clarified term, I then defined religion as a "cultural system" consisting of corresponding symbols that converge to form a model for reality. On the basis of this conceptual framework, I then attempted to draw a sketch conveying some concept of what Islam is.

The next step of my analysis, the theme of which will be the question of the cultural accommodation of change in Islam, will now be the model for reality provided by Islam for its adherents, from whom "surrender" to its religious content is demanded. The very word *Islam* is derived from the verb "to surrender." To be converted to Islam is expressed in Arabic as *aslama,* literally "he has surrendered." An elaboration of the Islamic model for reality will thus form the subject of Chapter 3.

To return again to conceptual analysis, the question will be asked at the end of Chapter 4, the task of which has been indicated above, whether a culture can promote change, reflect it, or even impede it. This question will be examined both at the conceptual level and using material from Islamic history and contemporary history, so that the answer sought will not merely be of a general nature but can be tailored to the particular conditions of Islam.

3

Basic Cultural Patterns for the Perception of Change in Islam: The Islamic Model for Reality[1]

We have already alluded to the cultural diversity in Islam and opened to question the monolithic notion of Islam that is to be found equally—albeit for different motives and with varying degrees of emphasis—in both anti-Islamic polemics and in the fundamentalist apologia of Islam itself: Islamic symbols are contingent upon both time and place, and the form they take varies accordingly. Social behavior also changes, both directed by these symbols and at the same time correlating to them. We can also speak of an Islamic canon binding for all Muslims but untouched by this real and manifest diversity. This diversity is connected to varying perceptions of the canon contingent upon time and place. Consistent with my line of argument in Chapter 1, I construe this canon as a pure system of symbols offering a model for reality. Actual existing symbols are derived from this pure symbolic system, becoming suffused with prevailing reality. It is thus entirely within the scope of the question as formulated in this study to outline the ideal model for reality, that is, the pure symbolic system of Islam. This may be abstracted from Islamic religious differentiation (the formation of sects and religious schools) or internal cultural differentiation[2] (the adaptation of Arab Islam to non-Arab cultures, or inter-Arab cultural diversity) at this level of analysis, with the model for reality of the religious commandments (*ta'alim*) forming the focal point. At various other levels of our analysis we shall become acquainted with forms of confrontation between this model and the reality that deviates from it.[3] For contemporary Muslims schooled in the rational discourse of reasoning it is hardly possible to overlook this tension between model and reality, provided their thinking is not hampered by dogmatism and fanaticism. It is hard to reconcile, for example, the religious proclamation "You are the best community (*umma*) created by God on earth" with the reality in which members of this very *umma* rank among the underdogs of this "feudal world order."[4] Many contemporary Muslim thinkers are similarly concerned with the vexing questions of history and revelation in Islamic teaching.[5]

To begin with, I shall proceed from the hypothesis that particular issues in contemporary Islam—in this case the relationship between Islam and development—need to be classified into two general spheres and dealt with accordingly. First, the fundamental issues of modern Islam can hardly be discussed without reference to the early form of this religious system, and second, contemporary Islam cannot be adequately interpreted without taking into account its confrontation with Europe, which by virtue of industrialization is superordinate to it and hence hegemonial.[6]

The first sphere by no means implies a historical review of early Islam, desirable though this may be, not only from the academic viewpoint. Throughout Islamic history, the first Islamic city-state of Medina, founded by the Prophet Muhammed, has been deemed the original Islamic community and therefore regarded by Muslims as the ideal for every future solution. When, in the "re-Islamization" literature that has been appearing on a massive scale in most Muslim countries during the last decade, there has been reference to the Islamic solution (*al-Hall al-Islami*),[7] this has invariably involved the concept of a sociopolitical entity based on the model of Medina. It is not, then, for reasons of theology and religious history but because of the temporal retrospective orientation of Islam itself that attention to the founding of Islam as a religion in the seventh century is central to the discussion of Islam and development.

The second sphere of issues, that of Islam and Europe, arises out of the classical Islamic doctrine of the *dar al-Islam* and *dar al-harb* (the House of Islam and the House of War), according to which the world is divided into Muslim and non-Muslim territory, characterized by peace and war respectively. In other words, Islam declares itself to be the ultimate and absolute monotheism, thereby claiming an absolute character correlating to the doctrine of Islamic dominance.

In Islamic history, therefore, non-Muslim territory was always identified with the *dar al-harb,* the House of War. This situation has changed in the modern age, which is characterized by the power of the European technological-scientific culture.[8] The cultural superiority of the Islamic Middle East vis-à-vis Europe during the era of the Arab Islamic empire, and the subsequent military and political threat to Europe posed by the invasions of the Ottoman Turks, have been supplanted by European dominance on a global scale in cultural, political, and military terms.[9] In this new relationship between Islam and Europe, there has also been a concomitant change in Islamic concepts of development.

The complexes of questions indicated so far are reflected in the internal structure of this chapter. The attempt to determine what the model of Islam is in light of the existing religious and cultural diversity leads us to concern ourselves with the essential religious content shared by all Muslims, defined here as the core of Islam. Because all aspects of this religious content have their roots in the original Muslim community of Medina and its legitimation through the Koran and the Sunna (the tradition of the Prophet), a consideration of early Islam and its concepts of political and social development is indispensable. I shall then proceed to examine the problems of development in the altered historical situation, which now favors Europe and to which modern Islam has tried to find an answer since the nineteenth century.[10]

The Islamic Religious Establishment and the Goal of Its Development

The historical situation in which Islam came into existence was marked by an absence of unity. At the world political level, the then two great empires of the Byzantines and of the Sassanids in Persia, were in a state of war. At the religious level, Christianity and Judaism were mutual rivals, whereas the Arabs, at that time polytheists, had no state structure of their own aside from the Arab vassal states of the world powers of that time (the Lachmids and the Ghassanids) and were organized on the Arabian peninsula in uncivilized, fiercely competing nomadic tribes. Seen in this light,[11] the demand on the part of the Islamic religious establishment for universal standardization becomes understandable. The Islamic doctrine of unity (*tauhid*) embodies this religious message.

After Muhammed's migration from Mecca as a result of political persecution in 622 (as described in Chapter 2), he founded in Medina the first Islamic political structure, the basic principles of which were laid down in the "municipal code of Medina." The leading international historian of early Islam, W. Montgomery Watt, states that this new code

> essentially represents a treaty of alliance in accordance with
> traditional Arab principles. . . . In addition to this, entry into the
> alliance became a strict prerequisite for the adoption of Islam. . . .
> Non-Arab Muslims had to become clients of Arab tribes, non-Muslim
> groups becoming "protected minorities." . . . It is stated in two
> Articles that in the event of disputes which could split the
> community, the people should turn to "God and Muhammed."[12]

It has already been suggested that the Islamic doctrine of unity (*tauhid*) was the linchpin of this political order. Islam interprets itself as a strict, uncompromising (*"la ilaha illa Allah,"* "There is no god but Allah"), and ultimate monotheism, recognizing no authority other than Allah, either in heaven or on earth. Allah is not an Arab, Muslim god, as may be read in medieval polemics against Islam, as this word has no other meaning than "God." On this point, the British Islamic scholar Watt has the following to say: "When speaking of Islam, the Arab word Allah is commonly translated as 'God'. This implies that the God whom Muslims serve is the God worshipped by Jews and Christians. There are several million Arab-speaking Christians who have no other word for God than Allah."[13]

On the basis of the Islamic doctrine of unity, Muslims interpret the city-state of Medina as the foundation stone of a universal political order governed by Islam. In other words, Islam does not start from an assumption of diversity, but solely on the basis of a single unified order. After a thorough textual analysis of the Koran, Bouman came to the conclusion that "the concept of uniformity dominates the message of the Koran like a constant factor."[14] The historical situation prevailing at the time of the foundation of Islam, as mentioned in the introduction, in which humanity was divided into a number of both monotheistic (Jewish and Christian) and polytheistic (Arab pagan) confessional communities, led Islam to claim that it was bringing definitive unity with its message. The goal of human development for Islam thus consists of guiding it to the point where it becomes a unified monotheistic community. It is in this sense that Islamic teaching, as we have seen in Chapter 2, is based on the Koran, revealed through the last of all the Prophets of God, Muhammed, in which "the final essential truth"[15] for mankind was definitively proclaimed.

Acceptance of Islam during the foundation of the city-state of Medina entailed both submission to God and unconditional recognition of his messenger (*rasul*), Muhammed, as arbitrator. Since that time it has also entailed acknowledgment of the Koran as the ultimate, definitive word of God, and the Sunna (tradition) of the Prophet and Messenger of God. This is the core of Islam.[16] The goal of development is declared to be the core of an international society. Out of this proceeds the doctrine of Islamic dominance. Apart from Muslims, Islam recognizes people of other faiths within its territory either as unbelievers (*mushrikun*) or as "people of the book" (*ahl al-kitab*). As Islam is not a missionary religion, it sees no goal in proselytism. "Unbelievers" are not tolerated, while Jews and Christians, as monotheists, are recognized as tribute-paying "protected minorities" under the umbrella of Islam. Non-Muslim territory is perpetually *dar al-harb,* the sphere of war, with which it is permitted to conclude temporary international peace treaties only in times of Muslim weakness.[17]

Within the Muslim community there can only be one concept of Islam. The Koran calls those Muslims of Medina who did not fully submit themselves to the Prophet "the hypocrites" (*munafiqun*). Turning away from Islam or conversion from Islam to another religion is not permitted and punishable according to Islamic penal law under the charge of apostasy (*radda*); apostates (*murtaddun*) may be executed.[18]

It is clear from the discussion so far that, on the one hand, the Islamic goal of the development of mankind is solely that of a united monotheistic community, achieved through the agency of Islam. It is incumbent on Muslims to move in this direction. That the original Muslim community of Medina remains an enduring model in perpetuity makes it obvious, on the other hand, that future development is oriented according to an ideal of the past, the municipal code of Medina (Pax Islamica). Orthodox Islam recognizes no utopia. Although there have been political movements in Islamic history that have proclaimed utopian notions of salvation—for example, the Karmathians (*Qarmata*)—Muslim orthodoxy has always rigorously opposed them as heresy and persecuted and executed their supporters.

In summary, therefore, we can state that Islamic doctrine has two conflicting concepts of development: a forward-looking option for the future and humanity, toward which one is supposed to work and within which humanity will become united under the banner of Islam; and a backward-looking interpretation of history, bound up with the aspiration of restoring the original Islamic community of the Prophet at Medina.

Religious Sources of the Islamic Doctrine of Development

Not only experts are aware that the Koran is recognized by all Muslims as the sole primary source of Islam, even by Shi'ites, who make the accusation of *tahrif* (falsification) against it, as we shall see. Inasmuch as the Prophet Muhammed was a messenger from God, he is acknowledged as arbitrator. The handed-down traditions of his verbal utterances and deeds are described as the practice of the Prophet (Sunna), having evolved after his death into a complementary, likewise undisputed, secondary source of Islam. Resting on the Koran and the Sunna, Islam interprets itself not only as a monotheistic religion, but also as a legislative code perceived within a theocentric context. The *shari'a*, the divine law of Islam, is part of the core of this faith.

According to Islamic doctrine, all past, present, and future development derives from these religious sources. It follows, therefore, that no interpretation of the relationship between Islam and development can avoid an analysis of the historical importance of the Koran, Sunna, and *shari'a.*

The Koran, Koranic Exegesis, and Sunna in the Past and Present

Within the Islamic perception, the Koran is in its present form an unaltered version since the revelation received by Muhammed. Watt and other Western Koranic scholars, however, working with the methods of historical and critical text analysis, have arrived at the hypothesis that some revision must have taken place. As evidence for this, Watt points out places in the text of the Koran where, for example, it is possible to discern "rhyming phrases that do not fit into the passage . . . , abrupt changes of rhyme . . . , the juxtaposition of apparently contradictory assertions."[19] Initially, Muhammed's followers, Muslims, learned the revealed Koranic verses by heart. In the time of Muhammed the text of the Koran was recorded on stones, on palm leaves, and above all with the aid of the "heart of man," meaning human memory. After Muhammed's death there was a group of *qurra'*, those Muslims who had learned the entire Koran by heart. But as important *qurra'* members met their deaths in military campaigns, the Prophet's successors, the caliphs, recorded the text of the Koran permanently on parchment. According to Watt, the edition of Zayd Ibn-Thabit, created between 650 and 656, is the version of the Koran that has been handed down to this day and that is regarded as authoritative by all Muslims with the exception of the Shi'ites. Shi'ites see in it evidence of *tahrif,* falsification, alleged to have come about when Sunnis removed those parts of the text in which the first Shi'ite imam, Ali, was appointed as caliph, or successor to the Prophet.[20] In other respects, however, Shi'ites also accept the Arabic text of the Koran.

Both those in political authority and ordinary individuals are obliged to express their Islamic faith by constantly striving to bring their actions into harmony with the Koran. For this reason alone, it was necessary to interpret the messages of the Koran, so as to be able to legitimate change. After the expansion of Islam and its worldwide dissemination during the era of the Umayyad caliphate (661–750) and above all during the period of High Islam (750–1258), when Islam evolved into a world civilization, there arose the urgent necessity to understand and cope with the complex political, economic, and social structures that had emerged. All the great Koranic commentaries stem from this epoch. After the collapse of the Arab Islamic empire in the thirteenth century, no significant Koranic commentaries were forthcoming until the nineteenth century.

The importance of the Koran for Muslims as the source of their perception of past, present, and future development can only be understood and its true position realized by taking into account Islamic teaching, according to which the Koran represents the word of God in both form and content. A former representative of the Arab league in Bonn, Hamdy M. Azzam, expresses this Islamic faith in his book on Islam: "The Koran as the word of God not only stems directly from Him in its content, but is also of divine origin in its form and in the structure of its language."[21] If we call to mind my previous remark that Islam is a strict, uncompromising monotheism, we can discern here the Islamic doctrine of theocentrism: God rules the world and directs it according to His will, that is, according to His word, contained in the Koran. Koranic exegesis is thus a means for coping with change and for understanding political, social, and economic evolution. This observation can also help explain attempts on the part of contemporary Muslims to comprehend problems of the modern age with which they have to cope through this medium of Koranic exegesis.[22]

Like other monotheisms, Islam also recognizes an afterlife as a prospective future in heaven for the whole of humanity (heaven and hell, with appropriate punishment or reward for life in this world). For this world, however, as has already been shown, it recognizes solely the original community of the Prophet as a guideline for development. The basis for this is to be found in the Koran and the Sunna, seen as its ideal. In other words, the Islamic concept of the future is retrospective, with the seventh century past as the yardstick for all political, social, and economic development. The Koran also constitutes the central source for orthodox Muslims for the purposes of coping with contemporary issues. "From the doctrine that the Koran is the word of God, the ordinary Muslim draws the conclusion that it is infallible in every respect, even on scientific and historical issues."[23] On the path of Koranic exegesis, all human actions are defined and all changes in society legitimated. Islamic theology (*kalam*) and jurisprudence (*fiqh*) are thus based primarily on Koranic exegesis. After the stagnation of the Islamic Middle East from the thirteenth to the nineteenth centuries, innovative Islamic thinkers then attempted to reopen creative Koranic exegesis to the modern, in an attempt to reconcile with the Koran the adoption of technological and scientific achievements from the West. This attempt formed the core of the Islamic modernism of the nineteenth century.[24]

Following Watt's research into the Koran, it is possible to discern "that the message of the earliest parts of the Koran relates mainly to the conditions prevailing in Mecca at that time,"[25] and that in general many verses of the Koran can only be correctly understood "if one is familar with the particular characteristics of Arab life, especially with life in the desert and with the Arab way of thinking."[26] Here again we are confronted with the problem of coping with change using a retrospective understanding of history. During the golden age of Islamic civilization, which received substantial impulses from the process of hellenization,[27] Islamic philosophers (chiefly Averroës) endeavored to resolve this problem by evolving a theory of the dual nature of truth.[28] This theory, which was rigorously opposed both by Muslim orthodoxy and later, after the spread of Averroism in Europe, by the Catholic church,[29] distinguishes between religious and philosophical truth, each of which has its own proper sphere,[30] what amounts to secularization. Today Muslim secularists (and I include myself among them), are attempting to interpret the Koran and the Sunna as the source of a divine ethic which belongs to the realm of inwardness (*batiniyya*), thereby derigidifying the scholastic understanding of the Koran.[31] Watt also deals with this complex phenomenon, showing that "many parts of the Muslim world still operate very conservatively. A person who pushes forward too quickly will perhaps encounter difficulties in one way or another. Although a reconciliation with modern thinking has been set in motion, much still remains to be done. Some paths that have been taken have proved to be dead ends. Others look promising, but so far no-one has gone very far along them."[32]

With regard to Islamic concepts of the future, the position of fundamentalism and integrism may be outlined as follows: Its followers insist that only the original community of the Prophet can be valid as a point of orientation. This tendency in modern Islam is thus known as *salafiyya,* for it accepts only the *salaf* (the "good old" original community of the Prophet) as the sole source for determining development.[33] We must note, however, that in contemporary Islam, *salafiyya* fundamentalism differs greatly from traditionalism insofar as the basic formulas of Islamic fundamentalists are imbued with modern concerns.

Law as a Social Regulative: Islamic Law (Shari'a) and Development

Legal sociologists define law as the regulative element in social development;[34] it both governs the forms of social interaction and renders them decipherable, so that processes of development may also be directed with the aid of law. No complex social system can dispense with legal norms, and even simple social systems have some legal basis. Such systems (for example, the precolonial, nonliterate cultures of black Africa) may not be familiar with written law, yet they do have customary law.[35]

Although the pre-Islamic Arabs had a written language, they had no written law. The most important pre-Islamic legal norm was the vendetta. In view of the absence of a central state power structure with legal norms at its disposal, the fear of blood revenge served as an equivalent for the directive function of law. Muhammed, the Prophet of God and political leader of the city-state of Medina,[36] initially assumed the function of arbitrator among disputing Arab bedouin; the Pax Islamica of Muhammed may be defined as a "federation of Arab tribes," established on the basis of the legal norms contained in the Koran.

Islamic law, as reflected in the Koran and the Sunna, was and is to this day a *lex divina;* in the time of Muhammed it had the character of a *lex talionis,* taking the place primarily of the ancient Arab, pre-Islamic customary legal norm of repaying an offence with a like punishment. What was new was that the Muslim community, the *umma,* now carried out the act of punishment—no longer did the injured party take justice into its own hands. The Muslim state as a central power monopoly had thus been born.

After the Muslim conquests and the unfolding of a process of civilization within the Pax Islamica, a *lex talionis* was no longer sufficient for the regulation of social interaction; the increasingly complex Pax Islamica necessitated a complex legal system. The developmental process of the Islamic legal system, which has been reconstructed by the Scottish legal historian Noel Coulson and the German-British scholar of Islam, Joseph Schacht,[37] nonetheless evolved within the confines of Islamic doctrine, based on the Koran and the Sunna. Islamic jurisprudence similarly rested on Koranic exegesis and the reconstruction of the Sunna of the Prophet through the medium of oral and written tradition.

In contrast to Christianity, in Islam jurisprudence not theology takes precedence; not the *kalam,* but the *fiqh* was regarded as the core of "Islamic knowledge" per se. In semantic terms *fiqh* means "knowledge," but legal knowledge is knowledge par excellence in Islam. Schacht correctly states: "It is impossible to understand Islam without understanding Islamic law."[38] The Muslim scribes, the *ulema,* who have come to represent a kind of Muslim clergy—even though Islamic doctrine does not recognize a clerical class—do not see themselves as theologians but as lawyers. *'Alim,* the singular form of *ulema,* means "scholar" in

Arabic. In Islamic history, the *ulema* were thus the embodiment of Islamic *fiqh* in its capacity as Muslim knowledge par excellence.

Unlike Christianity, Islam is not an ecclesiastical, but an organic religious system; it offers regulations for all spheres of life as an organic whole. Islamic law corresponds to this, embracing both the sphere of public worship, *'ibadat* and of business dealings, *mu'amalat.* Its essence is the regulation of what is permitted, *halal,* and what is forbidden, *haram.* External control over the observance of *haram* and *halal* takes the form of Islamic legislation (*tashri'*), whereas internal control takes the form of guidance during the course of the Muslim upbringing (*taujih*). We shall find out more about this in Chapter 5, which is devoted to *shari'a.*[39]

The Islamic legal system evolved between the seventh and ninth centuries. In addition to the Koran and the Sunna as primary sources, the legal techniques of *qiyas* (analogy deduction) and *ijma'* (consensus doctorum) also evolved as secondary possibilities for defining laws. If neither the Koran and Sunna nor these methods provided legal answers to problems of development, the methods of *ijtihad* (independent legal reasoning, or stretching of a point in individual cases) was permitted. By the beginning of only the tenth century, however, the developmental process of the Islamic legal system was considered by Muslim legal experts (the *faqihs*) to be complete and already to have reached a state of perfection. From that time until the nineteenth century, no further development occurred in Islamic law; it stagnated until, in the last century—with the onset of a confrontation with the developed, industrialized West, which had a technological-scientific culture at its command—it was not capable of coping with the imminent problems of development. Only then were the gates of *ijtihad* opened once again by some of the more enthusiastic innovators among Muslim scholars. They provided no solution, however. The result of this historical situation was the emergence of compound legal systems, such as Anglo-Muham-medan Law in the anglophone Muslim colonial region and the Droit Musulman in the francophone Muslim colonial region.[40]

During the era of High Islam, when economic prosperity[41] engendered a social structure with which a sacral legal system could hardly be expected to cope, various methods were evolved for legally circumventing the *shari'a,*[42] as will be discussed in Chapter 5. In the sphere of state politics, which according to the Islamic doctrine of *din wa daula*[43] (the correspondence between sacral and state spheres) should be subordinate to *shari'a,* the principle of *siyasa*[44] was elaborated. Literally, *siyasa* means "politics," but in fact it refers to administration, as it concerns the administrative measures of the Muslim ruler and in practical terms removes it from the sphere of *shari'a* legal control.

   This touches on a problem in Islamic history that persists to this day: How does law cope with the problems of development? The Islamic legal experts verbally attached the law to the revealed word of God, the Koran, and removed it from the possibility of adapting to development. *Shari'a* is thus conceived as being immutable, not subject to historical change.[45] Social change does take place, however, and the only remaining possibility is to acknowledge existing law verbally and then circumvent it legally in social practice. A cultural innovation in Islam as a cultural system, however, would open up other possibilities, as we shall see in Chapter 5 on Islamic law.

The Relationship Between Islam and Development Since the Confrontation with the Industrial West in the Nineteenth Century

   As has already been mentioned, Islamic doctrine does not recognize a clergy, although in the course of its historical development a Muslim clerical class, the *rijal ad-din* (men of religion) who as a rule belong to the *ulema* (scribes), has arisen. This new clerical class mainly came into its own in institutions that had likewise not been foreseen by doctrine and that evolved largely within the fold of Arab-Islamic law (as well as during Ottoman Turkish rule); these institutions still definitely exist today in a modified form (depending on the country): We have already seen in Chapter 2 that the West African Muslim *marabouts* fulfill the social function of a clergy.[46]

   In the section on Islamic law, the concepts of *tashri'*, legislation, and of *taujih*, guidance, were named components of the Islamic *shari'a*. The Islamic religious institution embraces both, the external law, and education.[47] This institution, writes Watt, is "in the first instance a juristic and a pedagogical institution. During the course of time, men with such an education were appointed to positions which in other religions would be occupied by priests, especially after property had been transferred to them in the form of pious institutions (*auqaf*)."[48] In the nineteenth century, these scholars of religion found themselves overwhelmed by the problems of the technological-scientific age.

   On the surface, the confrontation was a military one, but in essence it was a confrontation between civilizations. Its gateways were south-eastern Europe, where the Ottoman Empire had been pushed back into its Turkish heartlands by the now superior European armies, and Egypt, where Napoleon Bonaparte had attempted to block his English adversaries' route to India.[49] The military inferiority of the Muslims in this encounter led them to adopt first the European military inventions, but further cultural absorption inevitably followed.[50] The question is in what spirit these alien elements were adopted, and how the change instigated by this situation was perceived.

A Muslim imam is comparable to a Christian priest. Rifa'a Tahtawi, the first Muslim imam to go to Paris, accompanying a group of Egyptian students in 1826, was so impressed by the French culture that he himself wanted, and indeed obtained permission, to study. In his Paris diary, he writes of his astonishment that French teachers did not adhere to texts in order to find the truth, whereas Islamic scholars wrote merely "commentaries and supercommentaries" on traditional texts. With regard to the relationship between religion and development, Tahtawi's following observation should be mentioned: "When it is said of someone in France that he is a scholar, this does not mean that he is acquainted with religion but that he is familiar with some other field of knowledge. It is not difficult to see the superiority of these Christians over others in the sciences, and consequently also that in our countries many of these fields of knowledge do not exist at all."[51]

Tahtawi was the first Islamic scholar in the nineteenth century to recognize the conflict between Islam as a preindustrial culture and the demands placed upon it by the technological-scientific age.[52] He writes in his diary: "Naturally I approve only of that which does not contradict the tenor of our Islamic law."[53] This sentence demonstrates the concern of a Muslim with a traditional family and educational background who is aware that the Islamic Middle East has to learn and adopt elements from industrial Europe in order to overcome its backwardness, without relinquishing its own identity. This remains the central problem of modern Islam to this day. Are Muslims able to cope with social change and to accommodate it culturally without undertaking appropriate concomitant changes within their cultural system, that is, within Islam itself? Could Muslims adopt modern science and technology while retaining the metaphysical and theocentric world view described above? Could Muslims appropriate modernity while rejecting the world view related to it?

Recent events in Iran also serve to illustrate the problems inherent in the relationship between Islam and development.[54] On the one hand, the modernization attempts of the shah are evidence of the repeatedly expressed view that in the Islamic Middle East it is not possible to cope successfully with the problems of development using modernization instrumentally without including Islam and culturally innovating it in the process.[55] On the other hand, the experiences of the self-styled "Islamic Republic"[56] ruled by the Shi'ite clergy in Iran have shown that although it is possible to achieve a fanatical mobilization of the people solely with traditional methods for fostering religion, it is not possible to achieve a solution to the conflict between Islam and development that has dominated the Islamic Middle East since the nineteenth century.

4

Culture and Social Change: Is Underdevelopment a Given of Cultural Tradition? The Problem of Cultural Innovation in Sociology

In the now classic article "Cultural Sociology," originally published by Vierkandt in the *Handwörterbuch der Soziologie* (Handbook of Sociology), Alfred Weber defines culture as a "spiritual and intellectual expressional form within the substance of life, or a spiritual and intellectual attitude toward it."[1] Weber continues: "The social structure has hence been the most essential object of spiritual and intellectual formation throughout all ages."[2] At the end of the article, he states: "Coming to terms with traditions and the *ideal* or *religious* incrustations of existence is in every *new constellation*—as we would describe the new historical situation in a sociological, technical way—mostly at least *as important* as the endeavor to capture and form, or come to terms with, the new naturalistic, practical, and intellectual stuff of life."[3]

To this day the theme of this argument remains controversial within social science theory, which is persistently of a one-sided and indeed one-dimensional orientation, be this in the form of structuralism on the one hand, or behaviorism on the other. Frankfurt sociologist Gerhard Brandt's[4] call for a combination of these two approaches—the analysis of social structure *and* the theory of social action—on the grounds that both are equally essential for the development of theories oriented towards society as a whole, has not progressed beyond the level of an appeal. Although it is not possible to take up these theoretical and methodological questions here, they do nevertheless need to be mentioned when broaching the subject of the cultural accommodation of social change. There are still social scientists of the opinion that sociocultural norms and the attitudes associated with them are the direct reflections of an existing social structure or of the level of its development. As a rule, such concepts turn out to be *a priori* con-

structions and armchair theorizing without any empirical basis, since
such theoreticians are unable to explain how it is possible for cultural
norms to persist for centuries in certain cultures quite independently
of the prevailing level of socioeconomic development. In the Muslim
culture, for example, the virginity of female relatives is regarded as a
substantial mark of honor (*sharaf*). This sociocultural norm and the
often dramatic attitudes associated with it are as widespread today as
they were during the Middle Ages, as much part of a highly modern
urban environment as an archaic rural one.[5] Further examples could
be added; only lack of space and the need not to lose sight of the
essential issue prevent me from citing them here.

Just as prevalent as the materialistic reductionists criticized above,
certain social scientists are still of the opinion that changes in the
dominant procedure of socialization—with more recent norm systems
being internalized in place of the old ones—are sufficient in themselves
to bring about a dynamic change in a society. The idea that the
surmounting of underdevelopment signifies "The Passing of Traditional
Society," in the sense of a departure from handed-down norms, is thus
valid not only for the outdated work of Daniel Lerner.[6]

With regard to social science in the Federal Republic of Germany—
and unlike the English-speaking academic community—it is particularly
deplorable that social structure reductionists are classified as politically
"left," and those with a subjective-normative approach as "right."
According to this preconceived notion, a "leftist" social scientist working
on the Third World has to concern himself in the first instance with
the world market and with the "structural dependence" arising out of
it as the cause of underdevelopment. Scholars who focus their attention
on the internal factors conditioning underdevelopment are consequently
looked down upon with contempt, even if they do not lose sight of
external factors.[7] As far as the study of non-European regions and
cultures is concerned, social science in Germany—owing to lack of
professionalism and area studies specialization—is hopelessly weighed
down with normative preoccupations and frequently dispenses with
empirical substantiation altogether. It is not uncommon for the internal
political debates to be projected on to the remote non-Western world,
with which scholars are frequently unfamiliar.[8] As an extreme example
of this attitude, I could mention the position that sees in Khomeini's
Islamic revolution evidence supporting the thesis of dissociation from
the world market. It is not possible, however, to work seriously on non-
European cultures without knowing them from the inside. Without a
familiarity with their background conditions, we cannot hope to understand what is known in this country as the "Third World"—even
if we know the structure of the world market as well as a member of

the clergy knows the Bible or the Koran. The analysis of structures of underdevelopment includes research into the cultural systems of the relevant region. Clifford Geertz presents himself as a proponent of this and endeavors to explain why a scholar is unable to comprehend the conceptual structures of an alien world: "What in a place like Morocco prevents us from grasping what people are up to is not ignorance as to how cognition works . . . as a lack of familiarity with the imaginative universe within which their acts are signs."[9] After a number of fieldwork trips in Morocco, Geertz began to understand the people and their social setting: "The more I manage to follow what the Moroccans are up to, the more logical, and the more singular they seem."[10] It is difficult to grasp how a scholar can be an expert on developing countries without the benefit of this first essential, and yet there is an abundance of such "experts."

Still at a general level, at this juncture we ought to go beyond a critique of the normative-subjective or socioeconomic structural one-dimensionality of social scientific theory formation and take up the problem of the evolutionary unilinearity of development, in order to clarify whether rigid, nondynamic patterns of culture in fact represent a specific level of development or persistent forms. Both the theoretical traditions under criticism, despite their points of dissent, share an insistence on the notion of unilinear development, albeit described in different ways. For Marxist authors, the development of the means of production is an unstoppable process; it signifies the "collapse of the Old World," as Marx described it, for which at that time England, "whatever crimes it may have committed, was nevertheless the unwitting tool of history,"[11] by dissolving, as a colonial power, the precapitalist structures in its colonies. Modernization theorists of the colonial system described this in a similar way; for them, this system represented a modernizing force, since it undermined traditionality.

Following a spate of exertion within the materialist approach in the social sciences in Germany during the 1960s and 1970s, a certain weariness seems to have set in. It is noticeable in that modernization theories, which were previously subjected in the scholarly literature to sometimes cliché-ridden, but nonetheless in some cases pertinent, harsh criticism,[12] are currently enjoying a new reception, accompanied by the stated intention of formulating a "critical theory of modernization."[13] Even today, however, both conventional modernization theories and Marxist analyses still leave many questions of social change unanswered. I venture to speak here of a paradigm crisis (in the Kuhnian sense) in both these explanatory models, insofar as it is obvious that neither is able to resolve these unanswered questions (or anomalies).[14]

Although it is not the purpose of this book to take issue with these anomalies, nonetheless, to the extent that this book is, on the one hand, theory-oriented and attempts a conceptual exploration of the problem of how the Islamic culture copes with change, and because, on the other hand, modernization theory can—despite its shortcomings—make a significant contribution in this problem area, it would seem justified to take a closer look at an important attempt on the part of one *revisionist* modernization theorist, S. N. Eisenstadt, to redefine this approach in terms of the analysis of cultural traditionality. We shall therefore be examining this attempt while keeping a constant eye on our own theme.

Though American in terms of academic training, Eisenstadt[15] is a sociologist educated in the European tradition and familiar with the philosophical sources of modern sociology. In these he sees among other things the origin of a doctrine asserting the existence in history of a universal tendency toward development (evolutionism), which finds its fullest manifestation in modern sociology. Concepts still central to macrosociological analysis in classical sociology were at first, above all in the United States, ousted in favor of microsociological research. Not until the 1950s and 1960s was there a noticeable and abrupt increase of interest in formulating questions in macrosociological terms, a change that undoubtedly coincided with the renewed importance of those preindustrial regions collectively known as the Third World. Even today, holistic social analyses find more scope within the sociology of development than within analyses of industrial societies, which tend to be predominantly microsociological. In the United States, research in development is closely linked with the sociological investigation of social change. The new paradigm, modernization theory, is thus at the same time a theory of development.

First, let me summarize in three points Eisenstadt's critique of modernization theory: the validity of the tradition-modernity dichotomy, ahistoricity, and Euro-Americo-centrism. He assumes by means of his modification to have achieved a differentiation, and thereby a neutralization, of this dichotomy. He also makes a criticism of ahistoricity and likewise claims to have invalidated this through modification.[16] Eisenstadt understands "historical" to mean "different"; for him, reference to the diversity of developmental paths amounts to a historical line of argument. If one conceives of history as historical social science, however, then the connection between history and sociology lies in being able to demonstrate the historical genesis of a structure. But the depiction of underdevelopment as cultural traditionality and the "diverse" and "multifarious" dissolution and continued development of that traditionality as modernity far from constitutes a holistic, combined historical and sociological analysis. Nonetheless, one element of this "diversity" is historically determined, namely, that which affects the varying historical context of change, which now has the character of an international society, or—as Eisenstadt writes—constitutes an international environment. The latter not only "impinges in an undifferentiated way on a 'closed' social system" but moreover develops relations "among a series of international networks—cultural, economic, and political—that impinge on different aspects of these societies and evoke different responses within them."[17]

This particular problem is central to any theory of social change under the prevailing conditions of an international society, as change is exogenously induced; its driving force is, if only partly, external and hence perceived by the people concerned as an alien influence. It is from this that hostility to change arises. According to Eisenstadt, the crucial problem of non-Western societies lies not in the "relatively small extent of modernization, but rather in the lack of development of new institutional settings, the lack of regulative mechanisms and normative injunctions."[18]

Unfortunately, this insight is not conceptualized and consequently does not form part of Eisenstadt's frame of reference. Although the theoretical approach referred to here fails to deal satisfactorily either with the international or with the internal overall social structural factors of change, it is important in view of our own concern here to pursue it further, since the discussion of traditionality as a cultural manifestation is a central issue for Eisenstadt.

Of particular interest is the question of the extent to which a culture can either promote or impede social change. In this connection, Eisenstadt disputes the thesis that the Protestant ethic is an economic ethic and that social change is contingent upon it alone. After an extensive discussion of Weber, he arrives at the conclusion that the Protestant ethic coincided with other social factors and for this reason was able to exert such a transforming influence. He thus categorically refutes the thesis that the Protestant ethic alone could have induced change as a movement for modernization. This discussion is of special concern to the Islamic cultural sphere. The question why this old debate is being taken up once again today can be answered in terms of a reconsideration of the importance of Weber for the sociology of social change: "In the last fifteen years or so, with the upsurge of great interest in development and modernization beyond Europe, interest in this thesis has arisen once more. Many seek in the existence or nonexistence of some equivalent to the Protestant ethic the key to understanding of the successful or unsuccessful modernization of non-European countries."[19] Western readers may be surprised to learn that

Muslim thinkers explain the backwardness of the Islamic Middle East in terms of the absence of such an ethic. Islamic modernists see a new religious movement, such as that of the Reformation, and a reformer such as Martin Luther, who would establish a new Islamic ethic, as the only escape route out of backwardness into modernity.

Afghani[20] (1839–1897), the spiritual leader of recent Islamic modernism, active in the second half of the nineteenth century, stated in one of his seminal writings: "If we pause to consider the causes of the revolutionary transition of Europe from barbarity to civilization, we discern that this change only became possible through the religious movement initiated and carried out by Martin Luther. . . . He succeeded in propelling Europeans towards a reformed re-orientation."[21]

As a corrective to this assertion by Afghani, who hoped to overcome the traditionality of the Islamic Middle East by means of a revitalizing religious movement[22] in the style of the Lutheran Reformation, a fairly long passage from Eisenstadt is worth quoting:

> It is of course true that originally the Reformation was not a "modernizing" movement. It did not have very strong modernizing impulses; it did indeed aim at the establishment of a new, purer "medieval" sociopolitical religious order. Originally Protestantism was indeed a religious movement aiming at the religious restructuring of the world. It was just because of these strong "this-worldly" religious impulses that from the very beginning they were caught up with, and in, the major sociopolitical, economic, and cultural trends of change that European (and especially Western and Central European) society was undergoing from the end of the seventeenth century on: the development of capitalism, the development of Renaissance states, absolutism, and the consequent "general" crisis of the seventeenth century, the crisis between "state" and "society," the development of a secular outlook and science.[23]

This explanation clearly shows that a religious ethic can only exert a decisive influence on social change if it coincides with other sociopolitical and socioeconomic factors. Neither the definition of the development of the means of production among Marxists, nor the "subjective-normative preconceived notion" can be an alternative for the sociologist interested in social change. The interplay between sentiment and socioeconomic development in a specific social totality will have to move into the field of vision of the macrosociologist before substantial insights can be achieved. One example of a successful attempt of this kind was the analysis of the founding of the Islamic religion by the French sociologist of religion, Maxime Rodinson.[24] Eisenstadt gives some indication of how an economic ethic can operate in social terms but allows his cultural value orientation to dominate his essential arguments. Eisenstadt's cultural interpretation of the traditional society as one that defines itself on the basis of tradition and experiences its definition, would seem to be a very fruitful one, although it should be added that this only represents *one* dimension of the phenomenon of underdevelopment and does not embrace the problematic as a whole. If we remain at this sociocultural level of discussion, we may observe that religion is one of the central elements within traditionality. As Luhmann has shown in his study of the sociology of religion,[25] in modern societies there are functional equivalents for religion, in contrast to traditional societies, in which religion represents the "symbolic orientation" of an indispensable "collective identity."

In such societies, religion has not yet become secularized, forming part of the sociocultural and politicial order. Religious leaders see their task in the "formulation and formalization of their creeds and traditions so as to make them fully articulated and organized at a relatively differentiated cultural level."[26] Part of the process of formalizing religious principles and anchoring them at the organizational level includes both a forestalling of all forms of intellectualization of religiosity and the suffusion of religion and state as a legitimate ruling authority—Morocco and Saudi Arabia will be presented as case studies for this phenomenon in Chapter 11. Religious leaders saw—not without reason—"a threat to the maintenance of basic political loyalty" in free religious activity.[27] Eisenstadt is all too well aware how difficult it is to achieve generally valid statements through generalization, and he therefore specifies modifying empirical illustrations in support of his thesis. It strikes me as very dubious, however, to formulate assertions in the sociology of religion that are equally valid for monotheistic religions, such as Islam, and for entirely different religious forms, such as those of the Sassanids and the ancient Chinese. In the work of Eisenstadt all these religions are presented as such by empires.

As has been shown elsewhere, monotheistic religions require a varying frame of reference.[28] On the basis of the discussion so far, we can state by way of summary that the analysis of religion as a cultural system should occupy a central place in any attempt to explain the connections between existing norm systems and prevailing social structures or forms of rule in the nonindustrial societies of the Third World— including the forty Islamic countries. It thus becomes clear that the most important difference between so-called traditional and modern societies in this respect is that the former are characterized by religiocultural tradition, whereas the latter are secular and rational, their structures functionally related to one another. Like all other modernization theorists, Eisenstadt has nothing to say about the socioeconomical underdevelopment of the former and the high development of the latter, this in fact constituting the structure of the international society.[29] Admittedly, he does at one point assert that the world now represents the cardinal category of the social sciences, as it displays the hallmarks of a system,[30] but he does not analyze this social system. Within the sense of this general statement, however, I can point out together with Eisenstadt that "modernity was an indigenous development in Western Europe" that was later "foisted" on the whole world.[31] But I cannot go along with Eisenstadt in explaining that this modernity did not take a foothold in the non-Western world in merely cultural-normative terms. He does not depart from the level of the "preconceived normative-subjective notion," for which reason his argumentation leaves no room for the structure of underdevelopment. Holistic social analysis, however, must have at its disposal both structural analysis and a theory of behavior. Those sections of Eisenstadt's study concerned with behavior theory are far-reaching for a sociological analysis of social change, but they nevertheless convey only a limited view, as they stand in isolation.

Having pursued this discussion of the cultural dimension of social change, using as our theme Eisenstadt's definition of underdevelopment as a form of cultural traditionality, our concept of culture now crystallizes along the lines of the passage by Alfred Weber quoted in the opening remarks to this chapter: Culture forms an integral part of social structure, but is not a direct reflection of it. Cultural innovation can on the one hand further, or even accelerate, social change, but it cannot in itself bring change about. Cultural "encrustations," on the other hand, can inhibit social change. It is in this sense that I formulate here the thesis that the furthering of change calls for cultural innovations, the absence of which can give rise to stumbling blocks that prevent the pervasive transformation of the social structure.

But who are the instigators of such cultural innovations and what do we understand by the term innovation as it is used here? According to a notion still prevalent in scholarly writing on modernization theory, in spite of its obsolescence, innovation consists solely of adaptation to Western industrial cultural patterns, which supersede indigenous ones. As a counterview to this not only Eurocentric, but also quite simply false concept, innovation will here be taken to mean the evolution of new forms out of existing indigenous cultural patterns, as well as the latter's enrichment through the adoption of outside elements—not, however, the exchange of one for the other.[32] Over and above this, I am interested not in the modernization of elites through socialization but in the possible significance of such elites in the cultural innovations that are called for, which must be radical and not merely peripheral. In this connection, I have recourse once again to Eisenstadt, who shows, with reference to the latest research into elites, "that such transformative capacities are to be found primarily among elites who are relatively cohesive and have a strong sense of self-identity."[33]

Elites in traditional societies may be divided into those with traditional and those with Westernized education. Modern elites consist almost exclusively of Westernized intellectuals. Despite Eisenstadt's assertions to the contrary, the fostering of culture forms one of the main activities of modern non-Western elites. This does not result in cultural innovation, however, but in self-glorification[34] and in a rejection of the alien. At this point I may bring in König's concept of the defensive culture as an adequate explanation for such activities. Defensive culture is a countermovement that has its justification; it pertains to a counteracculturative tendency hostile to the prevailing processes of acculturation—without, however, being able to overcome them, as it consists only of a protest against a situation for which there is no clear concept.[35] König explains: "What is described as anti- or counter-acculturation is frequently one of the most significant consequences of *cultural defense mechanisms, in fact a defensive culture,* in which the indigenous and the exogenous are virtually indissolubly suffused. This defensive culture seems always to be set in motion when a hopeless situation arises in which the only two alternatives are redemption or destruction."[36] It emerges clearly, both from König's assertion, and above all from an examination of the literary products of non-Western elites, that the *fostering of culture,* in contrast with Eisenstadt's contention, is not only of interest to this elite but in fact forms the prime content of its dealings. The weak or even absent inner cohesion of these elites, a cohesion that forms one of the prerequisites for creativity and innovative ability, is conditioned both by this suggested objective situation, that is, the existential and structural tension between two parallel cultural entities in close proximity, and by the subjective inability of modern non-Western elites to assimilate change at the cultural level.

Maria Mies has undertaken a reconsideration of Durkheim's thesis of anomie so as to be able to interpret the absence of inner cohesion of these elites, who as a result of their Westernization have internalized cultural norms for which there are no corresponding social structures in their own societies. The result is cultural anomie.[37] The discovery of the indigenous culture assists in self-assertion against the invading culture. Preoccupation with culture thus takes the form of a defensive culture, a defense mechanism.[38] Modern elites are acquainted with modernity but are unable to assimilate it culturally. Parallel to them are still the traditional elites, whose prospects are far gloomier, as they are unable to exert an innovative effect, hampered as they are by tradition. The reactions of these traditional elites may be interpreted as "resistance to change," which is synonymous to the inability to redefine problems or permit new solutions. Where individual new solutions are permitted, they are mostly subsumed within one of the old solutions—in any case, the exclusivity of the old solutions is militantly defended, which can lead to new problems.[39] But it is precisely this "resistance to change" that, because it is culturally articulated, constitutes the content of a defensive culture. This general definition of the situation is fully valid for Muslim societies. These reflections on the thesis that cultural innovations instigated by elites are necessary for overcoming underdevelopment cannot be brought to an interim conclusion without calling to mind once again that in this book (Chapter 1) culture has been defined as a system of the symbolic dimensions of social behavior. Such symbols are valid for all members of a cultural sphere and are by no means peculiar to elites. Specifically with regard to Islam, we should also remember that religiocultural symbols form an integral part of reality, so that any understanding of culture that is innovative merely at the literary level alone is futile if it is not also socially pervasive in the Geertzian sense. Provided we are not advocates of either leftist (proletarian) or rightist (people's) populism, we can concede on the basis of a mere glance at the course of history that historical processes have always been directed by elites. It is precisely for this reason that Eisenstadt adopted his position, according to which the relevant elites are able to produce the required cultural innovations that bring about social change. To prevent such an assertion from taking on a purely appellative character—meaning that elites ought to bring about change—we must always bear in mind that the essays of scholars of religion do not form the focal point of this study. My central interest, like that of Ingo Mörth, is in everyday religious awareness.[40] If elites themselves change, bring about innovations, and are the mediators of a dynamic cultural direction, this still does not signify that a process of cultural change has been set in motion. Only when "everyday religious awareness" (Mörth) has changed, that is, when the "symbolic dimensions of social behavior" (Geertz) have changed, can we speak of cultural change in the anthroposociological sense. By the same token, the innovative or dynamic behavior of elites can only become manifest as an enduring element when a parallel sociostructural equivalent has been brought about in the context of transformation processes. We know from the Kemalist experiment with the secularization of Islam and the attempt to eradicate backward elements in Turkey,[41] for example, that this and similar attempts foundered through lack of sociostructural equivalents.

Social structural transformation, as a prerequisite for the development of social structural equivalents for cultural innovations, does not simply happen of its own accord or fall like manna from the skies. We find ourselves, then, confronted once again with the question of whether elites who are enthusiastic about innovation, characterized by inner cohesion, and equipped with the necessary degree of consistency for effective action, may be discerned as the possible instigators of social change in the Islamic Middle East. We have already seen in Chapter 2 that the legal Islamic tradition—in this case, a structural and predominantly urban tradition—and the parallel popular Islamic tradition—which is predominantly though not exclusively rural—have shaped the history of Islam so far. The scriptural definition of Islam is very hostile to change, whereas the popular Islamic tradition was and is a source of symbolic dimensions of social change that have quite often contradicted legal Islam. This de facto tension, however, is not apparent in everyday religious awareness, as this also rejects innovations in Islam. The Islamic term for innovation is *bid'a,* which is tantamount to heresy. The traditional Islamic wisdom pertaining to this cultural attitude says unequivocally *al-bid'a min al-dalal,* or innovation is misleading.

If we now ask where Muslim elites stand in relation to this complex, we can meet two extremes, of which only one exists today. One of these is the extreme of the over-Westernized elite, which recognizes Europe as its sole model and equates the word "Orient" with "backwardness." Exponents of Egyptian liberalism and early Arab-Fabian socialism at the beginning of this century[42] represent one example of this tendency, which is hardly encountered today. The other extreme, which still predominates and may be observed in all countries inhabited by Muslims, is that of politicized Islamic revivalism, correctly characterized by the Egyptian sociologist Fuad Kandil as a variety of "nativism."[43] To be sure, this qualification does *not* intend to suggest that Islamic revivalists are not affected by modernity. There is no question here of any effort toward cultural innovation—only of the retrieval of the traditional culture, as an alternative and as a prospect for the future. Kandil argues: "The aspect of the glorification and idealization of the past seems to be an integral part of the movements in question. They seek to master the present by resorting to 'tried and tested' solutions and watchwords, for all problems are seen as arising out of a considerable deviation from the norms of the traditional culture."[44] This is hardly the right way to meet the urgent need to cope with change in the Islamic culture.

PART THREE

Social Change and the Resistance of the Islamic Sociocultural System: Law, Language, and the Educational System

One of the ideas developed in this book so far, and central to it, is that cultural patterns are not simply reflections of social change that has already taken place; rather, they themselves are able to shape it, although at the same time they are products of it. Taking this idea through to its logical conclusion ultimately amounts to an appeal for cultural change in those structurally underdeveloped regions of the world to which the Islamic countries belong. The cultural world view of man can, but does not have to, change side by side with changing social structures: Sociocultural systems can prove resistant to change. The role of law in Islam is a prime example of this; one of the fundamental principles of the Islamic religious system is that it will not change, and indeed that it is not permitted to change, for it claims a definitive and final message or truth for the whole of mankind.

As an organic religious system,[1] Islam embraces all spheres of life and has strict commandments for conduct within them. Islamic law, the *shari'a,* is the expression of these sacral instructions, which claim to define and structure all aspects of human behavior. At an international Christian-Islamic conference, the Islamic supreme court judge Allah-Buksh K. Brohi, who was both a legal adviser to the late Pakistani dictator Zia ul-Haq and an Islamic professor of law, insisted on this point that the *shari'a* is immutable.[2] One of the most important lessons (that we recognize so far) to be learned from the models of "revolution from above"[3] is that social change can be forced but cultural change cannot. The Kemalist revolution in Turkey is an example of this lesson.[4] If we concede the resistance of cultural systems to instigated change, the question arises whether a change from the inside is possible or has any prospects for success.[5] Taking Islamic law as a specific example, this idea will be examined in Chapter 5 on the possibilities of integrating topical thinking.

The sources of Islamic law, the Koran and the Hadith, are Arabic language proclamations. As we have seen in Chapter 2, Islam is of a primarily Arab character as a result of its historical form. This observation does not mean imposing an Arabocentric interpretation on Islam, for it is part of the theological definition of Islam that its script, the Koran, and its rituals (including prayer) can only be recited or practiced in the Arabic language. Arabic is thus the medium of articulation in the Islamic sociocultural system. Even in pre-Islamic times, Arabic was already a sophisticated written language; among the cultural achievements in Arabic is the superb *mu'allaqat* poetry, which Jacques Berque has compared to that of Charles Baudelaire.[6] The Koran, however, is seen by Muslims as the culmination of the development of the Arabic language; Arabic has since then enjoyed the status of the Koranic language and is generally defined as a sacred one. We shall see in Chapter 6 that Arabic, like every other language, is subject to the factors of social change, and therefore changes with culture. In this context we will consider how this change is culturally received and how Muslims perceive the conflicts that flare up in this connection.

Law, in this case the *shari'a,* is the complex of theological and worldly regulations of Islam. Arabic is the medium of articulation in this sociocultural system. Islamic educational institutions are in addition the place in which this religiocultural tradition, practiced in Arabic, is passed on. The educational institution (*madrasa*) with which we shall be dealing in Chapter 7 is the key institution in Islam, next to that of independent legal reasoning. It is likewise subject to change, and clashes occur between the Islamic model for reality mediated within it and reality itself. The intrusion into the Middle East by technological-scientific civilization has magnified the crisis in Muslim education,[7] but the crisis itself dates from an earlier time and can in fact be traced back to the conflict between hellenized philosophy (*falsafa*) on the one hand and scholastic theology (*kalam*) and sacral law (*fiqh*) in Islam on the other.[8]

5

Social Change and the Potential for Flexibility in the Islamic Notion of Law: The Shari'a *as an "Open Texture," Legal Hermeneutics, and the Topics Thesis*

Some legal scholars attribute a universal character to law, without being aware that they take the term *law* to mean a tradition that has evolved within Europe and which predominates in that hemisphere only. Although we do have both an international society and its inherent international structures, we have no grounds for assuming the existence of a universally valid notion of law, although Article One of the UN Charter does provide for the settlement of international disputes by peaceful, that is, legal means. The UN is an international organization of all peoples, and international law is basically a European law of which there is nonetheless no universal legal awareness. Although there is only one international law, a diversity of legal systems parallel the existing diversity of cultures. The Oxford jurist H.L.A. Hart shows clearly how European-structured law becomes international law, binding for new states. "It has never been doubted that when a new, independent state emerges into existence . . . it is bound by the general obligations of international law. . . . Here the attempt to rest the new state's international obligations on a 'tacit' or 'infered' consent seems wholly threadbare."[1]

In terms of ideal type in legal dogma with regard to the procedure of lawmaking, a substantial distinction is to be made between modern European positive law and the traditional concept of sacred law prevalent in many non-European preindustrial societies, such as, for example, those of the Islamic Middle East. Modern European law is predominantly legislative, devised and codified by people, whereas sacred law is taken as God-given and practiced interpretatively. It is important to draw a

59

clear boundary between legal philosophy and legal practice. At the level of legal practice, the German civil code is intended to be administered in a manner similar to the text of the Koran in terms of legal dogma, although the *shari'a* is neither codified nor endowed with any legal institution independent of the ruler.

If, however, we follow Ralf Dreier's method of treating legal theory as a discipline whose subject is law in general, we can then add further important differences between positive and sacred law to the substantial difference already mentioned. According to Dreier, the three-dimensionality of legal theory consists of a logical and linguistic (or analytical) dimension, a sociological and a psychological (or empirical) dimension, and finally an ethical or political (or normative) dimension.[2] The question now arises whether such a concept of law, derived from modern European law, may be applied to non-European, sacred law. In other words, can the Islamic notion of law be renewed by means of a concept of law enriched by contemporized and intercultural perspectives, or must the *shari'a* be evaluated as a residue of preindustrial times? We know that recourse to the legal definitions of the *shari'a* in the course of the call for Islamization of the law is currently enjoying a certain revival in the forty Islamic countries, and that positive law is roundly rejected.

An aspiration toward innovating the *shari'a* and a parallel and equally desirable flexibilization of the Islamic notion of law aim not only at the adaptation of dominant cultural patterns to the modern, but are also of interest to world peace, inasmuch as intercultural communication and the cultural and legal structure of the global social pattern of interaction form one of its constituent elements. It is of interest here to take up the issue of "the potential for world peace through law"[3] raised by Reinhard May. I have already emphasized repeatedly that the world of today, since Europeanism conquered the world (to use Helmuth Plessner's phrase)[4] has become an international society.[5]

Cultures that were nonliterate prior to this process (for example, in Africa), have by now had European law superimposed upon them in toto.[6] Other societies, which once engendered advanced civilizations and elaborate legal systems, have been able to set a legal notion of their own against the invading European one. In the Islamic Middle East, for example, this has given rise to an internal conflict within the Islamic legal sphere, polarized into religious fundamentalists and secular modernists, that persists to this day.

Reinhard May, who draws upon the peace postulate of the Federal German Basic Constitution as a leitmotif for his treatment of Chinese law, observed at the outset of his research a significant impediment to the argument of a thesis for "world peace through law": the absence of a universal notion of law. There is, for instance, "hardly an adequately based concurrence between the Western and Chinese legal notions." An intercultural comparison of the two leads May to conclude:

> The urge toward achieving a generally valid cognition and foundation for the existence of man and the world, which characterizes the progression and regression of the Western intellectual tradition, conflicts with the imperative of the specific Chinese way of reasoning to find a counterpart for the prevailing state of affairs in a comparatively more open, flowing, and transient world view, without having to justify required change, or any alterations taking place, except in terms of the current state of affairs.[7]

Consonant with such a comparison, I may state here that the legal notion within the "Islamic intellectual tradition" differs considerably from the European one. One aspect of this difference in discourse may be illustrated using the example of legal terminology.

Theodor Viehweg characterizes the tradition of European legal terminology with the formulation: "Legal terminology specifically shows that, for easily discernible reasons, it prefers the assertive to the instructive form of expression, being able in this way to construct a legal reality of its own."[8] Islamic legal terminology may be characterized as the exact opposite of this, as its lines of argument make constant use of the instructive form of legal terminology. The distinction between *halal* and *haram,* between what is permitted and what is forbidden, is indeed central to the content of interpretative Islamic law,[9] which has never known a tradition of codification. The Koran, the substantial source of Islamic law, expressly sets forth the *halal* and *haram* forms in an instructive style; this cultural product of legal terminology has been handed down from the seventh century and continues to pervade contemporary Islamic legal thought. Despite the difference in the structure of legal terminology in these two traditions, however, similar parallels are also to be found in the history of European law.

In our international society we do not have a substantive cultural consensus on international law. The existing patterns of the latter are, as has been mentioned already, based on European law. Since the problems of the North-South gap, which likewise characterize this international society, have intensified, the formally existing international consensus on a basis for legal norms, and hence international law itself, have entered a state of crisis. Events in Iran (as when Iranian students held hostages in the U.S. Embassy in Tehran in 1979) have been only one variant of this phenomenon. An international society without a legal basis, however, would be not only a social entity without peace, it would be characterized by a state of barbarism and brute force. This realization motivates the search for common platforms for culturally differentiated notions of law in the sense of establishing an international, legally anchored consensus. Such platforms would constitute material substantiation for the principles contained in the UN Charter, which are in a certain regard postulative, yet such a consensus would be free from the premature integration of new states into an international legal order in the formation of which they have had no part and which came into existence without them, as described in Hart's quoted critique. In my essay "Akkulturation und interkulturelle Kommunikation," (Acculturation and Intercultural Communication) following the civilization theory of Elias, I appeal for a cultural platform of the international society that would *not* have an imitative Westernization process imposed upon it by a Western European culture, but would be able instead to retain and uphold the wealth of cultural diversity.[10]

It is precisely this aimed-for plurality amid consensus of mutually communicating cultures, with equal status and without global social asymmetries, that constitutes the perceptual interest of the following remarks on Islamic law. Fundamentalist-oriented Islamic jurists react to European dominance with an appeal to the old Islamic doctrine of the Pax Islamica, according to which the world consists of only two regions, the *dar al-Islam,* the House of Islam (literally, of peace), and the *dar al-harb,* the House of War, which is identical with non-Muslim territory.[11] This doctrine of Islamic dominance is no alternative and will be among the subjects of discussion in Part 5.

World peace on the basis of intercultural plurality is of course just as impossible under the dominance of such an Islamic notion of law as it is under the conditions of a world dominated by Europe. A more flexible, modern notion of Islamic law, however, would open the way for a different interpretation, reconcilable with both world peace and intercultural plurality. Nevertheless, in the interests of the societies of the Islamic Middle East, efforts for a renewal of Islamic law would be bound to be helpful, inasmuch as all these societies suffer under their structures of underdevelopment. Social change needs law in order to become institutionalized. Here, the concept of institutionalization is used in the sense of Samuel Huntington's political theory, which unfortunately does not include a legal dimension. Law is used in this context in Frank Rotter's sense, that is, as a component in the institutionalization of social change.[12]

In this chapter on Islamic law (*shari'a*) as an element of the Islamic cultural system, we are primarily concerned with a consideration of how it might be possible to make the Islamic notion of law more flexible and how an Islamic law conceived of in this way might contribute to the cultural accommodation of change. Although in what follows we shall have recourse to the impressive interpretation of law as an "open texture" by H.L.A. Hart, as well as to juristic hermeneutics, I should perhaps justify my somewhat selective concentration on the work of the German legal theorist Viehweg, with regard to his thesis of topical discourse in legal thought, especially as the topics discussion among German jurists now seems to be closed. Ralf Dreier quotes the assessment of G. Otte, "Zwanzig Jahre Topik-Diskussion," and points out: "This topics thesis . . . implies . . . that juristic thinking, even where it purports to be deductive, is in reality an inductive process of convincing decisionmaking, arising out of problematic circumstances and based on argumentations that are open to consensus."[13] Dreier regrets the absence of a theory of argumentation in Viehweg's work, commenting in the same passage: "The initial euphoria has now given way to a certain sobriety."

If, despite current theory, I refer to Viehweg's thesis of topical discourse, this is only inasmuch as it relates to my theme. Juristic discussion has revealed some limitations of this thesis as a frame of reference for the study of the European legal tradition in its present phase. Viehweg's approach of topical discourse in legal reasoning would nonetheless seem to be of use for indicating the potential for reform within Islamic law.

This chapter consists of two parts: In the first section I undertake to reconstruct the *shari'a,* and in the subsequent section I will consider possible ways of making the Islamic notion of law more flexible. I shall also be dealing with the Arabic language (*'arabiyya*) as the linguistic medium of the *shari'a,* albeit only in passing, as I will take up this subject later, in Chapter 6.

On the Genesis of Islamic Law: The Shari'a as a Form of Worship and as a Religious Legal System

Pre-Islamic Arabia (the Arabian peninsula) consisted, as indicated in Chapter 2, of acephalous nomadic tribes, organized in a segmentary fashion and reproducing materially by means of the "camel economy," as well as by making raids on merchant caravans (*ghazu* actions). No materially developed culture, and consequently no formal legal system, was able to develop within this bedouin milieu. The bedouin is unfamiliar with abstract thinking: "He is a realist, and the tough life in the desert has not prepared him particularly well for reflection on the infinite,"[14] writes the French scholar of Islam Maxime Rodinson in his portrayal of pre-Islamic Arab culture. In addition to the nomadic social organization of these ethnic groups, however, pre-Islamic society was also familiar with two relatively developed urban centers of trade, Mecca and Medina, out of which Islam emerged; for this reason the founding of the Islamic religion may be interpreted as the spread of an urban culture.[15] I should nonetheless note here that neither in the nomadic nor in the urban component of pre-Islamic Arab culture was there a tradition of written law; the prevailing law was the primitive customary law—which included the vendetta—among the acephalous tribes; in the two urban centers of Mecca and Medina social life was regulated by more developed forms of customary law.

The history of the founding of the Islamic religion is not simply a religious history but is also synonymous with the establishment of a Pax Islamica and thus with the birth of a new legal tradition, as is documented by *shari'a*. The new Islamic law, the *shari'a,* is a divine law and forms the substance of Islam. The great *shari'a* historian Joseph Schacht correctly states that it is impossible to understand Islam without understanding Islamic law;[16] he also points out, equally correctly, that *kalam* (Islamic theology) scholars have never been able to achieve the same status as *fiqh* (Islamic jurisprudence) scholars in Islamic history. Semantically *fiqh* means science, but juristic science is science par excellence in Islam. The term *'alim* (plural *ulema*) means scholar in Arabic. In Islamic history, the *ulema* have always been the guardians of legal Islam, which has been in a state of permanent antagonism with the very spiritually oriented Sufi *tariqa* Islam (Islamic mysticism) but has nevertheless always managed to keep the upper hand.[17]

Although pre-Islamic Arab culture was a literate one,[18] the Koran was in cultural terms the first great written document, on the basis of which an advanced Arab culture was able to unfold in due course. The Koran,[19] revealed between A.D. 610 and 632 (the death of Muhammed),[20] is the focal point here, for it constitutes the first primary source of Islamic law. The second primary source is the Sunna, based on the Hadith tradition, which consists of the lawmaking proclamations handed down by the Prophet. Two further components of Islamic law are acknowledged as complementary secondary sources: *ijma'* (*consensus doctorum*) and *qiyas* (conclusion by analogy).

Revealed Koranic truth is regarded in Islam as eternal and immutable; its jurisdiction is unlimited. The Islamic law derived from this truth claims to embrace all spheres of life and is theocentric in the sense that in its capacity as revelation it merely serves as an instrument whereby God governs the world and not as a means for people to regulate their social interaction. The history of Islamic law so far may be divided according to Coulson's research[21] into three phases; the *first* phase, comprising the course taken by the founding of the Islamic religion from the seventh to the ninth centuries, may be described as the formation phase, during which a coherent Islamic legal system was developed; the *second* phase, from the tenth to the twentieth centuries, documents the rigidity of this law, inasmuch as reality was seen as being determined by law, which claimed to be valid as divine truth for all times and was in no respect to be modified by history. Only in the twentieth century, after the formation of Islamic national states in what is now an international society, has a *third* phase been entered in the historical development of Islamic law. This phase has come about because modern states have been unable to cope with their system and its environment with the aid of classical Islamic law, this legal doctrine relating to historical conditions that are no longer true in modern times and are therefore obviously no longer appropriate to new legal requirements.

This problem did not arise for the first time in the twentieth century, however. Even during the golden age of Arab-Islamic culture, particularly in the period between the ninth and eleventh centuries, before the collapse of the Arab Islamic empire in 1258, new and complex social and economic structures that could not be regulated by means of the *shari'a* evolved. This difficulty was resolved by using a method characteristic for Arab Islamic history: through the legal circumvention of a legal dogma that was unlimited in its validity, namely, by means of a new type of law known as the *hiyal* literature. *Hila* (plural *hiyal*) means legal dodge in Arabic, in other words, a way of circumventing a legal norm by legal means. The Islamic *shari'a,* for example, prohibits the charging of interest; the *hiyal* literature led to legal ways of circumventing this prohibition.[22] Rodinson, who has researched this phenomenon, describes "medieval Muhammedan society . . . [as] an ideological society."[23] This feature is not only evident within the sphere of law, however. Clearly, the behavior of people who believe in an immutable dogma must in the course of the centuries deviate from dogma, if that dogma is not newly formulated and adapted to suit new conditions. But because that dogma claims not to be historically conditioned, and because it conceives of itself as eternally valid, a new restructuring would contradict the essence of that dogma. This is the substance of the great centuries-old gulf between legal philosophy and practice in the history of Islam. On the basis of his research in Morocco, the U.S. social scientist Waterbury developed the concept of "behavioral lag" (referred to earlier) which goes some way toward explaining the gulf between thought and behavior that arises out of the impossible adaptation of religious dogma to new conditions: "In this sense it is more important to understand what Moroccans really do and why they do it than to understand what they think they are doing."[24] This comment is also important to the analysis of Islamic law and its forms of validity. In the second section of this chapter, I will argue that the application of juristic hermeneutics can help us to understand this circular relationship between the imperative (although unconscious) nonhistoric preconception of Islamic legal sources and the belief in its immutability. Although there is only one Islamic law, there are nevertheless differing historical and geographical notions of Islamic law.

Arabic is obviously the language of Islamic law, inasmuch as the Koran is not merely formally a product of the Arabic language. Numerous verses of the Koran emphasize its Arabic character. Non-Arab Muslims must say their prayers and similarly recite the Koran in Arabic, for which reason the language used in non-Arab Koranic schools is also Arabic. All Islamic jurists are educated in Arabic.

In the same way that the language of the Koran is sacred and makes use both of the forms of commandment and prohibition, the language of Islamic law, as I have emphasized, is one of *instructive* rather than *expressive* form, which distinguishes Islamic from European law. Sacred law is brought to expression by means of the sacred language of the Koran,[25] so that one Islamic jurist feels justified in stating that "*'Arabiyya* [Arabic] is the symbol of Islam."[26]

Islamic jurisprudence, *fiqh,* equally embraces both the sphere of worship (*'ibadat*) and that of profane business (*mu'amalat*),[27] the *shari'a* thus to the same degree representing both a form of worship and a legal system, albeit a sacred one. Islam differs from Christianity chiefly in that it is an organic rather than an ecclesiastical religious system, and in its pronounced worldliness.[28] This explains why *fiqh* is central to Islam. The divine law, however, is not only concerned with the external aspects of life; Islamic *fiqh* thus distinguishes between the facts of the *tashri'* (legislation) and *taujih* (guidance), both forms relating to the ascertainment of what is *halal* (permitted) and what is *haram* (forbidden). Whereas *tashri',* as it is irrevocably laid down in the tradition of the four sources of the Islamic notion of law, is concerned with external control for the purposes of the observance of commandments and prohibitions, *taujih* relates to the internalization of these norms, that is, to the hearts of Muslims, which are not externally controllable by means of law. The Lebanese *fiqh* scholar Subhi Salih (killed by Shi'ite gunmen in Beirut in 1988) regarded *tashri'* and *taujih* as a single entity, asserting: "When the outer form becomes united and harmonized with the inner depths, then this unity forms a part of *the divine beauty,* which is not to be misinterpreted as pantheism, as it is by some who have deviated from Islam, but is to be seen as the divine beauty of which the Prophet of Allah was speaking when he said that God loves beauty."[29]

The content of *halal* and *haram* presents a further question. The Tunisian *fiqh* scholar Muhammad Ben Ashur, who has examined the goals (*maqasid*) of the *shari'a,* alludes to the twin concepts of *as-Salah* and *al-Fasad,* good and evil. From these two definitions the terms *al-Maslaha* and *al-Mafsada,* literally, the proper course and villainy, are linguistically derived. On the basis of this conceptual definition, Ben Ashur elucidates: "The highest goal of the *shari'a* is the realization of *good* and the aversion of *evil.*"[30] The former is identical to the interest of the Islamic *umma,* the Islamic community, while the latter is identical to damage to it. All is well with the *umma* provided Islam dominates in the spheres of *'ibadat* and *mu'amalat,* that is, as long as the spheres of worship and business transaction are controlled by the principles of the *shari'a.*

The development of the *shari'a*[31] between the seventh and ninth centuries occurred simultaneously with the Muslim conquests, during which the Pax Islamica expanded from a city-state to an empire. Muhammed founded the city-state of Medina[32] in 622, after leaving Mecca with his followers (the year of the *Hijra,* which marks the beginning of the Muslim era). Even in Muhammed's lifetime the *Pax Islamica* grew to comprise the whole of the Arabian peninsula, becoming an empire as early as the eighth century through Islamization by conquest.[33] The *shari'a* was thus confronted not only with the problems of regulating the internal affairs of a political order but also with those of war and peace between states. Islamic *fiqh* scholars such as Sabir Tu'aima propound the thesis that the *shari'a* offers no less than the fundamental formulation of international law.[34] Tu'aima writes:

> What is fundamental about Islam, is that it is a religion for the whole of humanity. Muslims hence have an obligation to proclaim Islam in order to bring all those whose hearts are open to Islam into its fold. . . . As long as Muslims proclaim their religion in order to disseminate it, Islam is in a state of either peace or war [*dar salam* or *dar harb*]. Circumstances falling between these two are regulated by means of international treaties.[35]

Tu'aima is referring to the ninth sura of the Koran, "Repentance,"[36] in which, on the one hand, there is a call for the military dissemination of Islam and, on the other, for the honoring of agreements already made (for example, a truce).

By way of transition to my attempt to integrate into Islam the resumed tradition of topical discourse of Viehweg, I would like to appeal for a reform of Islamic law. Such reform will not be able to limit itself to a renewed exegesis of handed-down law. Tu'aima's Islamic definition of an international law that lays claim to an imposition of Islam on the whole world—in blatant contradiction of the ideal of a pluralist world culture—ought in itself to highlight the necessity for reforming Islamic law. This much will also be conceded by culturally innovative Muslims. These remarks similarly point out the contrast between European and non-European law, as indicated by Reinhard May in using the Chinese example: "It has visible consequences, perhaps even undesired ones, for the Western conception of bringing about world peace through law."[37]

Perhaps a rapprochement between culturally divergent legal traditions, using the medium of symmetrical global intercultural communication, would do more to achieve world peace than the concepts propounded so far of a universal claim to validity on the part of a *single* legal tradition. Such proposed global communication[38] would of course have to embrace the legal sphere as well. For scholars such as myself, living and working as Muslims in a state of tension between Western and Eastern culture, the question arises whether Islamic legal discourse, with the great steps forward made by Europe in its own legal sphere, can be fertilized without at the same time sacrificing Islamic authenticity. A social transformation of the Islamic part of the world would today call for a modern notion of law, appropriate to social conditions, since any modernization of the social structures of the present Islamic countries is condemned to failure unless it also aims for a parallel attempt to regalvanize Islamic culture. Only reform from the inside, therefore, can bring any promise of success; it would also have to be incorporated into similarly structured Islamic institutions. The modernization of Islam must take place from the inside and be carried out by Muslims themselves. The remarks in the following section are shaped by this prior understanding.

The Reform of Islamic Law and the Potential for Flexibility in the Islamic Notion of Law

In the Islamic Middle Ages, which represented (as should be mentioned in passing) the golden age of an advanced civilization,[39] in contrast to the popularly held European view of the era, an Islamic philosophy was flourishing in which the central themes of ancient Greek philosophy were being assimilated. These influences are described using the concept of the "hellenization of Islam."[40] A conflict flared up within Islam between philosophy and sacred law (*fiqh*) after Islamic philosophers began, in the context of their "rationalization of the cosmos," to introduce hellenized scientific terminology, alongside sacred terminology, into Arabic.[41] The charge of heresy (*takfir*) was not long in coming, and the persecution of philosophers brought this process of the rationalization and desacralization of the Arab Islamic culture to an end. "No wonder in this case either that Muslim orthodoxy cursed both Avicenna and Averroës, burning both of them in effigy, that is via their works, as the Christian Inquisition was later to burn Giordano Bruno in body,"[42] writes Ernst Bloch, recalling and extolling Islamic philosophy. The Egyptian philosopher Mourad Wahba, who teaches at the Ain-Shams University in Cairo, has described how Averroës is honored in Europe, whereas he is condemned by Muslim orthodoxy even today; he calls it as "the Averroës paradox."[43] At the same First Islamic Conference on Islam and Civilization (Cairo, November 1979) at which Wahba spoke, I appealed for a secularization[44] of Islam and, using Luhmann's frame of reference,[45] emphasized that the functional differentiation of society, that is, the surmounting of underdevelopment, will entail reducing the religious system to a partial system, or secularization.

Islamic law is divine law revealed by God and not to be conceived of in historical terms; according to the Islamic cognizance of values it is immutable and eternally valid; in terms of the Islamic notion of law, the *shari'a* does not serve to help people shape their social life according to law, since its function is to govern human behavior as regards divine will. The purpose of the Islamic *fiqh* scholar consists exclusively in interpreting this will. We have already seen, however, that in the Islamic Middle Ages the *hiyal* literature relating to legal dodges and tricks was required to adapt Islamic law to the life of society. This occurred because it was not permitted to make any alterations to the norm itself. Legal practice was thus adjusted to the changed reality, but not the legal form itself. From the formal point of view, the deviation from the norm in practice also represents the starting point of every process of jurisdiction undertaken by a modern European jurist. Here, too, the principle applies: "The legal norm has an existence independent of social reality within its fundamental sphere of validity,"[46] even though it is applied by people and is not a divine revelation like the *shari'a*. The Islamic jurist could learn a great deal in this respect from the European jurist and from his way of dealing with legal norms. Both the theory of topical discourse and juristic hermeneutics could be integrated into a reformed Islamic legal system. We are concerned here not with theological argumentation but with the process of independent legal reasoning as a cultural discourse. We can therefore exclude the question of the origin of law (whether legislation or divine revelation) from our consideration, interpreting law instead in the sense meant by H.L.A. Hart, as an "open texture," a fixed written structure of norms, open to interpretation. Hart points out that all legal systems, whether traditionally handed-down or legislative in character, represent a compromise between two legal requirements, "the need for certain rules" and "the need to leave open," adding: "In every legal system a large and important field is left open for the exercise of discretion by courts."[47] Hart reminds us that recourse to the same handed-down law can have a different content in different times and different systems. Islamic legal history offers a classic example in support of this assertion.

Our deliberations pertaining to substantive legal reform in Islam have to proceed on the basis of the current situation in the Muslim countries—which, at least in ideological terms, is characterized by a rejection of the Western model in general and its legal model in particular—and by recourse to their own model, the *shari'a*. We must take this into consideration but at the same time vigorously oppose the classical Islamic legal means of the *hiyal* (legal dodges) as well as the verbal manipulation of Islamic law (for example, amputation of the hand as a punitive measure). Thus the question arises to what extent the potential for "flexibilization" of the Islamic notion of law exists. ("Flexibilization," a technical term currently employed in German juridical debate, refers to the nonrigid handling of legal norms. This is not tantamount to a bending of law at the interpreter's discretion; rather, flexibilization conveys the notion of a certain pliancy in the process of lawmaking and jurisdiction.) If one greets this cultural return of consciousness without at the same time acknowledging cultural ghettoization, and indeed defensive cultural chauvinism, then we can find no road here leading to intercultural learning processes, nor any prospect for substantive cultural change in the sense of developing patterns for the cultural accommodation of social change.

Change—even in legal reasoning—has always taken place in Islamic history, although the Islamic cultural system does not admit a category of "change." Yet change is related to legal practice and not to legal philosophy, as noted earlier. In this sense, the Islamic notion of law has always changed in opposition to its own sense of values. The flexibilization aimed for here would, unlike the former Islamic *hiyal* legal tradition, have to incorporate a consciousness of social and cultural change. The theory of law as an "open texture" in Hart's sense, the topics theory of Viehweg (to a certain extent still to be further clarified), and juristic hermeneutics could all be of great assistance in efforts to modernize Islamic law. The target is to establish an Islamic discourse of legal reasoning that runs—in the norm and in legal practice alike—from actual social givens to textual understanding.

In Islamic legal philosophy the text is the point of departure. I have already made my theme-related reference to Viehweg, even if I share Ralf Dreier's critical evaluation. I am concerned here, like Josef Esser, with "disclosing topical forms of thinking as an indispensable element in the channelling of metadogmatic assessment criteria and in ensuring accuracy."[48] It is only in this sense that I have recourse to Viehweg's theory of topical discourse, which is addressed, as Martin Kriele says, "not to the dogmatic system as such, but against the preconceived idea that a system can be perfect and definitive."[49] Advocating the adoption of topical thinking in the Islamic notion of law therefore amounts to advocating openness in the legal system.

In real historical terms there has been no lack of such openness. Viewed from historical periods in which the Muslim *ulema* enjoyed ideological supremacy, it *is* possible to find intellectual plurality in Islamic history. Both the tradition of hellenized Muslim philosophers, as well as the early debates from which the legal internal differentiation of Islam arose (the emergence of the four legal schools, the *madhahib*) may be mentioned in this connection.[50] Another important factor is the distinction in Islamic law between *taqlid,* submission to the authority of predecessors as *fiqh* scholars, and *ijtihad,* creative lawmaking through individual, independent legal reasoning (although of course also on the basis of the *shari'a*). Islamic modernism, which came into existence during the second half of the nineteenth century in Egypt,[51] and the efforts to reform Islamic law in this century[52] represent a revival of this *ijtihad* tradition in Islam.

One of the central ideas of Islamic legal reformers pursues the line that God as Creator would not bring His will to expression in the form of rigid laws and that it is a gross misreading of Koranic teaching to interpret it as a rigid legal doctrine: The Koran contains general principles that are intended to be understood as an Islamic ethic and that also allow for varying interpretations within the *ijtihad* tradition. This notion of the Koran as the source of Islamic legal ethics opens the way for the introduction of topical thinking into Islam. "Topics" here refers to "that technique of thought which focuses on problems,"[53] writes Viehweg, adding that it is "thus the technique of thinking in terms of problems."[54] Islamic ethics are of a thoroughly systematic character, so that separate problem orientations could arise and, on the one hand, take account of the needs of Muslim societies in the developmental process and, on the other, also lend themselves to integration within the Islamic ethical system without, however, having to lapse into the ossified tracks of scholastic *fiqh* doctrine. Viehweg advocates bearing in mind a dovetailing between system and problem,[55] emphasizing that "topics" cannot be understood without subsuming the integrity of the problem within some kind of order.

According to Viehweg, thinking in terms of problems should embrace the system as a whole, its components, and also the concepts and statutes of jurisprudence. For Islamic law, the adoption of this method would entail a notion of law deriving from the problems of Islamic societies and not primarily from texts. An introduction of topical discourse into Islam means grasping the idea that the function of topical themes lies in "serving the discussion of problems. . . . The topical themes, which intervene in an assisting capacity, derive their respective meanings from the problem itself."[56]

I have just cited Viehweg's central notion that problems must be integrated into an order. A highly comprehensive body of handed-down, established Islamic law is already in existence; this is not to be laid aside *ad acta,* but rather reconsidered in light of an awareness of problems. The introduction of topical thinking into Islamic law cannot entail starting from scratch and disavowing the traditions that have been upheld so far. Interpretation is itself an art that has always been predominantly the domain of Islamic *fiqh* scholars. Today it is a matter of cultivating this art in the wider context of the development of Muslim societies and with a problem orientation. Viehweg highlights interpretation as an element of "topics," arguing that this involves forging new possibilities for deriving meanings without damaging the old ones. This occurs by adhering to fixed designations that have already been made but shifting them into new angles that have often arisen in quite different connections and now offer an opportunity to give new applications to old precepts.[57] These aspects of topical thinking presumably render Viehweg's theoretical framework more acceptable to Muslim jurists, who fear for their heritage, especially because exegesis (*tafsir*) forms part of Islamic law. Exegesis does provide interpretation, but it is important to point out that, according to Viehweg, not every interpretation fulfills the requirements of topical thinking. To return to the definition cited above, Viehweg stresses: "Not every interpretation (explanation, exegesis, hermeneutics) does this, but every one is capable of doing it. It is part of topics."[58]

The researcher can find examples of interpretative patterns that may be construed as topical in the writings of Islamic modernists since Afghani—although I should qualify this by saying that most Islamic modernists do not depart from the basis of religious dogma.[59] One very important piece of Islamic writing, dating from 1925, the author of which was a *fiqh* scholar at the Muslim al-Azhar University and also a supreme court judge, does contain an interpretation of Islam that may be construed as topical in the sense defined by Viehweg. This work is Ali Abdelraziq's Cairo publication *al-Islam wa usul al-hukm* (Islam and forms of government),[60] in which the author, on the basis of an interpretation that fully qualifies as topical, reaches the conclusion that Islam is only a religion for the spiritual sphere, and not a system of government. In the Islamic Middle East, this counts as a revolutionary interpretation, which cost the author his material existence at the time. Abdelraziq nevertheless laid a most important foundation stone.

The introduction of topical discourse into Islamic law is of course unthinkable without corresponding concepts for reform. Orthodox Muslim *fiqh* scholars react fanatically against all reformers, not hesitating to invoke the weapons of *takfir* (pronouncement as a misbeliever) against culturally innovative Muslims. It would be instructive at the end of this appeal for the adoption of topical thinking in Islamic law to undertake a sample critique of an opponent of all forms of Islamic legal reform. This opponent is the Pakistani fundamentalist Muhammad Muslehuddin, who in fact has a Western education and is a graduate of London University. In the context of his (in some respects justified) criticism of Western Oriental studies, he takes issue with Malcolm Kerr, the political scientist from California who was researching into efforts toward reform in modern Islam and who was murdered by Muslim fanatics in Beirut in January 1984.[61] Muslehuddin discredits all reform attempts with the apodictic statement: "Those who think of reforming or modernizing Islam are misguided, and their efforts are bound to fail. . . . Why should it be modernized, when it is already perfect and pure, universal, and for all time?"[62] In his view, therefore, the task of jurists is solely that of interpreting the *shari'a* in order "to comprehend and discover the law and not to establish or create it."[63] Such a rigid definition of the work of jurists, who in this case cannot be scholars in the Weberian sense, clearly leaves no room either for topical thinking or for topically-oriented interpretations along the lines of Viehweg. The jurist interprets at a purely philological level, and, if this proves insufficient, the only other recourse is then deduction by analogy. Remote from all belief in modernization, we may discern here parallels between legal dogmatists who work with positive law but who do not proceed on a topical basis, and the Muslim *shari'a* jurist. In this connection, Viehweg alerts us that "frequent occurrence of deduction by analogy generally points to the absence of a perfect logical system."[64]

Muslehuddin's critique of Kerr focuses on the latter's rational, scientific working style, which attempts to comprehend Islamic law in terms of human categories—making him bound to fail, as this law is instead a divine law:

> Divine law is to be preserved in its ideal form as commanded by God, or else it will be devoid of its capability to control society

which is its chief purpose. The mistaken view of the Orientalists is
due mainly to the fact that the real good may be rationally known
and that the law should be determined by social needs, while all
such needs are provided for in divine law and God alone knows what
is really good for mankind.[65]

With the application of juristic hermeneutics, this statement col-
lapses as an ideology-laden assertion. Arguing in terms of *shari'a* law,
the text of the Koran is an expressly fixed body of directives for a
God-given order. The process of jurisdiction comprises the formulation
of a question, and its answer calls for an evaluation in accordance with
norms. This evaluation needs to be derived from the appropriate legal
text in which those norms are laid down—in this case the Koran. Esser
distinguishes between the historical and the problem-oriented precon-
ceptions of a text, thus resorting to juristic hermeneutics as a way of
representing the elements of understanding in the process of lawmaking.
Esser develops the thesis of "carrying over" a problem into the text,
"in that a specific current issue is carried over into the text. . . . and
a preconception of the problem is brought out of the text that does
not coincide with the historical preconception."[66] Such a cognitive
procedure, that is, one of deriving a nonhistorical preconception of a
text that is to be interpreted, such as the Koran, is inevitable according
to Hans Georg Gadamer's hermeneutics. The adoption of this herme-
neutic cognitive method would be an enormous enrichment of Islamic
law and signify an opening to innovation.

Notwithstanding the appeal I have made for an integration of
topical discourse into Islamic legal philosophy, I have not overlooked
that the cited position of Muslehuddin is more representative of Islamic
intellectual discourse in the legal sphere than the position being
propounded here. The juristic debate in Islam, the conflicts and tensions
of which manifest themselves in the legal system, is not aimed—as is
the European debate—at determining the substance of law but, rather,
exclusively at interpreting the will of God on the basis of *fiqh* sources,
in order to transform it into a "system of legally enforceable rights
and duties,"[67] as Coulson, one of the leading international experts on
Islamic law, stresses. As long, however, as the fundamentalist belief
prevails that Islamic society ought to be "the product of sacred law
and to be seen in an ideal way in harmony with its ordinances,"
resulting in the perception that Islamic law is immutable[68]—it is difficult
to imagine how Islam could evolve into a dynamic element of the
currently rapid social change in crisis-driven Islamic societies. The
adoption of topical discourse would increase the capacity of Islam to
become a sociocultural factor in the process of overcoming underde-

velopment. In contrast, the generally accepted application of Islamic law as an instrument of legitimation,[69] as is the case in many Islamic countries, leaves Islam in its archaic state, indeed making it resistant to change in societies where social change is taking place with such enormous speed and where the adaptation of sociocultural systems to altered conditions has become a matter of urgent necessity. The call for the Islamization of law[70] and the policies related to this call reflect a defensive cultural response to change and ultimately lack the needed willingness to cope with structural change. The so-called Islamization of law does not show any sign of cultural accommodation of change.

6

'Arabiyya *as a Sacred Language: Arabic as a Language Between Koranic and Historical Designations*

If language is, among other things, "an instrument of a quite specific nature that we use to cope with the reality of our lives,"[1] then we need to ask in this connection what effects the problems of the cultural reception of change in Islam have had on the Arabic language (*'arabiyya*). At the descriptive level we know that Koranic Arabic has shaped the Arabic language as a whole since the founding of Islam as a religion, and in the course of this study (Chapter 3) we have learned that according to Islam's own understanding of itself it will not submit to any form of change. Does this also hold for language? And, further, how can such a claim be sustained in the linguistic sphere in the face of the factual reality of continual linguistic change, side by side with and analogous to social change?

In the course of its thirteen centuries of history, Islam has so far twice been confronted with a substantial challenge, which is of interest to us here with regard to the cultural accommodation of change specifically within the sphere of language. The first challenge arose in the Middle Ages, when Muslim theologians and philosophers were beginning to respond to and adopt the cultural heritage of ancient Greece.[2] This meant the incursion of a cognitive, theoretical, and rational terminology into the Islamic culture, not only adding one more linguistic category to those already existing—the literary (poetry) and the sacred (Koranic Arabic)—but also stimulating substantial change and proffering alternative forms of linguistic articulation. The hellenization of Islam was itself affected by the collapse of the Arab Islamic empire in the thirteenth century (1258): The hellenization of Islamic thought failed to prevail beyond the epoch of High Islam and did not set deep roots. Not until the nineteenth century, with the onset of the modern confrontation between the West and the Middle East under the shadow of colonialism, was another sociocultural gauntlet thrown down, although this time under quite different historical circumstances.[3] These two challenges, both the earlier effects on Arabic of the hellenization of Islam during the classical advanced civilization phase of the Islamic Middle Ages and the ongoing language change of the modern period since the nineteenth century, form the focus of Chapter 6. Although I am not concerned here with linguistic analysis, I cannot entirely evade the scholarly controversy surrounding my theme.[4] On the one hand there is the school of thought of Paul Henle, more accessible to the social scientist as it sees a close connection between language, thought, and culture. On the other hand is that of my Göttingen colleague Gustav Ineichen, who defends a linguistic position that interprets change as being transposed into language from the outside, language thus being affected by change lexically but not syntactically. According to Ineichen, we must distinguish in linguistic analysis between the level of expression and the level of content, since a formal incongruence exists between the two. The level of content falls within the sphere of semantics and thus outside that of linguistics. We shall have occasion to refer to these controversial positions again in the course of our exploration.

The philosopher 'Aziz Lahbabi, who teaches at the Muhammed V University in Rabat, having completed his habilitation work in Paris and advanced as a result of his numerous publications, both in French and Arabic, to become an important contemporary Arab thinker, has the following to say in regard to the current state of Arabic: "Our language is closely bound up with our reality: *'Arabiyya* adapts itself to some extent to changed conditions, but sometimes it forms an obstacle to change. This language reflects both periods of opening up and of stagnation in our history. It is suffering today from an inability to adapt to change, renouncing its right both to innovation and to open itself up."[5] Lahbabi has put forward this position at numerous lectures in a number of Arab cities, reaching the following conclusion in the quoted collection from which this text is taken: "The Arabic language is undoubtedly in need of substantial changes today so that it can develop; it is subject—like everything human—to the imperatives of change."[6] What is striking here is that the Koranically-inspired claim to the perfection and hence "freedom from change" of Arabic is *implicitly* rejected.

Although still only at the beginning of our analysis, we find ourselves confronted once again with the methodological problem of determining what linguistic change in fact is. Ineichen cites the varying interpretations within linguistics of the connection between linguistic and social change, freely admitting that "the entire complex of questions

. . . [is] still open,"[6a] although insisting that change alters the grammatical structure of a language less than its lexical fund and its correlation of meaning. Social change affects "extralingual" situations. The grammatical structure of *'arabiyya* has indeed hardly changed at all in centuries. What is it that brings about this conservation of tradition in Arabic? In the High Islamic period, this language was still capable of assimilating the philosophy of ancient Greece; today it is not able to meet the needs of modern science and technology. During verbal discussion with Ineichen, he put forward the view that the sacred commitment of a language adversely affects its capacity for expression; this does not in turn affect its morphosyntactic structure, however. Helmut Seiffert criticizes modern linguistics for restricting its research horizons to language as an instrument of communication, defined as a "socially agreed system of signs." Historical issues are excluded on the grounds that they are extralingual; other "viewpoints," such as that of the nature of language as a historical or cultural product, are brought into discussion only as secondary to the study of language and are thereby underestimated.[7] The basic grammatical structures of *'arabiyya* have hardly altered at all in centuries. It would nevertheless be problematical to reduce linguistic change to the level of grammatical change, especially since this would lead to an exclusion of the historical elements of linguistic change. These reservations point to a need to combine linguistic with semantic analysis, and they are not compatible with the line of argument of the now long-discarded method of traditional Orientalists, namely, the philological criticism of texts. The latter can hardly contribute toward an illumination of our theme, whereas sociolinguistic and semantic approaches, in conjunction with a social scientific definition of culture and the inclusion of language in the context of thought and a sociological concept of culture, are of far more help. In view of the restricted horizons in such research, the great French scholar of Islam Maxime Rodinson, himself a researcher of sources and a professional in the methods of philological textual analysis, advocates the adoption of the social scientific formulation of questions and working techniques in Islamic studies, heralding "la fin de l'hégémonie de la philologie."[8]

Bearing in mind that linguistic and cultural norms are mutually interwoven both in the cultural and in the linguistic systems, we should perhaps recall here the position I formulated in Chapter 1, following Geertz, in which cultural patterns consist of cultural symbols that convey meaning. I insisted in this connection that cultural patterns and reality are not mutually reducible—reality is not a product of cultural patterns and cultural patterns likewise are not a reflection of reality. Both social reality and cultural systems are closely interwoven and are able to influence each other in both directions. This position may be transferred to the relationship between language and culture. Language is the medium in which cultural symbols are articulated. It is a product of social reality but at the same time "one of the factors . . . that affect perception and the general organization of experience."[9] Henle, who alleges a causal relationship among language, thought, and culture, accepting the idea that "certain linguistic characteristics can make certain kinds of perception more prevalent and more probable,"[10] similarly insists that this causal relationship can work in the other direction, insofar as it is dubious "whether one can gain a sufficiently close relationship with language without . . . a broader familiarity with the culture." Transferring this to our own theme, this assertion means that Islamic culture can hardly be accurately understood without familiarity with its cultural symbols, articulated through the medium of Arabic. Koranic Arabic is taken to be eternally valid, but culture is changeable and the perception of human beings is—to reiterate Henle—shaped by "certain linguistic characteristics." This suggests the question whether a language that perceives itself as resistant to change can in fact become an impediment to the cultural reception of social change, insofar as language shapes human perception. In other words: How can Muslims perceive change culturally if their perception is shaped by an *'arabiyya* that is ostensibly not subject to change? We can start with the reflection that "every culture correlates to some aspect of the language that accompanies it,"[11] at the same time emphasizing with Henle that we are not yet able to capture this "aspect" in a general concept. More work on this theme would seem to be the only way forward so far as this question is concerned. We have already stated that the basic grammatical structures of Arabic have so far remained virtually untouched by change. This resistance to change is particularly striking when compared to the development of European languages. One explanation for this is the "eternally valid" commitment of Arabic to the Koran as the ultimate and definitive divine revelation, whereby its linguistic form also achieves an equally definitive and unchangeable status among Muslims. European linguists carrying out interlingual research, such as Ineichen, stress the hermetic nature of *'arabiyya* in contrast with its elucidation by means of linguistics. This also illustrates how difficult it is to carry out linguistic modernization work in *'arabiyya*. So far this has not gone beyond the translation stage through the formation of new words. A European-educated Arab reading the Arabic translation of, for example, Marx's writings, is able to replicate the contents by surmising the original concepts behind the new Arabic words. For an Arab with a Muslim education, however, the translated text is as good as a closed book. W. Diem deals with this in an essay in which he evaluates a linguistic treatise published in 1969 by the European-educated Egyptian linguist A. Ayyub. In Diem's view, the piece under evaluation acquires special value because linguistic research at Arab universities is still in its infancy. This is undoubtedly on account of the socially determined backwardness of the Arab universities, the cause of which is deeply rooted in history. To this day, a stubborn belief persists that Arabic was predestined to be a superior language and that an Arab may acquire technical and scientific knowledge from Europe but can never acquire useful linguistic knowledge[12]—a view tirelessly propounded in apologetic literature. The Iraqi writer M. Ismail thus refers to some examples of the adoption of Arabic vocabulary in European languages in order to demonstrate the *original,* and hence superior nature of Arabic, as against the *artificial* nature of those languages that developed out of others.[13] The tendency of Muslims to see themselves as superior to others will be dealt with in more detail in Chapter 7, where these attitudes will be specified as a "psychological impediment" to learning from other cultures. More enlightened Muslims, however, no longer persist in this view, so that today, a decade and a half after the appearance of Ayyub's publication, we can speak of a penetration of the Arab Islamic Orient by linguistics. The renowned Centre d'Etudes et de Recherches Economiques et Sociales (CERES) of the University of Tunis not long ago published the proceedings of a large-scale scholarly colloquium on *al-lisaniyyat* (linguistics) and *'arabiyya.*[14]

In the Arab Middle East today is a fusion between two notions of language, each of different cultural origin: on the one hand the Islamic notion of *'arabiyya,* which we shall be looking at in more detail, and on the other the political notion, adopted from German Romanticism, of language as the hallmark of a community, as an essential element within a cultural community.[15] In this sense the Arab nation (*umma 'arabiyya*) is defined as a community of the Arabic language.

The following remarks will consist of an outline of the historical development of *'arabiyya,* in order to proceed in a separate section to an examination of the current discussion. In the subsequent parts the positions of two great Arab thinkers, Sati' Husri (the spiritual father of popular Arab nationalism) and Salama Musa (the early Arab socialist) will be presented, so as then to be able to formulate some definite theses.

Historical Changes in Arabic:
From Koranic Arabic to the Language of Science

In linguistics too, the concept of language awareness is invoked to describe the human sense of belonging to a certain community. Seen from this angle, the pride of Arabs in their language, leaving aside literature of a purely apologetic character, does have a material basis. Arabic is one of the oldest literary languages in the world. Long before the founding of Islam, the Arab tribes had their poets, who composed their poems in a sophisticated language, rich in vocabulary. Pre-Islamic poetry, disdained by Muslim historians as a literature of *jahiliyya* (ignorance), is in fact among our most valuable literary heirlooms.[16] The great French Islamic scholar Jacques Berque, as has already been mentioned, has attributed to *mu'allaqat* poetry, some parts of which he has translated into French, a literary quality comparable to the works of Baudelaire.

Pre-Islamic poetry did not plumb the depths of any great philosophical abstractions in the treatment of its themes—praise, chiding, grief, love, landscape, camels. This, however, has nothing to do with any "lack of capacity for abstraction" on the part of the Arab mind, in the sense of a constant anthropological characteristic, as some colonial ideologues assert. Its historical explanation is to be found rather in the stage of social development: Pre-Islamic poetry is the product of a partly nomadic, partly agrarian culture. The Arab bedouin were primarily concerned with coping with the harsh life of the desert and were "less prepared for reflection on the infinite."[17]

Arabic, which gave pre-Islamic poets an opportunity for expression that was powerful and rich in vocabulary, also contained the seeds for further development into a language capable of philosophical differentiation and abstraction, as the advanced Arab Islamic civilization was later to prove. As will be shown, Arab philosophers were able to shape the wealth of vocabulary of their inherited language in order to encompass the complex social content of their time. Even the language of the Koran itself, which does display hellenistic influences, despite assurances to the contrary by orthodoxy and Islamic apologetic literature, shows evidence of progress compared to the language of pre-Islamic poetry and hence also to the social conditions in which it arose. Muhammed—as Rodinson shows—"dazzled by the prestige of writings from the world of civilization and scholarship . . . , set his own cultivated rationality . . . against the barbaric rationality of the Meccans."[18] We must bear this in mind during our later examination of the reduction of Arabic to the language of the Koran in the wake of social stagnation in the Middle East. Although the Arabic of the Middle Ages, inspired by hellenistic philosophy, had a richer content than that of the Koran and was consequently more conducive to abstraction, this should not mislead us into assuming that the language of the Koran, sacred as it was, could boast no rationality. It should suffice here to refer to Rodinson's analysis of Koranic ideology: Rational processes of argumentation were lost during the suppression of hellenistic influences by orthodoxy.

T. J. de Boer characterizes the basic structure of Arabic as follows:

> The Arabic language, whose wealth of vocabulary, form and cultivable qualities have been a special joy to the Arabs themselves, was eminently suited to a position of world rank. It distinguishes itself in particular, for example, from ponderous Latin or pompous Persian, through *its short abstract formations, which proved to be of benefit for scientific expressions.* It is capable of the finest nuance, but on account of its richly developed synonyms tends to lure one *to deviate from the Aristotelian rule that in precise science the use of synonyms is not permissible.*[19]

Arabic, if further developed, facilitates the expression both of differentiated content as well as statements devoid of content, with a mere weight of words. The former can be found in Arab philosophy, the latter in sacred language, at least as it is handled by orthodoxy and in its literary form in Arabic poetry.

With the recording of the Koran, Arabic has been "immortalized" to this day; had it not been recorded, there would no longer be any Arabic today, in view of centuries of Turkish dominance and ensuing European colonialization. The handing-down of the Koran thus also meant that Arabic was kept alive in some form. With the recording of the Koran, however, Arabic acquired the designation of a sacred language, which continues to shape Arabic to this day. The attempt to go beyond Koranic Arabic is regarded as just as heretical today as it was in the early stages of advanced Islamic civilization in the Middle Ages, when Arab philosophers also attempted to go beyond the sacred and to reduce Islam to a cultural dimension by adopting Greek philosophy.

It is no coincidence that the branches of science were divided by Islamic scholars of the tenth century into Arabic and non-Arabic ones. Whereas linguistics in the traditional sense, that is, literary knowledge and doctrines of obligation and belief, were considered part of the Arab sphere of knowledge, all philosophical, natural science, and medicinal disciplines were treated as non-Arab branches.[20] This division, particularly between philosophy and linguistics, would at first seem nonsensical, but it does have a social function. Arabic was intended to remain a sacred language, a medium for handing down the Koran and religious scripture. Only in this context could linguistics remain an Arabic branch of science for Muslim orthodoxy. The coining of new words and the new meanings from Greek philosophy attached to them, it was feared with some justification, could only serve to undermine the faith. Some verbal forms, as de Boer reports, "originating from translators of foreign works, were abhorred as barbaric by purist language teachers. More widespread distribution than the scholarly research of language was achieved by the fine art of calligraphy, which, more decorative than constructive, like Arab art in general, evolved into fine noble forms."[21]

It did not stop with purist arguments, however: Arab thinkers who tried with the aid of Greek philosophy to break the boundaries set in the sacred language were persecuted as "heretics." The purist language school of Kufa, for instance, took a stand against the hellenist-inspired language school of Basra, whose advocates "had had their heads turned by logic in the view of true Arabs," having "gone much too far in the mastery of language."[22] An apologetic author of the tenth century expressed this in no uncertain terms, stating that it was a matter of the inviolability of the faith, and that rationalist philosophy contributed to undermining it; an adoption of its concepts into Arabic was the task of sacred Koranic Arabic. This was the point:

Anyone familiar with the finer points and depths of Arabic poetry and metrics knows that it surpasses everything that people are wont to cite as proof of their opinions, which labour under the misapprehension that the essence of things is cognizable: numbers, lines and dots. I fail to see the use of these things, unless despite the minimal use they provide, *they damage faith and result in things against which we must call on God's assistance.*[23]

Placing this view in the total social context, we can see that the maxim of orientation imposed by official Islam to assist believers' spiritual salvation does in fact have a function in the social order.[24] As is generally known, the Arabic language of science developed out of a quasisecular tradition, whereas the Arabic scholarship of the Middle Ages, above all philosophy, was alien to Islamic doctrine.[25] Philosophy, within which *'arabiyya* began to develop from a sacred language into a language of science, "was as dangerous in the Orient as the natural sciences in Italy after Galileo's trial."[26] For Avicenna, the great Arab philosopher, it was Aristotle, continues Bloch, and not Muhammed, who was the highest incarnation of the human spirit.[27]

In pointing out the conflict in Islamic history between philosophy as a secular and rational branch of knowledge and theology,[28] I must clarify my thesis, in order to avoid being forced into the same group as hack journalists whose dissemination of crude judgments and projections of the Muslim world contradict its true history: This conflict was not a struggle of "pure" ideas, between rationalism and irrationalism. Rodinson has devised the thesis, impregnable in its sheer breadth, that "the Koran leaves far more room for reason than the holy scriptures of Judaism and Christianity,"[29] and that this rationality applies equally to post-Koranic ideology.[30] As Rodinson rightly emphasizes,[31] the social backwardness of the Muslim world "may be attributed to any number of other factors, but not to the Islamic religion."[32]

It is possible in Islam to study theology (*kalam*) and philosophy (*falsafa*) as two warring traditions. Islamic philosophy adopted the Greek theory of cognition, whereas theology served by contrast as a source of legitimation for the existing form of rule. Religious ideologues had the task of admonishing the masses

> to resignation, to promise them comfort in the awareness of their piety and righteousness before God, and to encourage them at most to reverential expectations. This is the only way if they do not want to bring about the undermining and destruction of the order that is bound up with the ideology they defend. In this sense all religions, and by extension all state ideologies, are very definitely the opium of the people.[33]

Philosophy, on the other hand, pointed a way out of this condition by criticizing it. From this we can see that we are dealing here with the irrationality of a system of political rule that mobilized religion to legitimate itself, and not with the irrationality of the "holy scriptures" as such. These scriptures, though sacred and consequently limited to specific content, have left ample room for rationality. In short, the struggle between the advocates of these two traditions in Arab Islamic history, the theologians and the philosophers, did not revolve around religion; it was concerned with two different world views: a sacred one and a rational one based on a theory of cognition.

The philosopher- and heretic-hunts conducted by Muslim orthodoxy particularly benefited from signs of collapse within the Arab Islamic empire and from the re-agrarianization and geographical splintering of imperial territory.[34] The late phase of the Abbasid epoch marked the end of advanced Arab civilization. The prolegomena of Ibn Khaldun, dating from the fourteenth century, is the last really worthwhile work of social philosophy in Arabic. Ibn Khaldun's distancing himself from philosophy in this magnificent work,[35] denying its philosophical character, is a clear indication of the persecution of philosophers taking place at that time. From the examples both of Ibn Khaldun's prolegomena and preceding great philosophical works by Avicenna and Averroës, we can see the great extent to which Arabic had developed into a language of science and moved away from the sacral Arabic of the Koran.

The collapse of the Abbasid empire, the ensuing particularism of a variety of territorial states, and the subsequent domination by the Ottomans signified the end of this secular tradition and the restoration both of religion and archaic social structures. Wolfgang Freund has summarized the impact these had on the Arabic language:

> Because administrative correspondence was initially conducted in Turkish, and later in English and French, sophisticated written Arabic was left with no social functions at all. Nothing thus stood in the way of a linguistic lapse into the sole remaining binding element, namely the sacral text of the Koran. During all this, however, separate dialects were evolving among the peoples of the former Arab empire, developing out of medieval international Arabic. As these peoples were cut off from all forms of political power, however, these dialects were never able to evolve into written languages. A vulgarization of Arab dialects thus set in, similar to linguistic developments within the Latin-speaking world after the collapse of the Roman Empire.[36]

Unlike in Europe, cultural initiatives of various kinds were unable to make any headway at the regional level, so the language of the Koran remained the sole medium of cultural transmission. The clamp of the Koran held the language in its grip. The language of the Koran, however, is a sacred one, exerting a decisive influence on the semantic content passed on by following generations.

> Not a single aspect of human development, whether social, political, cultural or technological, could possibly flow into written Arabic under such circumstances. Furthermore, because these developmental aspects were of a highly complicated nature and would have required a written and at all times authentically reproducible form so as to be internalized in the collective memory of social groups, it was quite out of the question for Arab regional dialects to take over this function instead of the now sterile language of the Koran, as these regional dialects could not be written down.[37]

I would add to this account, however, that the intransigent dominance of the Koranic language after the suppression of Arabic scientific language in the Middle Ages was not the *cause* of cultural stagnation, but rather

an accompanying phenomenon. I should further qualify the cited
assertion with the remark that the stultification of written Arabic held
good for the morphosyntactic but not for the semantic structure of
'arabiyya (the levels of expression and content), as the latter continues
to correspond to changing situations, even in a stagnating society. I
can underscore, with Rodinson, the importance of studying socioeconomic conditions; "but these do not constitute a language, which makes
it highly unlikely that the structure of this system will prove funda-
mentally analogous to a language."[38] I return here to the position
outlined with reference to Henle, according to which there is a mutual
relationship between language, thought, and culture, in which language
shapes culture and culture also shapes the development of language.
Language is not, however, a reflection of culture, and culture does not
develop analogously with the structure of language.

'Arabiyya *in the Wake of the Second Sociocultural Confrontation with an External Challenge in the History of Islam*

We have seen that Islam as a civilization has been obliged to
face an external challenge on two separate occasions in its thirteen
centuries of history: first as a result of hellenization and second as a
result of European penetration of the Orient in the colonial era. We
have outlined the context and limits of the hellenization of Islam when
dealing with language and the conflict between Koranic and scientific
Arabic. We have also seen that the first sociocultural confrontation
produced an enrichment, especially in that it was not associated with
the establishment of a foreign power, as was the case in the recent
confrontation between West and East. In the linguistic sphere, the
effects of the modern European penetration of the Orient have been
much more far-reaching than they were in the case of hellenization.
With regard to language change in this context, I refer to two works
written partly under my supervision: the published doctoral dissertation
by the Tunisian Z. Chaabani[39] and the most remarkable dissertation
about translated German novels in Arabic by the Syrian Abdo Abboud.[40]
The process to which these works refer is now some century and a
half old, having been initiated in linguistics by the Egyptian scholar
Tahtawi,[41] who was the first Arab to study in Paris in the 1820s.

The first substantial organized group of Egyptian scholarship-
holders arrived in Paris in 1826. Rifa'a R. Tahtawi (1801–1873) accompanied this group, first as imam and then, after receiving appropriate
permission, as a student (he later came to be esteemed as one of the
greatest Arab thinkers of the nineteenth century). Returning to Egypt

in 1831 with the intention of disseminating what he had learned in Europe through Arabic translation, Tahtawi was forced to realize that he lacked the necessary linguistic medium. Centuries of stagnation in the Arabic language rendered him unable to find any equivalents for the historical, sociophilosophical, and natural scientific terms of European culture. Tahtawi was thus obliged to begin his project by setting to work on modernizing Arabic. He soon became aware, however, that the formal insertion of concepts lacking in Arabic using new word formations was insufficient. How could the subjects of a despotic power possibly be expected to grasp such concepts from bourgeois democratic revolutions as *liberté, humanité, fraternité,* when the substance of such things did not exist in their social world?

Arab thinkers of the nineteenth century were confronted on the one side by a Koranic language that had not progressed beyond the sacral and on the other by local Arabic dialects that had command of only atrophied grammatical structures and banal vocabulary. The difficulties of reflection under such conditions is exemplified by the work of Tahtawi, the great Arab modernist of the nineteenth century. In 1835, four years after his return from France, he was appointed director of the language school in Cairo, where he and his students translated European works into Arabic. In order to do this, it was first necessary to modernize *'arabiyya,* by then stagnant and reduced to the sacred language of the Koran. A glance at Arabic literature of the eighteenth century and its linguistic forms and content[42] ought to be sufficient illustration of the immensity of the task Tahtawi and his students had set themselves. Tahtawi himself criticized scholarly work, which had become degraded to the empty exegesis of theological texts, and the lack of expressive capacity in *'arabiyya* associated with it. Tahtawi derided those Oriental scholars who took such pains over the compilation of "commentaries and supercommentaries" instead of seeking knowledge systematically; it was characteristic of them "to register, collect, order, and comment on the conventional."[43] On the difference between the European bourgeois notion of a scholar and that of stagnant Oriental culture, Tahtawi stated:

> As far as their [the French] scholars are concerned, they are of quite a different ilk; they have perfect mastery of a number of disciplines and additionally devote their efforts to a further specialist branch, just as they illuminate many things and introduce may useful things that were never there before. These are in their view the qualities of a scientist. Not every teacher is a scientist in their eyes, nor does every author automatically count as a scientific lumen. . . . We should not suppose, for example, that scientists among the French are priests,

> since the clergy are versed solely in divinity. . . . The word 'scientist'
> is rather applied to someone versed in the rational sciences.[44]

In the following chapter on the Islamic institution of education and
change within it, I shall be dealing with this problem more fully.

Early Arab modernists such as Tahtawi, who were not yet able to
perceive Europe in colonial terms, were full of enthusiasm for European
culture.[45] They had no qualms about sacrificing sacral Koranic Arabic
in their efforts to develop Arabic into a medium for disseminating the
European ideas they had adopted. This lack of inhibition gave rise to
the translation movement in the nineteenth century, above all in Egypt;
deficient as it may seem to us today, it is nonetheless worthy of
considerable historical attention.[46]

Another intellectual stream of the nineteenth century in the Arab
Middle East was the literary renaissance of Greater Syria. This did not
primarily involve the translation and transmission of foreign ideas but
the revitalization of the classical Arab heritage by Westernized Syro-
Lebanese intellectuals, who through this work were later to become
the spiritual fathers of cultural Arab nationalism. These were predominantly Christian Arabs, for whom the revitalization of classical Arabic
literature and thus of the Arabic language—not the sacral language of
the Koran but the language of literature—meant their potential emancipation from Islam-legitimated rule. The fathers of cultural Arab
nationalism saw 'arabiyya as a national language. By using it as a
medium for the articulation of secular content, they were able to develop
the language into an instrument for the discovery of national identity,
especially because, as Christians, they could not identify with the
Ottoman Empire.[47]

At these two levels of the acculturative and secular revitalization—
that of the reception of European bourgeois, progressive culture by
Arab intellectuals and its dissemination via the medium of Arabic, and
that of the revitalization of the neglected Arab cultural heritage as a
national culture—the process of modernization of Arabic and its liberation from sacral forms and content in the nineteenth century was
prompted.

Although great progress may be noted since that time, the central
problems nevertheless still remain unsolved: The gulf between High
Arabic and the regional dialects persists. It is important to point out
that these dialects do not constitute diverse forms of expression of one
and the same language, as is the case in French or German, but are
rather virtually separate languages in both vocabulary and grammatical
structure, despite their nonwritten form and their restriction to everyday
use. With the growing development of modern Arab societies, they are

becoming more and more unsuitable for the formulation of abstract, theoretical ideas.

Similarly, local nationalists—such as the Lebanese nationalist Sa'id Aql[48]—have always tried to transform regional dialects into written languages, in the hope of distancing themselves from pan-Arab nationalism. Fortunately these efforts have so far not met with success. The atrophied regional dialects would be quite incapable of providing the basis for languages equal to the demands of change and international standards. On the other hand, there are still enough apologetic thinkers resting their arguments on purist ideology and the antiphilosopher tradition who bemoan the "decline of the Arabic language," as it is allegedly submerged under a deluge of foreign words and new terms with European content. This attitude is typical of the largest and most influential linguistic body, al-Majma' al-Laghawi al-'Arabi (the Arab Philological Society), which is officially recognized by all Arab lands and in view of its established position assumes the right to direct the renewal of the Arabic language. This body is composed of conservative Muslim Arab scholars who are anything but well-disposed toward modern tendencies. Curiously enough, it is greatly esteemed by European, especially German, Orientalists, who feel flattered in their association with it. Although these classically-inclined Orientalists, in particular the Germans among them, are not Muslims, they are if anything even more recalcitrant than traditional Muslims on the matter of purism in the Arabic language.

I can state with some relief, however, that the Arabic Philological Society exerts hardly any influence at all on intellectual life, for all its "language decrees" and official character. Books are translated from European languages on a daily basis, new content introduced into Arabic, and foreign words assimilated without the slightest regard to the society's suggestions. On the contrary, the latter, still oriented toward sacral Koranic Arabic, are fuel to the fire of the joker's imagination.

This has inspired one Arab author to a fierce call to avert the "destruction of *'arabiyya.*" In the official newspaper of the Arab Socialist Union set up by Nasser, the weekly *al-Shabab al-'Arabi,* Suleiman Thanyan wrote:

> O Arabs, how much longer will we lie in our deep sleep? How much longer shall we stop our ears and not hear the cry for help: "Help me! I am your language! I am your life, I am you, I am in peril; where are you? Help me before I fall into the abyss; take hold of my hand!" When will we finally hear this call, when will we finally go toward this grief-stricken, sorrowful voice? When will we become aware of our responsibility and mindful of the great peril?[49]

These phrases are not here solely for amusement. They document a mental attitude far from restricted to only a few, which therefore makes our analysis the more urgent.

Thanyan demands that Arab governments lend political authority to the Arab Philological Society. Were it to acquire such authority, the following scenario might result: In Arabic, one says and writes "television." This is a great offense to Thanyan and his kind. Therefore, the Arab Philological Society would simply recommend that the board of the television institution, on which "television" is written, be torn down and a new board erected with the word *marna*.[50] The majority of Arabs have no idea what *marna'* means, but they do, of course, know what "television" means. Although the Arab Philological Society would be unable to enforce this incomprehensible word formation, it would continue to insist on its demand. Thanyan calls for tougher measures,

> because if we do not proceed with severity in this matter, if we do not protect our language, in twenty years we shall have a language consisting of empty, paralyzed terms and a disintegrated mixture of words from the most diverse languages. Such a language would be useless. Please do not say no. . . . For the Arabization of foreign content through the adoption of Arabized terms spells death to the Arabic language—more than this, it contaminates the value of the Arab nation. This kirid of Arabization is no less criminal than the adoption of foreign words in Arabic in their original form. . . . It spells the destruction of both the Arabic language and ourselves.[51]

It was against such views that the great Arab thinkers of both the modern and secular national camps acted. To call this discussion to mind and to draw a balance, we shall look here at two teaching approaches: that of Salama Musa, the influential early Arab socialist, and that of Sati' Husri, father of popular, Germanophile Arab nationalism.

Salama Musa and the Modernization of the Arabic Language[52]

Salama Musa[53] was born in 1887 in the Egyptian village of Kafar-'Afi near Cairo, the son of a Coptic, petit bourgeois family. His Christian origin in itself destined him to follow in the footsteps of laical Christian Arab thinkers—all the more so, as has been mentioned above, because emphasis of the national and secular element in Arab culture, as against the religious and Islamic element, denoted both the discovery of an identity and emancipation for these Christians. Musa indeed latched on to this tradition in his boyhood, but he did not stop there. He developed still further the social-liberal, and thus no longer purely nationalistic, seed ideas of Syro-Lebanese, Western-educated intellectuals. Those intellectuals, among whom were Farah Antun (1874–1922) and Shibli Shumaiyil (1860–1917), had fled Ottoman oppression to work in Egypt. After the Anglo-French sojourn, Musa published in 1913, at the age of twenty-six, his first treatise of socialism in Arabic.[54] The ensuing years, until Musa's death in 1958, were marked by vigorous journalistic activity, in which he produced forty-five works and founded numerous journals, some of them only short-lived. These were complemented by his political activities, which included the founding of the first socialist party in Egypt in 1920. Such activities, directed against both British colonial rule and indigenous reaction in Egypt, landed him in prison on more than one occasion. Musa writes in his biography:

> I am fighting against this rotten Orient, which is being devoured by the worms of tradition. I am fighting against the yoke under which my compatriots suffer: that of ignorance and poverty. True, I am an enemy of the British, but I am at the same time also an enemy for thousands of my compatriots. I am an enemy of those reactionaries who are against science, modern civilization, and the emancipation of women, and who stifle themselves in mystification.[55]

Proceeding from this basic position, Musa also examines the problems of modernizing Arabic, stating that this can only be accomplished in the context of innovation in society as a whole, for harking back to the ancestral cultural heritage, such as is practiced only in apologetic literature, is unproductive. "We must . . . now create culture. . . . This cannot happen by evoking the cultural heritage of our ancestors, or by exhausting ourselves in the manner of al-Jahiz and Ibn Zaidun in coining cumbersome new terms, or by glorifying our old advanced culture and playing confidence tricks with our cultural origins."[56] Musa thus distances himself unequivocally from all revitalization tendencies, casting his eye toward the future and not the past, although still giving the past its due: "Only a corpse whose brain has ceased to function and whose vital force has been stopped can recall the dead; and only the poor and destitute, prostrate with fatigue, exhume the dead so as to clothe themselves in their shrouds."[57] The early socialist Musa is nevertheless arguing purely idealistically in asserting that only a modern, secular, future-oriented culture can offer a way out of misery, "for every social change necessitates a cultural one. Only agrarian peoples can live in a static, unchanging culture, because societies that are developing need a dynamic, complex culture. Herein lies the necessity for cultural innovation, in order to render possible a revolution within civilization."[58]

For Musa, the problem of language development and renewal falls within this context, language being "the basis of every culture, and [because] it is absolutely impossible to bring about a dynamic, developed culture with a stagnant, decayed language. The level of development of a culture points at the same time to the level of development of the language of that culture, and cultural progress implies renewal of language."[59] This emphasis of the correlation between language and culture leads Musa to a concentrated analysis of the language problem.

> We cannot emphasize enough the importance of language for a
> people, that is, a modern language capable of assimilating the arts
> and sciences and constantly expanding its vocabulary. We mean a
> language that does not confine the thinker as a result of its structure,
> which provides him with the potential for articulation by means of
> adequate terms, and which does not prevent him from comprehending
> complex scientific or philosophical content.[60]

Here Musa, as a Western-educated Arab intellectual, has put his finger on a problem that still remains to be solved. Western-educated Arab intellectuals have, through their adoption of developed languages, been able to dissolve the restrictions imposed on their thought by the stagnant Arabic language. Because they are primarily Western-educated, however, they are not sufficiently familiar with the "secrets of *'arabiyya*" (*asrar al-'arabiyya,* as Arab philologists and European Orientalists tend to mystify the Arabic language) to undertake attempts to articulate in Arabic the content they have received through the medium of learned European languages. Traditionally educated Arabs, on the other hand, generally have either no knowledge at all or only slight knowledge of European languages, although they do have full command of Arabic. They are nonetheless unable, because of the language barriers imposed on them, to replicate complex thought processes and comprehend them conceptually in Arabic. This problem is misinterpreted by traditionally educated Arabs, as is shown by their criticism of literary works by European-educated Arabs, whom they accuse of speaking "vulgar Arabic" (*'arabiyya rakika*) on account of their disregard for the strict grammatical rules and literary elegance of *'arabiyya*. Such critics thus fix the problem at a subjective level, reducing it to a matter of insufficient mastery of Arabic and judging that it would be eliminated if everyone had a better command of Arabic—as if the structure of Arabic permitted the formulation of complex content, and as if the objective inadequacies of Arabic were not brought to light by the Europeanized Arab intelligentsia in "vulgar Arabic." Salama Musa saw the problem clearly from the outset, deploring philological acrobatics that were devoid of content. In 1927 he wrote:

> Arabic language teaching in Egypt is still in the hands of traditionally educated teachers whose thinking languishes in the dim past of old Arab culture. If we want to reform our education system, we can do no better than to dismiss these people and transfer the teaching of Arabic to Europeanized intellectuals who have already immersed themselves in modern culture.[61]

It is important to mention here that Musa, who refused to cling doggedly to the outmoded forms and content of indigenous culture and who was so open to European influences, did not share the naive faith in Europe that the early liberal bourgeois intelligentsia of the Middle East had, but was fully aware of the ambivalence of European culture.

A socialist such as Musa was unlikely to set great store by a national language. He thus laments the decline of Latin into a dead language: "In our times, when our thought is acquiring a supranational dimension . . . and we are thinking of creating a world language, we can only regret the decline of Latin and its reduced use in universities, monasteries, and churches."[62] With today's exclusive dominance of national languages, however, if we want to further international communication we must press forward with the cross-fertilization of languages, the less developed languages of course adopting form and content from the developed ones. To nationalist authors who see the sacrifice of national identity in such a postulate, Musa responds that in those times when the Arabs were culturally more advanced than Europeans, the latter adopted a great deal from Arabic without having to relinquish their identity in the process. He quotes a number of examples, saying:

> We could continue this list of examples of the adoption of Arabic vocabulary by Europeans into their national languages virtually endlessly. This is simply an indication of how cultures adopt something from one another and how this adoption turns out to be a cross-fertilization and a step forward in mutual understanding among men. It can do us no harm, therefore, to adopt European terms that are associated with European achievements.[63]

In this context, Musa vigorously attacks the Arab Philological Society for its constant attempts to cling tenaciously to the purity of Arabic, even at the price of forming inadequate Arabic words for standard European terms so as not to have to adopt them in their original form.

For Musa this kind of purism is positively grotesque, since the terms devised by European science have become supranational, while resistance to their assimilation into Arabic creates the impression that "whilst the whole world has agreed to use common terms, we alone deviate from this trend by applying scientific terms other than those recognized throughout the world."[64]

To less insightful Muslim authors, such as the Egyptian writer 'Abbas Mahmud 'Aqqad, this position would be totally incomprehensible; they charge Musa with the evil motives of a Christian for laying aside Islam and for replacing the religious standpoint not only not with an Arab nationalist one but with an internationalist one. Despite Musa's tireless emphasis that, although of Christian origin he, as a socialist, did not profess any religion, such authors nevertheless latched on to his background: 'Aqqad went so far as to ask whether anyone who was prepared to relinquish the purity of *'arabiyya* could be an Arab at all.

Sati' Husri: The Renaissance of 'Arabiyya as the Renaissance of the "Arab Nation"

Sati' Husri (1882–1968) was far more influential than Salama Musa. After World War I he was regarded as the spiritual father of Arab nationalism, which at that time, in the wake of Anglo-French colonization, was developing from an Anglophone or Francophone into a Germanophile ideology. The German idea of nation obviously differs from the French and Anglo-Saxon ones in its adherence to the notion of a cultural community. For Johann Gottfried von Herder and Johann Gottlieb Fichte, the nation is not a nation-state, but a cultural community that can claim a national existence even in the absence of a state structure. We cannot examine in detail here either these correlations or their relationship to Arab nationalism, chiefly in the phase after World War I; they have in any case already been thoroughly examined elsewhere.[65] For the purposes of discussing Husri's views on modernizing Arabic, I shall limit myself to a few references to his significance and to the importance of language in his conception of nationalism.

On the basis of this conception, which drew considerably on the German concept of nation, Husri stressed that language forms the most important nonmaterial link among the members of a social group, giving rise to a certain way of thinking and common feelings among those who speak it, thus binding them to one another by means of a chain of intellectual and emotional relations, handed down from one generation to another.[66] If the language stagnates, then so does the consciousness of the group, Husri argued, conceiving of his own writings as a contribution to the awakening of the "Arab nation" and to the achievement of "Arab unity"—without realizing that in fact the reverse was true. For language only stagnates when the group itself stagnates. Husri, however, wanted to start out with the revival and modernization of Arabic, so that the Arabs themselves could flourish. Husri insisted on the *originality* of the language, even though *'arabiyya* was not his mother tongue: Although a Syrian Arab, he grew up in an Ottoman Turkish milieu and was for a time an Ottoman education official.[67]

Husri, who had had the benefit of a period of study in Europe and was familiar with the body of European social philosophical thought, touched on the problem of exogenous influence on a language, recognizing that every Arab "who immerses himself in the subject-matter of modern scientific disciplines inevitably begins to feel the inadequacy of the Arabic language as soon as he tries to articulate the content of those sciences in Arabic. This fact holds despite the fame of Arabic as a language rich in content."[68] My linguistics colleague Ineichen took the view on this matter that there are, within the structure of *'arabiyya,* specific obstacles to this kind of language that will not admit the influences aimed for by Husri. Compared with the European languages, which in any case constitute a family, the grammatical organization of *'arabiyya* in itself renders interlingual exchange difficult. With this assertion, Ineichen wanted to confine comment on sociocultural obstacles to a minimum and bring to the fore the manner in which the language itself is structured.

By way of elucidating his quoted assertion, Husri explained what he understands by the wealth of a language:

> The wealth of a language can be measured neither in terms of how many word entries have been recorded in dictionaries, nor in terms of the number of synonyms contained in them, as dictionaries are not only an inventory of living vocabulary, but also a graveyard for dead vocabulary. This is particularly true of Arabic dictionaries, which house a munificence of vocabulary that is no longer used and has lost its value. Those who point with pride at the enormous vocabulary of a language without distinguishing between living terms and dead ones are akin to those who take pride in the size of their country without distinguishing between the homes of the living and the graveyards of the dead.[69]

We can all the more appreciate the value of such a statement, particularly from the most influential representative of pan-Arab nationalism, if we are aware of the kind of arguments put forward in apologetic Arabic literature, where even today the superiority of Arabic over European languages is extolled with allusions to the wealth of vocabulary and grammatical complexity in 'arabiyya. In a somewhat different form, this applies even to authors with a European education, for instance the Lebanese philologist and literary historian 'Umar Faroukh,[70] who acquired a German university education in the 1930s, and who wrote an influential apologia for 'arabiyya.[71] Husri pointed to the historically conditioned weaknesses of Arabic, adopting, despite his nationalism, a position against the apologetics of Muslim and nationalist authors.

Although Husri severely criticized 'arabiyya apologists, accusing them of blindness in refusing to face the backwardness of Arabic, he rightly did not go to the lengths of some Westernized Arab intellectuals, who want to be more European than the Europeans. He did consider Arabic to be capable of development; he did not impute its unusability outright, so as to make an appeal for its replacement by European languages, but endeavored to find possibilities leading to the modernization of Arabic. "Whereas some Arab philologists go to the lengths of declaring 'arabiyya to be the richest language in the world, other [Westernized] authors go to the other extreme, asserting that Arabic is not capable of adopting the scientific terminology necessary for our generation. We share neither of these extremes."[72]

Husri then proceeded to offer some preliminary suggestions for the modernization of Arabic. First he stressed that efforts in this sphere need to be coordinated at the level of all Arab countries, all the more so because of the tendency for even written High Arabic to vary from one country to another as a result of the separate development of the language. "Not only among writers of different countries but even among those of the same country it is possible to observe a confusion in the formation and use of modern vocabulary."[73] Husri thus called for a cross-regional body to solve these problems, a task for which he considered the Arab Philological Society unsuited. In a discussion of how to create Arabic terms as general equivalents for modern social and natural scientific terms, a philologist versed in the Koranic sciences can only prove to be eminently dispensable.

In the 'arabiyya dispute referred to here, discussion has so far focused on the surface, scarcely departing from questions of whether or not the language is capable of development or whether Arab philologists trained in the Islamic sciences are equal to the task of linguistic renewal. According to linguistics, every language is theoretically capable of development, as it is able to express all content. When a language becomes sacral, however, this linguistically given capacity for expression is considerably reduced, as the language becomes bound to a single theme. In Islam, 'arabiyya is bound to the Koran, and for the orthodox Muslim it cannot be allowed to break the restraints set by its sacral nature. These restraints, however, are not boundaries, for they can be overcome through desacralization of the language. The liaison between Latin and scholasticism offers a historical example at the comparative level; the demise of scholasticism was the precursor of language development in Europe. Husri was a secularist, but for him secularism was purely a political matter and devoid of aspects pertaining to social or linguistic structure.

There is, perhaps, a lack of depth in Husri's concept of language modernization, however; anyone who calls for the enrichment of terminology alone is overlooking the need for phraseology when expressing terms. Terms are always expressed in a specific way using specific verbs and thus have bearing on phraseological structure. To carry out language renewal solely at the level of terminology would mean seeking to accumulate words without also improving the linguistic potential for expression.

Language Renewal as a Contribution
to the Cultural Accommodation of Change

As we shall see in more detail in Chapter 7, three kinds of science were distinguished in High Islam, during that period in Islam when the civilization was at its height: Islamic science (first Koranic and Hadith exegesis, or branches thereof), the science of the ancients (*al-Qudama'*, that is, of the Greeks, or philosophy and natural science), and finally literary science (*'ulum al-adab*).[74]

In fact, the orthodox Muslim *ulema* (scribes) and the hellenized Muslim philosophers shared a very low estimation of poetic language, which was often lacking in content and based on pun, but they nonetheless differed on the definition of the content of language. Their historical conflict was resolved in favor of orthodoxy, which, as we shall see in Chapter 7, was able to maintain or gain total control of all institutions of learning. In other words, the tradition of a language of science initiated in High Islam was unable to evolve, nor was it able to step beyond the sacral restraints imposed upon it, so that during their intercultural conflict with the modern, technological-science-oriented civilization of Europe, the Arabs had only a poetic or sacral language at their disposal. The linguistic and cultural reception of change had somehow to be contrived ad hoc during the conflict itself— a conflict for which they were unprepared and unarmed and which is in fact still in progress. The preconceived notion of the poetic or sacral nature of *'arabiyya* is still predominant, as I shall demonstrate.

The former head of the Bonn office of the Arab League, the leading Egyptian diplomat Hamdy Azzam, highlights the persistence of even the pre-Islamic poetic tradition in emphasizing that for the Arabs "language is not merely a simple means of communication but an aesthetic art, capable of inspiring the masses and transporting them into a euphoric state."[75] No Arab speaker, whether scientist, academic, official speaker, businessperson, or government spokesperson, can succeed in impressing an audience without demonstrating a mastery of language such as has been described. The enlightened Syrian philosopher Sadiq al-'Azm, who graduated from Yale University and today teaches at the University of Damascus, emphasizes the negative function the Arabic tradition of poetic language, a tradition evident, among other places in the political speeches of Arab politicians, took on during the Six-Day War of 1967. Al-'Azm stresses "that a concept of war, rooted in the days of chivalry, sword duels, personal feats of daring, and direct confrontation, still has a far-reaching effect on Arab thinking. One recalls the many poems heard on all radio stations and read in all publications—poems about the clashing of swords, galloping behind enemy lines, and other tribal forms of expression pertaining to individual feats of daring."[76] The crushing military defeat of the Arabs in the June War of 1967 was also related to such cultural attitudes.

To illustrate just how much hellenized Muslim philosophers despised poetry in High Islam, I quote Abu Nasr Muhammed al-Farabi: "The evidence whereby truth prevails over falsehood stems from rhetoric; the evidence in which falsehood prevails over truth stems from the writings of the forger, and the evidence that contains only falsehood is learned from the art of poetry."[77] The Arabs, then, consider poetry *kalam fadi* (speech devoid of content). This helps to explain the paradox that in the Arab Middle East skilled speakers are on the one hand greatly admired for their way with words and are on the other hand not taken seriously. This is a serious problem in the cultural reception of change in the Arab Islamic Middle East; we need to be aware that linguistic communication in Arabic does not always contain a factual statement.

To the poetic character of Arab thought as described above I may add the sacral definition of the language. We have already seen in Chapter 2 the extent to which everyday Arabic is laden with sacral terms. At a Muslim conference on "Muslim Education" in Mecca, the Saudi Prince Muhammed al-Faisal emphasized: "We shall maintain the Arabic language not because it is the national tongue of the Arabs but because it is the language of the Koran, and therefore the language of Islam."[78] S. Husain and S. A. Ashraf also argued along these lines in compiling the conclusions of the conference, stating that *'arabiyya* is the lingua franca of the Muslim world and concluding: "A Muslim should be able to read the [Koran] even without being able to understand the words, because the ability to read the Koran itself has been known

to evoke in people a response to the teachings of Islam which socio-
logically has been very valuable."[79] Clearly such a notion of the social
function of language is unsuitable for the cultural reception of impending
problems.

To recap, I cannot help but assess the secularist tendency within
Pan-Arab nationalism—as I have tried to evaluate it using the example
of Sati' Husri—as a positive cultural prospect for the reception of
change. It is regrettable that Husri's secularism has been pushed into
the background today with the revival of political Islam, as we shall
be examining in more detail in Part 4. In his works, Husri nevertheless
does not go to the lengths of the unreserved enthusiasm of some
Europeanized Arab intellectuals; he holds firm to the Arab heritage,
seeking only to submit this to a process of innovation. Within the
sphere of the modernization of Arabic, this position implies a conflict
both with conventional philologists, related to that of Muslim orthodoxy,
as well as with Europeanized intellectuals who want to relinquish
'arabiyya as a medium of articulation. Criticism nevertheless falls more
heavily on traditional Arab philologists, inasmuch as their resistance
to all modernization in Arabic presents an obstacle to further development of the language. These philologists, writes Husri, "ceased the
pursuit of worldly sciences centuries ago and have narrowed their
horizons of thought to a circle of philology and Islamic jurisprudence,
ignoring all other branches of knowledge. In this way, expression in
Arabic has become restricted to limited content, thus preventing change
from entering in and further development from taking place."[80] In the
eyes of these conventional philologists, philology must focus on the
sacral language of the Koran, whereas traditional jurisprudence is in
any case a theological discipline. Husri points out (as introduced in
outline in Chapter 6) that Arabic, having managed to develop into an
incipient scientific language in advanced Arab Islamic culture, has since
become reduced to a sacral language impoverished in terms of abstract
content. The change in the Islamic concept of science was closely
linked with this. We have already seen that the Arab philosophical
milieu was in a critical state during the Middle Ages. For the Arab
philosophers of the "Aristotelian left," religion was regarded as the
"people's way of thinking." The polished thinking of the scholar, capable
of abstraction, was thus only able to serve philosophy, not the medium
of religion.[81] The Muslim philosopher was always, as Bloch comments,
"Doctor, not monk, naturalist, not theologian."[82] It is not surprising,
therefore, that these philosophers soon found themselves in blatant
conflict with religion. Their philosophical systems were nothing short
of "heresy" in orthodox eyes, a just accusation inasmuch as this

philosophy provided a rational rather than a sacral interpretation of the cosmos. De Boer writes of Ibn Rushd (Averroës):

> In general there are three great heresies that place Ibn Rushd in opposition to the theology of the three great world religions of his day: first, the eternal nature of the physical world and of the spirits that move it; second, the necessary causal nexus of all world events, there thus being no room left for prophesy, miracles, and the like; and, third, the transitory nature of everything individual, which thus eliminates individual immortality.[83]

During the decline of the Arab Islamic empire and the associated restoration of Muslim orthodox authority, the concept of science typical for Arab laical philosophy was ousted in favor of another, in which science consisted of the Koranic sciences. I have already quoted Tahtawi's remark after his stay in Europe during the first half of the nineteenth century—his amazement that there science was taken to mean the secular branches of knowledge and not theology. These remarks offer us the key to understanding contemporary Arab culture and thus also the problems of language renewal. Both socially critical Arab thinkers, such as Salama Musa, secular pan-Arab authors, such as Sati' Husri (who nevertheless contrast sharply with Muslim orthodoxy in their progressiveness), grasped this. The modernization of Arabic calls for a vision of the future and the defeat of the *salaf* orientation (the time-honored ways of the forefathers), the ideology of *salafism*. The Tunisian sociologist R. Boukraa argued at the CERES colloquium on linguistics: "The concept of modernization implies here the structural transformation of *'arabiyya* and a departure from old theories. This linguistic view is opposed to the traditional one that *'arabiyya* is constant and does not have to change."[84]

Without either disputing the partial autonomy of language structures or mechanically reducing language change to social change, I stress here that the stagnant expressive capacity of Arabic, once a language of science, and its reduction to a sacral one, that is, to post–fourteenth-century Koranic language, should not be viewed as an isolated process but as part and parcel of an all-embracing process of social development. Even language renewal in the Arab Middle East cannot be understood as an isolated process. The *salafiyya* mold of Muslim traditionalists is an all-embracing one and is not to be broken solely at the level of language renewal.

Language development in the Arab culture is a matter of innovation in society as a whole, inasmuch as the problem is not simply of a sterile scientific nature but of a sociopolitical one. Language renewal denotes a confrontation with influential Muslim institutions and the *salafi* ideology that holds sway within them,[85] and above all an acceleration of secularization within the education sector.[86]

7

Institutions of Learning and Education in Islam: Their Historical Contribution to the Cultural Accommodation of Change and Their Current State of Crisis

Every culture is transmitted by various agents of socialization, ranging from the family to the social institutions of training and education (institutions of learning). These agents compete with one another in the socialization process, and which of them has the greatest influence is an empirical question.[1] The school and university are institutions concerned not only with cultivating and passing on tradition but also with evolving new cultural patterns to help accommodate change that is taking place or has already taken place. Islam has evolved patterns of training and education of its own and has been able to retain them for many centuries. Since the nineteenth century, however, these institutions have been in a deep state of crisis, and their outward form has altered radically as a consequence of European influence. A classic example of this is the Muslim al-Azhar University in Cairo, which since substantial reform in 1961 (see Chapter 9) hardly differs from any standard European or U.S. university, apart from its *shari'a* legal disciplines. It nonetheless still retains its essential, decisive characteristic: Only Muslims may study there.

To answer the question of the contribution to the cultural reception of change made by Muslim institutions of training and education, and also better to understand their present state of crisis, I shall deal in the first section with the historical genesis of these institutions. In the subsequent section we will examine the consequences of introducing the university institution, a modern one originating from Europe, into the Islamic Middle East, and we will conclude with the question of how Muslim authors perceive the "crisis in Muslim education" and what solutions they can put forward for dealing with them.

The Historical Genesis
of Islamic Institutions of Education

In the introduction to Part 3 I stressed that Islamic sacral law (*shari'a*) determines the content of the Islamic sociocultural system, which is articulated through the medium of Arabic (*'arabiyya*), and that the training institution—next to that of law—is not only the second most important institution in Islam but is also the unequivocal hub for transmitting and handing down Islam.

Notwithstanding their developed written language, pre-Islamic Arabs had no formal system of education. This was not developed until the foundation of the Islamic religion, the central institution termed an "institution of learning" by George Makdisi, a historian of the Islamic education system. The place where Islamic ritual was fostered, the mosque, also became the classical seat of Islamic learning. Classical Islam still distinguished between two categories of mosque: the *masjid,* the mosque in which Muslims could recite the prescribed five prayers daily, and the *jami',* the mosque in which Muslims performed collective prayer after the ritual sermon on Friday, the Muslim day of rest. In other words, *jami'* mosques were only used on Fridays in classical Islam and could therefore be set up as educational premises, or *madrasa,* for the other days of the week. In mosques such as these, learning was pursued in the form of a *halaqa* (learning circle), with the students sitting on a carpet in a circle around the teacher. In classical Islam, these learning circles in Damascus, Cairo, and Baghdad were, in addition to those of the *zawiya,* the predominant organizational form for learning and are to be distinguished from the *maktab* or *kuttab,* which are freely translatable as Koranic school. Unlike the *maktab,* the *madrasa* was a seat of higher learning. Koranic school, in practical terms a primary school, was attended only by children for the purposes of learning reading and writing using the text of the Koran. Some Islamic historians translate the term *madrasa* as university, which is plainly incorrect: If we understand a university as *universitas litterarum,* or consider, without the bias of Eurocentrism, the cast of the *universitas magistrorum* of the thirteenth century in Paris, we are bound to recognize that the university as a seat for free and unrestrained inquiry based on reason, is a European innovation in the history of mankind, as we shall be seeing in more detail later. The Islamic *madrasa* is not concerned with a process of investigation or unrestrained inquiry but with a learning process in the sacral sense. A *madrasa* is a place for the cultivation of Islamic science, that is, the Koran and the Hadith (the tradition of the Prophet), exegesis, and related disciplines (language teaching, grammar, and so on), in contrast to the *dar al-'ilm* (academy of science), where "foreign," i.e., non-Islamic (meaning Greek or Hellenized) branches of learning are taught and studied. We shall see that this institution was unable to flourish within Islam and that the *madrasa* became the Islamic educational institution par excellence until the onset of the modern period.

In speaking of Islamic "institutions of learning," with reference to Makdisi,[2] I must also mention those branches of knowledge not without prestige in their day. For classical Islam, I cite the classification of the sciences used by Ibn Bultan in the eleventh century, which distinguished three branches: the Islamic sciences, philosophy and natural science, and the intellectual or literary sciences.

Open-minded authors, with the best of intentions but nevertheless incorrectly, often take the term "Islamic sciences" (*al-'ulum al-isla-miyya*) to mean the philosophical and natural science tradition in Islam, based on the Greek heritage and its reception, in order to show that there were also scientific traditions outside Europe. This term, however, as experts in the field are aware,[3] is limited solely to exegesis of the Koran and Hadith and those branches of knowledge stemming from it. In classical Islam, philosophy and natural science were designated as "foreign science" or the "science of the ancients," that is, the Greeks (*'ulum al-qudama'*). They were unable to gain a foothold in Islamic educational institutions, as Makdisi has shown.[4] During the phase when philosophy and natural science were being encouraged by Abbasid caliphs, the *dar al-'ilm* was where they were cultivated. The Mu'tazilites, those hellenized Muslim theologians who introduced philosophical discourse into theology, were protected against Muslim orthodoxy above all by the Caliph al-Ma'mum in Baghdad. They instigated a tradition of Islamic rationalism that was unfortunately rigid and dogmatic and could not establish itself on a permanent basis.[5]

Within Islamic education the impediments to establishing branches devoted to the free acquisition of rational knowledge and unrestrained inquiry were precipitated on the one hand because the system was financed by private endowment (*waqf*), and on the other because of the encroachment by the institutions of the *kadi* and later of the *mufti* during an advanced stage of state development. In both cases the access of rational science (natural science and philosophy) to Muslim institutions of learning was obstructed. A fairly lengthy passage from Makdisi, in which he summarizes his original research, based on primary sources, is worth quoting here, as it is instructive on many outstanding issues:

> The Islamic sciences had total control over the institutions of learning, their ascendancy beginning to take place definitively after the failure of the rationalist-led inquisition of al-Ma'mun, and reaching its height by the time the fifth/eleventh century had moved to its mid-point. In this division, Islamic law was crowned queen of the sciences. . . . The sciences of the Ancients, that is of the Greeks . . . were studied in private, and were excluded from the regular courses of Muslim institutions of learning. *The religious sciences were at the forefront of education.*[6]

In order to understand how the hellenization of Islam[7] was possible between the ninth and twelfth centuries despite the continued domination of the Islamic education system by Islamic science, it is important to bear in mind the existence of a distinction between institutional and noninstitutional learning in Islam, and equally important to realize that rationalism in Islam represents a historical phase in which the unimpinged reception of the Greek heritage was possible. The conflict between the two branches of learning—Islamic science and philosophy/natural science—was resolved in favor of the former.[8] Ernst Bloch makes an impressive comparison between the burning of the works of Avicenna and Averroës by Muslim orthodoxy and the bodily burning of Giordano Bruno by the Christian Inquisition.[9] This tradition of rationalism, instigated by Avicenna and Averroës as well as by the Mu'tazilite school, found no access to the institutions of learning, thus remaining exiled from the institutional sphere of education even in its heyday. At that time, though, there were chairs for Koranic exegesis (*mashyakhat al-Koran*), Hadith exegesis (*mashyakhat al-hadith*), and for grammar (*mashyakhat an-nahu*). The relevance of Arabic grammar is to be understood here in the context of exegesis. Muslim philosophers, natural scientists, and hellenized theologians (*kalam* theologians) lacked a comparable institutional structure beyond that of the brief flowering of the *dar al-'ulum*. Their groups were thus informally organized intellectual ones: The *suhba* relationship,[10] or informal groups of teachers and students, constituted their structure. It was in this noninstitutional way that what Bloch has called the "Aristotelian left" was able to blossom. Within the institutional learning sector, by contrast, only sacral content dominated, with sacral law, the Islamic *shari'a* as the focal point, for "Islam is a religion based on a system of law. God is the sole legislator. There is no clerical hierarchy. Only the jurists count as interpreters (of the will of God as documented in the law). In this sense the crucial goal of Islamic learning consists of educating within the context of divine law, which embraces all spheres of life."[11]

In its early stages, the Islamic education system was, as has been mentioned, financed by private endowment (*waqf*). Sponsors looked upon the "foreign sciences," philosophy and natural science, as godless and excluded them from the institutional educational sphere.[12] This domain was nonetheless highly pluralistic, as it was a source of many initiatives and allowed differing opinions on religious doctrine to be represented. The Islamic principle of *ijtihad,* that is, the free inter-pretation of law—beyond exegesis—in order to interpret the will of God, permitted the development of controversies and a flowering of Islamic theology, in spite of the rigid boundaries of the institutional educational sphere. All professorships of the Islamic *madrasa* were financed privately through the disposition of *waqf.* This came to an end in the thirteenth century, however, with the introduction by the Islamic state of the state-paid office of *mufti,* an official who had the right to pronounce generally valid and binding *fetwa*s (legal opinions). This marked the end of the room for maneuver[13] previously enjoyed by the Islamic *madrasa*s as centers of socialization within the Islamic legal system—and indeed as a way of life. Islamic law, which is interpretative rather than legislative in character (God counting as the sole legislator), provides detailed codes of behavior for every sphere of life, even sexuality. The days of the privately financed *madrasa*s permitted diversity, and every interpretation of a legal provision was potentially open to dispute. The appearance of an institutional estab-lishment in Islamic 'law—brought about by the introduction of the office of *mufti*—and hence also of the Islamic educational sphere eliminated this diversity, as state provisions then counted as the pro-visions of God. The same thirteenth century saw the fall of Baghdad and the disintegration of the entire Islamic empire. A period of stagnation that was to last for centuries set in, not even to be alleviated by the flowering of the military feudal empire of the Ottoman Turks. During this decline of Islamic civilization, European civilization was bur-geoning.[14] Within the sphere of education, a new form of learning was unfolding for the first time, the *universitas litterarum,* which was to make an incursion into and leave its trace in even the stagnating Muslim world during the period of European conquest, as we shall see in the following section.

This account of Islamic educational institutions should not be concluded without posing the question, on the basis of the historical material I have presented and interpreted, of the extent to which Islamic education enables the individuals who have been socialized within it to accommodate change culturally. If we look at the curriculum of educational institutions in classical Islam,[15] it is clear that the room for creativity was very limited. There were always set texts that could not be questioned or inquired into; it was purely a matter of interpreting them. God was seen as the Creator (*khaliq*), and man the creature (*makhluq*), who was not permitted to create. Man's task was to accept what God had created; he could only attempt, by means of interpreting the word of God (*kalamu'l-Allah*), to understand creation better. Islamic learning methods were thus structured accordingly:[16] rote learning, a "constant feature of education in medieval Islam"; repetition; text comprehension; testing of one's own memory by being checked by another or by reciting a text in front of someone else (*mudhakara*); and writing down the words of the teacher. To sum up, therefore, traditional Islamic learning consists of both a written record and the learning of sources by heart.[17] Using these methods, however, one cannot learn either how to think in terms of problems or how to inquire into them. So this was the dominant learning method in the classical Islamic educational institution. Only in the noninstitutional branch of Islamic culture, influenced by hellenization, was the way open for a rationalization of the cosmos and for reasoning on the subject of man and his environment. This tradition was unable to evolve in Islam. The tradition of Muslim orthodoxy, which prevailed over the ruins of Islamic rationalism, could transmit no educational content that would facilitate the cultural accommodation of social change by Muslims.

The Universitas Litterarum *as a European Educational Institution: Its Universalization and Incursion into the Islamic Middle East*[18]

Neither the institutional form of the hellenized *dar al-'ilm* (academy of sciences) nor the noninstitutional *suhba* group of Hellenic-influenced Muslim scholars, but the institution of the *madrasa* historically shaped higher education. After the demise of the Muslim caliphate of Baghdad and the accompanying stagnation of Islamic civilization, Ibn Bultan's eleventh-century triclassification of science was narrowed to a purely Islamic definition of science, to Koranic and Hadith exegesis pure and simple. All other branches of knowledge were then derived from these Islamic sciences.

By the time Europe, by then a developed continent, colonized even the Muslim region in its conquest of the world, the Muslim education system was characterized exclusively by the *maktab/kuttab* at school level and the *madrasa* at the level of higher education. The Oriental ruler Muhammed Ali, who came to power in 1805 in the aftermath of Napoleon's Egyptian expedition, began to build a modern state, soon realizing, however, that he would not be able to achieve his goal on the basis of the existing structure of the traditional Muslim education system. He began in the 1820s, therefore, to send scholarship-holders to Europe. The following passage, quoted from the Paris diary of the leader of the first Egyptian student group to travel to France, is a striking illustration of the notion of science still predominant in those days. The author of the diary, Tahtawi, whose contribution to the renewal of the Arabic language has been recorded at length in Chapter 6, notes in Paris: "When in France it is said of someone that he is a scholar, this does not mean that he is versed in religion, but that he is familar with other sciences. It is not difficult to see the superiority of these Christians over others in these sciences, and therefore also to realize that in our countries many of these sciences do not exist at all."[19] In Arabic, the status of scholar is called *ulema*, in the singular *'alim*, or scientist. This refers to clerical scholar, however, whose knowledge is limited to Koranic science. Because the Koran is regarded by orthodox Muslims as the absolute source of knowledge, its exegesis is the object of science in general. When Muslims speak of Islamic science they mean the content outlined here and not what Europeans understand by the term "science."[20] The *ulema*, or scribes, and especially the *faqih*, or jurists, among them are hence the true scientists in this understanding of the term.[21]

Science in Arabic is *'ilm*, from which the term *ulema* is derived, but *fiqh*, Islamic jurisprudence, is science par excellence. The higher *madrasa*s of Islam, especially the oldest and today the most highly esteemed, such as al-Azhar in Cairo, Zeituna in Tunis, and Qarrawiyin in Fez, were seats for the training and instruction of scholars of religion. If we take a look, from the perspective of culture-specific diversification with regard to concepts of higher institutions of learning, beyond the Islamic Middle East, we are bound to make a distinction between cultures with a particular notion of such institutions, analogous to the Islamic example, and cultures unfamiliar with such higher institutions of learning before contact with Europe.[22] Illustrations of the first category of cultures may be found in many Asian countries. The nonliterate cultures of Africa may be cited as an example of those with no higher institutions of learning prior to the process of acculturation with Europe or with Islamic culture. We know from ethnology that magicians fulfilled the function of guardians of knowledge in such cultures. In those parts of Africa where Islam has succeeded in gaining a foothold, a combined magical and clerical function came about. The *marabout*, the African Muslim scribe, embodied both Islamic Koranic science and the required skill of controlling nature by magical means.[23]

In terms of the history of culture, the *universitas litterarum*, as a seat for the preservation and cultivation of human knowledge that is not limited to the functional sphere, constitutes a European innovation—although this remark should not be taken to mean that no non-European culture was previously acquainted with science in the European sense. From Islamic history, for example, we know that both natural scientific and great philosophical contributions by Islamic scholars prior to High Islam arose out of the scientific tradition—albeit not from the one that was institutionalized within the education system. These great achievements, however, did nothing to modify the Islamic notion of the institution of learning itself, in which the sheikh or *ustadh* (professor) transmits to his students traditional sacred science, neither searching for truth through research nor passing on practical knowledge for the cultural reception of the natural and social environment. The relationship between the *marabout* and his *talibés,* that is, between teacher and pupil, represents the equivalent of this in the Islamized parts of African culture.

A glance at universities outside Europe today, however, is sufficient to show clearly that the European notion of a university has prevailed worldwide. Even in the Muslim world the great classical, highly esteemed universities such as al-Azhar are peripheral in terms of educational policy compared to the new universities set up on the European model, and the traditional seats of learning are even establishing departments that recognize the content of the positive sciences. In regard to this observation, we might ask ourselves why world development has taken on such a pattern and why the European notions of science and the university have come to dominate worldwide. The question assumes some urgency when we consider the problem of the role of the university in the development process. I shall not go into this question in any depth here, however, but will limit myself to a quotation from Helmuth Plessner, who speaks of how "Europeanism conquers the world," arguing:

> Under its banner the non-European peoples are rising up out of their
> medieval, archaic view of life. The massive differences in level
> between Europe, the Orient and the Tropics are disappearing. . . .
> This expansion is only made possible and practically unlimited by the
> fact that scientific findings are becoming merged with their potential
> applications, and the use of apparatus and machinery is bound up
> with the notion of theory, but not with the notion of the humanistic
> ethos of theory. . . . Only at the price of its mechanization and
> instrumentalization is Europeanism conquering the world. This
> capacity for transferral to non-European cultures is becoming its
> destiny.[24]

The outcome of this Europeanization of the world is at all events the current structure in which we live, which may be called an international society. The crucial burden we are trying to overcome today, the world economy–related North-South gap between the industrial countries of the North and the nonindustrialized societies of the Third World, is a historical feature of this penetration.[25]

In view of the international social structure in which the non-European developing countries are embedded, the researcher is bound, in the context of fulfilling the impending tasks in these countries, to raise the issue of the significance of educational institutions in the development process. I do this with reference to a European university tradition, although without any Eurocentric undertones. The worldwide North-South gap is widening all the time, and the problems of Muslim and other developing countries in the south of the international society are becoming increasingly dramatic. Neither moralizing invective, such as is to be found in the 1981 report of the North-South Commission (sponsored by the UN and chaired by German ex-chancellor Willy Brandt), nor modish theoretical constructions, such as "autocentric development" or "dissociation from the world market," can be deemed much of a contribution to alleviating the misery of what is known as the "Third World." Moralizing invective may help some metropolitan individuals to appease their self-induced feelings of guilt, just as theoretical models regaled in seemingly fascinating conceptual apparatus may assist other individuals to promote their professional careers as experts on the developing countries and poverty—but they definitely do not offer any viable solution to impending problems. The international society is a structurally fixed reality, and any idea of escaping it can only be described as wishful thinking in the comfort of the armchair.

What is the nature of this reality in relation to university structures in the Muslim and other developing countries, and what role may be expected from the university as an instrument for self-help in the development process? We may proceed first from the empirical observation that virtually all universities in the developing countries display traces of the process described by Plessner as the conquest of the world by Europeanism. New cultural material is being adopted and, in the absence of an appropriate infrastructure, is coexistent with the old structures. In Muslim societies, where higher institutions of learning have a deeply-rooted procedure of rote learning, the content of positive sciences adopted from Europe is treated in a similar fashion. Verses of the Koran are learned by heart because they are infallible and not to be inquired into. Immanuel Kant's *Critiques* or David Hume's *Inquiry,* now available in Arabic translation, are learned by heart in a similar manner and not conceived of in terms of their nature as problem-oriented inquiry.[26] Not only contemporary universities in the Muslim world are characterized by this feature, however: Many universities in the developing countries are rote-learning institutions even for matter that criticizes rote learning. They are also institutes for equipping students with academic, although not very valuable, degrees. This gloomy reality goes hand in hand with a third- and fourth-class ranking of their own making in the international university scale. In many developing countries an examination certificate from London or Paris is estimated far more highly, even by indigenous authorities, than a formally higher academic grade from a home university. This practice has led to an upgrading of study abroad and a concomitant downgrading of study at home—despite all rhetoric to the contrary—that is far from conducive to the development process but nonetheless not the cause of it.

All Arab Islamic and black African universities I know of have courses of study based solely on the capacity for rote learning in order to pass successfully. In view of climatic conditions and the extreme shortage of accommodation (a room of one's own is a dream) in most developing countries, rote learning takes place in public and can be observed by anyone on the street or on the edge of town. Those acquainted with developing countries will be familiar with the sight of students at exam time, walking up and down certain streets, learning by heart the books in their hands, or of African pupils studying under streetlights. After study of this kind, a pupil is equipped with a certificate but not with any substantial qualification that can be usefully applied within the development process. Studying is regarded by most people as a bread-winning ticket or admission to the circles of the better-off. In conversation even with academic authorities in Muslim and other developing countries, scholars are not generally asked first about their fields but about which academic degrees they have achieved and, most important, at which universities these were obtained. Only then is an academic ranked accordingly.

It is striking that in many Muslim countries, especially in those with a French colonial heritage, the arts and law faculties are the most important, the *faculté des lettres* and the *faculté des droits* making up virtually the entire campus. Graduates of these courses have command of a general knowledge, one too general to be of any practical use and that was learned by rote, without focusing on problem-solving. The Malayan sociologist Syed Alatas, who teaches in Singapore, has bitterly condemned the lack of a "spirit of inquiry" among intellectuals of the developing countries.[27] To put it crudely, these courses may be regarded as a synthesis of the shortcomings both of the European (that is, too wide a general education) and of the U.S. education system (that is, too specific a training). As a scholar socialized in Europe, I feel far more affinity with the European interpretation of the university as a place for general study (*Bildung*) than with the U.S. notion of the university for vocational training (*Ausbildung*). The idea of general study can, however, be carried too far, even to the point of dysfunction, in that an academic who can claim to be able to speak about everything is no longer master of anything specific. This is unfortunately the case today in the Federal Republic of Germany in many of the arts disciplines that dispense with all functional differentiation. U.S. training, however, produces only *Fachidioten* (literally, "specialized idiots," that is, over-specialized specialists), to use polemically the 1960s student-revolt term.

Graduates of a training system are, on the other hand, generally experts who are fit for employment and who have mastered their subject. At many universities in Muslim and other developing countries, courses do resemble training insofar as the curriculum is laid down; and the assessment of performance is as strict as at U.S. universities. What is to be learned, however, is often as general as in European courses of study, so that mastery of the material does not amount to a professional qualification. This type of mastery, moreover, does not denote cultural accommodation but simply the ability to learn by rote. Again, to put it crudely, a student educated at one of the universities of today's Muslim countries has command neither of the expert knowledge of the U.S. graduate, nor of the rigorous, problem-oriented thinking of the European liberal arts scholar.

In Europe the development of science and technology has enabled people to build new social structures within which they have been able to meet their own needs. Science is as utilizable as it is instructive; neither of these definitions can be separated from the other. Most Muslim and other developing countries import science in ready-made form. Learning processes in agrarian societies still take the form of learning by rote; the acquisition of education is generally pursued with the aim of obtaining a certificate with which to seek a privileged job. The only reason students learn their books by heart is to obtain good exam results. But only a few weeks later they have forgotten what they learned, as knowledge learned by rote, but not assimilated, cannot be retained.

The Crisis of Muslim Education: Islamic Perceptions of the Crisis and Prospects for the Future

The preceding remarks clearly show that the education system, next to the institution of law, forms the second mainstay of the Islamic religious system and its transmission. The *shari'a,* the Islamic *lex divina,* determines the content of Islam; the *maktab* at the elementary level and the *madrasa* at the higher level are the Muslim educational institutions that guarantee the handing-down of the legal provisions of the *shari'a*. In this sense, therefore, the *madrasa* cannot yet be understood as a university, inasmuch as the latter serves the unrestrained free pursuit of truth and inquiry into the nature of the world by means of human reason, but not solely the handing-on of already existing, sacrally determined knowledge. As the European notion of learning and the educational institutions associated with it have become universal in the wake of the European conquest of the world, the Muslim educational system has been in a state of crisis: The tension between holding firm to the traditional and adopting new knowledge or adapting to changed circumstances now characterizes the gruelling test that this system has faced since its confrontation with Europe. Before passing on to a closer examination of the Islamic perception of this crisis, I should first clarify my concept of education and the institutions that correlate to it.

Education may be defined as a social system or as an institution, this system in fact forming a subsystem within the total social system. Interaction takes places between this subsystem and other institutions of the respective social system. Within an educational system, people are socialized according to a culturally determined orientation. Such a system is nevertheless also influenced externally, specifically in the context of interaction with the environment, both by the national and, in our own age of the international society, by the international system. The well-known educational sociologist Theodor Hanf has developed the following interesting definition:

> On the one hand a process of socialization can be given an orientation at the international level. . . . On the other hand such a process also includes unintended content and effects as well as intended ones. . . . In addition to national political systems, the international system ultimately also stands both in direct and indirect relationship to the education system. . . . The term political socialization is understood to mean that process whereby an individual acquires fundamental orientations toward the political system. . . . The cognitive aspect pertains to the transmission of perceptions of the political system, the affective aspect to the transmission of value orientations and the behavioral aspect to the shaping of political attitudes.[28]

Applying this definition, from an expert who is also familiar with the Middle East,[29] we see that the process of socialization in Muslim learning institutions transmits a specific *orientation,* which does not prepare for *change* but for *stabilization,* as those values internalized in a Muslim education system are defined as those eternally valid for all places and all times and not subject to change, inasmuch as their substance is divine revelation. This statement is pertinent insofar as the intentional determination of the Islamic orientation is concerned. At the unintentional level, however, Islamic values are nonetheless redefined by change that has occurred: The education system is not free of changes that take place in the social environment. In Islam, however, these changes are received and integrated into the system at the unintentional level. The history of Islam offers ample material to support this assertion. The Muslim education system is characterized by a lack of conscious cultural reception of change, for in Islam man, as a *makhluq* (creature of God), is supposed to live solely according to the unalterable divine commandments proclaimed in the Islamic revelation.

Applying, within Hanf's cited general definition, the additional dimension of the international system as a determinant of change in the educational system provides us with even deeper insight into the problems to be overcome by the contemporary Muslim education system. The Islamic system today has to face not only the demands of change in the systemic environment but also, and above all, those proceeding from the environment of the international society.

On an empirical basis we can first observe a duality, with former patterns of socialization existing side by side with those that have penetrated from the international environment and have been adopted. As we have already seen, a student thus learns natural science or technology exactly as if it were sacral knowledge from the Koran and the Hadith. As a functional equivalent for the fear of God in learning the latter, the colonial inferiority complex operates during the study of positive science from Europe.

The question becomes whether this simultaneity of the unsimultaneous, the existence at the same time in the educational systems of Muslim societies of two patterns stemming from two historically different formations, is perceived and culturally coped with as such. A look at some of the most important Islamic publications may help us to answer this question.

The well-known Egyptian professor of pedagogy on the faculty of education at Ain-Shams University in Cairo, Sa'id Isma'il 'Ali, constantly stresses in his publications the apologetic assertion: "The Koran is the constitution for life in Muslim society."[30] For this very reason, he argues elsewhere, "we are only acting consistently with the truth (*haqiqa*) in according first place to the Koran, and it is from this very primary source that we have to derive the definition of our Muslim education."[31] How this definition is to be derived is left open. In a more recent publication, Isma'il 'Ali speaks of the crisis in modern Muslim education, a crisis that has arisen out of the "unrest" (*qalaq*) that accompanies the difficulty in finding a solution to the *"mushkilat al-yaum,"* the problems of the present day. Isma'il 'Ali then asks courageously: "Can today's Muslim pedagogue find help in this situation in the traditions of his fathers and forefathers? Scholarly integrity compels us to answer no to this question."[32] Isma'il 'Ali then amplifies upon the prospect of developing a Muslim culture in tune with the times that would be capable of going beyond the alternatives that have prevailed so far. Muslim warriors (*al-fariq al-Islami*) have indeed held firm to Islam, he continues, but have failed to keep up with the challenges of the age. Those, however, whose thinking has kept up with the times, are no longer Muslims. Isma'il 'Ali offers a solution: "We must work very hard and invest energy in finding a way to harmonize these two positions, by developing a culture that not only retains the central values of the Islamic heritage . . . but that at the same time renders possible an opening to Western culture, so as to be able to embrace everything that will give us strength and propel us forward."[33]

Although this quotation comes from an Arab publication of 1982, it is necessary to add that such an open-minded notion of primary sources, that is, the Koran and the Hadith, no longer prevails today. One of the many negative secondary effects of oil wealth has been that the Saudis, who must be ranked among the fundamentalists, if only at the level of their legitimating style, have their own notion of the crisis in Muslim education, which they are also in a position to propagate with appropriate means.[34] The first World Congress on Muslim Education was thus held at the Saudi university of Abdulaziz in Mecca. The subsequently published proceedings in English, *Crisis in Muslim Education*,[35] and the resulting volume from the same university, *Education and Society in the Muslim World*,[36] distributed widely by the British publishing industry, contained quite a different concept, both of the crisis itself and of the ways to combat it culturally, than that of Isma'il 'Ali just quoted above.

The secularization and division of knowledge into the subdivisions of humanities, natural and social sciences, as contained in the well-known declaration U.S. university presidents made at Harvard after World War II, was criticized at the conference in Mecca. In the absence of a more profound acquaintance with their own much-lauded heritage, that is, with the classification of science put forward by Ibn Bultan in the eleventh century (see the first section in this chapter), the congress foresaw in such a division the seed of a rift between faith and inquiry. The congress also asserted that the Muslim world would be harmed by this seed:

The Muslim World too has been invaded by this Western form of
civilization. This feeling of rootlessness has already entered Muslim
society because our intellectuals are now being educated in the West,
being brainwashed and returned to their own countries after reading
text-books which are all filled with ideas in conflict with their
traditional assumptions. Even in Muslim countries the traditional
Islamic education system has been superseded by a modern one
which has been borrowed from the West.[37]

This, then, is the Saudi diagnosis of the crisis in Muslim education,
the surmounting of which can only imply a rejection of this Western
influence: "Muslim intellectuals are expected now to justify their
methods and at the same time restate their traditional ideas in the
context of the new, and formulate new concepts for recent branches
of knowledge by reasserting the spiritual realization of Truth as en-
shrined in revelations from God."[38] On the surface there would seem
to be no difference between these two quoted positions: Both call for
a renewed adoption of Islamic sources in tune with the times. On
closer examination, however, we can see that in the first position,
although the Koran is insisted upon as the primary source, the reply
to the question of whether answers to contemporary problems are to
be found in the sacred sources is no. Here, therefore, recourse to the
Koran is to be interpreted in the sense of finding purpose and developing
ethical principles. The fundamentalist position is not satisfied with
stopping there. The demand that textbooks be written "on the basis
of Islamic concepts"[39] clearly ranks among the postulates of the Muslim
world congress on education—in other words, physics, chemistry, and
modern technology, as well as the social scientific methods of all
branches of knowledge, must rest on the basis of revealed Koranic
truth. This position is writ typically large in the case of the Egyptian
pedagogue Mahmud Sayyid Sultan, who insists that the Koran does not
contain solely a set of ethical principles or a religious view of the
world: "Because the Koran is a method for living and a constitution
for the whole of humanity, without temporal or spatial limitations of
any kind. The Koran is furthermore also evidence of creation by miracle
[*i'jaz*] and is an all-embracing encyclopedia of science, and a compilation
of the history of the whole of humanity."[40] In Sultan's view, the essential
task of the educational system consists of accommodating "every teaching
method, every curriculum, and every scientific truth" to the "Islamic
definition of the cosmos" imparted in the Koran.[41] Any critic of such
a fundamentalist interpretation of the Koran takes the risk of being
declared an "unbeliever" (*kafir*), and any attempt to disavow the Koran
as an inexhaustible encyclopedia of science involves the danger of

being accused of heresy (*kufr*). The consequences for the offenders in either case are not to be overlooked. It would be wishful thinking not to admit that the fundamentalist position, and not the secular modernist version, dominates the debate on the crisis in Muslim education. Although there are many modern educational institutions in the Muslim world imparting apparently secular knowledge, the overall fabric of the educational sector is strained by the awkward heritage of Islamic institutions of learning, with the result that "science" is only to be found there in the form of a ready-made, imported product. There is still no discernible, deeply-rooted scientific tradition that could modify the substance of the educational sector in the Muslim countries. The duality between knowledge that is handed down unquestioned and knowledge that has been adopted in a cumulative fashion does not permit the practical application of education to the cultural reception of change. A discussion with my frequently quoted Freiburg colleague Theodor Hanf[42] on the penultimate draft of this chapter focused on the following two points: (1) the view held by many Muslims that they can adopt modern technology and science, but not the wider framework that goes with them; (2) the Muslim theological doctrine that the Islamic *umma* (community) is the best ever created by God leads us to assume that there is "a psychological barrier" among Muslims to learning from other cultures, to which they feel superior. My colleague, the late Richard Mitchell,[43] discussed the first of these points in his presentation "Islam and Modern Technology"[44] at the First Islamic Conference on Islam and Civilization in Cairo. Mitchell was heavily censured for arguing that modern technology does not consist of technological goods severed from their social context, that it also embraces a specific social organization in life and corresponds to specific attitudes that arise in that context. Applying this to the educational sector, I can state that in Muslim educational institutions neither the social organization referred to above nor, concomitant with adopted ready-made technological-scientific knowledge, the prerequisite psychosocial attitudes are conveyed.

Researchers working in the comparative sphere will be aware that in other, non-Islamic, but preindustrial cultures today there is also a tendency toward synthesizing preindustrial sociocultural systems with the ready-made products of technological-scientific civilization. The possibility of calling such a synthesis into question, as I have done in numerous articles,[45] does not, however, amount to the assumption that a *world culture* exists, or could exist. I continue to argue in the Herderian sense in favor of a plurality of cultures, though I am fully aware that this is only feasible at a symmetrical level. A prerequisite for such a state would be that all cultures become technological and scientific, in other words, acquire the capacity to handle creatively, and to produce for themselves, technology and science. The mere adoption and cumulative handling of these phenomena would rather tend toward a deepening of the existing gulf.[46]

There is a further consideration connected with this particular postulate: namely, that criticism of Eurocentrism should develop into general criticism of all ethnocentrism. The Islamic teaching that Muslims are the best and hence the superior community (*umma*) on earth represents not only a "psychological barrier" (Hanf) with regard to education; it also represents an obstacle preventing Muslims from seeing the other and the different as equal in value. This misconception of Muslim superiority blatantly contradicts the call for equality and plurality within the international society—a call that comes in the first instance from the "Third World." The Muslim education system, which imbues its offspring with a feeling of superiority, moreover prevents them from properly perceiving realities that do not correspond to this self-image, and therefore also deprives them of the ability to cope with those realities and to contribute substantively to their change.

PART FOUR

The Politicization of Islam as a Cultural System and the Topicality of Islamic Revivalism: Islam Today

Having defined contemporary Islam as a cultural system and clarified its most important elements, I now turn to the question of how this cultural system is politicized, how a political ideology is developed out of it. It would seem appropriate at this point to recap the stages of argumentation and analysis so far, as a reminder of the level at which the politicization of religiocultural symbols being discussed here will be approached. In Part 1, following Geertz, I interpreted religion as a cultural system and on the basis of this *preliminary* understanding developed a concept of Islam. Rejecting reductionism to a superstructure-basis formulation, in Part 2 I posed the question of the interchange between culture as a system of symbols and social reality as a social structure. In this context I observed that cultural symbols correspond to a specific level of social development in a dual sense, in that the prevailing cultural system can both reflect and decisively influence that level. Against the background of this discussion, I reconstructed the basic patterns of the Islamic perception of change. These fundamental analyses served to prepare the ground for an examination in Part 3 of the central elements of the Islamic cultural system: law (*shari'a*), language (*'arabiyya*), and the education system.

The outstanding feature of the forty Muslim societies in the modern world is that they are in some cases subject to extremely rapid and uneven social change.[1] Unfortunately the current politicization of Islam, as we shall see in the case studies, is not concerned with developing an innovative prospect for the future in the context of which the existing cultural system is adapted to changed conditions, or new elements created with its help. Instead, there has been a political call for the suppression of development, that is, making reality, condemned as a deviation from Islam, conform to the ideal cultural system. Underlying contemporary political Islam,[2] therefore, is the fundamentalist demand that Islamic symbols remain immutable and that reality be structured after them. The perceptive reader will recall the concept of religion as a model for reality, developed in Chapter 1. The political programs derived from this cultural system are motivated accordingly. Political Islam provides no innovative prospects for the future but solely a vision of the future as a restoration of the past, obtained from the "good old" ways of old (*salaf*), hence the term *salafiyya* (Salafism-integrism). Political Islam may therefore—with some restrictions—be interpreted as a backward-oriented utopia. This demand and reality nevertheless continue to clash: The Islamic past is perceived as the *primeval* democratic form of government of the people, to be regarded as a divine order and to be restored precisely for this reason. This is clearly not a traditionalist view of politics. We shall be seeing in detail in Chapter 8 how modern terms (for example, *nizam,* or system) are projected back on to Islamic history and culturally understood or perceived as authentically Islamic. Thus, Islamic fundamentalists are not traditionalists. Without preempting that discussion here, I do want to ask what political form of government developed parallel to the foundation of the Islamic religion, so as to be able to assess accurately the claim to authenticity of contemporary political Islamic integrists. In the study of this question, the available works by Orientalists of the old school have unfortunately also proved of little help, as they study reality solely with the aid of exegesis of classical sources, without examining the political structures of the time. Historical reality is not a text, however, and cannot be adequately grasped simply through research into sources. The two-volume work of the German Orientalist Tilman Nagel may be cited in support of this assertion.[3] In contrast to this, the social historian Reinhard Bendix, who was born in Germany and had to flee to the United States in 1933, has been able to produce profound insights into this question in his magnificent work *Kings or People.*[4]

In my earlier work, *Crisis of Modern Islam,* I showed that the founding of the Islamic religion was accompanied by an Islamic process of civilization in the sense meant by Elias, during the course of which a central authority, a state, was established out of the "regulated" anarchy of the pre-Islamic Arab tribes.[5] Contrary to the projected claim of Islamic integrists, however, there was not yet any democracy in the seventh century. The form of government practiced in Medina during the founding period may today be interpreted in Bendix's sense, as a "charismatic prophecy." It was out of just this "conjunction of pre-Islamic tribal traditions" with the religious message, according to Bendix, that the Islamic interpretation of royal authority emerged.[6] Within Islam we have both Sunni and Shi'ite traditional interpretations of the charismatic prophecy of Muhammed: In Sunni Islam the "caliphate of the patriarchs" is the legitimate form, the caliph being a "king," a successor to the Prophet. The Prophecy is unique and cannot be either passed on or repeated. The Shi'ites, on the other hand, with their notion of the *imamate* (the succession of the imams), insist on the passing on of charisma. Until the time of the Safavids (1501–1722) and Khomeini's Iran in modern times, Shi'ite Islam remained primarily underground, whereas the royal tradition in Islam was of a Sunni character.[7]

In Bendix's view, the conflicts in Islam pertained to the "legitimation of royal rule derived from *historical events*. The caliph was an absolute ruler, whose duty was to be the guardian of the people, and if necessary to force them to obey the law. Muslim jurists imposed on men the duty of complete obedience to the ruler."[8] The ruler was for his part obliged according to dogma to make his political conduct conform to the Islamic *shari'a*. We know, however, from the research of the Iraqi historian Abdalaziz Duri, that the political ideals of Islam were not practiced because of a lack of appropriate institutions.[9] The Muslim jurist (the *faqih*) possessed no autonomy vis-à-vis the ruler, as a result of which law was generally interpreted in conformity with the existing form of government, which has been characterized by the Syrian scholar Muhsin Shishakli[10] as a sultanic form (*al-hukm al-sultani*). The prescribed dogmatic combination of government and law thus remained ineffective in Islam. Islamic integrists today, aided by the politicization of cultural symbols, contest absolute rule in the context of a *search for meaning* within the *crisis of meaning* arising out of a situation of rapid change, and by means of the projection of modern concepts on to the past, as we shall see in more detail in Chapter 8. An alternative, along the lines of development policy, for coping with the burning social issues is not offered, however.[11] Islamic fundamentalism seldom goes beyond the confines of romantic social protest in its ideology, or beyond terrorism in its actions.

After a general cross-regional interpretation, based on the sociology of religion, of the repoliticization of Islam in Chapter 8, we shall proceed in the two subsequent chapters to selected case studies on Egypt (Chapter 9) and Iran (Chapter 10). In order to show that the politicization of Islam serves the interests not only of religiopolitical opposition movements but also those of existing orders, Part 4 also contains an analysis (Chapter 11) of the two Islam-legitimated monarchies still existing, Morocco and Saudi Arabia.

8

A Religiosociological Interpretation of the Politicization of the Islamic Cultural System: Political Islam as a Defensive Cultural Reaction to Rapid Social Change[1]

It is self-evident to the sociologist of religion that a scientific examination of Islam, or indeed any other religion, can never hope to be achieved through a mere study of sources; although familiarity with these sources is an acknowledged prerequisite, it cannot be seen as an end in itself.[2] A study of Islam in the sociology of religion cannot be anything other than the investigation of this religious system as a *fait social* in the Durkheimian sense. This basic methodological position in and of itself leads the sociologist into conflict with two other kinds of experts on Islam, who, though long-standing enemies, nonetheless share a very similar methodological starting-point: The basic assumption of the existence of an "essence of Islam" is propounded equally both by traditional Orientalists and Islamic fundamentalists. This cannot be of any special interest to the sociologist of religion, however, as it pertains to texts and not to Islam as a *fait social*.

For the Islamic fundamentalist, any *fait social* inconsistent with the essence of Islam, as derived from the texts, ranks among the endless list of deviations from Islam.[3] Although the category of deviation is not part of the vocabulary of the traditional Orientalist, such a scholar will nevertheless not dispute that only research into sources can provide an adequate understanding of Islam.[4] The sociologist of religion is distinguished methodologically from these two in focusing on how religious commandments become embedded in social relations, that is, how people perceive a religion and in what way they comply with it. Seen in this light, Islam in Indonesia is a different object of study from Islam in Morocco, even though both invoke the same dogmatic sources.[5] A competent sociologist of religion must of course also be familiar with the sources; criticism of the Orientalists' approach is not to be understood as a denial of the necessity for studying Islamic sources.[6] A sociologist who knows Islam only as a *fait social* is not more likely to provide an appropriate understanding of the subject than a traditional Orientalist. The researcher must be familiar with both the texts *and* the sociostructural reality that corresponds to them in order to achieve an adequate understanding of how that sociocultural system functions.

This preliminary methodological comment helps us to place accurately the interpretation offered here of the repoliticization of the sacred in the Islamic Middle East. It also defines my theme. I am not concerned here with a "re-Islamization" of the Muslim countries. This concept, which has become established in the German-speaking world as a description of what is happening in those countries and which I, regrettably, at one time also used myself, is not adequate.[7] The term "re-Islamization" presupposes—from the semantic viewpoint—that Islam was once suppressed and that a return to it is now taking place. Those familiar with the Islamic Middle East will know that Islam as a system of belief has never lost significance for its adherents. A political superseding of Islam did take place following the fall of Islamic modernism from the sphere of political ideologies in the Arab East (*mashrek*), after which Islam as a political ideology has had to quit the field in favor of secular ideologies such as nationalism and socialism.[8] But Islam has nevertheless forfeited none of its influence as a cultural-normative orientation for Muslims. The current reemergence of Islam as a political ideology is not therefore to be defined as re-Islamization, but more accurately as political revitalization, or as the *repoliticization of the sacred.*

Ultimately, in the majority of Muslim countries this new process consists of militant political groups or numerous political writers and pamphleteers raising the claim that Islam is not only a religion but also a *din wa daula* (a religion fused with a state order). More freely and aptly expressed in Balandier's terminology, it is "a correspondence between the sacred and the political." From this comes the assertion of a *nizam Islami* (*an-nizam al-Islami*), which is defined as the content of a political ideology and a political oppositional program.[9]

This chapter consists of two sections. The first will outline the sociopolitical factors behind the repoliticization of Islam and its raising to the status of *political ideology,* and the second will pose the question whether Islam as a *religiocultural system* provides a foundation for a political system or whether fundamentalists are projecting this expectation onto Islam, as has already been assumed in the introductory text to this chapter.[10]

The Sociopolitical Factors Behind the Political Revitalization of Islam

So as better to understand the process defined here as the *re-politicization of Islam,* it will be necessary both to place it within its wider context and to define it historically. It will be useful first to recall what "modern Islam" is and what in fact makes up its central problems and issues.

Maxime Rodinson has been insistent on comprehending Islam historically and differentiating between various periods in its development.[11] In theological terms, Islam is understood, as we have already seen, as the ultimate divine revelation, which is superior to all previous revelations on the grounds of this characteristic. The Koran identifies the Muslim Prophet Muhammed as *"rasul Allah wa khatem an-nabiyyin"* (Messenger of God and Seal of the Prophets).[12] In Arabic, the word *khatem* not only means "seal" but also implies that the Messenger of God is the "final seal" in the history of the Prophets.[13] This context has already been fully elaborated in Chapter 2 with reference to the research of Johan Bouman, who has done a textual analysis of the Koran. It will therefore suffice here to remind ourselves that in Islam the superiority of Muslims over other religious communities derives from this Koranic definition of the Prophet as the Seal in the history of the Prophets,[14] according to which Muslims have at their command the ultimate and eternal divine revelation in the history of mankind. After its foundation in the seventh century, Islam rapidly gained a superior position in the history of the world, which it has retained these many centuries—albeit under various conditions and in various forms.[15] This self-perception thus appeared to be corroborated by history.

Since the eighteenth century, the problem of modern Islam as a religious system has developed out of its confrontation with a power that was superior in science and technology, namely modern Europe. In this asymmetrical encounter, Muslims have been the underdogs not only in terms of civilization but also politically and militarily. Their notion of themselves as described above thus entered a state of crisis, which is also the crisis of modern Islam.[16] In 1930 a leading Islamic modernist, Shakib Arslan, posed the question, "Why are Muslims backward, while others have developed?" and made this the title of his major treatise. His answer was straightforward: Muslims were backward because they had deviated from Islam.[17]

In my earlier monograph on this crisis, I developed the following periodization scheme of the asymmetrical encounter between the now industrial West and the comparatively backward Middle East, in order to ascertain the position of Islam during the course of this development.[18]

1. The first phase was based on a revitalization of Islam as an indigenous culture so that it could assert itself against the expanding new power, Europe, which was making an incursion into the Islamic religion. Islam thus positioned itself as anticolonialism and as an ideology of *jihad* (holy war)[19] against European colonialism. This revitalization had both *modernist* components (the integration of modern science and technology in Islam) as well as *millenarian-nativist* components (a return to primeval Islam as a defensive culture against the alien).[20]

2. In the course of this cultural incursion of the Muslim countries, new Western-educated elites evolved who were better able to lead the anticolonial struggle. The ideologies of secular nationalism and socialism replaced the political ideology of Islam. If by secularization we understand both a transformation of the social structure in the sense of *functional differentiation of the social system* as well as a *redefinition of the sacred* to suit the altered situation, then it will be necessary to supplement the thesis of the dominance of secular ideologies with qualifying and modifying statements. Although an adoption of secular ideologies from Europe did take place in the Islamic Middle East, there was neither a process of secularization nor a theological reformation.[21]

3. The third phase, which forms the subject of this analysis, may be characterized as the suppression of secular ideologies in favor of a resurgence of Islam as a political ideology. The thesis that Islam is only a religion, propounded even by al-Azhar scholars such as Ali Abdelraziq[22] during the period when secular ideologies were predominant, was now rejected. In its place arose the call for *an-nizam al-Islami,* for the political order of Islam.[23]

Inasmuch as those countries which are inhabited predominantly by Muslims (forty states) are integral parts of the international system Luhmann designates as the "international society" (on the basis of the "worldwide interaction" that has been achieved through the networks of transport and communication),[24] the sociologist of religion working on Islam is obliged to go beyond the boundaries of the discipline and take account of international relations.[25] For the political revitalization of Islam, in other words, the recourse to an indigenous system of coordinates for the articulation of political content, has been brought about not only by factors within Muslim society itself, but also by the international society.

It is my central thesis that since the 1970s the Islamic Middle East has been undergoing a crisis brought about by both internal and external factors. Islam has the best symbols to offer in this crisis situation, inasmuch as these symbols fulfill a dual function. On the one hand, Islamic cultural symbols offer an indigenous form for the articulation of political content in a situation in which the outside, or non-Muslim, world is perceived as a threat to Muslims' own identity. On the other hand, the political content being articulated has a chance that secular ideologies, as an elite body of thought, do not have, to reach and mobilize broad sections of the population. Political Islam has more appeal than any of the secular ideologies, which are in any case propounded only by elites and perceived by the illiterate majority of the population as an imported product. Some spread of secular ideologies among the Western-educated social strata has taken place in the Islamic Middle East, but there has been no secularization as such, as I have pointed out. In light of this observation it is not difficult to explain how secular ideologies have so easily ended up in a legitimacy crisis.[26]

This crisis began immediately after the sweeping defeat of the Six-Day War. Both Arab nationalism and Arab socialism of the Ba'athist and Nasserist type lost their glamor with the defeat of the political regime they had exploited for legitimation purposes and fell into a legitimacy crisis.[27]

Of course it is not only a question of ideology here: The Arab Muslim countries are also partners in the worldwide North-South conflict between industrial and nonindustrialized societies. One of the academic debates on the possibilities for resolving the problems of underdevelopment was conducted under the slogan "South-South Relations."[28] Regional integration was deemed an important road to improving the position of the South in the North-South conflict. Those familiar with the Middle East will agree with John Waterbury in his assertion that the practical policy of the Arab political regimes is in all too stark contrast with daily pan-Arab rhetoric.[29] The ideology of Arab unity on the basis of a secular Arab nation that would include both Arab Christians and Muslims is now perceived as an ideology legitimating the political regimes of defeat; it is set against the idea of an Islamic *umma* (a community of all Muslims). Militant groups point to the great victories and successes of Islam in the days when the Islamic *umma* was united, comparing these achievements in rousing fashion to those of the secular regime that collapsed in the Six-Day War of 1967.

Further exploring the thesis that the repoliticization of the sacred is not so much connected with Islam as a religious system as with a system of belief as a *fait social,* and that, moreover, the factors behind it are to be sought not only internally but also in the international society, leads us to discern the following realities conditioning the phenomenon of the political revitalization of Islam:

1. a deterioration in the position of the Muslim countries in the worldwide North-South conflict;
2. rapid social change in Muslim societies and its disruptive consequences;
3. a legitimacy crisis within secular-oriented political systems, which is blocking any participation in the decisionmaking process.

These three factors will be examined in the following discussion.

To anticipate my elaboration of the effects of the worldwide North-South conflict for societies with a predominantly Muslim population, I will emphasize at this point that the thesis of dependency theory, according to which underdevelopment and social deformation in the Third World is attributable to external factors alone—that is, to the European incursion—is an empirically untenable one. Although the greatest achievement of dependence theory is in having drawn attention to the external factors behind underdevelopment, some of its advocates, chiefly in the German academic community, propound this interpretation monocausally, thereby reducing it to absurdity. The ultimate expression of this absurdity is the statement that only the neutralization of these external influences by means of "dissociation from the world market" will eradicate the development problem in the Third World.

In the context of this discussion, it will be seen that the worsening of the position of the Muslim societies in the North-South conflict is only partly determined by external factors and that it is also one of the elements that foster the repoliticization of Islam. To maintain, however, that the industrial nations are solely responsible for the poverty in those countries would be to drop the level of scientific discussion closer to that of Muslim neofundamentalists, which can only be described as downright xenophobic. I therefore will not go into the current debate among left-wing German social scientists, in which an attempt at "dissociation from the capitalist world market" is read into the process of "re-Islamization" inasmuch as it is directed against the West.

At the descriptive level, the integration of predominantly Muslim countries into the international social structure can only be presented as a feature of their underdevelopment. This is not the place to take up the debate initiated by the Oxford historian Roger Owen whether the Middle East is underdeveloped in itself or only seems so in comparison with Europe—after its penetration and integration into a structure dominated by Europe.[30] Suffice it to say that underdevelopment is also, indeed primarily, an endogenous phenomenon that must nevertheless be included within an international social framework. This very asymmetry, which existed before the incursion into the non-Western world, made that incursion possible in the first place, later itself becoming a structural feature of the new international social fabric.

The worldwide North-South gap became increasingly wider in the 1960s and 1970s. Criticism of the monocausality of dependence theory does not at all deny that dependence structures are one of the most important factors in the impoverishment of the Muslim peoples; it merely points out that endogenous factors are equally important structural elements in this process. But how do the people concerned themselves perceive this *fait social*? The privileged and politically dominant strata of Muslim societies as a rule consist (with the exception of Saudi Arabia) of Westernized or Western-educated, socialized and acculturated elites. The impoverished majority of the population feel that these elites do not belong to the indigenous structure. They perceive the industrial West and the industrial East (if they come into contact with these at all) as the cause of their impoverishment and judge indigenous privileged elites in the same way. The population similarly sees as alien the secular ideologies propounded by these elites, which are without any internal social substrata, as these societies are not completely industrialized and therefore not functionally differentiated. The more blatant the consequences of the widening North-South gap become and the more Muslims become aware, as a result of the communications network arising out of the international society, of the contrast between European and U.S. lifestyles and their own poverty, the greater their hatred of the alien will become and the greater their need to have an indigenous medium of articulation in order to express these intensifying anti-Western attitudes. Islam is the best form of articulation for this purpose. In a very interesting lecture he gave at a symposium in Washington, D.C., Philip Khoury pointed out that not Islam itself but corresponding political and economic demands lie behind the political manifestations of Islamic fundamentalists, for whom Islam is useful as a "most convenient, readily available ideological instrument."[31]

We are concerned here, therefore, with the development of Islam as a form of articulation for the Muslim peoples in the North-South conflict, helping both to express dissatisfaction and to compensate for the suffering of poverty. In addition to these, Islam can also fulfill another function, that of a political ideology of the opposition against existing political regimes.

This brings us to a discussion of the nature and consequences of the disruptive, rapid social change taking place in the countries of the Islamic Middle East. Before moving on to this, I should give an account of the analysis by Michael Hudson,[32] whose results are a good illustration of the statement made in the opening text of this chapter, that Islam can be mobilized *both as an ideology of opposition and equally for the legitimation of political power.* In Morocco, for example, where the king is legitimated through Islam as the *amir al-mu'minin* (the commander of the faithful) and is thus sanctioned by the *ulema* (the Muslim scribes), it would be difficult for an opposition to invoke Islam,[33] whereas it would be possible in Tunisia, where the deposed former head of state, Burguiba, had the secular legitimation of "combattant suprême."[34] Despite this qualifying remark about the limitations of Islam as an oppositional ideology, it should nonetheless be remembered that even a religiously sanctioned social order can be opened to question by religious revivalist salvation movements. This was indeed the case in the Islam-legitimated monarchy of Saudi Arabia, when in November 1979 the mosque in Mecca was occupied by Islamic revivalists.

We know from Norbert Elias's grand design of the civilizing process[35] that in Europe social change took place within society itself. One of the significant features of such a process of social change is that attitudes and norm systems (psychogenesis) change concomitantly and parallel to changing social structures (sociogenesis). Undoubtedly in this case too there have been situations in which the dominant interpretation of the world has entered a state of deep crisis. We may recall in this connection, for example, Franz Borkenau's research into the "transition from a feudal to a bourgeois view of the world."[36]

The type of social change that took place in the non-Western societies, which during the nineteenth century were being forcibly integrated into a global structure dominated by Europe, is of a completely different order. Since that time social change in these regions has been primarily exogenously induced,[37] the factors behind it forming a complex of both external and internal elements. Crucial as it is to point out external factors, we must guard against deducing everything monocausally from dependence structures. One of the hallmarks of such primarily exogenously induced change is that it is perceived by those affected as a threat from outside. Norms and values with substrata in social structures that existed before this change and that are substantially upset and altered by it, persist; they do not alter analogously with structural change, as is the case with one type of social change, which is so to speak organically determined and not exogenously induced. Thus, we can observe a simultaneity of the unsimultaneous, that is, the parallel existence in the same society of norms and values of a no longer existing historical formation along with newly evolved social structures. Norms and values do not change as fast as structures do.

In a changing world, people have to protect their identity. Their environment no longer seems *determinable;* they need to define it if they are to safeguard their identity. In such a context, religion acquires a crucial function. This social process, which is empirically observable in many non-Western societies, is manifest with particular intensity in societies with a Muslim culture. *The more rapid the social change, the more indeterminable the environment becomes for individuals as personal systems living in a state of transition, and the more marked the need for religion to maintain identity in the process of change.* Change is perceived as an out-and-out threat, and a longing for the past is cultivated as a result. The restoration of what has been repressed by the alien, a return of overlaid indigenous elements, and a parallel reorientation of thought is raised to the level of a program of political action. This background may help to explain the appeal of militant Islamic groups specifically for those superficially modern strata who are most affected by change and its effects. It is no coincidence that Islamists are predominantly urban university students suffering urban anomie, and are not impoverished peasants. They side with the Koran on behalf of the *mustad'afun* (the oppressed), this Koranic expression translated by Islamists in Tunisia, for example, with the word "proletariat." Even Marxism is dispensable for such non-Western movements that purport to be revolutionary; after all, it comes from the West, which is rejected and militantly opposed.

Niklas Luhmann has investigated such a phenomenon at the conceptual level, highlighting the importance of religion for the social system, religion having the function of "transforming the indeterminable . . . world into a determinable one." He sees the individual as disoriented in an apparently indefinable environment: "The person in transition is 'both-and' or 'neither-nor,' and indeed simultaneously. His identity becomes blurred and indeterminable. This situation renders of some urgency the problem of determining the indeterminable." Religion is able to solve this problem: Islam has an optimal capacity both for "determining the indetermined" and for absorbing disappointments— both of these being component functions of the religious system in a transitional situation, as defined by Luhmann.[38] All ideologies of a Western stamp, from nationalism to Fabian socialism or even Marxism, pale into insignificance compared to an alternative capable of such component functions. In short, without investigating the disruptive, rapid processes of social change and its consequences (dislocations, and so on) taking place in the Islamic Middle East, the social scientist cannot hope to acquire an adequate understanding of the political revitalization of Islam.

This specific appeal of Islam as an indigenous cultural asset and as a system of coordinates explains the intensity of the legitimacy crisis in secular-oriented political regimes in the Islamic societies of the Middle East. At the level of political agitation, Islamic neofundamentalists compare the achievements of these regimes to those of the city-state of Medina founded by the Muslim Prophet Muhammed, which managed within half a century to extend "from the banks of the Loire to the Indus, from Poitiers to Samarkand."[39] Set against such idealized and overtly promising historical recollection based on an extremely selective view of the past, these secular-legitimated political systems, which in any case lack the support of an appropriate sociostructural substrate,[40] are bound to appear as corrupt political orders, blocking all forms of participation and propped up both socioeconomically and sociopolitically by the rule of minority parasitic social strata, and Islam presents itself as a tried-and-true ideological weapon to combat them. The current alternative is *an-nizam al-Islami* (the Islamic system). My task in the following section will therefore be to explore and assess the nature of this alternative.[41]

An-nizam al-Islami *as a Backward-looking Political Utopia of Islamic Political Revivalism*

In order to explain what *an-nizam al-Islami* (Islamic system) may mean, we have to return to the sources and study them. First, of course, we have the Koran. Anyone researching into the *nizam* concept, however, will look for it in vain in the Koran, although it forms the most central category of Muslim neofundamentalism. With regard to the concept of *nizam,* the great scholar of religion Wilfred C. Smith, who taught at Harvard until his retirement, stresses: "This term . . . does not occur in the Qur'an, nor indeed does any word from this root; and there is some reason for wondering whether any Muslim ever used this concept religiously before modern times. The explicit notion that life should be or can be ordered according to a system, even an ideal one, and that it is the business of Islam to provide such a system, seems to be a modern idea."[42]

I could now raise the objection that the concept of *nizam,* or its synonyms, may have developed on a Koranic basis only later in the course of Islamic history. This would bring us to the discussion of political thought in classical Islam. We know that in Sunni Islam there is the discussion of the political heritage of the caliphate[43] and in Shi'ite Islam the countertradition of the *imamate.*[44] In Shi'ite Islam every ruler is illegitimate in the absence of the imam. In Sunni Islam it is purely a matter of determining how the ruler was to be legitimated and how his rule was to be brought in line with the norms of the Islamic *shari'a*. With few exceptions (for example, al-Farabi), there is no tradition of political theory apart from the *shari'a* to be found in classical Islam. The work *Al-ahkam al-sultaniyya* by Abu al-Hassan al-Marwadi, which elaborates a systematic definition of the caliphate as an Islamic form of royal authority in the sense defined by Bendix, is one of the few exceptions. Hamid Enayat, the late Persian Oxford scholar, refers to the "absence of independent political thought in Islamic history. It was only under the trauma of European military, political, economic and cultural encroachments since the end of the eighteenth century that Muslim elites started to write separate works on specifically political topics."[45]

The majority of treatments by Muslim neofundamentalists do belong to such a category, reinterpreting the caliphate as an "Islamic system," thus projecting the category of *nizam* back onto Islamic history.[46] Even the classical author Mawardi is currently enjoying something of a renaissance.[47] A *fan al-hukm fi al-Islam*[48] (Islamic art of government) is being developed as a foil to *asalib al-ghazu al-fikri* (the methods of intellectual penetration), against which *an-nizam al-iqtisadi wa al-siyasi al-Islami* (the Islamic political and economic system) is regarded as offering the best protection.[49] *Al-Islam wa al-siyasa* (Islam and politics) are now seen as an inseparable unity.[50] The struggle between "left" and "right," which is nowhere mentioned in Islamic sources, as classical Islam is not familiar with these European concepts, is now also projected onto Islamic history: *Al-Yamin wa al-yasar fi al-Islam* is now one of the important political writings of Islamic political revivalism.[51] These modern projections into an extremely selective use of the past indicate a crisis situation in which a search for meaning takes place to maintain identity and to unite a group (community).

We may now proceed to the conclusion that there is no specifically Islamic political system and that this is thus a new ideological construction based on a projection into the past—a product of the politicization of Islam, which is a cultural system. Even the great al-Azhar scholar Ali Abdelraziq indicated in his now classic book *Al-Islam wa usul al-hukm*[52] that the caliphate state was an Arab system of government for the ideological legitimation of which Islam was invoked. In his view Islam knows no system of government, as it is a religion. We may wish to reject this interpretation of Islam, published in Cairo in 1925 and widely opposed, on the grounds of its modernity. The historian will be hard pressed, however, to show just what is specifically Islamic about the classical Islamic caliphate state.

Today we live in the age of the national state.[53] The theocratic universalism is now, in Islam as in Christendom, a thing of the past.[54]

The claim to Islamic statehood now also includes the concept of *umma* (the community of all Muslims), to which 800 million Muslims throughout the world belong. I now pose the question whether the concept of *umma* also has political or sociological implications, so as to reach an assessment.

First, however, it will be necessary to clarify my terms. The translation of the Arab Islamic term *umma* (prior to the foundation of the Islamic religion the Arabs were a *qaum,* organized ethnotribally) as "community" fully corresponds to the content of the term. If we recall the definition of community, in the German sense of *Gemeinschaft,* as distinct from society, as may be found in Ferdinand Tönnies, we can say conversely that the idea of *umma* as a community repudiates both plurality and diversity. Only righteous believers (*al-mu'minun*), among whom there may be no dispute as to what Islam is, belong to the *umma.* This is no more than an ideal, however. Such a community has never existed in real terms since the very beginnings of Islam under the Prophet in the city-state of Medina. Islam is only monolithic if one understands by Islam the sources and the perception of those sources held by European Orientalists and Muslim fundamentalists alike. As a *fait social,* Islam has always been characterized by complexity and diversity.

So far we have always used the plural term "Muslim societies," and sometimes the synonym "societies with a Muslim population or culture." This term, however, has no distinct content, evoking neither specifically Muslim nor specifically Christian societies. The term basically applies only to those societies whose members profess Islam. Once we become aware of the cultural diversity in Islam, as has been emphasized by Geertz, it is easy to see that the attribute "Islamic" cannot at all be applied to any existing cohesive entity.

To return to the *umma* concept, we might ask whether the unilateral use by neofundamentalists of the Islamic concept of *jihad*[55] has any reality behind it—that is, whether such clarion calls for Muslim solidarity can be backed up by the existence of any cohesion among the world's 800 million Muslims. The U.S. political scientist Leonard Binder posed a similar question more than two decades ago and came up with an adequate answer that has lost none of its validity since. He begins by stating—thereby confirming the research results of Montgomery Watt and Louis Gardet—that Muslims feel a very deep psychosocial bond with Islam and to its adherents as fellows in faith. He then adds:

> this attachment had little political efficacy, that is, it did not
> determine the limits of the political community. To put their views in
> our own terms, the concept of the *ummah* served as a referent for the

identity resolutions of individual Muslims throughout Islamic history.
But, as we have pointed out, identity was a religious and not a
political category of concern until recent times. It is with the
politicization of identity and the posing of the problem of the
individual and the political community that Islam and politics have
had to be reconciled within a new framework.[56]

Everywhere in those parts of the international society inhabited
by Muslims we can hear the call for a *nizam Islami,* that is, for an
Islamic system, not only in the heartlands of Islam, in the Arab Islamic
Middle East, but also in black Africa (for example, in Senegal)[57] and
even in countries where Muslims do not form an absolute majority of
the population (such as Malaysia)[58]—and even calls for a unified Islamic
umma. It is indisputable that during the last decade Saudi Arabia and
Libya have been undertaking activities to this effect, which continue
to be furthered by an influx of petrodollars.[59] It would be oversimplifying,
however, to attribute the political revitalization of Islam to "petrodollar
activities" alone, much as the researcher may overlook them.[60]

The analysis so far has shown that the political revitalization of
Islam has been directed to a large degree by both internal and
international social determinants. A closer examination of this phenomenon under the auspices of this general interdisciplinary analysis—
within the confines of a conceptual combination of sociology of religion
and international relations' area studies[61]—is the task of empirical case
studies. Area studies[62] can point up a number of regionally specific
details in the political revitalization of Islam. At the general level,
however, they will confirm the validity of our analysis of the sociopolitical
factors behind this phenomenon, as of our discussion of the sociological
and political scientific truth behind the terms "Islamic system" (*nizam
islami*) and "Islamic community" (*umma islamiyya*) respectively. Area
studies may serve to modify these general findings and specify them
in regional terms. The following three chapters in the final part of this
book will undertake this task.

9

Oppositional Religiopolitical Underground Organizations and the Islam-legitimated Establishment in Egypt: The Roots of the Political Resurgence of Militant Islam

When speaking generally of Islam as a cultural system and of its politicization as a symptom of the articulation of social and political concerns within the fabric of Islam, we should not overlook how this phenomenon constantly adopts different guises at the regional level. Awareness of these differing varieties calls for regional research (along the lines of U.S. area studies).[1] The politicization of Islam in Egypt,[2] although it represents a microcosm within the Muslim world, is nevertheless historically singular in terms of the existence of specific, overall historical and structural factors.

When, more than a thousand years ago, the oldest Muslim "university," al-Azhar, was founded by the Fatimids at the same time as the city of Cairo, it was, consistent with its founding fathers, a Shi'ite institution of learning and remained so for some two centuries, until Sunni Islam was reintroduced into Egypt by Saladin when he conquered the Fatimids in 1171. Today, al-Azhar (literally, the blossoming one) is on the theological plane a bastion of Sunni Islam. Both for this reason and because Egypt has since the end of the eighteenth century born the brunt of the intercultural confrontation between the technological-scientific West and the preindustrial Middle East, Cairo still remains by and large the center of religio-ideological reaction against European incursion into the region. In this sense, it is also the center for the production of ideologies. Although the most important shrines for Islam as a whole are to be found in Arabia, in Mecca and Medina, the intellectual center of Sunni Islam today is Egypt. When Napoleon arrived there, he attempted to win over al-Azhar intellectuals by prefacing every declaration with "in the name of Allah, the Almighty," but this did nothing to avert their revolts. The founder of modern Egypt, Muhammed Ali, attempted to build a modern state on the ruins of Napoleon's rule, which although short-lived was to have far-reaching effects.[3] Modern Egypt presents us with a regional, historically modern variety of royal authority in the Islamic mold, such as I attempted to describe, with the aid of Reinhard Bendix, in the introduction to Chapter 4. The *ulema* are the legitimators, and religion their legitimation. Fouad Ajami states in his analysis of this theme: "An inquiry into religion in Egypt is really, and has to be, an inquiry into the nature of authority in that country."[4] Later he adds: "To the extent that Egypt's Islam forms the cultural system of the country, it will always matter. Rulers and opponents alike will phrase their concerns in Islamic categories. While there are some things which this cultural system will not tolerate . . . beneath that 'cosmic' level, cultural limits—in Egypt (and elsewhere)—can be stretched to accommodate a wide range of things."[5] We shall see that the politicization of the Islamic cultural system in Egypt has been and continues to be evoked and exploited both for the purposes of legitimating the government—whether monarchical, as before 1952, or "revolutionary republican," as later under Nasser—as well as for the oppositional aspirations of underground movements.

Sunni Islam has no institutional clerical organization of the religious system at its disposal, except for *waqf* (the institution of pious endowments), nor does it have any marked religious underground tradition, which applies much more to Shi'ite Islam and other sectarian offshoots. In social terms the mosque (*jami'*, that is, a meeting place in many respects) is central. The leading lights of the *jami'* are the *ulema*, the Muslim scribes. The survival of this tradition can still be observed in modern Egypt,[6] where there were and still are private endowments, financed by the well-to-do faithful, and state-run mosques. During the period of the monarchy, the political system was content with winning over the rector of the al-Azhar University (sheikh al-Azhar), who as the supreme religious authority became the chief legitimator, and with keeping his sphere under their control. An indoctrination of Islam in the sense of an interpretation to suit the regime hardly took place, unless we interpret as such the attempts of the Egyptian king to proclaim himself caliph in the context of the caliphate movement (after the dissolution of the Ottoman Empire). Since the seizure of political power by the "Free Officers"[7] and the abolition of the monarchy, however, we can discern a state religious policy determined on the basis of doctrine related to the ideology of the political regime. This policy became particularly apparent during the 1960s, when the function of sheikh al-Azhar was held by the cleric Mahmud Shaltut. Shaltut[8] was as much one of the religio-ideologues of Nasserism as the al-Azhar sheikh 'Abdalhalim Mahmud, who later served as a legitimator under Sadat.[9]

Parallel to this utilization of religion to legitimate the state and to ensure a loyal attitude toward the rulers (who were equally kings and president-kings) among the Sunni *ulema,* we can also observe a divergent tradition of social forces within Egyptian Islam that was directed against established religio-institutions, in particular against the al-Azhar University, and that mobilized Islam as an ideology for an oppositional underground movement. The *al-ikhwan al-muslimin* (the Muslim Brotherhood),[10] an underground movement set up by Hassan al-Banna in 1928, is the most important religiopolitical movement within Sunni Islam in this century. In view of the central position of Egypt in Sunni Islam, it acquired a political significance that extended far beyond Egypt's boundaries and remains to this day an important cross-regional movement. Rulers and opponents alike, the latter working underground, made equal use of the mosque both as an object and as a forum for their activities. We shall therefore be examining this in more detail.

As a rule, every mosque has an imam. This title does not have a sacred meaning in Sunni, as it does in Shi'ite Islam.[11] A Sunni imam is purely and simply a reciter and Friday preacher and the person who takes care of the administration of the mosque. In Egypt the majority of imams are al-Azhar graduates in the employ of the *awqaf* ministry (the Ministry for Religious Affairs). As is documented in the empirical research of Morroe Berger, during the military regime of Nasser the Egyptian government did not, for example, attempt to pursue a policy of secularization, as is sometimes falsely asserted in the literature. It merely pursued a religious policy of indoctrination. Its dual goal was to bring the mosques (in this case the private ones as well) under government control and to institutionalize a reformist interpretation of Islam, that is, one suitable to the military regime.[12] In other words, it was a question of exploiting Islam as an instrument of legitimation for government purposes.

Despite concerted policy efforts at the government level, including a reform of the al-Azhar University during the Nasser regime (of which I shall have more to say later), even in those days private mosques far outnumbered others: In 1964 there were still 14,000 private as against only 3,000 state mosques. Under Sadat—under the aegis of an intensified politicization of Islam, both on the part of the existing regime (against leftist and secular opposition) and on the part of fundamentalists in the face of a social and economic crisis in Egypt[13]—

the figures shifted even more in favor of the private mosques: In 1970 there were 20,000 of them. By the time Sadat was assassinated (October 1981), the number of private (*ahli*) mosques had risen to 46,000, compared to 6,000 state ones. Hamied Ansari, who has provided these figures and who conducted fieldwork on Muslim underground organizations in Cairo, writes us that the mosque serves both as a place for the political activities and as a recruiting station of these militant fundamentalist underground organizations.[14] One of these underground organizations, *al-jihad* (holy war), was behind the assassination of Sadat. This *jihad* group and many other similar organizations, collectively known as the Muslim groups (*al-jama'at al-islamiyya*), are for the most part splinter groups of the original Muslim Brotherhood Movement, which no longer seems sufficiently radical to young militants.

These young fundamentalists, as Hamied Ansari goes on, are for the most part members of the lower middle class,[15] which lacks urban roots, having acquired its social form in the context of the rural exodus to Cairo. Members of this class do not understand their new environment and perceive all social ills as the result of Westernization and deviation from Islam. Return to Islam seems to them the only alternative for a better future with any prospect of success. They reject their social environment, which is the source of their cultural anomie as well as their socioeconomic problems (unemployment). They declare this environment to be *jahiliyya* (pre-Islamic ignorance) and search for a new meaning.

When Sadat took office after Nasser,[16] he faced a powerful opposition. He therefore tried to mobilize on his behalf the Muslim fundamentalists who had been interned in concentration camps under Nasser. Prior to the Free Officers' takeover of power on 23 July 1952, Sadat, himself a member of the group, had been its link with the Muslim Brotherhood, as he writes in his autobiography.[17] Because Nasser had in his day disappointed the expectations of the Muslim Brothers, they had made an unsuccessful attempt to assassinate him in 1954, after which he had had dozens of their leaders hanged. After their abortive coup attempt in 1965, thousands of Muslim Brothers found their way into prisons and internment camps and were not released until Sadat came to power. The repoliticization of Islam under Sadat therefore has this underlying internal political reason in addition to those cross-regional structural factors analyzed in Chapter 8, both of which considerably predate Khomeini's takeover of power in Iran. After Sadat's assassination by the very Muslim militants he had courted, many experts asked, despite the facts just mentioned, whether Iranian events might not be repeated in Egypt in a spillover effect.

We know that some kind of spillover effect of the Iranian revolution into the surrounding regions was not merely the fear of many political observers. It was also, indeed, the declared aim of the Iranian revolutionary leadership.[18] Yet, the contemporary variant of political Islam did not evolve in Iran but in Egypt. The defeat in the Six-Day War of 1967 brought about a considerable legitimacy crisis in all Arab countries, on the one hand weakening the then dominant secular ideologies (nationalism, socialism, liberalism) and on the other hand creating favorable conditions for a resurgence of Islam.[19] Nevertheless it was in Iran and not in Egypt that the Islamic revolution took place. The two countries differ from each other not only in that Iran, unlike Egypt, is not part of the community of Arab states but also in that in Egypt, unlike in Iran, orthodox, Sunni Islam and not Shi'ite, sectarian (to translate literally) Islam dominates. But these remarks are not sufficient in themselves to preclude entirely the possibility of a spillover effect.

Of greater significance is that the history of modernization in Egypt spans a substantially longer period than that in Iran, which did not in fact begin until the founding of the Pahlavi dynasty. The discovery of oil in 1908 and the wish of Reza Shah, who had come to power in 1925, to deal with oil concessions centrally so that he would also benefit from revenues, lay behind the construction of a modern, centralized state, which had not existed before.[20] In Egypt, on the other hand, the history of modernization had begun in 1805 with Muhammed Ali's reforms, which followed Napoleon's expedition. Even during Napoleon's sojourn, the religious authorities of the al-Azhar University had revolted against the reforms he introduced. The same occurred under Muhammed Ali himself, who considerably curbed the political power of the *ulema,* also enlisting it for his own legitimation.[21] As I have argued above, Egypt is thus the cradle both of the adaptation of Islam to the modern (the Islamic modernism of the second half of the nineteenth century) and of Islamic fundamentalism, or the defensive cultural rejection of the modern (the Muslim Brotherhood).[22] The political scene in an independent Egypt in 1922 was directed by liberal secular parties[23] until the 1952 coup d'état by the Free Officers. The Muslim Brotherhood remained active underground, but despite its growing political strength, it never had an opportunity to seize power through a revolution. It is important to recall again that Sunni Islam, which dominates in Egypt, has, unlike Shi'ite Islam, a legitimatory tradition, its religious institutions having always formed part of the political establishment. Shi'ite Islam, on the other hand, with its doctrine of the "vanished imam," disputes state legitimacy as long as the Twelfth Imam lives in hiding.[24] Shi'ite Islam, in other words, has always tended to take an oppositional attitude toward existing rule. The al-Azhar

University, the authoritative seat of Sunni Islam, has generally shown itself willing to legitimate the ruler of the time. The Muslim Brothers, on the other hand, although Sunni, are opposed not only to the existing political establishment but also to the religious establishment, which they regard as corrupt.

During the years of the military regime under Nasser, both these Islamic tendencies in Egypt were politically neutralized or defused. The al-Azhar University, which prior to its "reform" had been autonomous and had only embraced the Islamic sciences (Koranic exegesis; Hadith science, meaning work with the traditions of the Prophet; and *fiqh,* Islamic jurisprudence), was made directly subordinate to the office of president, acquiring through reform legislation in 1961[25] additional faculties of medicine, engineering, agricultural science, economics, and a number of secular arts disciplines. It thereby lost its exclusively religious character, although it is still the most authoritative seat of learning for all Sunni Muslims, as the sheikh al-Azhar (the rector) is the highest authority in *fatwas* (legal opinions). Nasser had already suppressed the Muslim Brotherhood movement in the 1950s using broad-based political persecution.[26] He nevertheless continued to evoke Islam in its functional capacity and did not, like Atatürk, declare himself to be a secularist. His Islamic legitimation, however, served as a bolster for his populist ideology, which was secular in real terms. Until the defeat of 1967, Nasser remained a celebrated hero throughout the whole Arab region. To avoid misunderstanding here, it is important to point out that although Islam was depoliticized under Nasser, it was by no means excluded from public life. Islam as a popular religion[27] remained dominant even under his rule, continuing to exert an influence on public life in Egypt. Today's return to Islam is a return to *political* Islam, not a return to Islam pure and simple. All that is new is its repoliticization.[28]

Political Islam has been in the ascendancy again since 1967. I have mentioned that Sadat mobilized Islam as a legitimating force by having the Muslim Brothers released from prison and granting them complete freedom of movement. Not until Camp David, and above all since the Iranian revolution, did this marriage of convenience break down, coming to a definitive end with Sadat's assassination by militant Muslim fundamentalists.

Neither Sadat nor the Muslim Brothers themselves had ever seen this alliance as anything other than a tactical matter: For Sadat, the Muslim Brothers were a pawn in the game against the Nasserist-Marxists, who were perceived in almost paranoid terms; for the Muslim Brothers the alliance formed part of their attempt to reestablish themselves after roughly a decade and a half of total political suppression. The well-known French journalist Eric Rouleau reports from a reliable source a meeting of Sadat and his security advisers toward the end of 1979, at which Sadat was advised to destroy the strengthening fundamentalist groups before it was too late. Sadat is alleged to have retorted angrily: "I am not the shah of Iran, and our Muslims are not Khomeinists." The adviser who had made the remark was dismissed the following day.[29]

In addition to the work by Ansari quoted earlier in this chapter, we also have valuable eyewitness accounts by Egyptian social scientists on this subject. Of particular importance is the work by Saad Eddin Ibrahim,[30] who teaches at the American University of Cairo and who led a research team that, with permission of the Sadat regime, interviewed Muslim fundamentalists imprisoned in Egyptian jails. These were not Muslim Brothers but members of more fanatical groups, such as *takfir wa hijra,* whose ideology, like that of the Muslim Brothers, may be described as simply the setting up of a system *(an-nizam al-Islami)* based on sacred law (the *shari'a*). There is no need for us to lose ourselves in the ramifications of this ideology; instead, we shall focus our attention on political and social issues. What lies behind this political religio-ideology?

Since the nineteenth century, Egypt has been undergoing a process of rapid and uneven social change.[31] One of the characteristics of such processes is *asymmetrical urbanization*, which mostly affects Cairo. At the end of World War II, Cairo had some two million inhabitants, whereas today there are already over fourteen million. Around 56.1 percent of Egyptians still live on the land, but the rate of rural-urban migration is very high.[32] This already high rate of migration to Cairo was exacerbated after the Six-Day War in 1967 by an additional approximately two million refugees who poured into the city from the canal zone. Any European unfamiliar with conditions in the Third World would be appalled on arrival in Cairo at the sheer masses of people on the streets and would scarcely be able to comprehend that people (some 200,000 of them) even live in the cemetery. Given the chronic housing shortage in Cairo, migrant peasants have no choice: To be able to have a roof over their heads in any of the poor quarters of Cairo seems a luxury to them by comparison.[33]

The sociological data provided by Saad Eddin Ibrahim and Nazih Ayubi[34] indicate that members of fundamentalist groups generally come from the lower middle classes and that they mostly either have an academic education or are in the process of obtaining one. The data also reveal that although these people live in Cairo, they are not of urban origin but of rural stock and have only recently migrated to Cairo. These people, uprooted from their rural milieu, feel foreign and lost in a noisy, densely populated, and extremely dirty city where everything is anonymous. They have left in the expectation of creating a better future for themselves by migrating to the city and acquiring an academic education, but they find themselves in a situation of cultural anomie.[35] Their occupational frustrations become politicized. Islam, in the understanding of a political ideology, provides the form of articulation for these sociopolitical concerns.

Superficially, Cairo looks like a Western city; its outward appearance is dominated by neon-lit advertisements and the trappings of modern technology (automobiles, buses, and so on). In the fundamentalist perception, the West, one of the three "enemies of Islam" (next to communism and Zionism), is to blame for this situation. Only a return to Islam and a total casting off of everything that has been adopted from the West can in their view bring salvation. In this sense, therefore, Islamic fundamentalism is a doctrine of salvation. The call for a return to pure and primeval Islam ought not to be misinterpreted as a variety of traditionalism: Islamic fundamentalists are not traditionalists, as their recourse to Islamic "fundamentals," "basics," and "essences" is highly selective and greatly affected by the conditions of modernity.

In order to distinguish these underground movements (the *jama'at al-islamiyya,* the Islamist groups) from the original movement of the Muslim Brotherhood, I call them "neofundamentalists." Here we shall leave aside the subtle, for some confusing, distinctions between fundamentalists and neofundamentalists and concentrate instead on whether they constitute a social movement or are merely peripheral groups, whether Islamists represent a mobilizing force or whether they are likely to remain a merely peripheral phenomenon after all. The existence of these Muslim militants is not only linked with the situation described above: Under Nasser the once exemplary Egyptian education system was expanded and at the same time levelled, with the result that many academics are now equipped with a maximum in terms of social expectations and a minimum in terms of professional qualifications. In a poor society such as Egypt, this potential could undermine the entire political system, as the latter is unable to meet the occupational expectations related to academic education. Nasser attempted to escape the results of this disproportionate expansion of his education policy by guaranteeing jobs—although with minimal salaries—for all graduates. Today they are the plague of Egyptian society. Are these members of the lower middle classes, having migrated to Cairo from rural areas, capable of mobilizing other social groups?

The research of Ibrahim, Ayubi, and Ansari, as well as my own experiences on campus in Cairo, have confirmed that these fundamentalists have very scant knowledge of the Islam whose alleged system they wish to establish. On the other hand, they do exert a powerful attraction on students, which Ibrahim explains as follows: "The militant Islamic groups with their emphasis on brotherhood, mutual sharing, and spiritual support become the functional equivalent of the extended family to the youngster who has left his behind. In other words, the Islamic group fulfills a de-alienating function for its members."[36]

Ibrahim discerns similarities between these Egyptian groups and the Iranian *mojahedin* and believes that a success by the Iranian revolution in overcoming the effects of rapid social change would strengthen the position of Egyptian militants. Its failure, however, would detract from the ideology of an "Islamic system" that is propagated by these groups. Today, some years after this prognosis, we can already speak of a collapse of the Iranian revolution and yet still see that these militant Muslim groups remain just as much of a danger in Egypt as they did before.

Although Sadat's assassin (Khalid al-Istanbuli) was an army officer, I would put forward the thesis that militant Muslim groups exert little influence in the army and that their sphere of influence, besides that of the mosque, continues to be predominantly the underground and the university campus. In order to become politically relevant to a change in the existing system, they would have to be able to mobilize at least three other social groups: First the army, then the rural population and rural-urban migrants, and finally they would also have to win over significant elements of the Egyptian political elite. Ansari asserts, however, that militants exert no political effect either on the rural or on the urban elites.[37]

One does not have to know much about Egypt to notice its all-pervading religiosity as soon as one sets foot in it. Is a fundamentalist movement capable of mobilization in such an atmosphere? To answer this question, we shall need to recall the distinction between Sunni and Shi'ite Islam. In Egypt, al-Azhar is the pillar of Islam. Authorities from al-Azhar, sometimes even the sheikh al-Azhar in person,[38] are heard on Egyptian television almost daily, speaking against these Muslim groups, branding them as misled or as falsifiers of "true Islam." The ruling National Democratic Party, inherited by Hosni Mubarak from Sadat, publishes the weekly newspaper *al-liwa' al-Islami* (The Islamic Banner), in which members of the religious establishment, which backs the government, likewise write about and define what "Islam" is. The Islamic interpretative monopoly is thus firmly on the side of the Mubarak government.

One circumstance specific to Egypt should also be mentioned here, namely, that it has a Christian population—the Egyptian Copts—constituting 10 to 12 percent of the total population.[39] These are only a minority in the denominational sense, for in ethnic terms they are a homogeneous part of the Egyptian population. The sectarian conflicts of this country are not comparable, for example, with minority conflicts in Malaysia or Sri Lanka, where problems of this kind relate to an ethnic component. In this respect, therefore, the formation of an "Islamic Republic" along Iranian lines would be inconceivable in Egypt, much as the politicization of Islam unleashes bitter interdenominational conflicts.[40]

In Iran the modern, Western-educated elite is a very thin stratum and is hardly rooted in the wider society at all. In Egypt, however, as is also the case in Turkey, the beginnings of this Western-educated elite go back to the start of the nineteenth century. The first important Egyptian group of scholarship-holders, led by none other than an imam (at-Tahtawi) who was later to translate Rousseau and Voltaire, went to Paris in the 1820s (see Chapter 7). In an empirical piece of research on the bourgeois elite in Cairo, Raymond Hinnebusch has found that the members of this elite continue to favor the "secular, liberal democratic" road and alliance with Western industrial states.[41] In other words, a second Iran is not to be expected in Egypt.

Under Mubarak the fundamentalists no longer have the room for maneuver they once enjoyed under Sadat. Although the regime does invoke Islamic values,[42] it does not overdo this in an effort to consolidate its own legitimacy. Egypt remains a Muslim society without Iranian excesses.[43] The question whether the Iranian model could repeat itself in Egypt or whether the oppositional religiopolitical underground organizations or the Azharite *ulema,* as legitimators of the establishment, could shape the future direction of Islam in Egypt, is of an entirely political nature. The central issue of this book will not permit me to conclude this case study of Egyptian Islam without asking whether the various bearers of Egyptian Islam have ever undertaken successful attempts to make it capable of a cultural accommodation of change, in particular in Egyptian society, which has been undergoing extremely rapid and disruptive social change.

Leaving aside for a moment the founder of the Muslim Brotherhood, al-Banna, and the spiritual father of the same movement, Sayyid Qutb,[44] as well as many Muslim militants, I can state that in general the ideology of political Islamists does not go far beyond a politicization of the Islamic cultural system and beyond their defensive cultural recourse to Islam. The Azharites remain the foremost Islamic scholars; compared to them, the Islamic militants have for the most part only a superficial and inadequate knowledge of Islam. In short, I can limit my inquiry to the Azharite *ulema,* without touching on the general question whether fundamentalists are innovative or not. I will focus instead on efforts toward the cultural accommodation of social change with respect to Islam as a cultural system.

The thesis has often been put forward that the *ulema* have always been and still are legitimators of existing rule, and that we can therefore speak of a religiopolitical alliance. It has also been suggested that until Nasser's reforms of 1961 rulers contented themselves with legitimation through the Azharites, scarcely attempting to indoctrinate this traditional seat of Islam. Since Napoleon's expedition and the ensuing establishment of Muhammed Ali's rule, Egypt has been undergoing processes of rapid social change that have substantially altered both the social structure and the culture of the country. We are compelled to ask whether the al-Azhar sheikhs have incorporated these new circumstances into their image of Islam, or, to couch it in scholarly terms, whether their Islam-shaped world view has ever undergone a substantive change. Most scholars working on this question have reached a negative conclusion. One of them, Daniel Crecelius, concludes from his analysis that the responses of the *ulema*

> to the challenges of modernization have been predictably, instinctively defensive, characterized by a strong desire for self-preservation. . . . Unwilling or unable to direct change, or even to make an accommodation to it, they have in the end been overwhelmed by change which inexorably penetrated first the government and the ruling elites, then their own institutions and other social groups.[45]

According to Islamic dogma, anything new that is added to the primary sources (the Koran and Hadith) is pejoratively called *bid'a* (literally, "innovation," but with the connotation of "heresy"). The *ulema* at al-Azhar have always reacted in this way. If they ever did assent to a change, however, it was always in the sense of legitimating an action of the respective ruler without thereby relinquishing their own attitude of rejection. In this context, Crecelius terms as "obscurantism" the simultaneous legitimation and rejection, in the inner al-Azhar circles, of an innovative government measure. Even the radical reform of al-Azhar initiated by Nasser proved unable to bring about an affiliation between the crudely medieval culture of al-Azhar and the modern. The al-Azhar authorities thus, for instance, at the same time both assented to and undermined state birth control aimed at solving Egypt's most serious problem—overpopulation. Crecelius judges capably and to the point when he writes that the *ulema* has successfully managed to delay the process of modernization, but at a terrible price for Islam and the *ulema*.[46] We can see from this that there has been no contribution by the al-Azhar University to the cultural accommodation of change since the onset of the historical phase of rapid social change. Legitimation hand-in-hand with obscurantism characterizes the dealings of the *ulema,* who, together with the Western Orientalists they oppose, take Islamic culture to mean the philology of the Arabic language and the exegesis of traditional sources perceived as sacrosanct. There has been no attempt to adapt the prevailing Islamic world view to the changed conditions of our scientific-technological age, nor is such a needed development in sight for the immediate future. The recent, authoritative two-volume work of al-Azhar, published under the auspices of the new al-Azhar sheikh, no longer incriminates innovations as *bid'a* but rather warns of a sweeping use of this Islamic formula against change. This open-mindedness does not, however, go so far as to culturally promote and accommodate social change.[47]

10

The Iranian Shi'ite Variant of Religiopolitical Revivalism: The Mullah Revolution in Iran

The choice of Egypt and Iran as case studies was made in order to contrast two different variants of Islam and two differing sociohistorical backgrounds to the politicization of Islam. This will enable us to understand why no religioculturally legitimated revolution was able to take place in Egypt, the intellectual and theological bastion of Sunni Islam, whereas it was possible in Iran, where the majority of Shi'ite Muslims live.[1] Valid as the already indicated religiopolitical differences between Sunna and Shi'a (the legitimacy and illegitimacy respectively of political rule) may be, they are not in themselves sufficient to explain the specific difference between Egypt and Iran. In both countries, a repoliticization of the sacred is evident. Referral to the Islamic sources can hardly help to elucidate this phenomenon, although political and social structural analysis can provide us with substantial information about the general conditions and manifestations of the political revitalization of Islam.[2] Thus, for example, the homogeneity of the Egyptian population and the long-standing Egyptian tradition of central state authority, in Elias's sense, compared to the absence of these two factors in Iran, are not to be understood in terms of the difference between Sunna and Shi'a, but simply in terms of social history. Here the limitations of religioscriptural exegesis become apparent. The differing religious traditions in the two countries, however, both have social historical and theological-political dimensions that should be taken into account.

The Iranian Ulema as a Shi'ite Clergy

The schism that occurred after the founding of the Islamic religion has already been briefly described in Chapter 2. There it was shown that in 661 the Umayyads, after the murder of the fourth righteous caliph, Ali, whom the Shi'ites regard as their first imam, established a tradition of Sunni Islam as a form of Islamic rule in a kingdom with Damascus as its capital (661–750). The Shi'ites went underground and became enemies of the ruling Sunni Muslims on the grounds that they were "usurpers." Since that time, a number of different Shi'ite sects have evolved, but we shall leave these outside our consideration, since we wish here to concentrate on Twelver Shi'a, that is, the Shi'ite sect that prevails in Iran. The Islamic schism was not at first ethnically determined; in the course of historical development, however, it did acquire an ethnic aspect, as many Persians, treated as second-class Muslims (*mawali*) by the Umayyads (who gave strict preference to blood descent from Arabs) went over to the Shi'ite sect.[3] Prior to the Islamization of Iran, the Zoroastrian Sassanids had ruled, who were defeated by the Arab conquerors. There is a legend in Twelver Shi'a Islam that Hussain, the younger son of Ali, whose party (Shi'at Ali) the Shi'ites (partisans) joined, married Shahrbanu, the daughter of the last Sassanid emperor, Yazdigird III. Hussain is third in the line of the twelve holy imams in Twelver Islam. This legend gives Shi'ite Islam a Persian nationalist stamp.

The Twelfth Imam is said to have been living "in hiding" since the ninth century (873 or 874); within the minor occultation, he is said to have been represented up to 940 by the *wakils* (representatives), but since that time the Hidden Imam can only be represented by the Shi'ite clergy (the major occultation), which consists of the *mujtahids*. In the absence of the Twelfth Imam, all rule is illegitimate according to Shi'ite doctrine. During the Safavid dynasty (1501–1722), Twelver Islam was invoked for the first time in history to legitimate rule. We know from research by the historian Nikki Keddie,[4] however, that the *ulema* that supported the legitimacy of Safavid rule, although Shi'ite, must have been "imported" and did not originate from the indigenous official Shi'ite clergy. This does not mean that the millenarian tradition of Shi'ite Iranian Islam, hostile to existing rule, was interrupted during the Safavid era. The Khomeini revolution is the first time in the history of Iran that a religiously legitimated regime, a "mullahcracy," has come about with the aid, and indeed under the leadership, of the Shi'ite clergy. For this purpose, Khomeini developed his own interpretation of the Shi'ite doctrine of *vilayat-e faqih* (mandate of the jurist), so as to be able to propound the doctrine of *hokumat-e islami* (Islamic government). I shall have more to say about this later.

Just as al-Azhar in the Sunni tradition of the *madrasa* (See Chapter 7) represents the intellectual stronghold of Sunni Islam, so Qum in the Iranian city of the same name represents—as a *madrasa*—a comparable authoritative seat of learning in Shi'ite Islam in the counterpart tradition. Khomeini himself came from Qum. In his investigation of this *madrasa,* Michael Fischer writes that Qum "is the religious heart of Shi'ite Iran; what happens in Qum has national importance."[5] The term "national" refers here to Shi'ite Islam as the religion of the Iranian people. Compared to the Sunni *ulema,* who historically hardly ever served as anything other than legitimators of existing rulers, the Shi'ite clergy has proved more resistant to existing rule in the course of history and has hardly ever allowed itself to be politically exploited, although this statement requires modification in isolated instances. What are the causes of this difference? Reference to doctrinal and theological differences is not sufficient to explain this reality.

The validity of the statement, often repeated throughout this study, that there is no such thing as abstract Islam, as this religious system has always had historical forms that manifested sociopolitical constellations and forms of expression representing concerns prevalent at the time, holds true also for Shi'ite Islam, with its specifically underground tradition. As a result of its different theology and the history that went with it, Shi'ite Islam produced a clergy that has proved more autonomous and resistant to the existing rule of the day than the Sunni *ulema* position has been. Keddie[6] identifies as the reasons for this both the distance between theology and the regime (the latter's illegitimacy during the occultation of the Twelfth Imam) and the underground traditions associated with it. It may be added that the Shi'ite clergy is economically much more powerful than the Sunni *ulema,* who, although they have their *awqaf,* could historically always be controlled both politically and economically by the political rulers of the time. The Shi'ite clergy were able to finance not only Khomeini's return to Iran but also, prior to that, his extensive activities in France.[7] This leads us to the relationship between the Shi'ite *ulema* and the tradespeople, the *bazaaris.* Recent history in Iran documents repeated fruitful alliances between the Shi'ite clergy and the *bazaaris* resulting in political success. Khomeini's Islamic revolution represents the latest link in this chain of events.

Earlier *bazaari-ulema* alliances were the Tobacco Uprising[8] of 1891-1892 and the Constitutional Revolution of 1905–1911. Up to a point, the National Front under Mohammed Mosaddeq,[9] who was able to win the elections of 1950 and exile the shah during the oil crisis of that time until the latter's CIA-backed return in 1953, also involved cooperation with the clergy. But not until the *bazaari-ulema* alliance under the leadership of Khomeini, initially promoted by these two groups and eventually backed by a broad mass base, did the bond lead to a total seizure of power. We know that this revolution rapidly lost its mass support. The *pasdaran* (revolutionary guard) replaced the

SAVAK secret service, and the bourgeoisie around Basargan was soon kicked out. The Iranian mullah regime only managed to stabilize itself on the basis of the undoubtedly very welcome Iran-Iraq war from 1980 to 1988, that is, by the fabrication of another enemy image. I do not want to go into this issue here; of more interest in this context is how the Shi'ite doctrine of the illegitimacy of rule during the absence of the Twelfth Imam is now being applied to the legitimation of a regime—by the very clergy, in this case the Shi'ite *mujtahids*,[10] who allegedly represent (although not politically) the Vanished Imam.

Roger Savory energetically stresses that in Twelver Shi'ite theological doctrine there is not a shred of support to be found for a reconciliation between the doctrine of the illegitimacy of rule, whatever form it may take, and the function of the Shi'ite *mujtahids*, that is, the clergy in a state.[11] That in Iran today a regime—without the "masses" and even without the *bazaaris*—has been inaugurated by the clergy would seem to be a paradox, even if Savory is also aware that the Shi'ite *mujtahids* would never willingly relinquish the power they have seized. The late Oxford scholar Hamid Enayat, however, put forward the thesis at a London Symposium of the Royal Institute for International Affairs that just such a reconciliation—at least in literary terms—is so unique in Khomeini's writings. In Khomeini's reinterpretation of the Shi'ite doctrine of *vilayat-e faqih,* (the representation of the Hidden Imam by jurists), the *faqih* (jurist, *fiqh* being Islamic jurisprudence: see Chapter 5) appears as the "supreme overseer, judge, and guardian"[12] of the entire state administration, as all "legislative, judicial, and educational institutions of the Islamic republic are expected to take their shape under its direct influence."[13]

We are thus witnessing today the emergence of an entirely new tradition in Shi'ite Islam, in which a change in the function of the clergy is taking place—a change from opposition to political rule to mullahcracy. It would be incorrect to assume that the differences between Sunni and Shi'ite Islam have been eliminated by this change, for what we see now in Iran is a dictatorship of the clergy, which has never existed in Sunni Islam. Although there is historical evidence of Sunni rulers exercising what is interpreted by Bendix as an "Islamic conception of royal authority,"[14] this rule was always in the hands of the laity. The Sunni *ulema* merely provided religious legitimation for the caliphs: They never held this office themselves; they were always subordinate to the holders of power. In Iran it was only under the leadership of Khomeini[15] and other *ayatollahs* that the Shi'ite clergy, who had held all regimes of the previous thirteen centuries to be illegitimate, themselves came into power. According to a reinterpretation of the doctrine of *vilayat-e faqih,* this occurred, moreover, in the name of the Twelfth

Imam himself, whose occultation, according to the original doctrine, makes all regimes illegitimate.

Let us now proceed to the question of how this clergy managed to topple the shah, regarded as a powerful oriental despot, and what the underlying factors were. Central to our analysis is the question of whether under the shah the requirements of social and cultural change were mutually reconciled and the problems associated with them overcome.

The Modernization Experiment of the Shah: Rapid Social Change Under the Conditions of Oriental Despotism

Research may lead us to reject the modernization experiment of the shah without making us join the chorus of those demonizing the shah and levelling monotonous complaints against his regime. I can agree with Robert Graham, who, after giving an account of the shah's experiment, reaches the conclusion "that the Iranian system of government was incapable of launching a dynamic process of development" but who would have us consider that "to cast the Shah as the villain is in one sense misleading. There is nothing to suggest that another leader or group of leaders in Iran would have done better or behaved much differently under the circumstances. . . . The Shah's critics decry his authoritarianism, but there is scarcely a liberal tradition in Iranian history."[16] The Iranian modernization experiment needs to be understood in structural terms: Autocratic rule by a shah is itself an element of these given structural conditions. It is difficult to see what makes the undoubtedly reprehensible oriental despotism of the shah any worse than other dictatorships in the region, such as, for example, that of the Iraqi president, Saddam Husain, or that of the Libyan autocrat Qadhafi, or indeed that of Khomeini himself and his mullahs.

By the time the Pahlavi dynasty was founded in 1925 by Reza Khan, an officer of the Iranian Cossack brigade, Iran had already been a centralized state under the former Qajar dynasty (1794–1925), but the Qajar rulers did not wield the required state central authority to exert sovereignty over the entire territory. When, after successful prospecting, oil production began for the first time in the whole region in 1908, the European oil companies were able to circumvent the central government and negotiate on oil deposits directly with regional political leaders. One of the central aims of the founder of the Pahlavi dynasty, whose enthusiasm for Kemal Atatürk's experiment has been documented,[17] was the strengthening of central authority and the consolidation of its control over the whole of Iran. Oil revenues, which the central government was not able to obtain without considerable struggles to assert itself, were put to full use in pursuit of this aim.[18] We should bear in mind that at that time the Iranian population was for the most part still nomadic and that there were not yet even the beginnings of urbanization, the side effects of which we are well aware. Urbanization must be seen as a result of the effects on the land of oil production; in this respect, Iran is not at all comparable to Egypt.

The modernization of Iran did not begin with the deposed shah; it had already been instigated by his father. But because this section covers the immediate history of the Iranian revolution, we are interested primarily in developments following the first oil crisis of 1973/74, in the course of which oil revenues in Iran increased fourfold within a few short months as a result of the associated price rises.[19] The Iranian Five-Year Plan of 1973–1978 should be mentioned here, as it was financed—and indeed inspired—mainly by increased revenues. The phase of development that occurred between the first and second oil crises, that is, between 1973 and 1979, may be described simultaneously as the zenith of the Pahlavi regime and the historical period leading up to the Iranian revolution.

In sociological terms, this phase was one of rapid social change and in terms of the political science perspective a phase of political decay. In the Iranian context these categories will be explained in more detail. Suffice it here to point out that during this phase the rate of increase in industrial production and mining rocketed to 18 percent, that there was an overheated economic boom accompanied by rising inflation at the expense of domestic investments, and that "by early 1975 the Iranian economy was almost out of control."[20]

The terms *social change* and *political development* will be used as key categories here with reference to Huntington's[21] theory of institutionalization. Social change implies an alteration in socioeconomic structures, relating to corresponding political and social forms of organization. Huntington's central thesis is that the setting up of new institutions is a prerequisite for coping with the dissolution of traditional social structures in the context of social change. Through the absorption of the social forces unleashed by the transformation processes that have occurred, these institutions channel the newly arisen potential for conflict, introducing new democratic forms of mediation. Where social change takes place rapidly without the prerequisite building of institutions the outcome is not modernity but political decay. This frame of reference would seem to offer the necessary conceptual assistance for examining the phase of Iranian development from 1973 to 1979.

The shah's modernization experiment focused both on agriculture and on industry and was characterized by two features: a concentration on the political strengthening of the center (Tehran) and the predominance of power-political considerations over specialized plans in the modernization program. Fred Halliday has made a comprehensive study of Iranian industrial policy, showing that although increased oil revenues made the means available to finance such a policy, there was a lack of necessary infrastructure, particularly as regards an organizational and institutional framework, of appropriate personnel with specialist training.[22] This lack was one of the factors behind the failure of this policy, although there were of course others. In the agricultural sphere, the shah's modernization plans produced largely negative results, chief among which were the uprooting of peasants, an escalation in rural-urban migration, and even a drop in productivity. Prior to the implementation of this project, Iran had been self-sufficient in terms of foodstuffs, even with half its territory incultivable. Subsequent to the project, the population could not be fed without importing food or without state subsidization of foodstuffs.[23] As a result of the modernization measures introduced, aimed as they were at strengthening the center, the rural-urban gulf widened, a phenomenon known in development theory as structural heterogeneity.

With reference to Karl Wittfogel, I have called the political system under whose aegis this experiment was carried out "oriental despotism," that is, a specifically oriental form of regime that may be described as autocracy. The expert advice necessary for reform was absent, since the objective was a political one. Graham concludes: "The Shah and Hoveida [his grand vizier] showed a certain contempt for the economists who could not see beyond problems to a broader vision of an industrialized Iran."[24] The shah even reacted disdainfully to the warnings of a group of experts sent by the International Monetary Fund (IMF), who saw a connection between the overheated boom and the increased inflation rate; these technocrats, with their narrow scientific vision, could hardly be expected to grasp the sweeping political visions of the shah.

Applying the concepts we have just borrowed from Huntington, we can complete the empirical picture using the Iranian example: Through modernization, structures were dissolved and new social and political potential unleashed (social mobility in a traditional society) without the building of the prerequisite political institutions. The political system under the shah was autocratic, providing only a central ruling authority, identical with the shah himself. "The monarchy is the country's only institution, around which all power revolves without any formal checks and balances,"[25] writes Graham, who is not familiar with Huntington's work but who has nevertheless grasped the problem in Iran through his own observations. It would be instructive to complement Graham's descriptive account with Wittfogel's conceptualization. Graham regrets the personification of power under the shah, showing that in the absence of institutionalization the sole pillars for the personified monarchy were the security services: "Over twenty years the security services have become a central pillar of the Shah's system of government. . . . They are the Shah's eyes and ears and, when necessary, his iron fist, neutralizing all those disloyal to the regime."[26]

Wittfogel does not base his argument on a particular example: He sets out to define in the abstract the form of rule of oriental despotism, in which there are neither institutions, judicial structures, nor a division of power. The ruler can reach subjects only by means of naked power, unlike democratically legitimated politicians, who mediate with their citizens through institutions. The oriental despot has the "means to destroy his victims. . . . He has unlimited power over the army, police, and information services. He has prison warders, torturers, executioners, and all the necessary tools with which to apprehend, torment, and kill suspects."[27] This abstract definition provides an optimal depiction not only of the shah's security services, SAVAK and the Imperial Inspectorate, but also of Khomeini's *pasdaran*.

An examination of this autocratic system of course comprises only one part of the attempt to explain the failure of the Iranian modernization experiment. But the contradiction between the effects of rapid social change and the existing political structures of personified power, in the absence of appropriate institutionalization, is central to this attempted explanation. At this point it is apt to cite, by way of conclusion, Graham's interpretation, which encompasses the full complexity of the phenomenon: "Iran's rapid economic development tended to be grafted on to old structures rather than replace them. A modern sector grew up side by side with the traditional rural economy but the two existed in relative isolation. The size of the country, disparateness and widely dispersed nature of the population, coupled with a cumbrous corrupt bureaucracy and poor communications reinforced this gap."[28] Iran's crash development resulted in a simultaneity of the unsimultaneous, that is, in a parallel existence of both old and new structures—without, however, their being related to one another. Thus, this development contributed to social and cultural disruptions, but not to modernity. Such a comprehensive interpretation of this complex reality seems to me far more reasonable than monocausal ones of a purely economic or sociocultural nature.

Islam as an Ideology of Mobilization Against the Shah System and the Iranian Variant of the Politicization of the Sacred

In the eyes of the Iranian population, the shah's modernization program was Western, although we have seen that the shah's regime was of an indigenous type, representing, that is, only one variant in the long history of oriental despotism, albeit a modernized one. Opposition to the shah was consequently bound to arise by means of a recourse to indigenous elements. Unlike other oriental despots, for example the rulers of Morocco and Saudi Arabia, whose rule we shall be examining in Chapter 11, the shah had not legitimated his regime in Islamic terms, so that Islam, in masterly fashion, formed a united front as an oppositional ideology to mobilize against the shah. As we have seen, Shi'ite Islam had been an oppositional movement against Muslim orthodoxy since its very inception. I have also quoted from recent Iranian history those cases in which a politicization of Islam as a mobilization ideology against existing rule had already occurred: the Tobacco Uprising and the Constitutional Revolution. On both occasions the *bazaaris* allied themselves with the *ulema* in order to implement political and economic change. The Iranian revolution of 1979 documents the third *bazaari-ulema* alliance against existing rule in recent Iranian history; this time it was directed against the Pahlavi dynasty and succeeded in toppling it.[29] It has been shown in the preceding remarks that no institution-building took place parallel to the modernization policy of the shah. The only remaining spheres of political activity, therefore, were religious institutions, that is, the mosque, and the underground. V. Petrossian points out: "The Shah's destruction of all viable alternative political leadership made it inevitable that both the revolutionary protest and post-revolutionary Iran should be led by the mosque, and the mosque, in turn, by its most activist member, Khomeini."[30] Underground, political agitation stemmed largely from leftist and radical leftist movements, mainly the communist Tudeh party, although it would never have found as much response among the Muslim population as the *ulema* were able to find. The absence of political institutional structures enabled the Iranian revolution to gain control of religious forces, which did have such structures at their disposal. The Twelver Shi'ite doctrine of *vilayat-e faqih,* in its new interpretation, was invoked to transfer political power entirely to the clergy, this principle then being consolidated in the "Constitution of the Islamic Republic of Iran."[31]

Just how Islamic is the Iranian revolution? As I have already shown in detail, in Iran we have to assess the historical experiment of an oriental despot (an autocrat with neither constitutional nor institutional controls) who wanted to adapt backward Iranian society to the European standard from above and by decree, without inquiring into the needs of the population or even considering the possibility of including the Iranians in his plans. The oil boom after the oil crisis of 1973 encouraged the shah of Iran to implement his plans even more forcibly than before, as they could now be financed comfortably with oil revenues. The result of this policy of forcible modernization from above and by decree, without the participation of those concerned or regard for the suitability or adaptational capacity of the new measures (such as the introduction of agribusiness into Iranian agriculture), led not to the modernization of the country but to uncontrolled urbanization, massive rural-urban migration, and, not least, to a threat to and even elimination of the material existence of Iranian small traders, the *bazaaris,* and of small farmers and others. These social strata thus became the victims of the new policy. As Udo Steinbach observes: "In Shi'ite Iran, Islam was . . . the only hope of the petite bourgeoisie and all those who could not hope to achieve a social position in which they would escape the pressure of exploitation and their total absence of rights."[32] Islam was thus both the *form* of resistance and its ideology; the *content,* however, is to be sought in the social, economic, and political problems of Iranian society.

All experts on Iran agree that Khomeini's seizure of power was initially backed by a broad consensus among the population. In the course of clerical rule so far, however, during which the country has gone to ruin, experts observe that this consensus has been lost. The Iran-Iraq war, which on the one hand signified for Iran the exacerbation of its economic poverty, on the other served to stabilize the Islamic republic of Iran by detracting attention from domestic problems. The war united all mutually hostile Iranian factions against a single external enemy—Iraq.[32a] From the analysis so far, we may conclude that the Iranian revolution had an Islamic religious impulse but does not constitute a specifically Islamic phenomenon; rather, it is a political and social manifestation articulated in Islamic terms.

In its day, the shah's modernization model had the wholehearted support of U.S. social scientists, despite its being entirely devoid of any social or economic planning and ignoring the cultural specificities of Iran. The shah overlooked the fact that without Islam any modernization policy would be bound to meet the resistance of the population, and that a modernization program called both for accurate social and economic policy research on a sound expert basis and for the inclusion of corresponding sociocultural implications (Islamic culture). All this was missing under the shah, with the result that uncontrolled social change took place without the prerequisite parallel cultural accommodation of its effects.

Social change without cultural accommodation leads to anomie, and modernization without the participation of the population and the building of an institutional structure to absorb the social forces unleashed by modernization can only lead to political decay. The shah's experiment ought to be ample enough proof that modernization that consists simply of imitating the Western developmental model and ignores the social and cultural conditions of those it concerns can only come to the kind of end it did.

Both modern innovative Muslims[33] as well as open-minded experts on Islam[34] are vehemently propounding today the necessity for studying Islam as a sociocultural system, in order to find ways of introducing innovations and modernization attempts capable of being integrated into the Islamic culture. Changes in Islam itself must also be undertaken in this process, so as to open it to innovation in terms of developing patterns for the cultural accommodation of change. Muslim fundamentalism, however, is reactive and fails to provide the needed framework for such modernizing interpretations of Islam.[35]

Shi'ite Reform and the
Cultural Accommodation of Change

The balance of the Iranian revolution is clear; it would be superfluous to carry out major research to find out the results so far of this revolution, with its sacral-political program. The slum-dwellers of Tehran, who pinned such hopes on Khomeini's promises, are not even supplied with water at the end of the fast days in the month of Ramadan. Many among the underprivileged in Iran look back with nostalgia on the hardly glorious days of the oriental shah-despot—an indication of just how catastrophic the present situation must be.

During the course of this investigation, we have seen that Khomeini's greatest intellectual achievement was to reformulate the doctrine of *vilayat-e faqih* in such a way that the clergy, who up to now were obliged to reject as illegitimate all regimes during the "major occultation" of the Twelfth Imam, are now themselves permitted to exercise power. Some of Khomeini's critics will insist that there are other figures in Shi'ite Islam apart from Khomeini, pointing above all to Ali Shariati, with the intention of proving that among the Shi'ites there have been the beginnings of a "cultural revolution," that is, to use the terminology of this study, the beginnings of a cultural accommodation of social change. The following remarks will be addressed to this matter, with the idea of surmounting underdevelopment as the conceptual background. It will be apparent from my comments so far that surmounting underdevelopment embraces not only sociostructural development but also cultural change, which may not, however, consist of imitation and also may not be coupled with loss of authenticity—as occurred, for example, under the shah, whose modernization program was unable to produce either changes in the North-South gap to the advantage of Iran or innovations of any kind. Has the Iranian revolution, with its politicization of the sacred, any positive contribution to show in this respect? The Iranian revolution was sustained by a *bazaari-ulema* alliance, as it was first based on a coalition between these two groups. In the Tobacco Uprising, similar coalitions had arisen of "nationalists, reformers, and religious leaders, whose opposition to the government masked very different aims—a legacy which still shows strong signs of life as late as the present,"[36] as Keddie writes in her book on the Tobacco Uprising, published in 1966. We can extend her "present" to include our own present. Such a coalition, however, endured only from 1979 to 1981. Today, the Shi'ite clergy rules autocratically, monopolizing power at all levels, thus justifying the use of the term "mullahcracy." The post-Khomeini era marks no change in this regard. There have been no attempts at cultural innovation issuing from Khomeini's party; in the years of the alliance they issued from other factions, for example, from the group around Bani Sadr,[37] who managed briefly to rise to the post of president, and from adherents to the ideas of the reformer Ali Shariati.[38] In the case of Khomeini, and those *ayatollahs* on his side, cultural innovation in Islam was never even an intention. Set against this, during Bani Sadr's presidency, a kind of Iranian "cultural revolution" (in Farsi, *engelab-e farhangi*) was instigated. Apart from this there were supporters of the European-educated, Islamic Iranian reformer Ali Shariati (1933–1977), who attempted in his writings to develop what he called a "reformed and renewed Islam."[39] Neither of these tendencies has influence any more today, and yet it is interesting to evaluate them in order to make a historical assessment.

The Farsi term *engelab-e farhangi* (cultural revolution) was coined by the former Iranian president Bani Sadr and the commander of the *mojahedin-e khalq* (holy people's fighters), Masud Rajawi, who have since fallen out. If we call to mind the analysis of this cultural revolution, made by the competent Persian expert on Iran Rouholla Ramazani,[40] from which it emerges that this revolution resulted from the power struggle between Bani Sadr and Rajawi on one side and certain leading *ayatollahs* on the other, then the religiopolitical accents of this revolution become easier to understand. Three principles were central to this cultural revolution: first, "the unitized community," which, second, was to be brought about by "pious men," in order third, to eradicate the "idolatrous order." The first principle soon revealed its totalitarian content, since the *umma* community being aimed for will not tolerate within itself people who think differently. The principle of "pious men" rapidly backfired on its originators, both Bani Sadr and the members of the *mojahedin-e khalq* being mercilessly persecuted by the "pious men" of the clerical-fascist troops of the *pasdaran* as alleged lackeys of the "idolatrous order." The latter order originally referred to that of the shah's regime with its Americanisms instigated from above. Exclusive and intolerant political slogans can easily shift their accent and even recoil on their originators.

The worthwhile writings of Ali Shariati, which also had their supporters in the Iranian revolution, deserve to be taken more seriously than the "cultural revolution" of Bani Sadr and Rajawi. The thoughtful reader of Shariati's main writings,[41] some of which have now become available in English, will be impressed by the enlightened quality of this authentically Islamic thinker and will likewise admire his courage in criticizing the traditional *ulema* that upholds Iranian Shi'ite Islam. But it is difficult to agree with Shariati in his thesis that Islam alone, indeed more precisely "the true Shi'a Islam," could be a guide for all humanity. Shariati's appeal for a "new concept of Islam" does nevertheless point the way for Muslims in their efforts to accommodate social change. Ideas do not make history, but they can affect the course it takes. In this regard we could ask why Shariati's ideas did not exert an influence on the Iranian revolution, especially since he has many supporters among the Persian intelligentsia. The Iranian historian Mangol Bayat, after a critical examination of Shariati's writings and despite admiring them, comes to the sober realization that Shariati "had no program to offer, only fiery revolutionary rhetoric and an inconsistent sociological analysis of religion."[42] This is not to denigrate Shariati, for a single Muslim can hardly be expected to accomplish what whole generations of Muslims have not managed to achieve in centuries. Bayat's assessment can help us to understand in part, however, why Shariati's ideas were so ineffectual and powerless in the face of the political programs of the *ayatollah*.

The same historian, Bayat, informs us that there is at present in Iran "no reform-minded theologian willing to undertake seriously the task of doctrinal reforms."[43] We cannot evade the conclusion, therefore, that the Iranian revolution has made *no* contribution to the cultural accommodation of change in Islam. This "revolution" did manage to topple one powerful form of oriental despotism, but only so as to replace it with an even more repressive clerical dictatorship, what I have called a mullahcracy, which may be described as a Shi'ite variety of this very oriental despotism.

11

Islam as Legitimation for "Royal Authority": On the Relationship Between State, Religion, and Politics in the Islam-legitimated Monarchies of Morocco and Saudi Arabia[1]

In the introduction to Part 4, I adopted an interpretation of the caliphate as the "Islamic conception of royal authority"[2] from the fascinating sociohistorical comparative research of Reinhard Bendix. In the general religiosociological definition of the contemporary political revitalization of Islam (Chapter 8), we discovered that Muslim fundamentalists are not traditionalists; they do not at all want to restore the caliphate but rather to convert Islam into a populist form, onto which they project their concerns. They thus employ Islam as a formula for the legitimation of opposition to existing regimes. In the case study on Egypt (Chapter 9), we found empirical material to support not only this thesis but also the assertion that the politicization of Islam arose out of a process of rapid and disruptive social change that had not been culturally accommodated. If we resort to the interpretation in which Islam, in historicopolitical terms, was initially a charismatic prophecy and later became the legitimation for royal authority, we are bound to be surprised that an Islamic republic came into existence in Iran using just this religious system as its legitimation. It is important to repeat here, however, that the tradition of the "Islamic conception of royal authority" is a Sunni one and that in Shi'ite Islam, except during the Safavid dynasty in Iran (1501–1722), there is no tradition of royal authority. It has also been shown with reference to the research by Nikki Keddie that the exploitation of Twelver Shi'ism by the Safavids was not authentically Shi'ite, having occurred by means of imported theologians. Furthermore, the Shi'ite doctrine of *vilayat-e faqih* does not permit the legitimation of any regime. Khomeini's reinterpretation of this theological doctrine into the "Islamic Republic" is his own invention. Michael Fischer indeed goes so far as to say that the political ideas of Khomeini and the other leaders of the Islamic Republican party (IRP) and the evocative language they use in articulating these ideas are "contemporary constructions rather than simply reaffirmations of ancient ideas and words."[3] As I commented in Chapter 10, we are evidently witnessing here the emergence of an entirely new ruling tradition in Shi'ite Islam.

Since the abolition of the last Islamic sultanate-caliphate in 1924 following the Kemalist revolution in Turkey and the definitive disintegration of the Ottoman Empire[4] brought about by World War I, not a single Muslim ruler has claimed to be caliph, even though some Arab rulers aimed at obtaining this title. The Sunni Muslim tradition of royal authority nonetheless lives on in two Islamic monarchies that legitimate themselves in the traditional Islamic way without Western adaptations—such as, for example, the transformation of *vilayat-e faqih* into an "Islamic republic" in Iran. These traditional monarchies are Morocco and Saudi Arabia.

In this chapter, the central focus of which will be the relationship between Islam and the state, both historically and conceptually, these two Islam-legitimated monarchies will be examined. A general historical overview and an attempt to develop a conceptual approach to the subject will precede the empirical analysis, which will be followed by a discussion of the future prospects of Islam as political legitimation in the modernization process. If we retain the hypothesis that modernization signifies a functional differentiation of the social system, in the course of which the religious system is reduced to a part-system of the society,[5] then we need to ask whether the Islam-legitimated political order of the monarchies we are about to analyze will be able to persist in a complex social system.

Islam and State in Historical Perspective[6]

The toppling of a secular-legitimated monarchy in Iran and the declaration of an "Islamic republic" by the Muslim clergy there raises the question of the relationship between Islam and the state. The researcher will look in vain for the term "Islamic republic" in either Sunni or Shi'ite Muslim sources, for in both content and wording the term is—as has already been shown—a new invention documenting European influences on Islam. Republic is a European, not an Islamic concept. Sunni (orthodox) Islam knows only the caliphate, and Shi'ite (sectarian) Islam knows only the imamate. The theocratic city-state that was initially founded by the Prophet of Islam in Medina and developed in the course of history into an empire was based on the principle of *shura* (consultation). Muhammed the political leader, who, as Rodinson suggests, "combined in one person the qualities of Jesus and Charles the Great," allowed himself to be advised in his decisions by a tiny elite of his followers (*as-sahaba*). The *shura* principle is put forward by Muslim scholars as proof of an Islamic primeval democracy, notwithstanding the substantial differences between *shura* and parliamentarianism. After the death of Muhammed, two further principles of Islamic rule came into existence: *ikhtiyar* and *bay'a*. *Ikhtiyar* means selection; a successor to Muhammed had to be selected from among his followers (*as-sahaba*). The successor (caliph) had to be confirmed by the *bay'a* (oath of loyalty). The four successors of Muhammed, who are described as the "righteous caliphs" (*al-khulafa' al-rashidun*), were all selected consultatively and legitimated by *bay'a*. After the murder of the fourth caliph, Ali, and the ensuing conflict between his supporters, who opposed the hegemony of the Arab Quraish tribe (Ali himself was a Quraishite), and the aristocracy of that tribe, the Umayyads, the latter prevailed, introducing the dynastic principle into the caliphate as an Islamic tradition of royal authority. The caliphs were all recruited from the Umayyad dynasty, which was abolished by force in 750 by the Abbasids, who established their own dynasty, which persisted until the collapse of the great Islamic empire in 1258. The supporters of Ali (*shi'at Ali,* the party of Ali) brought about the first and so far most important schism in Islam. Since that time, the Sunni notion of the state has been characterized by the caliphate and the Shi'ite notion by the imamate (the legitimacy and illegitimacy of rule respectively). Ali was declared the First Imam, and Shi'ite Islam took on in the course of its development in a later period the form of an *Iranized national religion.* According to the doctrine of Twelver Shi'ism, the world awaits the return of the twelfth, vanished Shi'ite imam,[7] who will save the world as a Messiah. All forms of political rule until that time have been declared illegitimate.

After the collapse of the Abbasid empire, the Muslim world dissolved into regional kingdoms that acted as territorial states until the Ottomans restored the Islamic empire under the umbrella of their imperial state in the fourteenth century. After the Kemalist revolution and the abolition of the caliphate in 1924, efforts to restore a pan-Islamic empire (for example, the founding of the caliphate movement)[8] were useless. Since that time, however, there has not been a caliphate.

This introductory historical overview sheds light on the question of the classical relationship between the state and Islam and its relevance to the present.[9] In the above remarks we have become acquainted with *shura, ikhtiyar,* and *bay'a* as elements in the Islamic form of government.

In High Islam, during the Abbasid dynasty, the first attempts were made to develop Islamic constitutional law.[10] During this epoch, a fourth element in the Islamic form of government was added to the three already mentioned. Religious scholars, who continued to develop Islamic law on the orders of their rulers, were consulted as (dependent) advisers, as "people who loose and bind" (*ahl al-hall wa al-'aqd*), who then of course simply supplied a religiously founded legitimacy for the ruling elite.

The Syrian lawyer Adib Nassur,[11] who is concerned with Islamic constitutional law and is also thoroughly familiar with the tradition of European political philosophy, points out that Islamic teaching on political government[12] comprises no more than *shura, ikhtiyar, bay'a* and consultation of the people of the *hall wa al-'aqd,* commenting that political philosophy was very underdeveloped among Muslim Arabs aside from the few works by Mawardi, al-Farabi, and Ibn Khaldun.[13]

Within the Arab Islamic region of the international society today there are three monarchies, of which two are Islam-legitimated: Morocco and Saudi Arabia (I shall leave aside here the tribal Gulf sheikhdoms). The third monarchy, Jordan, was inaugurated by the Hashemite dynasty, whose incumbents are regarded as *ashraf* (notables legitimated by descent from the family of the Prophet). This kingdom, however, is not legitimated in explicitly religious terms,[14] for which reason it falls outside the scope of the present analysis. Without recourse to Islam, the majority of government systems in the Arab world cannot be adequately understood, especially as no secularization process has taken place there. Even "republican" military dictatorships legitimating themselves in "revolutionary" terms, such as Libya, for example, base themselves on Islam and interpret it along their own lines.[15] The analysis here is limited to monarchies that legitimate themselves using religion because of the explicitly Islamic consolidation of rule in these states; the ruler reigns as *amir al-mu'minin* (commander of the faithful), deriving his right to rule from the Koran and the Sunna, with the Muslim *ulema* serving as legitimators.

The traditional approach of Orientalists and scholars of Islam to this issue has proved unhelpful on numerous occasions, in particular because these disciplines have no developed methodological apparatus at their disposal and lack analytical concepts. The classification of Arab political systems by the German Orientalist Werner Ende may serve as an illustration here: In his view,[16] there are rightist *salafiyya* systems (such as Saudi Arabia), leftist *salafiyya* systems (Algeria and Libya), and moderate *salafiyya* systems (equally valid for Tunisia, Lebanon, and, intermittently—according to Ende—for Egypt). Apart from its intellectual naiveté, this classification can be used to describe a personal perception of reality but not reality itself.[17] Less naive but more problematical is the oversimplified classification of Soviet Marxist authors in the German Democratic Republic's handbook on the Arab world,[18] according to which these countries may be divided into "national democratic, progressive" and "reactionary, pro-imperialist" regimes.

Before turning to the subject of my empirical analysis, I shall attempt to elaborate a conceptual framework, with the aid of which Islam will be interpreted as a simple, not yet functionally differentiated social system, to facilitate a more appropriate classification of the empirical configurations in Morocco and Saudi Arabia. By way of conclusion, I will discuss the future prospects of religiously legitimated monarchies in the modernization process.

A Conceptual Framework for the Study of the Relationship Between Islam and the State: Islam as Political Culture and as a Simple Social System

Leaving aside the attempts at secularization that have been undertaken in the recent modernization process in the Middle East, which have in any case failed to achieve what they set out to do, then I can state that Islam constitutes the primary determining factor of political culture in the Arab Middle East. Islam, however, is itself a historical manifestation; it has taken on historically varied and regionally specific forms in the course of its development. The Islam of the tribes in the Arabian peninsula cannot therefore be equated with that of the Atlas tribe in Morocco. And there is another difference: If we concede that Islam as a system of belief and values has influenced the political culture of elites and political authority in the Arab countries, we are starting out at odds with some scholars of Islam, for whom Islam consists of the Koran and the Sunna. Systems of belief and values change with history, so that the actions of men cannot be derived from these systems, even if we take change into account. This statement is particularly true for Islamic culture, in which there is a noticeable gap between religious dogma and the realities prevailing at any given moment. We know, for example, that the payment and charging of interest (*riba*) are strictly forbidden in Islam, but that in the body of juristic and religious writings there is a type of literature concerned with ways and means of circumventing this prohibition. *Hiyal* means legal tricks and dodges, and "can be described, in short, as the use of legal means for extralegal ends, ends that could not . . . be achieved directly with the means provided by the *shari'a.*"[19] We may ask at this point why prohibitions are stipulated, the circumvention of which is then theorized about in religious writings. Maxime Rodinson informs us that "medieval Muhammedan society . . . was an ideological society."[20] During his fieldwork in Morocco, John Waterbury was able to discern a similar gap between proclamation and action in the present day. From this Waterbury methodically draws the conclusion that in the analysis of political culture in Morocco—as a case in point—we must bear in mind a feature of that political system as a whole, namely, that political culture consists of the system of "empirical beliefs, expressive symbols, and values which defines the situation in which political action takes place."[21] It is in this sense, therefore, that it is much more important to understand what the Moroccans *really do* than it is to understand *what they think* they are doing.[22] By way of analogy to the concept of *cultural lag,* Waterbury develops the concept of *behavioral lag,* whereby he seeks to explain why the collective behavior patterns of members of a political culture deviate from the systems of belief and values those people have internalized.

This is the phenomenon generally rehashed by less scrupulous journalists into a form laden with value-judgment by applying the feuilletonistic expression "Arab rhetoric." The term "behavioral lag" can be used to interpret an essential anthropological feature of Muslim culture that lies at the heart of this study: The norm is not permitted to change and may likewise not be adapted to change, but the actions of those involved do not remain as constant as the norm would appear to be. The term behavioral lag[23] can contribute to an understanding of the Islam-specific phenomenon that the *held norm* is not in harmony with *everyday action.* This does not filter into the awareness of the people concerned, however, as belief in the norm would thereby be endangered. This is precisely the social phenomenon for which the phrase "cultural accommodation of social change" has been coined in this book.

When I state that Islam is the central component of the political culture in Arab political systems, this does not of course mean that I am dealing with a unified monolithic political culture. With reference to the thesis I have already formulated—that Islam in history cannot be properly understood in terms of dogma, as the latter is fixed forever, whereas Islam as a cultural system is constantly changing—I can put forward the hypothesis that there is no unified political culture[24] valid for all Arab political systems, though these systems share certain central features, despite historically determined differences.

This observation about political culture holds true as well for my attempt to define the nature of the social system characterizing a particular historical configuration of the political system. Although all Arab social systems may be described (although not in an evolutionist manner) as preindustrial, being based on a correspondence between the sacred and the political,[25] some differentiation will have to be made in the empirical analysis. Egypt, whose social structure is the most developed in the region, has a correspondingly more complex political system than Libya or Iraq, although it has in common with these two countries the formal characteristic of being an Arab republic. It would seem useful in the first place to examine the problem of rule and legitimacy in Islam, so as to permit an understanding of what I derive from my empirical analysis.

The traditional Islamic order system may be regarded as an organic, religiopolitical system dominated by a correspondence between the sacred and the political. The ruler is a worldly figure, who is nevertheless legitimated by the clergy, the *ulema*—the guardians of the Islamic *shari'a*, the divine law.[26] The political ruler bears the religious title *amir al-mu'minin* (commander of the faithful) and is thereby incontestable. Although Arab political systems vary, we may characterize the social system that unites these political forms of government as one that displays no functional differentiation.[27] If we adhere to Luhmann's system theory, a social system does not become functionally differentiated until the religious system, as a result of development in the social structure, is reduced to a partial system of the society, that is, when this system becomes secularized.[28] In Luhmann's view, "secularization [is to be regarded] as the consequence of the high degree of differentiation modern society has achieved."[29] There are calls for secularization at the literary level in the Arab Middle East, but none of the existing systems can be described as secularized. The correspondence between the sacred and the political continues to exist not only in the religiously-legitimated monarchies but also in the republican forms of government.

It would seem pertinent to specify more closely the concept of the nonfunctionally differentiated system for the analysis of political systems in Muslim countries. Political systems arising out of functionally differentiated social systems may be described as developed. The most important indicator for this is the degree of institutionalization. Developed political systems are defined here, along the lines of Samuel Huntington's theory, as institutionalized ones, as distinct from underdeveloped ones, those with a low degree of institutionalization.[30] In this sense, political development may be understood as a process of institutionalization. In the Arab Muslim countries we can encounter differing underdeveloped systems, systems with various levels of underdevelopment. Egypt has the most highly developed Arab political system so far, although even it is underdeveloped.[31]

A political system whose institutions are adaptable, complex, autonomous, and coherent may be described as institutionalized.[32] An institution is adaptable when it is able to reorient itself constantly to societal adjustments brought about by social change; it is complex when it is not monolithic and displays differentiated segmentation into sub-organizations; it is autonomous when its procedures are independent and self-sufficient; finally, it is coherent when a consensus is to be found within it, particularly with regard to the resolution and settlement of disputes. An institutionalized political system has at its disposal institutions that display these features; power in such a system is attached to law, that is, to legal and binding norms, not to persons. Power is thus in this case legal and neither charismatic nor traditional, to cite the ideal types of Max Weber.[33] I could interpose here that Islam-legitimated political systems are formally institutionalized insofar as they are based on Islamic law, the *shari'a.* In a traditional social system based on a correspondence between the sacred and the political,[34] however, there is *no division of power;* the legal system, inasmuch as one exists, is largely dependent on the rulers. These general assertions can be supported in the case of Islam by the research findings of Fritz Steppat. In High Islam, during the period of the Abbasid dynasty, the *shari'a* was institutionally fixed with the setting up of a judicial system. The Muslim jurists, the *faqihs,* were consulted as judges (*kadi*). "This judicial system, however, was not an institution independent of the caliphate; the judges were subject to the orders of their rulers . . . This process did win over the major part of the *ulema* class to the state, but as officials, as pliant, dependent tools."[35] The religious dogma of Islam does not recognize a clergy, but the Islamic religious system as a component of the social system in Islamic history, as Nikki Keddie[36] and Arnold Green[37] have shown, does acknowledge the *ulema* as an institutional, virtually clerical power, in alliance with political authority and subordinate to it. This alliance substantiates the correspondence between the sacred and the political, as we shall see in the empirical research findings from Morocco and Saudi Arabia. Islamic law, which is interpretative law and thus not codified, has to this day never formed a juristic basis for a legalization, that is, an institutionalization of the political system.[38] This legal function in a political system is discarded as being in contradiction to the Islamic understanding of jurisprudence (*fiqh*) as a divine discipline.

Political systems with a low degree of institutionalization may be subdivided into traditional ones, in which political authority is trans-mitted through religion, and praetorian ones, in which political authority is inaugurated through an oligarchical or radical government or one sustained by a mass movement. The Moroccan and Saudi Arabian monarchies, as well as the tribal Gulf sheikhdoms, are traditional political systems. All Arab military regimes[39] are radical praetorian systems with weak institutionalization in the terms defined by Huntington.[40]

These features characterize the prevailing dominant forms for settling conflicts.[41] Political loyalty is not bound to institutionalized norms (Weber: "set rules"), but to persons. This helps to explain why personalities play such a paramount role in the politics of Muslim countries compared to developed political systems: Because this kind of politics is personified rather than institutionalized. It is possible to reconstruct the contemporary history of the Middle East from individual biographies, as has been attempted by Majid Khadduri, and before him by Anis Sayigh.[42] Successful politicians such as Nasser inaugurated a charismatic leadership and are not professional politicians in Max Weber's sense of the term.[43] Precisely this charismatic leadership, however, undermined all tendencies toward institutionalization, Nasser's Egypt being a classic example.[44] The absence of an institutionalization of power I have pointed to here likewise correlates to the correspondence between the sacred and the political even in republican Arab Islamic states such as Egypt, where "political culture, government legitimacy and national identity are all infused with Islam,"[45] as Bruce Borthwick has written.

So far we have been able to ascertain that Islam shapes the political culture in Arab Islamic states and defines, in its capacity as a system of religion, the social system as a whole, which is not yet functionally differentiated. Islam knows neither enlightenment on the cultural level nor the division of power on the politicosocietal level. Islamic law therefore had a purely legitimating function and was unable to become a vehicle for the institutionalization of social change, as has been the case for a function of law in the process of social change in European development since the French Revolution. Although Islamic law (*shari'a*) forms the central element in Islam, Islamic history knows no constitutional state. The empirical analysis of Islam-legitimated monarchies will give an account of two historical forms of relationship between Islam and state.

Islam and the State in Morocco and Saudi Arabia

In both Morocco and Saudi Arabia, political rule is legitimated through religion, the political leader also embodying religious authority, recognized by the Islamic scribes, the *ulema*. In both countries the head of state is at the same time a Muslim king, who makes political decisions autocratically, performing the role of *amir al-mu'minin* (commander of the faithful) in Morocco and *khadem al-harameyn al-*

sharifeyn (servant of the holy shrines of Mecca and Medina) in Saudi Arabia. Both kings also provide religious orientation. A specifically Arab component of this traditional correspondence between the political and the sacred is that the holder of power not only must combine these two characteristics but also must be the tribal chief in a segmented society consisting of rival tribes. Despite the characteristics Morocco and Saudi Arabia share, however, there are also significant differences, as will be explained.

The Moroccan royal house is a very old one, having been recruited from the Alawi dynasty, which has ruled in Morocco since the middle of the seventeenth century (1666). This dynasty consists of sherifs (in Arabic, *sharif,* pl. *ashraf*), that is, notables who legitimate their status as descendants of the Prophet Muhammed. In contrast to Egypt, where central state authority has been uncontested since the days of the pharaohs, in Moroccan history the conflict between *bilad al-makhzan* and *bilad as-siba* has been central, and remains relevant even today for the analysis of the political system there. In Morocco the state is known as a *makhzan* (warehouse), which demonstrates its presence through military might; its tasks include both the collection of taxes and the pacification of tribes that are to some extent mutually hostile and to some extent hostile to the state. The designation *bilad al-makhzan* describes the sphere of de facto exercised sovereignty of state power, whereas *bilad as-siba* constitutes those regions in which the central power is not present in military form and where the rebellious tribes, who refuse to pay taxes, therefore have the upper hand. It is certainly worth mentioning here that the Spanish Sahara, partly controlled by the Saharan liberation movement, the Polisario, is known today as *bilad as-siba.*[46]

Unlike Saudi Arabia, where the Koran itself is regarded as the constitution, Morocco so far has a tradition of three written constitutions, patterned, albeit only formally, on the Western model.[47] The texts of each constitution contain a paragraph in which the king is legitimated as *amir al-mu'minin,* that is, as a religious authority. The Koran contains no verse with an equivalent content, although the king in Saudi Arabia is an imam in a similar sense (in the Sunni understanding); the legitimation of this is taken care of by the religious leaders, the *ulema,* who interpret the Koran accordingly.

The Alawi dynasty is very old compared to the Saudi Arabian one but has similar problems in retaining mastery over the political sphere, in its case with maintaining political power in the face of rival and rebellious tribes. The founder of Saudi Arabia, Ibn Saud (1881–1953) was only able to establish a central power this century in a struggle against the tribes. The Alawi dynasty has been obliged to assert its authority against the tribes since the seventeenth century. In Saudi Arabia the king is also known as the *sheikh al-mashayekh* (the sheikh of sheikhs), or the supreme tribal leader. In Morocco the rule of each new sultan or king must be reconfirmed through the traditional *bay'a* (oath of allegiance or loyalty), which is sworn by the tribal leaders at his enthroning ceremony.[48] Prior to this, however, the new ruler must demonstrate his military dominance and the associated presence of the *makhzan*. In this context we can understand the action of King Muhammed V some years before his death in appointing his son, the present king, as commander-in-chief of his fighting forces in 1957. In both Morocco and Saudi Arabia political rule has to be confirmed both sacrally by the *ulema* and tribally by the tribal leaders. In Morocco, however, rule is not as simple as in Saudi Arabia, as Moroccan society is more complex and characterized by a developed system of client-patron relationships.[49] In addition, Morocco also has a Westernized modern elite who influence the political life of the country. This explains why Morocco has a formal constitution as well as a party political system, neither of which is to be found in Saudi Arabia.

In their work on the role of political parties in the process of social change, Myron Weiner and Joseph LaPalombara have shown that "the political party . . . [is] both an indication of and a prerequisite for a move forward into the modern."[50] In this sense a party is a social institution. In underdeveloped societies, none of which has at its disposal a fully institutionalized political system, political parties are "no more . . . than limited cliques or oligarchies"[51] in the judgment of Weiner and LaPalombara, who elucidate: "The fact that a small oligarchic group has created an organization on paper does not make this organization a political party."[52]

The Moroccan political system, with its political parties, is undoubtedly superior to that of Saudi Arabia, with its monolithic structure, although this remark only makes sense when we bear in mind the evaluation of Weiner and LaPalombara. The Moroccan system of client-patron relationships reproduces itself in the political parties, which are more or less clienteles.[53] The Moroccan king can only rule successfully as long as he is able to maintain a proper balance among the clienteles and assert himself as a political leader, or *za'im*. After his research in Morocco, Waterbury rephrased the watchword "divide and rule" into "divide and survive."[54] The parties are tools for the king in his balancing act. Insofar as Moroccan society, like all underdeveloped countries, displays a marked rural-urban gulf (that is, heterogeneity), the political process has to adopt different forms in rural regions from those in the metropolitan centers. Political parties in Morocco are an urban phenomenon. On the Moroccan periphery, the king is obliged to deal differently with the tribal leaders so that the presence of the *makhzan* remains ubiquitous and the periphery does not lapse into *bilad as-siba.*

To this day the tasks of the state continue to be tax collection and military pacification. The Moroccan political system is "a stable system with continuity of power," as Waterbury characterizes it: "Collect taxes to pay the army to crush the tribes to collect still more taxes."[55] This state as *makhzan* is personifed in the king, who is the political and religious leader at one and the same time. In his capacity as *amir al-mu'minin*, he is empowered to bestow divine blessing, the *baraka.* This is central to the notion of the political culture of Morocco. The legitimacy crisis and the two *coup d'état* attempts of 1971 and 1972 were not overcome with military might alone.[56] The king's survival of two assassination attempts was, in the minds of Moroccans, proof that he was not only a *za'im* but also a sacral authority in possession of *baraka.*[57]

The stability of the Moroccan political system lies not only in the fully developed military and police apparatus of the *makhzan* but also in just this sacralization of political power accepted by the bulk of the Moroccan population. The Alawi dynasty embodies this sacral quality. Together with Waterbury,[58] however, I should point out here that additional, to some extent diffuse, religious authoritative sanctions exist, between rural folk Islam and urban legal Islam. The primacy of royal authority, however, is not contested.

Like the Moroccan *makhzan,* the Saudi Arabian system is based on the royal family, the *ulema,* and the military (the "white army," which exists side by side with the regular fighting forces). Unlike the Alawis, however, the Saudis are a young dynasty, whose kingdom was established through a union between the political and the sacral (an alliance with the Wahhabis)[59] and through the paramilitary use of that sacral-political authority in the struggle against rival tribes (the founding and implementation of *ikhwan*).[60] The numerous tribes of the Arabian peninsula may be described as segmentary, acephalous societies that were forced into constant fighting among themselves by the harsh conditions of life in the desert. There was no centralized power on the Arabian peninsula prior to the founding of the Saudi kingdom. Ibn Saud, the founder, had to fight not only against the Hashemites and the British colonial power but also and above all against wild tribes.[61] As a result of military actions and military agrarian settlements of the *ikhwan,* he was able to set up centralized authority and pacify the tribes. In this respect his work resembles that of the Prophet Muhammed, especially as the Arabian peninsula had known segmentation of a similar form before the founding of the Islamic religion.[62]

Wahhabism was initially a purely religious movement, founded by Ibn 'abd al-Wahhab and aimed both against the Ottomans as the then holders of Islamic legitimacy and against deviations from primeval Islam. In what is hitherto the best concise account of this movement, Richard Hartmann suggests that

> Wahhabism as a religious movement is no more than a natural reaction, understandable in the light of the social conditions prevailing in Arabia, which had hardly altered substantially since the time of the Prophet, to the adaptation of Islam to complex cultural conditions, which clearly at the same time mostly meant a weakening of the basic ideas of the religion's founder and a certain Westernization.[63]

The Saudis, who prior to the founding of Saudi Arabia ruled only over the Nejd province, allied themselves (1744) with the Wahhabis through marriage. Until the beginning of the twentieth century, this by then politicized religious movement only achieved intermittent success: It was put down in the period from 1811 to 1818 by the Ottomans with help from Muhammed Ali's Egypt. Under Ibn Saud, the Wahhabis were politically revived; they developed into a paramilitary group, the *ikhwan,* who managed through missionizing on the one hand and agrarian military settlements on the other to elaborate Wahhabi religious dogma into an ideology of mobilization, by means of which they pacified rival tribes. Gary Troeller characterizes the *ikhwan* as a religio-military, fundamentalist movement aimed at settling the nomadic bedouin so as to subordinate them to central government authority.[64] The *ikhwan* were in fact traditionalists and not fundamentalists. They were so conservative that they fanatically opposed all innovations, such as radio and other modern appliances; it is reported that they burned the first trucks they encountered. Ibn Saud came into military conflict with them and neutralized their movement in 1930. In 1932 Saudi Arabia was proclaimed the central power of the Arabian peninsula; the neutralized *ikhwan* were forcibly integrated into the new kingdom.[65]

We would be justified in asking here how intricate the political system of Saudi Arabia is. Although the new monarchy may seem so in comparison to the Saudi sultanate of the Nejd, it can by no means be described as a complex system. Power is embodied in the king as political and religious leader.[66] One monograph on the political system by a Saudi Arabian political scientist states: "The government of Saudi Arabia consists of several major elements. The first is the Royal Family; the second the *Ulama*; the third, its military institutions."[67] In other words, the monarchy has a sultanate form of rule at its disposal that, over and above the legitimating religious leaders and the traditional military forces protecting them, is devoid of any of the functionally differentiated institutions characteristic of a complex political system. The author of the Saudi Arabian work just cited emphasizes the correspondence between the political and the sacred and the substance of legitimation of the Saudi monarchy, showing how this emerged from the religiopolitical alliance: "That first alliance was both political and religious in nature and clearly emphasized the true notion of the state in Islam; that is, state and religion are inseparable. The Kingdom of Saudi Arabia is an example of an Islamic state governed by the Holy *Quran*. This fact reflects the important role of the *Ulama*."[68]

The alliance between the royal family and the *ulema* (the correspondence between the political and the sacred) constitutes the legitimation of power, which is held at the military rather than the institutional level; the royal family, the *ulema* (sacral legitimation), and the military (physical and technological might) are the pillars of the traditional monarchy in Saudi Arabia. If we leave the level of legitimation and military might and shift to that of policymaking, then we need to take into account a further social group, the tribal leaders.[69] Although the latter are not permitted to share in government, without them the pacification of the tribes, as elements of political stability and the continued existence of central power, cannot be maintained. Formally the king holds a *majlis* (meeting) with the tribal leaders, in which he acts in a tribal manner as a *primus inter pares* (first among equals). This cannot, however, be considered as participation in the political system, because the *majlis* does not fulfill such a function.

To sum up, the Islam-legitimated monarchies examined here may be characterized as simple, preindustrial systems, the state being the incarnation of the correspondence between the sacred and the political. A specific feature of both monarchies is that this correspondence correlates to tribal social structures. The Islam-legitimated state cannot be sustained on the basis of an alliance between the Muslim clergy (the *ulema*) and the monarchic ruler alone; it also needs the acclamation of the tribal leaders. We may thus speak of a politico-religio-tribal alliance. Legitimation of the state, however, is primarily Islamic, for which reason we may define these monarchies as Islam-legitimated states. Whether this traditional form of rule, derived from a simple, preindustrial (in the functional rather than the evolutionist sense) social system, will be able to survive unscathed the process of rapid social change to which these societies are currently exposed, will be discussed in the following concluding remarks.

Islam-legitimated Monarchies and Rapid Social Change: State and Modernization

The perceptive reader nearing the end of this book will be justified in asking whether the formulation of the central issue in this book, the "cultural accommodation of social change," is not perhaps just another way of saying "secularization." This would be only partly accurate, however, as "secularization" is a manifestation of the *historical effect* of change on the cultural system, not, however, of the *process of actual cultural accommodation* of change called for at each historical phase. Muslim traditionalists and fundamentalists alike in any case will not permit the concept of "secularization," for in their conception it is incompatible with *the* Islam.[70] Neither the historical substance of "secularization" nor the historical determination of change is culturally grasped, as suprahistorical concepts are always used.

A religio-normative argumentation constantly found in Islamic writing is that secularization and the separation of the political from the sacred in general is an exclusively Christian phenomenon, unknown in Islam. Behind this separation of the two in Europe is said to be the "concealed hand of Jewish thought,"[71] according to one Arab-language academic publication by a university professor. The author goes on to explain:

> The separation between religion and politics can be traced on the
> basis of its emergence and development to purely Christian conditions.
> Of far greater danger in this new creation, however, is its adaptation
> by global Zionism, whereby it has acquired considerably more
> destructive forms. . . . Its aim is the establishment of a Jewish world
> government after the eradication of the other religions.[72]

This quoted passage may serve to give an impression of the level of Muslim conspiracy-driven discussion on the relationship between the sacred and the political.

According to the norm, the state is only Islamic when Islamic law, the *shari'a,* is dominant in it. The *ulema,* an institution that has developed historically, though in fact it has no right to exist in terms of the norm, are the custodians of Islamic law. Michael Hudson, who has coined the term "modernizing monarchies"[73] for the remaining kingdoms from the viewpoint of their legitimation emphasizes: "The ideal Arab monarchy, perfectly legitimized, entirely congruent with the values of the traditional political culture, would be an Islamic theocracy governed by the ablest leaders of a tribe tracing its lineage to the Prophet."[74]

In a functional sense, such a political system is appropriate to a preindustrial society whose social system knows no functional differentiation. The question therefore arises how this system develops analogously to social change. We know from the theoretical discussion within the discipline of international relations that we live today in an international society[75] in which political, cultural, and socioeconomic interactions are structurally fixed and social change exogenously induced. Traditional political systems do not fall into a state of crisis on account of the gulf between the traditional form of the state and changes in the social structure in the course of rapid social change: The reception of new ideas through the modernization of education, and above all through study abroad, also contributes to the undermining of legitimacy in existing state forms. The director of the Center for International Affairs at Harvard, Samuel Huntington, predicted even before the fall of the shah that the modernization of traditional monarchies would cost the latter their security: "The principal threat to the stability of a traditional society comes not from invasion by foreign armies but from invasion by foreign ideas. The printed and the spoken word can move quicker and penetrate further than can regiments and tanks. The stability of twentieth-century traditional monarchies is endangered from within rather than from without."[76] This is linked to the lack in traditional monarchies of hardly any choice but "to attempt to promote social and economic reform."[77] This very reform, however, is undermining the traditional foundations of power and legitimation, as the case of Iran has shown.[78] To argue in this way does not in the least imply the uncritical adoption of the position of modernization theory or to accept its evolutionism, according to which secularization constitutes a precondition for modernity in conformity to a preconceived model. It is acknowledged today that there is a need to formulate the secularization question in another way and that the religious system, which forms part of the debate, should be heeded in the process.[79] Yet this still leaves untouched the question of whether Islam-legitimated monarchies will be able to survive the conditions of rapid social change with a politicized cultural and religious system that, according to their own self-perception, is unalterable.

In both Morocco and Saudi Arabia social change is being accelerated by the existence of important raw materials, the export of which calls for intensive exogenous influences. Saudi Arabia is the largest exporter of crude oil in the world, controlling more than a quarter of the world's known oil reserves;[80] Morocco is the third largest producer and the largest exporter of phosphate.[81] Unlike Saudi Arabia, Morocco underwent colonization, in the course of which the traditional structures were upset and a modern Westernized elite formed.[82] In Saudi Arabia, today, however, as a result of oil wealth, a new middle class is emerging that is at variance with the political-sacral-tribal alliance that sustains the political system.[83] The Islam-legitimated monarchy of Saudi Arabia, though, does not have an institutional framework available with which to absorb this new social stratum. Institutional reform so far has not accompanied the structural effects of the three major planning periods (1970–1985). Petrodollar wealth, although decreasing owing to the drop in oil prices, is accelerating social change, but the political system is not assimilating changes within the social structure. John Entelis, who has researched the potential for a democratization of Saudi Arabia in the wake of petrowealth and the structural changes associated with it, comes to an unequivocally negative conclusion at the end of his research.[84]

The democratic constitutional state owes its political stability to existing, legally established mechanisms, legitimated by consensus, for the resolution of conflict. Where these do not exist, the result is either civilian mass violence or severe forceful repression, as Eric Nordlinger has shown.[85] Traditional monarchies lack available institutions capable of absorbing the social forces released by social change; they bridge the emerging gap by exercising total executive authority.[86] A situation like this cannot persist indefinitely, however, as the Iranian example has shown. The absence of religious legitimation of the Iranian monarchy explains why it collapsed so rapidly, especially because the absence of the sacral in politics had no balancing counterpart in the existing nonindustrial social structure. The massive repression of the traditional monarchy in Iran has today been replaced by mob violence in the form of a dictatorship by the clergy, for which I suggested the term "mullahcracy" in Chapter 10.

The Islam-legitimated Arab monarchies in Morocco and Saudi Arabia will survive longer than the secular Iranian kingdom of the Pahlavis, until in the long term they likewise take their place in the list of toppled Arab Islamic monarchies: Egypt (1952), Tunisia (1956), Iraq (1958), Yemen (1962), Southern Arabia (1967), and Libya (1969). In addition to the sacralization of power, the intertribal balance policy of the Moroccan *makhzan* and the size (3,000 to 4,000 princes) and effective organizational form of the royal family in Saudi Arabia speak in favor of a *relatively* long existence of the religio-tribal-royalist state form in these two monarchies. Despite the oil-price slide, Saudi Arabia still controls a considerable petrodollar surplus in the world economy. This immense petrodollar wealth enables the monarchy to link its domestic and foreign policies to appropriate financial measures that are temporarily able to neutralize destabilizing elements at both levels. Saudi Arabia today forms the center of gravity of the Near East regional subsystem.[87] The Saudi royal house has indeed so far been able to "buy itself out of" all dangers (to use the words of Peter Scholl-Latour). The social scientific question concerning the extent to which a traditional religio-tribal-royal form of government can outlive the conditions of extremely rapid social change[88] remains to be answered, and the social substance of that question will certainly not be charmed out of existence by petrodollars.

PART FIVE

Conclusions and Future Prospects: Asymmetries in the International Society, "Demonstration Effects," and Globalized Intercultural Communication as the Structural Framework for Rapid Social Change in the Islamic Middle East

The inquiry pursued in this book took as its starting point the definition of religion as a cultural system along the lines of the anthropology of Clifford Geertz, to which this study is indebted, despite the effort taken to go beyond it in considering the international environment of culture. One of the levels at which this was attempted was the interpretation of the contemporary world as an international society. Recent globalizing socioeconomic structures, as well as the conditions created by modern transport and communications technology, are all contributing to the embedding of all cultures in a given structural framework of interaction. This statement, however, is too general and therefore open to misunderstanding. It is therefore important to emphasize that I am not propounding here the existence of an international society with unified and coherent structures such as those of a national society. Nor do I overlook the fact that despite the generally valid assertion of a growing network of interaction on the global scale there are still widely differing interactions, which differentiate among themselves. Here, however, the subject itself should form the focus, and not the theories employed to investigate it, as this discussion has already been carried out elsewhere.[1] The questions arising with regard to determining both conceptually and empirically the position of Islam within the wider issue of the cultural accommodation of social change, relate primarily to three subject areas:

1. Change in global conditions: whether the preindustrial culture of Islam would be able, once the existing asymmetries in the contemporary world have been overcome

(although there is no prospect of this at present) to become integrated into a kind of *culture universelle* and thus, as it were, phase out questions of

2. Repoliticization of the sacred: whether the current cross-regional repoliticization of the sacred represents solely a resistance to this process of integration into a universal entity, whether it is opening up new prospects for the independent development of a region that may be classified as Islamic, or whether it is purely and simply a romantic and regressive resistance to change as such, and finally

3. Cultural secularization: the concluding remarks of the study as a whole on modernization, secularization and on the relationship between religion and social change in general.

Competing Models of the Future: The Middle East as Global Center of an Islamic Umma, an International Culture Shaped by the West, or Cultural Pluralism?

At many points in this book, the Islamic world view has been presented as one proceeding from the universality of Islam as the ultimate divine revelation, valid for all people and for all times. The *umma* concept in Islamic doctrine recognizes neither limitations nor exclusivity. Any person who is converted to Islam can become a member of this *umma,* and all Christians and Jews can live as protected minorities under Islamic tutelage. This model is of no significance at all for reality nowadays, although it remains binding for more than 800 million Muslims living today and represents a program to go with the banners of many religiopolitical groups in this period of repoliticization of the sacred. The widely dispersed Muslims are after all part of the asymmetrical structure of the worldwide North-South gap—to use the conceptual framework of Johan Galtung, they are among the "underdogs" of the international order, which is dominated by the European and U.S. or East European "top dogs." Orthodox Muslims characterize this situation by the term *inqilab al-mawazin,* which may be freely translated as *reversal of circumstances.* Even for the greatest Muslim reformer of the nineteenth century, Afghani,[2] the primary characteristic of Islam consisted of its "dominance and superiority."[3] It is not the purpose of this investigation to criticize contemporary Western dominance from such a viewpoint. My perspective, a self-confessedly normative one, is based on an egalitarian definition of cultures, even though the latter today display different levels of development that are leading to the emergence of structures of global dominance among them. Despite my unequivocal rejection of the Islamic claim to dominance on the grounds both of its anachronism and of my inclination toward intercultural open-mindedness based on cultural pluralism (but *not* relativism), I must nonetheless stress, glancing back over history, that Islamic dominance of others in High Islam did not incur the kind of destructive actions or deformation of other cultures that have often marked, for example, the European conquest of the world. The author of a recent, well-informed publication on the *Third World and Western Civilization,* written for a general readership, reflects on the relationship between Europe and the non-Western world and suggests in a somewhat moralizing tone: "The arrogance of Europeans toward people in other cultures poisoned the atmosphere and hindered or impeded those normal processes of mutual acquaintance and positive cultural encounter that had often occurred in the history of the world previously."[4] Just this historical reminder, still topical even in the postcolonial age, gives the author cause for concern about the possible threat of an international culture of European stamp; he appeals to his broad readership:

> The current economic gap between the countries of the Third World and Western civilization must not only be reduced in order to overcome poverty and hunger but also in order to preserve cultural plurality on earth. The political differences and tensions should be weakened and cultural differences strengthened, despite many tendencies to the contrary, for it is not a unified international society . . . but the continuous interplay between many different, equal, and economically viable cultures that represents the best prerequisite for what all people want above all: peace.[5]

Democracy in the liberal Western sense means "droit à la différence," the right to be different from others. There is no such tradition in the German political culture, characterized by the concept of a unified community,[6] which makes it all the more welcome when a German author makes such an appeal for an international intercultural order—although it should apply equally to the author's own society. This concept of a unified community characteristic of German society can be traced back to Herder, although this German philosopher, whose cultural philosophy is deeply indebted to the Western Enlightenment, speaks out against the levelling of cultures. Despite his polemics against "the fashion books from Paris," Herder adopted the liberal idea of pluralism and carried it over into the world of nations. "Every nation has its own way of looking at things all the more deeply imprinted upon it because it is their own, kindred with their heaven and earth, sprung from their way of life, bequeathed to them by their fathers and forefathers."[7] Part of the idea of pluralism is the equally liberal conception of equality; this demand implies equality and democratization both within the society itself and in global terms. The concept of a democratized international society characterized by egalitarian structures, with no more worldwide structural North-South gap but also without cultural uniformity, is an idea I discussed in some depth with Reinhard Bendix at Berkeley (who read the early draft of these conclusions). In his view this meant overlooking a model of a historical process of modernization that came about in England and France in the eighteenth century and that since then has, comparatively speaking, put all other societies into a position of "backwardness." Although African and Asian societies have made "ad hoc adoptions of items of modernity" (Bendix), this does not amount to an overall modernization.[8] In one section of this concluding part, Bendix's modernization concept will be discussed in detail; many of his positions form the intellectual background to my line of argument. I responded to this justified criticism of the model of an asymmetrical egalitarian international society with the argument that today we are already living in a global society characterized by globalized structures and networks of interaction, but which is nevertheless not egalitarian. Bendix proposed that such a general conception of an international egalitarian society would bring about the misunderstanding of a world order based on cargo concepts, by creating the impression that equality meant the distribution of existing wealth without regard to the historical processes in which it came into being and was reproduced. This justified criticism compels me to clarify my ideas more precisely and to state emphatically that the idea of equality in global terms means here no more than a plea that access to the conditions that render modernization possible should be democratized. Without reducing the process of modernization to the development and handling of modern science and technology, I should like here to place the accent on both elements of the modernization process.

Only the Western and European peoples, in whose region the industrial revolution took place, are able to produce and handle science and technology; through these they have freed themselves from the power of nature. The mastery of nature, which is no longer explained in religious terms, is one of the essential features of the industrial societies. A consequence of this process, and related to it, are the radical changes in the world view of Europeans in the modern age.[9] In contrast to this secular Christian-Western world view, Islamic culture is still defined in preindustrial, religious terms.[10] This feature both of Islamic and other non-Western cultures is also one of intercultural asymmetry, embedded in unequal structures in which intercultural communication processes take place in our international society. The latter system is not as homogenous as a national social system, and yet its component parts are bound together structurally; it embraces segmentary structures and cultures of various levels of development, which are nevertheless all structurally bound together by worldwide interaction.[11] Following Luhmann, I distinguish here between simple and complex, that is, segmentary, stratified, and functionally differentiated social systems.[12] Unlike Luhmann, however, I see a close connection between the functional differentiation of a social system and the degree of industrialization of a society. If we interpret the international society using a central-periphery model, then we may define all central cultures as technological-scientific and those of the periphery as nonindustrial. In this sense the worldwide North-South gap also has a sociocultural dimension. This involves a sociocultural conflict between industrial and nonindustrial cultures, insofar as the former dominate the latter by virtue of their technological-scientific character. I may mention in support of this thesis the example of the repoliticization of the sacred in Muslim societies, insofar as it documents a sociocultural protest movement and a counter-acculturation.[13] I shall be developing this thesis in a general conceptual way, although always with special empirical reference to the Islamic part of the international society, which is conceived of by some scholars as a "Muslim world" of its own.

It would be appropriate at this point to problematize the development concept used here in light of intercultural conflict formation. Development is a vague concept without specific content in its general form; it is open to any of us to read our own perceptions into it and thus present it as our own concept of development.[14] In the Western hemisphere, Eurocentrists understand by development the transfer of their societal systems to the non-Western world; in Africa we can see the opposite extreme, where many politicians interpret development in the context of their particular ethnocultural authenticity. Concepts such as *ujamaa* or *négritude,* for example, define development as a restoration of the precolonial conditions of the agrarian subsistence economy. For Muslim fundamentalists, development means restoration of the Muslim order. These ideas involve romantic development ideologies of decolonization[15] and may best be described as a cultural perception of underdevelopment.

If we abandon these normative fillings for the development concept, we may wonder at its social scientific definition. Scholarly inquiry into the issue of development goes back to the nineteenth century, when the social philosophical concept of evolution, borrowed from biology, was beginning to crystallize into a tradition of evolutionism, being adopted chiefly by social anthropology and ethnology.[16] The latter were social science disciplines that in their day represented the higher branches of research (in contrast with subordinate "hothouse" disciplines such as Oriental studies) and had the monopoly on scholarly investigation of the non-European regions.

Since the 1960s, the process of decolonization has made a decisive contribution toward changing this situation, as well as toward the establishment of a new focus of research in social science; it may be described as the birth of more recent research into developing countries (development studies), which flourished first in the United States and then also found its way into German universities.[17] Above all in U.S. research, the nineteenth-century concept of evolution was adopted and applied to the developing countries. The title of the well-known study by Daniel Lerner, *The Passing of Traditional Society,*[18] illustrates this approach, in which underdevelopment—understood as traditionality—represents merely a passing stage in the processes of social change. I have already introduced this discussion using the example of Eisenstadt's notion of underdevelopment as cultural traditionality in Chapter 4. I refer to it again here only to avoid two possible misunderstandings:

1. If here the intercultural conflict within the international society is defined as a conflict between industrial and nonindustrial cultures, this is by no means to interpret nonindustrial societal conditions as a transitional or development stage. The line of argument being pursued here is *not an evolutionist one.* Muslim nonindustrial societies could of course always retain this definition, but this would also mean a retention of the North-South gap.

2. The second possible misunderstanding concerns my concentration on the sociocultural dimension of underdevelopment. This could raise the criticism that in this study the socioeconomic monocausality of some Marxist authors is simply being replaced by another monocausality. For this reason it would seem necessary to point out that any attempt to interpret reality must be *multidimensional.* This includes economics and politics as much as culture and social structures. In this sense, therefore, the structure of underdevelopment also has political and sociocultural dimensions; none of them alone can help us toward a comprehensive interpretation of the phenomenon.

The concept of underdevelopment is a category acquired through comparison, for those societies it classifies are only ranked as underdeveloped in comparison to the industrialized parts of the world. In this sense, the discussion whether, for example, the Middle East was at all underdeveloped prior to its contact with Europe or whether it in fact became underdeveloped as a result, has already been excluded.[19] My own starting point is the European conquest of the world and the latter's restructuring into an entity dominated by an industrial center.

Industrial development in Europe, for which England and France supplied the model, thus became a yardstick for global development in the non-European regions as well. As much as I adhere to my normative orientation, that is, to a preference for the option of global cultural pluralism (but *not* relativism), I must nevertheless pay heed to the danger of distorting my analysis with wishful thinking. The choice of the path ahead must be made within the given framework of existing structures, and cannot overlook these. This comment may at first seem to contradict the model of the egalitarian international society for which I appealed in the introduction, since global societal equality is only possible on the basis of comparable and equally developed structures. This is not the reality at the moment, however, and there are no indications that such a goal could be achieved in the near future. It nevertheless seems justified for us to adhere to such a concept as a normative orientation, without allowing ourselves to be seduced into some kind of egalitarian cargo cult.

The process of civilization described and analyzed by Norbert Elias[20] has become globalized in the context of the European conquest of the world. How did it come about that Europe was in a position to make such a conquest, whereas in the previous history of mankind other civilizing processes also had highly differentiated levels of advanced culture but were still unable to achieve such a historic feat, or only to a very limited extent? Elias gives the following explanation: "What lends the civilizing process in the West its special and unique character is the fact that here the division of functions has attained a level, the monopolies of force and taxation a solidity, and interdependence and competition an extent, both in terms of physical space and of numbers of people involved, unequalled in world history."[21] In the context of the European colonization of the rest of the world, these processes were exported from Europe and became universal. The spread of this mechanism of socioeconomic complexity and competition throughout the whole world represents in Elias's view "the last wave of the continuing civilizing movement that we are able to observe,"[22] and "the contrasts in conduct . . . are reduced with the spread of civilization; the varieties or nuances of civilized conduct are increased."[23] For this part of Elias's analysis I have developed the term *globalization of the civilizing process,* arguing that differing variants of cultural patterns can emerge out of this process, yet remain integral to it.[24] We should not overlook the great deal of destruction this globalized civilizing process has left in its wake, nor the crimes against other cultures it has generated. The wheel of history, however, cannot be turned back, and the universalizing effects—of both a socio- and a psychogenetic nature—of this process are now features of our reality. Realistically speaking, the demand for cultural pluralism can only mean striving to increase the scope for more varieties within the sociocultural sphere, at the same time dismantling contrasts, above all in structural differentials. This conclusion leads me to the second focal point of my discussion, namely, an assessment of the repoliticization of the sacred and its pursuit of a sociocultural disconnection from the global structure.

An Islamic Ghetto of the International Society or a Component Region Integrated into It and Inhabited by Muslims?

In Chapter 8 of this study I proposed a religiosociological interpretation of the repoliticization of the sacred in the Islamic region of our international society. There is no need to reiterate the conclusions of this interpretation here; my concern at this point is to assess this phenomenon in the global context, having defined it from the perspective of the societies involved as a result of rapid social change that has not been culturally received.

Since the Iranian revolution, scholarly and journalistic literature on this phenomenon, known in the English-speaking world as Islamic resurgence, has proliferated to such an extent—especially in the United States—that some observers have commented ironically that the number of publications by Near East experts in both academia and journalism exceeds the number of fundamentalist pamphlet authors in the Muslim world itself. In the Federal Republic of Germany there has also been an "Islamic boom," which, interestingly, has been closely followed by Near East experts of the German Democratic Republic, who even evaluated its salient features.[25] In many of these publications the reader will find new versions of old prejudices about Islam. In the German Federal Republic, for example, left-wing Third World development theorists have seen their wishful thinking about a "dissociation from the world market" fulfilled. The Iranian revolution, it seems to them, has made their political dreams come true.

One of the most highly regarded and influential scholars of Islam in the United States, the Princeton scholar Bernard Lewis, refers to the current variants of Islamic political revivalism as an expression of the "return of Islam."[26] Lewis advocates a careful observation of events. In his remarkable book *The Muslim Discovery of Europe,*[27] Lewis relates the currently observed phenomenon to the broader context of the Muslim-European encounter with a focus on modern times.

Although some authors may view the repoliticization of Islam as a grave threat to the West—or even to NATO—[28] other authors, as we have already mentioned, see a great liberation from imperialism through

Islam. The complex of problems and issues I have been investigating during the course of this book, on the interrelationship between social and cultural change, seems irrelevant to such authors, who see in Islam the fulfillment of their own positively assessed wishful thinking: For them Islam is nothing more than an ideological mask; all that remains is for "re-Islamization" to bring about the hoped-for "dissociation from the world market." One of these authors, Uwe Simson, states baldly that the consequences of this process under discussion

> can be described without using the term "Islam" in an Islamic sense; home market–oriented development on the internal level corresponds externally to a decoupling from unconditional integration in the world market and global communication combined with retention of a selective cooperation with the developed countries. Here, therefore, we find the central elements of . . . the dissociative development strategy aimed at decoupling from the capitalist world market put forward by Dieter Senghaas.[29]

Islam is thus reduced to the mere articulation of economic demands; nothing remains of it as a cultural system shaping the entire sphere of interaction in all Muslim societies.

Reaching beyond the Eurocentric mentality of some Orientalists or the dilettantist homage of wishful thinkers, the social scientist must investigate the problematic of Islam and social change, that is, the interrelationship between the cultural system and the particular societal structure—not only structurally and in terms of a critique of ideology but also in the context of the anthropological theory of culture—so as to be able to arrive at viable statements on the subject. This study will therefore conclude with a conceptual analysis of this interrelationship, built upon the basis of previous empirical studies.

Modernization and Secularization: Religion as a Cultural System and the Processes of Rapid Social Change in the Islamic Middle East

For every social scientist—whether sociologist, anthropologist, or political scientist—who works on social structures or belief systems, the category of change always stands at the forefront of a striving for knowledge. In his empirical, comparative study of Islam as reality in Morocco and Indonesia, Clifford Geertz rightly points out that admission of the category of change is problematic for every religion, for the idea that religion could be subject to change is in itself a heresy,[30] Assertions regarding the embedding of religion in social reality are today universally valid and recognized sociological findings. For societies exposed to externally induced rapid social change, such assertions must be of even greater relevance. This is because for any analysis of the "relationships between religion and society in the countries of the Third World . . . social change becomes both the central theoretical and empirical problem of analysis of the current situation,"[31] as one article on the sociology of religion, in a handbook of empirical social research, emphasizes. The formal content of religious symbols may be found in the scriptures of the particular religion, for which reason many scholars of Islam maintain that their subject can be understood through the textual, critical examination of sources, thereby overlooking that "the content and significance of religious symbols can only be derived from the context of their specific application."[32] Religion is not merely an ideological form of articulation, interchangeable with and secondary to understanding of real processes, and yet it only becomes adequately comprehensible in the context of change. The religious foundations of sociocultural change, which form part of social change, must always be a central component in analysis.

The present situation in which the sacred is being politicized, a situation not limited to Islam, is for its part bringing about a crop of salvation movements that see themselves as religiopolitical action groups. Four circumstances are put forward in the literature on the subject as general preconditions for this.[33] Prior to the crisis situation, that is to say, historically, there must have been a "moral order" that could be resorted to as an ideal. To this is added acculturative contact with a supraordinate structure—in this case, the industrial West—which in turn causes social tensions (rapid social change and the disintegration of existing structures), which arouse corresponding dissatisfaction. Westernized educational elites, who feel particularly affected by the acculturative contact, are as a rule—even in modern Islam—those indigenous elements who, in the context of the dissatisfactions arising out of the existing social tensions, tend to ideologize by resorting to the "moral order" that existed prior to this situation. Religiopolitical secret societies in the contemporary Islamic Middle East, such as those we have examined using the Egyptian example (Chapter 9), may thus be classified as salvation movements in this sense.

Any perceptive reader will immediately, and rightly, ask whether it is not Eurocentric to characterize protest movements in the Third World, even those with religiopolitical program content, as salvation movements. This thought does have some justification, for reaction to rapid change does not always have to involve recourse to an old "moral order"—even that of the ideal city state of the Prophet Muhammed in Medina. In the course of the cultural reception of change, other, future-oriented perspectives, in other words, ones not aiming for a romantic restoration of the past, can also be developed. It is therefore sensible to call to mind the conditions and the content of the modernization processes taking place, so as to be better able to reflect on this question within the proper context.

Starting from the present state of scholarly findings and research, I will spare myself the necessity of taking up outdated modernization theories. In his comparative social historical studies, Reinhard Bendix has overcome and gone beyond the old, almost scholasticized debate between the conceptual pair of traditionality and modernity. He impressively demonstrates that the concept of modernization is vague, at the same time insisting on its usefulness. This usefulness is retained only if the researcher knows how to avoid "confusion between scientific constructions and actual development."[34] If we abandon the level of a preconstructed observation of reality, then we are able to discern "that modernization does not necessarily lead to modernity. Moreover the modernization process itself is neither uniform nor universal, for the economic and political breakthrough made at the end of the eighteenth century in England and France has put every other country in the world in a situation of relative backwardness."[35] The processes of social change in contemporary Muslim societies cannot therefore be understood in the sense of the evolutionist model as transitory, nor can they be defined as catching up with a process that has already taken place in Europe. As in other Third World societies, so here, too, rapid social change is exogenously induced. A solution to the problems thus brought about cannot be that of ghettoization, or its more positive formulation, "dissociation," as the overall context of change is irrevocably of a global social nature. Not to take account of this is to succumb to the tendency to confuse reality with scientific constructs manufactured at the desks of scholars.

This overall context of the processes of rapid social change currently taking place in Muslim societies confronts the latter with the task of modernizing their structures on the one hand, and on the other with the many conflicts this creates. Each one of these societies is faced with "the problem of fusing its historically handed-down structure and typical tensions . . . with the effects of ideas and techniques coming from outside. . . . Each one must bring the gravitational pull of the developed societies into harmony with the values contained in its own traditions."[36] This general theoretical formulation comes from a text by Bendix presented at the World Congress of Sociology in 1966, at a time when it was still believed that modernization consisted of the wholesale adoption of structures, which were thought to be incompatible with indigenous cultural elements in every respect. The collapse of the

Iranian modernization experiment under the shah, which had been characterized by just such a preconception, freed the social sciences from false estimations and constructions of this kind. Even in those days, Bendix was ahead of his time. In his comparative social historical study, which appeared under the title *Kings or People* and contained sections on both early Islam and the contemporary situation, the assertions cited here are substantiated.

Bendix captures a crucial feature of contemporary Muslim societies in seeing social change there as characterized by "continuously repeated conflicts between nonindustrial and industrial ways of life."[37] Entanglement in tradition and the structural gravitational pull of the new explains why Arab Muslim elites are torn "between appeals to the great Islamic tradition they know to be popular and efforts to bring about economic change that, along with secular political institutions, tend to undermine that tradition."[38] The choice between the two has to be made "in a world of alien superpowers and a modern technical civilization."[39] Bendix assesses the situation correctly in viewing the surmounting of this dilemma as dependent on the ability of these elites "to blend restored traditions with the demands of modern development under the conditions of the twentieth century."[40]

In his Max Weber lectures in Heidelberg, Bendix develops historically the concept of "spiritual mobilization," discussing it in the context of social change in the non-European societies, which on the basis of the "demonstration effects" called for by modern communication methods are structurally exposed to European development. What is viewed as recommendable from the perspective of "progress" is often seen from the angle of indigenous tradition as "a danger to national independence"; the researcher must therefore understand the "peculiarities" of these societies so as to be able to assess "how they will come to terms with the ideas and institutions of the industrially and politically influential countries, or, conversely, how they could fail to do so."[41] It will depend on the spiritual mobilization of the elites of these societies whether they will be able to cope culturally with and be equal to these historically impending challenges. The level at which Bendix treats this problematic is that of historical reality. The criticism of scientific Eurocentrism may be levelled against Bendix and against me. The argument that Third World cultures, including Islam, can only be adequately understood in their own terms, however, would be based on a serious misunderstanding of the essence of Eurocentrism: Science is related to human reason and is the common property of all mankind, and is therefore applicable to the analysis of Third World cultures as well. I would identify the following interpretations, then, as Eurocentric: the belief in progress arising out of European development and the conviction of modernization theory that all cultures are on the road to development in the same direction as the European model. I would dispute the latter by asserting that there are various paths of development and that industrialization represents only one of the prospects for overcoming underdevelopment, but that it by no means necessarily has to be carried out. All this depends on the given structural circumstances and above all on the ability of the elites in question to cope culturally with change that has taken place in non-Western societies or, as Bendix would express it, to become spiritually mobilized. The preempted criticism that could be made against Bendix and myself assumes an ethnocultural fixation of knowledge that can nevertheless be rejected as a subjective, if well-intended, "racism in reverse." There are various cultural paths to knowledge, but there is no ethnocultural variation in patterns of rationality to which essentially different kinds of sciences (for example, Islamic science) are related. Conceding cultural diversity does not at all signify contention with the existence of a single form of human rationality. I shall have to leave this theme at this point, however, so as not to lose the thread of my concluding thoughts.

Discussion of "spiritual mobilization" raises the question how this issue is approached by the Muslim elites themselves. A dialogue on this theme has been underway for years between European and Arab social scientists within the scholarly forum of the Euro-Arab Social Research Group, of which I am a member. The issues arising here were taken up particularly in the context of the regional conferences on "Patrimoine Culturel et Mémoire Collective" in Marrakesh and "Cultural Identity in Time" in Cairo.[42] In Marrakesh the discussion concerned how the goods of a technological-scientific culture can be successfully adopted without at the same time changing the existing sociopolitical institutions and the dominant sociocultural attitudes of a preindustrial culture and its related world view. Unfortunately, the problem of "cultural identity" was dealt with only in terms of cultural theory, in a quasi-literary manner, without the prerequisite social theoretical level. Among Third World intellectuals there is often an articulated fear of losing their cultural heritage in the process of social change; this forms the background to debates that hardly ever depart from a vicious circle of modernity and authenticity.

In contrast, the Cairo discussion was more fruitful. The Cairo philosopher Mourad Wahba, who led the conference, insisted that there are no "cultural constants," as culture is always closely connected to "time." The definition of cultural identity was in accordance with this: In this sense, there can be no conflict between cultural identity/authenticity and modernity, especially where elites are capable of the cultural reception of modernity and do not simply, imitatively adopt ready-made products from industrial societies.

Were I to concede the argument that cultural systems such as Islam can only be adequately understood in their own terms, then the assessment that my discussion so far has bypassed the real theme would be an appropriate one. Even my concept of change, my central category, would be inadmissible, for Islamic scripture would forbid its use as heresy. Such an assessment would similarly apply to all sociology of Islam[43] and to all social historical investigation of it.[44] Nevertheless the "rationalization"[45] of recent times permits even the scientific probing of religion as a cultural system. The inherent danger is of succumbing to blind faith in science and progress and thereby subordinating the infinite, religion, to the finite, that is, science.

Can Islam be adequately understood with non-Islamic, scientific concepts? It has become almost a fashion—even among some Western scholars—to dismiss such efforts as "Orientalism." An anthropologist such as Ernst Gellner[46] would dispute this, although he himself is unable to remain consistent with this view in his own studies. Is Islam undergoing certain stages of development, as other religions allegedly do; is the cultural reception of change in Islam inconceivable except as the development of an Islamic Protestantism?

Parson's translation of Max Weber's *Protestant Ethic* in 1930 formed the background to the application of the Weberian thesis to one of the central paradigms of U.S. evolutionist modernization research, thereby merging two fields of research, as Constans Seyfarth and Walter Sprondel note in their account of Weber's thesis on Protestantism and capitalism. "Attempts that seek analogies to ascetic Protestantism often fail to see that it is quite a different question whether and to what extent 'religion,' even non-Christian religion, is exerting an influence on the emergence and development of industrial and postindustrial societies today."[47] Even Weber made a distinction between these two research questions. "It is beyond question that for Weber ascetic Protestantism played a significant role in social development. The question remains unanswered, however, whether it is in itself a stage in the development of religion as such."[48]

My remarks so far contribute more to an increased awareness of the complexity of my theme than toward answering the many outstanding questions even this book, whose author is ever mindful of the limitations of science, is unable to answer satisfactorily. On the one hand, analyses so far have amply demonstrated that scripturalist Islam does not enable its believers to assimilate change culturally. Although change is continually taking place, Islam refuses to admit the category of change into its doctrine. Muslims are therefore obliged to react to changed situations with a cultural system that in their own eyes is definitive and unchangeable. On the other hand, I have perceived, together with Reinhard Bendix and Norbert Elias, that the globalizing process of civilization proceeding out of Europe is exerting considerable and substantial effects on the process of social change in the countries of the Islamic Middle East. This new historical situation calls for changes in the Islamic cultural system to enable Muslims to assimilate at the cultural level the rapid change taking place in their societies. Nonetheless, in my rejection of evolutionism I have already regarded with some skepticism the idea that Protestantism represents a stage within religion that Islam must necessarily undergo in order to catch up with the contemporary situation. Following all these reservations is the question what changes must be carried out in Islam so as to render its adherents capable of the cultural accommodation of change. I am not thinking here of social strategy suitable either for public-policy consulting or for direct implementation. This book represents no more than an attempt at unrestrained scholarly inquiry that just happens to have been made first in German and now in English. As such it was addressed to a Western scholarly readership by way of developing an interculturally comparative sociology of development and of religion— but *not* because these readers are the ones to whom these efforts at reform are directed.

The question at this point, by way of conclusion, is whether a secularization of Islam, added to the "demonstration effects"[49] alluded to by Bendix, could form part of our contemporary scene, which would moreover be shaped according to the essential model. Gellner[50] reminds us that Islam is unfamiliar with the Christian separation of the sacred from the profane ("Render unto the emperor . . ."). Many influential Muslim authors, for example Muhammed 'Imara, argue in this respect that the modernization of Muslim societies would by no means lead to their secularization.[51] But even authors such as T. G. Carroll, who distance themselves from the secularization that has so far been regarded as universal,[52] have their doubts whether orthodox Islam, with its organic notion of society will, like Catholic fundamentalism, be capable of keeping a harmonious pace with the structures of modernity. Nevertheless, if we pay heed to contemporary critiques of civilization and science, which do not deny the existence of what is being criticized but simply wish to point out its limitations, then we are obliged, despite the reservations stated here, to assess the secularization thesis more skeptically than hitherto. In my earlier book *Crisis of Modern Islam,* I interpreted secularization along the lines of Luhmann's sociology of religion[53] as a by-product of a process of functional differentiation in the religious system—a process in the course of which religion is reduced to a part-system within society as a whole. In spite of all the reservations conceded here, I still hold firm to this interpretation, although I would wish to provide it with further differentiation and nuance.

Two thematic spheres need to be emphasized here. The first of these is the correspondence between the sacred and the political in Islam and the necessity for desacralizing politics in a broad sense. The second is concerned with the possibility of developing an Islamic variant of technological-scientific culture that would involve a reduction of the term "Islamic" to the ethical and cultural sphere, and hence a process of desacralization. A doctrinal renunciation of the Islamic claim to superiority would appear inevitable from the perspective of cultural pluralism. This is in any case a doctrine that today has no material underpinning. As a source of an ideology of intolerance it stands in the way of establishing a true cultural pluralism.

With reference to modern European social history, it is possible to point out that the secularization of Christianity[54] brought about by industrialization did not bring about its disintegration: Western industrial culture remains essentially Christian in character, despite being secularized. Muslims are anxious for their religion and identify secularization with atheism. It should be self-evident today, however, that overcoming underdevelopment is only possible through industrialization, which brings about secularization as a by-product, as is documented by the examples of societies already industrialized. Muslim scholars refuse to recognize that a backwards-looking contemplation of Islam alone, that is, the revitalization of the sacred, is important from the social psychological viewpoint (in resolving identity problems) but that it is no alternative to an urgently required strategy for overcoming underdevelopment. Another factor to be considered is the level of the international society and in this context the aimed-for symmetrical interaction between cultures that can become technological and scientific without ceasing to be cultural varieties in their own right. Within this context would fall the necessity for an Islamic renunciation of the doctrine of superiority. The realization of Herder's guiding principle, already quoted, whereby a cultural pluralism of various distinctive but peacefully coexisting peoples is aimed for, is difficult to imagine in an unequal international society. The Western peoples, who form the "upper stratum" (as Norbert Elias calls it) of the contemporary world, owe their privileged position to the technological-scientific culture they have developed. The equalization and thus democratization of international social relations can only consist of other peoples' integrating these technological-scientific components into their own cultures—although while altering their world view.

The Muslim societies are all underdeveloped and based on a correspondence between the sacred and the political. Adopting science and technology from the developed West and developing a secular Islamic variant of technological-scientific culture should not mean simply aping the West. By the same token, a backward-looking cultural reexamination of Islam such as propelled the Islamic clergy, as guardians of the religious culture, to power in Iran in the context of an Islam-legitimated uprising, as we have seen in Chapter 10, can for a short time appear to be attractively promising but is incapable of offering real solutions. This critique should in no way be interpreted as an argument against religious culture per se, much as it *is* an appeal for a desacralization of Islamic culture. With this question in view I will try to differentiate my terms.

In one of his interesting essays, the Harvard sociologist Daniel Bell proposes a restriction of the term secularization to that of a return to its original content. At one time, it meant simply a separation of religion from political life. In the course of the last two centuries, however, it has acquired a further dimension in Western societies— that of profanation, or what Max Weber, quoted by Bell, calls "de-magification" (*Entzauberung*). In Bell's view, underlying this idea is the belief that man can penetrate and master everything with the aid of science and his own instrumental reason: Total modernism implies nihilism.[55] Bell seeks not to restrict the concept of culture to its anthropological implications, that is, to how people live and cope with their lives. For him, culture means the "modalities of response by sentient men to the core questions that confront all human groups in the consciousness of existence."[56] Although science is capable, as Bell goes on to argue, of contributing to the mastery of nature, it is no substitute for the imbuing of culture with meaning through religion.[57] It is important to add here that Bell has no specific religion, and definitely no exclusive religion in mind here, as this would in his eyes be a political religion and would therefore neither correspond to his notion nor fulfill the function of providing answers to the fundamental questions of human, that is, universal human, existence. To concede, with Bell, the limitations of science should not mean succumbing to some kind of irrationalism.

The democratization of access to science and technology is a contribution toward overcoming the worldwide North-South gap. The preindustrial cultures of the South, such as Islam, can then participate in the processes of intercultural communication at a symmetrical level with the now dominant industrial cultures—albeit in the absence of claims to superiority and dominance. The secularization of religion will not do away with it: By helping to desacralize politics, a secularization that is not a profanation will protect religion from exploitation for political purposes, thus preserving it as an answer to the questions of human existence. In a free, symmetrical world, however, there cannot be uniformity, as freedom is unthinkable without diversity. Cultural diversity would also correspond to such religions, to the capacity for providing answers to the intrinsic questions of human existence. But this appeal for an international societal plurality of cultures on a symmetrical basis does not absolve the individual cultures from their outstanding internal social tasks. The globalized European civilizing process has produced historically a "standard of civilization in the international society"[58] with which the nonindustrial cultures must inevitably be confronted by means of "demonstration effects." The "dissociation" recommendation propounded by some Western researchers is pie-in-the-sky; with the monocausal vision of dependence theory, they see the dominance of the industrial West as merely the cause of underdevelopment. Without wishing to deny the negative, indeed destructive and deforming, effects of this dominance in the non-Western parts of the world, in light of our current improved state of knowledge we are now obliged to stress internal factors (and not purely economic ones), besides the external causes of underdevelopment, as an object of research. The lack of a cultural accommodation of social change in many "developing" countries is exacerbating the inability of people living there to come to terms with the existing structural framework of international societal asymmetries and with the demonstration effects proceeding from the industrial center. Neither the adjustment to change in terms of conformism,[59] nor the aggressive defensive-cultural response[60] to the disruptive effects of rapid change evince signs of cultural accommodation of social change. Underdevelopment is not only related to structural economic backwardness[61] or simply to a stage of political development[62] (a low degree of institutionalization) but rather to a very complex combination of economic, political, and cultural constraints. This book has been an effort to explore the latter—without reducing the cultural constraints of underdevelopment to cultural tradition[63] or separating them from the economic and political factors with which they are intermingled.

Notes

Introduction

1. B. Tibi, *Die arabische Linke,* Frankfurt/M, 1969. Reviewed by Hisham Sharabi in the *Middle East Journal* vol. 24, 3 (1970), pp. 391–392.

2. B. Tibi, *Nationalismus in der Dritten Welt am arabischen Beispiel,* Frankfurt/M, 1971.

3. B. Tibi, *Arab Nationalism: A Critical Inquiry,* trans. Marion and Peter Sluglett, New York, 1981. Reviewed by Michael Hudson in *International Journal of Middle East Studies* vol. 17, 3 (1985), pp. 292–294; and by George Atiyeh in *American Political Science Review* vol. 76 (1982), pp. 183–184. A second, substantially enlarged edition of *Arab Nationalism* was published by Macmillan Press, London, 1990.

4. See B. Tibi, "Islam and Modern European Ideologies," *International Journal of Middle East Studies* vol. 18, 1 (1986), pp. 15–29.

5. B. Tibi, *Militär und Sozialismus in der Dritten Welt,* Frankfurt/M, 1973. Reviewed by Peter von Sivers in *Muslim World* vol. 67, 3 (1977), pp. 236–237.

6. For more details, see Morroe Berger, *Islam in Egypt Today,* Cambridge, 1970.

7. See the introduction in John L. Esposito (ed.), *Islam and Development: Religion and Sociopolitical Change,* Syracuse, 1980, and in particular the chapter by Michael Hudson, "Islam and Political Development," pp. 1–24. See also Michael Hudson's book, *Arab Politics: A Search for Legitimacy,* New Haven, 1977, pp. 47–55.

8. B. Tibi, *Krise des modernen Islams,* Munich, 1981. U.S. ed. B. Tibi, *Crisis of Modern Islam: A Preindustrial Culture in the Scientific-Technological Age,* trans. Judith von Sivers, with a foreword by Peter von Sivers, Salt Lake City, 1988. Reviewed by Fred Halliday in *The Times Literary Supplement* no. 489, April 14–20, 1989, pp. 387–388. The original German publication of *Crisis of Modern Islam* was reviewed by Barbara Stowasser in *The Middle East Journal* vol. 37, 2 (1983), pp. 284–285.

9. English ed. *The Civilizing Process,* trans. Edmund Jephcott, 2 vols: vol. 1, *The History of Manners,* New York, 1978; vol. 2, *Power and Civility,* New York, 1982. On the meaning of Elias's work for the study of Islam, see Tibi, *Crisis of Modern Islam,* pp. 22–31. It is very unfortunate that in the seminal works of the leading historical sociologists Tilly and Skocpol there is no reference to the pathfinding publication of Elias, even though the *Civilizing*

Process has now become accessible in English translation. See Charles Tilly, *Big Structures, Large Processes, Huge Comparisons,* New York, 1984; and Theda Skocpol (ed.), *Vision and Method in Historical Sociology,* 4th printing, Cambridge, 1987.

10. A skimming reviewer of the German edition of *Crisis of Modern Islam* (see n. 8 above)—Gudrun Kraemer in *MERIP-Reports*—claimed to find a confusion between the terms "culture" and "civilization" in my book. In fact, I use culture in the anthropological sense of a framework for the social production of meaning, whereas "civilization" denotes the historical standard of development in a societal formation in terms of *sociogenesis* and the *transformation of social behavior.* I do not use the terms culture and civilization interchangeably. There exist on the one hand *a wide range of basically different cultures within Islam* extending from Africa to Asia, but on the other hand there is only *one Islamic process of civilization* related to the foundation of Islam. With the spread of Islam beyond Arabia this process has been globalized, although not to the extent that the European process of civilization has reached in mapping the entire globe into a single structure. See also my contribution to *Arab Civilization,* cited in n. 12 below.

11. Hedley Bull draws a clear distinction between the *international system of states* (structure) and world society (a normative consensus about the rules). When I refer to *structure* in this book I use the terms *global society* and *international system* interchangeably, in view of the fact that the focus of my analysis is not the system of states but rather the global structures that cannot be confined to the political level of the state system. See Hedley Bull, *The Anarchical Society: A Study of Order in World Politics,* New York, 1977. I agree with Bull, however, "that the shrinking of the globe . . . does not in itself create a unity of outlook and has not in fact done so. . . . Humanity is becoming simultaneously more unified and more fragmented" (Bull, p. 272). To be sure, the reference to the international system as a global society is far from being in accord with the equally simplistic and reductionist approach of Wallerstein of an economically determined monolithic world system. On the contrary, I reject this approach of Wallerstein. See Immanuel Wallerstein, *The Modern World System,* 2 vols., New York, 1974 and 1980.

12. For a further discussion of this thesis see B. Tibi, "The Interplay Between Social and Cultural Change: The Case of Germany and the Middle East," in *Arab Civilization: Challenge and Responses,* ed. G. Atiyeh and I. Oweiss, Albany, 1988, pp. 166–182.

13. See Leonard Binder (ed.), *The Study of the Middle East,* New York, 1976; and the more updated B. Tibi, "Der Amerikanische Area Studies–Approach in den International Studies," in *Orient* vol. 24, 2 (1983), pp. 260–284.

14. I owe Clifford Geertz a great many insights. My encounter with him during my term as a visiting research fellow at Princeton University in 1986–1987 and our ensuing debates form the background to my essay on his work, which is included in the German edition of his *Islam Observed,* Clifford Geertz, *Religiöse Entwicklungen im Islam beobachtet in Marokko und Indonesien,* with an essay by B. Tibi, Frankfurt/M, 1988. This acknowledgment notwith-

standing, my framework goes beyond Geertz, insofar as I do not confine my analysis to "culture," but rather attempt to place "culture" in the global society that forms the wider environment of any culture in the modern world. Geertz noted ironically during one of our enlightening communications at Princeton that "anthropologists view cultures as if they were islands," thus failing to discern the surrounding international society.

Part One

Introduction

1. See B. Tibi, *The Crisis of Modern Islam: A Preindustrial Culture in the Scientific-Technological Age,* Salt Lake City, 1988. See also the review by Fred Halliday in *The Times Literary Supplement* no. 489, April 14–20, 1989, pp. 387–388.

2. See the texts in John L. Esposito (ed.), *Voices of Resurgent Islam,* New York and Oxford, 1983; and the interpretation of B. Tibi, "The Renewed Role of Islam in the Political and Social Development of the Middle East," in *The Middle East Journal* vol. 37, 1 (1983), pp. 3–13 (originally given as a paper at the Middle East seminar of Harvard University, spring 1982; see the account in *Orient* vol. 23, 2, [1982], pp. 183–192).

Chapter 1: Religion as a Model for Reality and the Interaction Between the Two: Islam as a Cultural System

1. Clifford Geertz, *The Interpretation of Cultures,* New York, 1973, pp. 87ff.

2. Ibid., pp. 93f.

3. See the theoretical introduction by Geertz, ibid., pp. 3–30.

4. E. E. Evans-Pritchard, *Theorien über Primitive Religionen,* Frankfurt/M, 1968.

5. See Johan Bouman, *Gott und Mensch im Koran. Eine Strukturform religiöser Anthropologie anhand des Beispiels Allah und Muhammad,* Darmstadt, 1977.

6. Our question thus goes beyond that of Rodinson's formulation in his early but important essay (1961) "L'Islam, doctrine de progrès ou de réaction," in Rodinson's collection of essays, *Marxisme et Monde Musulman,* Paris, 1972, pp. 95ff.

7. Geertz, *Interpretation,* p. 93.

8. Ibid., p. 125.

9. T. W. Adorno, *Stichworte, Kritische Modelle 2,* 3d printing, Frankfurt/M, 1970, p. 189.

10. This line of thought also concerns Ernst Bloch in his book *Thomas Münzer als Theologe der Revolution,* Frankfurt/M, 1972, pp. 51ff., in which

he uses it strictly to repudiate the purely economic view, and specifically the inference of "convictional complexes . . . of a religious nature" (p. 55).

11. See B. Tibi, *Crisis of Modern Islam,* Salt Lake City, pp. 11–31.

12. See the published habilitation thesis of Franz Steinbacher, *Kultur, Begriff – Theorie – Funktion,* Stuttgart, 1976.

13. Geertz, *Interpretation,* pp. 29–30.

14. See Ch. 8 in Dale F. Eickelman, *The Middle East: An Anthropological Approach,* Englewood Cliffs, N.J., 1981, pp. 175ff., in which this concept is elaborated.

15. The great extent to which the political thinking of modern Muslims is pervaded by religiocultural symbols is documented in anthologies by John J. Donohue and John L. Esposito (eds.), *Islam in Transition: Muslim Perspectives,* Oxford, 1982 (see also my review in *The Middle East Journal* 4 [1982], pp. 614–616); and by Kemal Karpat (ed.), *The Political and Social Thought in the Contemporary Middle East,* 2d (substantially revised and expanded) ed., New York, 1982.

16. A review of these various approaches is made by Friedrich Fürstenberg (ed.), *Religionssoziologie,* Neuwied, 1964. See also the article by F. Fürstenberg and I. Mörth in vol. 14 of the *Handbuch der empirischen Sozialforschung,* ed. René König, 2d printing, Stuttgart, 1979, pp. 1–84; and the introduction by I. Mörth, *Die gesellschaftliche Wirklichkeit von Religion, Grundlegung einer allgemeinen Religionstheorie,* Stuttgart, 1978.

17. Geertz, *Interpretation,* p. 90.

18. Clifford Geertz, *Islam Observed: Religious Development in Morocco and Indonesia,* 2d printing, Chicago, 1971.

19. Dale F. Eickelman, *Moroccan Islam: Tradition and Society in a Pilgrimage Center,* Austin and London, 1976 (see also n. 14 above).

20. Gerhard Endress, *Einführung in die Islamische Geschichte,* Munich, 1982, p. 106.

21. Ibid., p. 31.

22. See N. J. Coulson, *A History of Islamic Law,* 3d printing, Edinburgh, 1978, pp. 139ff.

23. Geertz, *Interpretation,* p. 95.

24. Ibid., p. 99.

25. Ibid., p. 106.

26. Islam is also among the empirical subjects of Geertz's research (see n. 18 above); the essay cited here, however, dates from 1966, so that at that time he could not yet have been familiar with the phenomenon of "Islamic resurgence" (see n. 2 to the introduction to Part 1).

27. See Chapter 9 of this book and the essays by Ansari, Ibrahim, and Ayubi cited there.

28. Niklas Luhmann, *Funktion der Religion,* Frankfurt/M, 1977, p. 115.

29. Geertz, *Interpretation,* p. 109.

30. Ibid., p. 112.

31. Ibid.

32. Ibid., p. 123.

33. See Maxime Rodinson, *Islam und Kapitalismus,* Frankfurt/M 1971 (see my review in *Archiv für Rechts- und Sozialphilosophie,* vol. 59 [1973], pp. 155–158); and, more recently, Maxime Rodinson, *La Fascination de l'Islam,* Paris, 1980.

34. Edward Said, *Orientalism,* Cambridge, 1978; and E. Said, *Covering Islam,* New York, 1981.

35. On the Orientalism debate, its stock themes and exponents, see B. Tibi, "Orient und Okzident, Feindschaft oder interkulturelle Kommunikation? Anmerkungen zur Orientalismus-Debatte," in *Neue Politische Literatur* vol. 29, 3 (1984), pp. 267–286.

Chapter 2: What Is Islam? Islam in the Past and Present

1. See my detailed account of this in *Orient,* vol. 23 (1982), pp. 370–377 (on this point, pp. 375ff.). See also the report of the most important Dakar daily newspaper on this, "Islam et Cultures Africaines" in *Le Soleil* of 30 June 1982.

2. Mukti Ali, "Islam and Indonesian Culture," in Mourad Wahba (ed.), *Proceedings of the First Islamic Conference (19–22 Nov. 1979),* Cairo, 1982, pp. 15–34; and also my report, "Islamische Weltkonferenz über islamische Philosophie," in *Entwicklung und Zusammenarbeit* vol. 21, 2 (1980), pp. 11–12.

3. On these pillars of Islam, see the chapter by Alford T. Welch, "Das religiöse Leben der Muslime," in W. Montgomery Watt, *Der Islam I,* Stuttgart, 1980, pp. 262ff.

4. The Koran is quoted here in comparison to the Arabic original and with appropriate modification of the translation by N. J. Dawood, 4th revised ed., Harmondsworth, Middlesex, 1974.

5. In the Koran (sura 12, verse 2) it is written, for example, that God revealed the Koran "in the Arabic tongue." See also verse 16/103 and 26/195; B. Tibi, *Crisis of Modern Islam,* p. 62.

6. Rodinson develops this theme systematically with wide use of historical material in his work *Mohammed,* Lucerne and Frankfurt, 1975. See B. Tibi, "Religionssoziologische Anmerkungen zur Entstehung des Islam als einer mobilisatorischen Ideologie. Maxime Rodinsons Mohammed-Biographie," in *Archiv für Rechts- und Sozialphilosophie* vol. 64 (1978), pp. 547–556.

7. For details on this, see Watt, *Islam I,* pp. 17ff.; and Maxime Rodinson, *La Fascination de l'Islam,* Paris, 1980, pp. 19ff.

8. Theses on such an attempt are contained in B. Tibi, *The Crisis of Modern Islam: A Preindustrial Culture in the Scientific-Technological Age,* Salt Lake City, 1988, pp. 22ff., 57ff., and 67ff.

9. The life and work of Muhammed are examined in the two seminal works by W. M. Watt, *Muhammad at Medina,* 6th printing, Oxford, 1977, and *Muhammad at Mecca,* Oxford, 1953. See also W. M. Watt, *Muhammad, Prophet and Statesman,* 4th printing, Oxford, 1978. There is now also a very interesting

commemorative work for Watt, A. T. Welch and P. Cachia (eds.), *Islam: Past Influence and Present Challenge,* Albany, 1979.

10. The most comprehensive, reliable, and brilliant cultural history of Islam so far is contained in the life's work of Marshall G. S. Hodgson, *The Venture of Islam,* 3 vols., Chicago, 1974.

11. See on this S.H.M. Jafri, *The Origins and Early Development of Shi'a Islam,* London and Beirut, 1979. See also Moojan Momen, *An Introduction to Shi'a Islam,* New Haven, 1985, pp. 11ff, and 23ff.

12. Pierre Rondot, *Der Islam und die Mohammedaner von heute,* Stuttgart, 1963, pp. 211f.

13. A detailed account appears in J. J. Saunders, *A History of Medieval Islam,* 2d printing, London, 1978, pp. 95ff. Also worth reading is Abdalaziz Duri, *Arabische Wirtschaftsgeschichte,* trans. Jürgen Jacobi, Munich and Zurich, 1979, pp. 73ff.

14. Rodinson, *La Fascination,* p. 58.

15. B. Tibi, "Orient und Okzident, Feindschaft oder interkulturelle Kommunikation? Anmerkungen zur Orientalismus-Debatte," in *Neue Politische Literatur* vol. 29, 3 (1984), pp. 267–286.

16. On this and the following see B. Tibi, *Arab Nationalism, A Critical Inquiry,* London and New York, 1981, pp. 53ff., 62ff., and 135ff.

17. R. Hartmann, "Die Wahhabiten," in *Zeitschrift der Deutschen Morgenländischen Gesellschaft* vol. 78 (1924), part 2, pp. 176–213, particularly p. 177.

18. The American Afghani editor Nikki Keddie thus calls her collected texts *An Islamic Response to Imperialism,* 2d printing, Berkeley and Los Angeles, 1983.

19. On this see B. Tibi "Management und Kultur im Entwicklungsprozess, Bericht über eine entwicklungspolitische Konferenz in Kairo," in *Entwicklung und Zusammenarbeit* vol. 25, 3 (1984), pp. 29–30.

20. See Othman Amin, *Ra'id al-fikr al-misri. Mohammad Abduh* (A pioneer of Egyptian Thought: Mohammed Abduh), Cairo, 1955, pp. 141ff.; and also Charles C. Adams, *Islam and Modernism in Egypt,* 2d printing, New York, 1968 (first published in 1933).

21. This happened to me in Cairo when I expounded views along these lines in a paper on "Islam and Secularization" presented at the Islamic World Conference on Philosophy (see n. 2 above). (After hefty debate and corresponding delay, this lecture—see *Proceedings,* as in n. 2 above, pp. 65–80— was published in Cairo.)

22. An example of this is Ali al-Shabi, *al-Shi'a fi Iran* (Shi'a in Iran), Tunis, 1980, p. 5 and (in more detail) pp. 169ff.

23. Annemarie Schimmel, *Mystical Dimension of Islam,* Chapel Hill, 1978.

24. See case studies in Philip H. Stoddard, et al. (eds.), *Change and the Muslim World,* Syracuse, 1981.

25. In contrast to the philological research of Islamic scholarship, in anthropological research Islam as it is practiced forms the focal point of interest.

By way of contrast see the anthropological work of Michael Gilsenan, *Recognizing Islam: Religion and Society in the Modern Arab World,* New York, 1982; and the oriental scholarship publication of Peter Antes, *Ethik und Politik im Islam,* Stuttgart, 1982.

26. John Waterbury, *The Commander of the Faithful: The Moroccan Political Elite,* New York, 1970, p. 5.

27. R. A. Nicholson, *Islamic Mysticism,* 4th printing, Cambridge, 1980, p. 3.

28. Ibid., p. 50.

29. Ibid., p. 79.

30. Husain Ibn Mansur al-Hallaj, *Märtyrer der Gottesliebe,* Annemarie Schimmel (ed.), Cologne, 1968, p. 37.

31. Nicholson, *Islamic Mysticism.*

32. See B. Tibi, "Islam and Secularization, Religion and the Functional Differentiation of the Social System," in *Archiv für Rechts- und Sozialphilosophie* vol. 66 (1980), pp. 207–222; also printed in Mourad Wahba (ed.), *Youth, Violence, Religion, Secularization and Desecularization,* Cairo, 1983, pp. 69–86.

33. J. Spencer Trimmingham, *The Influence of Islam upon Africa,* London and Beirut, 1980, p. 5.

34. Ibid., p. 8.

35. See J. Spencer Trimmingham, *The Sufi Orders in Islam,* Oxford, 1971.

36. Trimmingham, *The Influence,* p. 9.

37. Ibid., p. 46.

38. Ibid., pp. 48ff.

39. Ibid., p. 74.

40. More on this in Dale F. Eickelman, *Moroccan Islam: Tradition and Society in a Pilgrimage Center,* Austin and London, 1976, pp. 65ff.

41. For the legal science perspective, see Brun-Otto Bryde, *The Politics and Sociology of African Legal Development,* Frankfurt/M, 1976, pp. 108ff. (see also my review of this in *Kölner Zeitschrift für Soziologie* no. 4 [1979], p. 821); as well as a general account in J.N.D. Anderson, *Islamic Law in Africa,* 2d printing, London, 1978.

42. M. Piamenta, *Islam in Everyday Arabic Speech,* Leiden, 1979, p. 1.

43. Well worth reading on this is the short but illuminating essay by Ernst Bloch, *Avicenna und die aristotelische Linke,* Frankfurt/M, 1963, which has unfortunately not been reprinted.

44. Johan Bouman, *Gott und Mensch im Koran, Eine Strukturform religiöser Anthropologie anhand des Beispiels Allah und Muhammad,* Darmstadt, 1977, p. 19.

45. Ibid., p. 30.

46. Ibid., p. 73.

47. Ibid., p. 229.

48. Ibid., p. 208.

49. Ibid., p. 101.

50. Ibid., p. 180.

Part Two

Chapter 3: Basic Cultural Patterns for the Perception of Change in Islam: The Islamic Model for Reality

1. The text below largely contains the results of my overview "Islam et Développement," prepared at the request of the Commission Française pour L'UNESCO. The survey served as a preparatory document for "Rencontres entre les Communautés Culturelles." See my report in *Orient* vol. 22 (1981), pp. 532–537.

2. These processes of internal differentiation within the Islamic religious system form the subject of Part 2, pp. 74ff., in B. Tibi, *Crisis of Modern Islam,* pp. 55ff.

3. See C. H. Becker, *Islamstudien, Vom Werden und Wesen der islamischen Welt,* 2 vols., 2d printing, Hildesheim, 1967 (originally published in Leipzig, 1924 and 1932).

4. These concepts originate from Johan Galtung, *Strukturelle Gewalt,* Reinbek and Hamburg, 1975, pp. 108ff., esp. pp. 120f.

5. The perception of these vexed questions in the works of six modern Islamic thinkers is analyzed by Rotraud Wielandt, *Offenbarung und Geschichte im Denken moderner Muslime,* Wiesbaden, 1971; on this see my review article in the collection of articles B. Tibi, *Internationale Politik und Entwicklungsländer-Forschung. Materialien zu einer ideologiekritischen Entwicklungssoziologie,* Frankfurt/M, 1979, pp. 136–140.

6. This confrontation forms the central stock theme in modern Muslim thought; for representative examples see the works of Hichem Djait, *Urubba wa'l-Islam* (Europe and Islam), Beirut, 1980 (U.S. ed., Hichem Djait, *Europe and Islam: Cultures and Modernity,* Berkeley, 1985); and Abdallah Laroui, *Azmat al-muthaqqafin al-'Arab* (The Crisis of Arab Intellectuals), Beirut, 1978 (French ed., *La Crise des intellectuels arabes,* Paris).

7. The only quoted representative documentation of this is the very widely distributed work of Yusuf al-Qardawi, *al-Hall al-Islami, farida wa darura* (The Islamic Solution is a Duty and a Necessity), Beirut, 1974. See also n. 23 to Chapter 8 below.

8. See H.A.R. Gibb and H. Bowen, *Islamic Society and the West: A Study of the Impact of Western Civilization on Moslem Culture in the Near East,* 2 vols., London, 1950 and 1957.

9. In the context of a comprehensive cultural history of Islam, this matter is dealt with in vol. 3 of Marshall G. S. Hodgson, *The Venture of Islam,* 3 vols., Chicago, 1974; see also Bernard Lewis, *The Middle East and the West,* 2d printing, New York, 1966.

10. An example of such an attempt to answer this question is the work, originally published in 1930 and still influential today, available in reprint, by Shakib Arslan, *Limadha ta'khara al-muslimun wa taqaddam gheirahum?* (English trans., *Our Decline and Its Causes,* 2d printing, London, 1952.)

11. An exhaustive account of this situation is given by Maxime Rodinson, *Muhammed,* Frankfurt and Lucerne, 1975, Chs. 1 and 2.

12. Montgomery Watt in conjunction with A. T. Welch, *Der Islam I,* Stuttgart, 1980, in the chapter entitled "Ursprung und Werden des Islams," pp. 39–161; see p. 97. (On Watt, see n. 9 on Chapter 2 above and the literature given there.

13. Watt and Welch, "Ursprung und Werden," p. 46.

14. Johan Bouman, *Gott und Mensch im Koran, Eine Strukturform religiöser Anthropologie anhand des Beispiels Allah und Muhammad,* Darmstadt, 1977, p. 226.

15. Ibid., p. 229.

16. See W. M. Watt, *What is Islam?* new ed., London and New York, 1979.

17. This *shari'a* legal position was representatively propounded by Sabir Tu'aima, *al-Sha'ria al-Islamiyya fi 'asr al-'ilm* (Islamic Law in the Age of Science), Beirut, 1979, pp. 208ff.

18. Thus in Iran the people's *mojahedin* (*mojahedin-e khalq*) are condemned and executed as *murtaddun* (apostates) even if they are lying wounded on the street.

19. Watt, *Der Islam I,* p. 170; see also R. Bell and W. M. Watt, *Introduction to the Qur'an,* 2d printing, Edinburgh, 1977; and Rudi Paret, *Mohammed und der Koran,* 4th printing, Stuttgart, 1976.

20. On the early epoch of the Islamic schism between Sunna and Shi'a, see S.H.M. Jafri, *The Origins and Early Development of Shi'a Islam,* London, 1979. See also Moojan Momen, *An Introduction to Shi'a Islam,* New Haven, 1985.

21. Hamdy M. Azzam, *Der Islam, Plädoyer eines Moslem,* Stuttgart, 1981, pp. 130f.

22. On modern Koranic exegesis, see J.M.S. Baljon, *Modern Muslim Koran Interpretation (1880–1960),* Leiden, 1968; and J.J.G. Jansen, *The Interpretation of the Koran in Modern Egypt,* Leiden, 1974.

23. Watt, *Der Islam I,* p. 17.

24. See Charles C. Adams, *Islam and Modernism in Egypt: A Study of the Early Modern Reform Movement,* 2d printing, New York, 1968 (originally published in 1933).

25. Watt, *Der Islam I,* p. 17.

26. Ibid., p. 75.

27. See W. M. Watt, *Islamic Philosophy and Theology,* 5th printing, Edinburgh, 1979, pp. 37ff.

28. At the First Islamic Conference on Islam and Civilization, the Egyptian philosopher Mourad Wahba first coined the term "the paradox of Averroës" (*mufaraqat Ibn Rushd*), whereby he sought to describe the positive evaluation of Islamic rationalism during the European Renaissance and the contempt in which it was held in the Islamic Orient. See Mourad Wahba, "The Paradox of Averroës," in *Archiv für Rechts- und Sozialphilosophie* vol. 66 (1980), pp. 257ff. See the article in *Historisches Wörterbuch der Philosophie* (ed. J. Ritter), vol. 1, pp. 724ff. (on Averroism) and vol. 2, pp. 585ff. (on the dual nature of truth).

29. See Wahba, "The Paradox of Averroës."

30. Details may be found in T. J. de Boer, *Geschichte der Philosophie im Islam,* Stuttgart, 1901. The Arabic translation of this work, *Tarikh al-falsafa fi'l-Islam,* Cairo, 1957, by the Egyptian professor of philosophy Muhammed 'Abdulhadi Abu-Zaida (University of Cairo), is similarly regarded in Arabic as a standard work on Islamic philosophy.

31. See B. Tibi, "Islam and Secularization, Religion and the Functional Differentiation of the Social System," in *Archiv für Rechts- und Sozialphilosophie* vol. 66 (1980), pp. 207–222.

32. Watt, *Der Islam I,* p. 232.

33. Right-wing radical militant Islam is as a rule the consequence of this definition. See G. H. Jansen, *Militant Islam,* New York, 1979; and the now classic study on the Muslim Brotherhood that has even been translated into Arabic: Richard P. Mitchell, *The Society of Muslim Brothers,* Oxford and London, 1969; and, more recently, E. Sivan, *Political Islam,* New Haven, 1985.

34. See Frank Rotter, "Verfassungsrechtliche Möglichkeiten der Institutionalisierung des sozialen Wandels," in *Jahrbuch für Rechtssoziologie und Rechtstheorie,* vol. 2 (1972), pp. 87–137.

35. The literature on this is given in n. 41 to Chapter 2.

36. See W. M. Watt, *Muhammad, Prophet and Statesman,* 4th printing, Oxford, 1978.

37. See Joseph Schacht, *An Introduction to Islamic Law,* 5th printing, Oxford, 1979; and N. J. Coulson, *A History of Islamic Law,* 3d printing, Edinburgh, 1978, as well as Chapter 5 of this book.

38. Schacht, *Introduction to Islamic Law,* p. 1.

39. But see Subhi al-Salih, *Ma'alim al-Shari'a al-Islamiyya* (Basic Features of Islamic Law), Beirut, 1975, p. 116.

40. Schacht, *Introduction to Islamic Law,* pp. 94ff.

41. An economic history survey is provided by the Iraqi historian Duri in the introduction to his book, which appeared in Arabic in Beirut in 1969 and is now available in German translation: Abdalaziz Duri, *Arabische Wirtschaftsgeschichte,* Zurich and Munich, 1979.

42. Maxime Rodinson, *Islam und Kapitalismus,* Frankfurt/M, 1971, pp. 64ff. (originally published as *Islam et capitalisme,* Paris, 1966).

43. See Sa'id Bensa'id, *Daulat al-khilafa* (The Caliphate State), ad-Dar al-Baida' (Casablanca), no date; as well as the general account given by Thomas W. Arnold in *The Caliphate,* 2d printing, London, 1965 (originally published in 1924).

44. Schacht, *Introduction to Islamic Law,* pp. 54ff.

45. This issue will be discussed in detail in Chapter 5.

46. See n. 33 and n. 35 to Chapter 2.

47. See Chapter 7 of this book.

48. Watt, *Der Islam I,* p. 24.

49. On both these aspects of the encounter between the Middle East and the West under new global conditions, see B. Tibi, *Arab Nationalism: A Critical Enquiry,* ed. and trans. Marion Farouk-Sluglett and Peter Sluglett, London, 1981, pp. 53ff. and 70ff.

50. See Lewis, *The Middle East and the West.* See also Bernard Lewis, *The Emergence of Modern Turkey,* 2d ed., Oxford, 1979, Chapter 3 "The Impact of the West," pp. 40–73; and Tibi, *Arab Nationalism.*

51. Rifa'a R. At-Tahtawi, *Takhlis al-ibriz ila talkhis Baris* (The Refinement of Gold Toward the Summarizing Description of Paris), German trans. Karl Stowasser, *Ein Muslim entdeckt Europa, Die Reise eines Ägypters im 19. Jh. nach Paris,* Munich, 1989, p. 150 (originally published in 1834).

52. See Tibi, *Crisis of Modern Islam* and Tibi, *Arab Nationalism.*

53. Tahtawi, *Ein Muslim entdeckt Europa,* p. 9.

54. See Chapter 10 of this book.

55. See "Conclusions: Future Prospects for Islam," in Tibi *Crisis of Modern Islam,* pp. 127–148.

56. Recent insightful works on the "Islamic republic" established by the leader of the Iranian revolution, the late Khomeini, include Cheryl Bernard and Zalmay Khalilzad, *"The Government of God": Iran's Islamic Republic,* New York, 1984; R. K. Ramazani, *Revolutionary Iran: Challenge and Response in the Middle East,* Baltimore, 1986; Said Amir Arjomand, *The Turban for the Crown: The Islamic Revolution in Iran,* New York, 1988.

Chapter 4: Culture and Social Change: Is Underdevelopment a Given of Cultural Tradition? The Problem of Cultural Innovation in Sociology

1. Reprinted in Hans Peter Dreitzel (ed.), *Sozialer Wandel,* Neuwied, 1967, pp. 239ff., particularly p. 242.

2. Ibid., p. 243.

3. Ibid., p. 244.

4. Gerhard Brandt, "Industrialisierung, Modernisierung, gesellschaftliche Entwicklung, Anmerkungen zum gegenwärtigen Stand gesamtgesellschaftlicher Analysen," in *Zeitschrift für Soziologie* vol. 1, 1 (1972), pp. 5f.

5. On the virginity issue and sexuality as a cultural dimension in Islam, see Dale F. Eickelman, *The Middle East: An Anthropological Approach,* Englewood Cliffs, N.J., 1981, pp. 127ff. and 141 ff.

6. Daniel Lerner, *The Passing of Traditional Society,* Glencoe, Ill., 1958.

7. In the article "Nord-Süd-Konflikt" by B. Tibi in W. W. Mickel (ed.), *Handlexikon zur Politikwissenschaft,* Munich, 1983, pp. 313–318, an attempt is made to define the highly complex and multidimensional structures (economy, politics, culture) of underdevelopment and to make a plea for overcoming monocausal, unidimensional explanatory models.

8. See B. Tibi, "Entwicklungspolitik ist kein Feld für exotisch-romantische Sehnsüchte," in *Entwicklung und Zusammenarbeit (E+Z)* vol. 23, 2 (1982), pp. 2–4; and B. Tibi, "Wissenschaft kontra entwicklungspolitischen Dilettantismus, Nachbemerkungen zur entwicklungspolitischen Wissenschaftsbörse in Bonn," in *E+Z* vol. 24, 2 (1983) pp. 7–8.

9. Clifford Geertz, *The Interpretation of Cultures,* New York, 1973, p. 13.

10. Ibid., p. 14.

11. Karl Marx, "Die Britische Kolonialherrschaft in Indien," in Marx and Engels, *Werke,* vol. 9, East Berlin, 1960, pp. 127ff., particularly p. 133.

12. W. Hauck, "Das Elend der bürgerlichen Entwicklungstheorie," in B. Tibi and V. Brandes (eds.), *Unterentwicklung,* Cologne, 1975, pp. 36–63; and Walter L. Bühl, *Evolution and Revolution, Kritik der symmetrischen Soziologie,* Munich, 1970. See also B. Tibi, *Militär und Sozialismus in der Dritten Welt,* Frankfurt/M, 1973, pp. 11ff.

13. Hugo C. F. Mansilla, *Entwicklung als Nachahmung. Zu einer kritischen Theorie der Modernisierung,* Meisenheim/Glan, 1978; and F. Nuscheler, "Bankrott der Modernisierungstheorie?" in D. Nohlen and F. Nuscheler (eds.), *Handbuch der Dritten Welt,* vol. 1, Hamburg, 1974, pp. 195ff.

14. Thomas Kuhn, *Structure of Scientific Revolutions,* Chicago, 1962.

15. S. N. Eisenstadt, *Tradition, Wandel, Modernität,* Frankfurt/M, 1979.

16. Ibid., p. 136. It is for this reason that Eisenstadt is considered to be a historical sociologist in the work of Theda Skocpol, the leading exponent of historical sociology as a new school of thought. See the chapter on Eisenstadt by Gary Hamilton in *Vision and Method in Historical Sociology,* ed. Theda Skocpol, 4th printing, Cambridge, 1987, pp. 85–128.

17. Eisenstadt, *Tradition,* p. 373.

18. Ibid., pp. 92f.

19. Ibid., pp. 237f. A relevant monograph on this is Bryan S. Turner, *Weber and Islam,* London, 1974; and, more recently, the proceedings of an international conference on *Max Webers Sicht des Islams, Interpretation und Kritik,* ed. Wolfgang Schluchter, Frankfurt/M, 1987. See also my critical review of this volume in *Kölner Zeitschrift für Soziologie und Sozialpsychologie* no. 4 (1988), pp. 808–810.

20. On Afghani, see the biography by Nikki Keddie, *Sayyid Jamal ad-Din al-Afghani,* Berkeley and Los Angeles, 1972; as well as the selected texts of Afghani edited by Keddie and published under the title *An Islamic Response to Imperialism,* 2d printing, Berkeley and Los Angeles, 1983.

21. Afghani, *al-A'mal al kamila* (Collected Works), one vol. Muhammed 'Imara (ed.), Cairo, 1968, p. 328.

22. See B. Tibi, *Arab Nationalism,* pp. 62ff.

23. Eisenstadt, *Tradition,* pp. 242f.

24. Maxime Rodinson, *Mohammed,* Frankfurt and Lucerne, 1975.

25. Niklas Luhmann, *Funktion der Religion,* Frankfurt, 1977.

26. Eisenstadt, *Tradition,* p. 206.

27. Ibid., p. 208.

28. B. Tibi, "Religionsstiftung, Islam und Psychoanalyse," in *Psyche, Zeitschrift für Psychoanalyse und ihre Anwendungen* vol. 33 (1979), pp. 773–783.

29. See the pathfinding work of Hedley Bull, *The Anarchical Society: A Study of Order in World Politics,* New York, 1977; and *The Expansion of International Society,* ed. Hedley Bull and Adam Watson, 3d printing, Oxford, 1988.

30. Eisenstadt, *Tradition,* p. 137.

31. Ibid., p. 277.

32. In this context see B. Tibi, "Cultural Innovation in the Developmental process of the Islamic Middle East as a Future Perspective," in *Archiv für Rechts- und Sozialphilosophie* vol. 67 (1981), pp. 545–550.

33. Eisenstadt, *Tradition,* p. 359.

34. With reference to Arab forms of self-glorification as a cultural variant of this phenomenon, see B. Tibi, "Von der Selbstverherrlichung zur Selbstkritik," in *Die Dritte Welt* vol. 1 (1972), pp. 158–184.

35. This form of protest ends in romanticism and nostalgia.

36. René König (ed.), *Aspekte der Entwicklungssoziologie,* Cologne and Opladen, 1969, p. 30 (italics in the original).

37. Maria Mies, "Kulturanomie als Folge westlicher Bildung," in *Die Dritte Welt* vol. 1 (1972), pp. 23–38. See the recent monograph on this issue, Marco Orru, *Anomie: History and Meaning,* London: 1987.

38. See the introduction in B. Tibi, *The Crisis of Modern Islam: A Preindustrial Culture in the Scientific-Technological Age,* Salt Lake City, 1988, pp. 1–8.

39. Eisenstadt, *Tradition,* p. 352.

40. Ingo Mörth, "Vom Pluralismus zum Integrismus, Aspekte religiösen Alltagsbewusstseins," in *Schweizerische Zeitschrift für Soziologie* vol. 9, 3 (1983), pp. 559–578; and also I. Mörth, *Die gesellschaftliche Wirklichkeit der Religion,* Stuttgart, 1978.

41. See B. Toprak, *Islam and Political Development in Turkey,* Leiden, 1981.

42. On the Egyptian variant of Fabian socialism see the remarkable monograph by Vernon Egger, *A Fabian in Egypt: Salamah Musa and the Rise of the Professional Classes in Egypt, 1909–1939,* Lanham and New York, 1986.

43. Fuad Kandil, *Nativismus in der Dritten Welt, Wiederentdeckung der Tradition für die Gegenwart,* St. Michael (Austria) 1983. The empirical part of Kandil's study is concerned with Egyptian Islam.

44. Ibid., p. 21.

Part Three

Introduction

1. On the definition of Islam as an organic religious system, see B. Tibi, "The Renewed Role of Islam in the Political and Social Development of the Middle East," *The Middle East Journal* vol. 37 (1983), pp. 3–13, particularly pp. 4f.; see also Donald E. Smith, *Religion and Political Modernization,* New Haven, 1974.

2. See my comprehensive report on this Bonn meeting of the Christian-Muslim dialogue in *Orient* vol. 22 (1981), pp. 172–176.

3. See the case studies in Ellen K. Trimberger, *Revolution from Above,* New Brunswick, N.J., 1978. Recent research on social revolutions highlights the structural component of change. Moreover, this structural transformation is being made into an element of the definition of a social revolution. See the remarkable work by Theda Skocpol, *States and Social Revolutions,* 11th printing, Cambridge, 1987.

4. The great importance of Islam in contemporary Turkey, in spite of Kemal Atatürk's "secularization from above," is shown by B. Toprak in *Islam and Political Development in Turkey,* Leiden, 1981; see especially pp. 20ff.

5. See B. Tibi, "Cultural Innovation in the Developmental Process of the Islamic Middle East as a Future Perspective," in *Archiv für Rechts- und Sozialphilosophie,* vol. 67 (1981), pp. 545–550.

6. A personal comment at the Association of Arab American University Graduates (AAUG) conference in Boston in 1971; see, however, the translation of one of these pre-Islamic ballads by Jacques Berque, *Cultural Expression in Arab Society Today* (originally *Languages arabes du présent*), Austin and London, 1978, pp. 110ff. (pp. 337ff., Appendix A, in the French).

7. See B. Tibi, *The Crisis of Modern Islam: A Preindustrial Culture in the Scientific-Technological Age,* Salt Lake City, 1988, Chapter 7, pp. 95–112.

8. Ernst Bloch, *Avicenna und die aristotelische Linke,* Frankfurt/M, 1963, in which this conflict is explained superbly.

Chapter 5: Social Change and the Potential for Flexibility in the Islamic Notion of Law: The Shari'a *as an "Open Texture," Legal Hermeneutics, and the Topics Thesis*

1. H.L.A. Hart, *The Concept of Law,* 2d printing, Oxford, 1970, p. 221. I am greatly obliged to my Göttingen colleague Ralf Dreier of the law school for his critical reading of an earlier draft of this chapter and for his valuable comments, which contributed to this revised version. The problem underlying the relevance to world peace of the urgently needed reform of Islamic law, in terms of *rethinking Islamic legal philosophy,* is that on the one hand we have an international law of clearly European origin, and, on the other, that we must deal with varieties of cultures, each of which has its own legal tradition. Islam is in this respect only a case in point. See the classic, fortunately reprinted, work by F.S.C. Northrop, *The Taming of the Nations: A Study of the Cultural Basis of International Policy,* 2d ed., Woodbridge, Conn., 1987. The basic issues of international law are discussed by Terry Nardin, *Law, Morality and the Relations of States,* Princeton, 1983.

2. Ralf Dreier, *Recht – Moral – Ideologie. Studien zur Rechtstheorie,* Frankfurt/M, 1981, p. 24.

3. Reinhard May, *Frieden und die Aufgabe des Rechts. Rechtstheoretischer Versuch zur Friedensforschung im rechtsvergleichenden Bereich unter Einschluss einer Darstellung chinesischen Rechtsverständnisses,* Wiesbaden, 1979, preface, pp. 4ff.

4. Helmuth Plessner, *Die verspätete Nation,* Frankfurt/M, 1974, p. 35.

5. See Niklas Luhmann, "Die Weltgesellschaft," in *Archiv für Rechts- und Sozialphilosophie,* vol. 57 (1971), pp. 1–35.

6. See Brun-Otto Bryde, *The Politics and Sociology of African Legal Development,* Frankfurt/M, 1976; as well as my review in *Archiv für Rechts- und Sozialphilosophie,* vol. 65 (1979), pp. 433f. Bryde elucidates the dominance of customary law but shows parallel to this the superimposition of European and Islamic law. Studies on Islamic-African legal variations in individual countries are contained in the volume by J.N.D. Anderson, *Islamic Law in Africa,* 3d printing, London, 1978.

7. Reinhard May, *Frieden,* p. 22.

8. Theodor Viehweg, *Topik und Jurisprudenz. Ein Beitrag zur rechts- wissenschaftlichen Grundlagenforschung,* 5th printing, Munich, 1974, p. 118.

9. For an authentic account, see Subhi Salih, *Ma'alim ash-shari'a al- islamiyya* (Essential Characteristics of Islamic Law), Beirut, 1975, pp. 122ff.

10. On this discussion, see B. Tibi, "Akkulturation und interkulturelle Kommunikation," in *Gegenwartskunde,* vol. 29, 2 (1980), pp. 173–190.

11. W. M. Watt, *Islamic Political Thought: The Basic Concepts,* Edinburgh, 1969, p. 91.

12. On Huntington's concept of institutionalization, see his work *Political Order in Changing Societies,* 2d printing, New Haven, 1969; and Frank Rotter, *Verfassung und sozialer Wandel,* Hamburg, 1974, especially pp. 59ff. On the discussion as a whole, see B. Tibi, "Schwache Institutionalisierung als politische Dimension der Unterentwicklung," in *Verfassung und Recht in Übersee,* vol. 13, 1 (1980), pp. 3–26, especially Part 4.

13. Dreier, *Recht – Moral – Ideologie,* pp. 116–117.

14. Maxime Rodinson, *Mohammed,* Lucerne and Frankfurt, 1975, p. 27.

15. See B. Tibi, *The Crisis of Modern Islam: A Preindustrial Culture in the Scientific-Technological Age,* Salt Lake City, 1988, pp. 57–66.

16. Joseph Schacht, *An Introduction to Islamic Law,* 5th printing, Oxford, 1979, p. 1.

17. For a detailed account, see contributions in Nikki Keddie (ed.), *Scholars, Saints and Sufis: Muslim Religious Institutions in the Middle East Since 1500,* Berkeley and Los Angeles, 1972; see in particular the editor's introduction.

18. See n. 6 to the introduction to this Part 3.

19. On the Koran, see Rudi Paret, *Mohammed und der Koran,* 4th printing, Stuttgart, 1976; as well as the internationally leading monograph by R. Bell and W. M. Watt, *Introduction to the Qur'an,* 2d printing, Edinburgh, 1977. Interesting interpretations of the Koran are given by Johan Bouman, *Gott und Mensch im Koran. Eine Strukturform religiöser Anthropologie anhand des Beispiels Allah und Muhammad,* Darmstadt, 1977.

20. On the interpretation of revelation in Islam, see W. M. Watt, *Islamic Revelation in the Modern World,* Edinburgh, 1969.

21. See the introduction to N. J. Coulson, *A History of Islamic Law,* 3d printing, Edinburgh, 1978.

22. Ibid., pp. 139ff. On the economic history of this period of flowering, see the German translation of the work by the Iraqi historian Abdalaziz Duri,

Arabische Wirtschaftsgeschichte, trans. Jürgen Jacobi, Zurich and Munich, 1979 (originally published in Arabic in Beirut, 1969).

23. Maxime Rodinson, *Islam und Kapitalismus,* Frankfurt, 1971, p. 77. See also my introduction ("Maxime Rodinson, der Islam und die westlichen Islam-Studien") to the 2d ed. of this book (1986) on the work of Rodinson, pp. ix–li.

24. John Waterbury, *The Commander of the Faithful: The Moroccan Political Elite,* New York, 1970, p. 5.

25. I shall be dealing in Chapter 6 with the conflict between scientific and sacral language in Arab Islamic history. On the relationship between law and language, see T. Viehweg and F. Rotter (eds.), *Recht und Sprache,* Wiesbaden, 1977 (supplement no. 9 of *Archiv für Rechts- und Sozialphilosophie*).

26. Salih, *Ma'alim ash-shari'a,* pp. 89ff.

27. Ibid., pp. 113ff.

28. On this distinction, see the introduction in Donald E. Smith (ed.), *Religion and Political Modernization,* New Haven and London, 1974.

29. Salih, *Ma'alim ash-shari'a,* p. 116.

30. Mohammed T. Ben-Ashur, *Maqasid ash-shari'a al-islamiyya* (The Aims of Islamic Law), Tunis, 1978, p. 64.

31. I may mention here, as the best problem-oriented introductions to the *shari'a,* the two internationally known monographs Schacht, *An Introduction;* and Coulson, *A History.*

32. See W. M. Watt, *Muhammad at Medina,* 6th printing, Oxford, 1977.

33. Marshall S. G. Hodgson, *The Venture of Islam,* 3 vols., Chicago, 1974.

34. Sabir Tu'aima, *ash-Shari'a al-islamiyya fi 'asr al-'ilm* (Islamic Law in the Age of Science), Beirut, 1979, pp. 208ff.

35. Ibid., p. 223.

36. See N. J. Dawood's translation of the Koran, 4th revised ed., Harmondsworth, Middlesex, 1974, pp. 320ff.

37. May, *Frieden,* p. 23.

38. See Tibi, "Akkulturation."

39. The cultural history of the golden age of High Islam is dealt with by Hodgson, *The Venture;* the economic history by Duri, *Arabische Wirtschaftsgeschichte;* and the philosophical history by T. J. de Boer, *Geschichte der Philosophie im Islam,* Stuttgart, 1901; as well as by T. Tisini, *Die Materieauffassung in der islamisch-arabischen Philosophie des Mittelalters,* East Berlin, 1972.

40. W. M. Watt, *Islamic Philosophy and Theology,* 5th printing, Edinburgh, 1979, pp. 37ff. and 91 ff.

41. On the problem of the sacral definition of Arabic, see Chapter 6 of this book.

42. Ernst Bloch, *Avicenna und die aristotelische Linke,* Frankfurt/M, 1963, p. 45.

43. M. Wahba, "The Paradox of Averroës," in *Archiv für Rechts- und Sozialphilosophie* vol. 66 (1980), pp. 257–260.

44. B. Tibi, "Islam and Secularization, Religion and the Functional Differentiation of the Social System," in *Archiv für Rechts- und Sozialphilosophie* vol. 66 (1980), pp. 207–222.

45. Niklas Luhmann, *Funktion der Religion,* Frankfurt/M, 1977.

46. Josef Esser, *Vorverständnis und Methodenwahl in der Rechtsfindung,* Frankfurt/M, 1970, p. 32.

47. Hart, *The Concept of Law,* p. 102.

48. Esser, *Vorverständnis,* p. 153.

49. Kriele quoted after ibid., p. 153.

50. On this see Schacht, *Introduction,* pp. 57ff.

51. See Charles C. Adams, *Islam and Modernism in Egypt: A Study of the Modern Reform Movement,* 2d printing, London, 1968 (first published in 1933).

52. See Norman Anderson, *Law Reform in the Muslim World,* London, 1976.

53. Viehweg, *Topik und Jurisprudenz,* p. 31.

54. Ibid., p. 31.

55. Ibid., p. 34.

56. Ibid., p. 38.

57. Ibid., p. 42.

58. Ibid. It is possible to say today that the topics thesis has made inroads into juristic hermeneutics: The influence of philosophical hermeneutics is clear. See Erwin Hufnagel, *Einführung in die Hermeneutik,* Stuttgart, 1976; and the useful reader by Otto Pöggeler (ed.), *Hermeneutische Philosophie,* Munich, 1972 (including contributions by Dilthey, Gadamer, et al.).

59. See B. Tibi, "Islam und sozialer Wandel im modernen Orient," in *Archiv für Rechts- und Sozialphilosophie* vol. 65 (1979) pp. 485–502; or the English version, "Islam and Social Change in the Modern Middle East," in *Law and State* vol. 22 (1980), pp. 91–106.

60. Ali Abdelraziq, *al-Islam wa usul al-hukm,* Cairo, 1925 (reprinted Beirut, 1966), French trans. in *Revue des Etudes Islamiques* vol. 7 (1933) and vol. 8 (1934). On Abdelraziq, see B. Tibi, *Arab Nationalism,* New York, 1981, pp. 144ff.

61. Malcolm Kerr, *Islamic Reform: The Political and Legal Theories of Muhammad Abduh and Rashid Rida,* Berkeley and Los Angeles, 1966. Kerr was murdered by Muslim fanatics in Beirut in January 1984.

62. Muhammad Muslehuddin, *Philosophy of Islamic Law and the Orientalists: A Comparative Study of Islamic Legal System,* Lahore (Pakistan), undated, p. 247.

63. Ibid., p. 242.

64. Viehweg, *Topik,* p. 40.

65. Muslehuddin, *Philosophy of Islamic Law,* p. 242.

66. Esser, *Vorverständnis,* p. 135.

67. N. J. Coulson, *Conflicts and Tensions in Islamic Jurisprudence,* Chicago, 1969, p. 2; see also Coulson, "The Concept of Progress and Islamic Law," in Robert N. Bellah (ed.), *Religion and Progress in Modern Asia,* New

York, 1965, pp. 74–92; as well as N. J. Coulson and Norman Anderson, "Modernization: Islamic Law," in Michael Brett (ed.), *Northern Africa: Islam and Modernization,* London, 1973, pp. 73–83.

68. Muslehuddin, *Philosophy of Islamic Law.*

69. See, however, the uncritical contribution by George M. Baroody, "The Practice of Law in Saudi Arabia," in Willard A. Beling (ed.), *King Faisal and the Modernization of Saudi Arabia,* London, 1980, pp. 113–124.

70. For a very insightful, knowledgeable, and sound interpretation of Islamic law, see Ann Elisabeth Mayer, "Law and Religion in the Muslim Middle East," in *The American Journal of Comparative Law* vol. 35, 1 (1987), pp. 127–184.

Chapter 6: 'Arabiyya *as a Sacred Language: Arabic as a Language Between Koranic and Historical Designations*

1. Helmut Seiffert, *Sprache Heute,* Munich, 1977, p. 14. The draft from which this chapter emerged was discussed with my Göttingen colleague, the Swiss linguist Gustav Ineichen, to whom I am also greatly indebted for his critical reading of the revised draft. I owe him some important sociolinguistic insights.

2. See W. M. Watt, *Islamic Philosophy and Theology,* Edinburgh, 1961, pp. 37ff., and 91ff.

3. Walther Braune, *Der islamische Orient zwischen Vergangenheit und Zukunft,* Bern and Munich, 1960.

4. See Gustav Ineichen, *Allgemeine Sprachtypologie,* Darmstadt, 1979, Chapters 1 and 10; and Paul Henle et al., *Sprache, Denken, Kultur,* Frankfurt/M, 1975, especially Chapter 1.

5. Mohammad A. Lahbabi, *Ta'ammulat fi al-laghu wa al-lugha* (Reflections on Linguistics and Language), Tunis, 1980, p. 104.

6. Lahbabi, *Ta'ammulat,* p. 141.

6a. Ineichen, *Allgemeine Sprachtypologie,* p. 14.

7. Seiffert, *Sprache Heute,* p. 14.

8. Maxime Rodinson, *La Fascination de l'Islam,* Paris, 1980, p. 106. See the discussion on this in B. Tibi, "Orient und Okzident. Feindschaft oder interkulturelle Kommunikation? Anmerkungen zur Orientalismus-Debatte," in *Neue Politische Literatur* vol. 29, 3 (1984), pp. 267–286, particularly pp. 272ff.

9. Henle et al., *Sprache,* p. 32.

10. Ibid., p. 31.

11. Ibid., p. 39.

12. See W. Diem, "Über eine Einführung in europäische Sprachwissenschaft auf Arabisch," in *Welt des Islam* n.s., vol. 13, 1–2 (1971), pp. 11–19.

13. Muhieddin Ismail, "Ma'al al-'Arabiyya fi 'araqatuha" (*'Arabiyya* in its Original Form) in *al-Adab* vol. 16, 8 (1968), pp. 25–27.

14. CERES (ed.), *al-Lisaniyyat wa al-lugha al-'Arabiyya* (Linguistics and the Arabic Language) Lisaniyyat series, vol. 4, Tunis, 1981.

15. On the role of language in the concept of German popular nationalism and on the influence of this concept on Arab nationalism, see B. Tibi, *Arab Nationalism,* New York, 1981, pp. 101–111 and 117–122; see also the discussion of my theses by Stephan Wild, *Sprachpolitik und Nationalismus,* Leiden, 1975.

16. See Hanna Fakhuri, *Tarikh al-adab al-'arabi* (History of Arabic Literature), 3d printing, Damascus, 1960, pp. 20–32. See also pp. 58ff.

17. Maxime Rodinson, *Mohammed,* Lucerne and Frankfurt, 1975, p. 27.

18. Maxime Rodinson, *Islam und Kapitalismus,* Frankfurt, 1971, p. 131.

19. T. J. de Boer, *Geschichte der Philosophie im Islam,* Stuttgart, 1901, pp. 34f. (my italics).

20. Ibid., p. 34.

21. Ibid., pp. 37f.

22. Ibid., p. 36.

23. Quoted after T. J. de Boer, *Geschichte,* p. 37 (my italics).

24. See W. S. Freund, "Religionssoziologie und sprachkulturelle Aspekte des Entwicklungsproblems in der Islamischen Welt," in *Internationales Jahrbuch für Religionssoziologie* vol. 7 (1971), pp. 105–126.

25. For details see Chapter 7 of this book.

26. Ernst Bloch, *Avicenna und die aristotelische Linke,* Frankfurt/M, 1963, p. 62.

27. Ibid., p. 18.

28. Ibid., p. 45.

29. Maxime Rodinson, *Islam und Kapitalismus,* p. 131.

30. Ibid., pp. 140ff.

31. Ibid., pp. 160f.

32. Ibid., p. 91.

33. Ibid., p. 78. See also the second edition of this book by Rodinson and my introduction.

34. On the social history of the Islamic Middle Ages, see S. G. Goitein, "The Rise of Near-Eastern Bourgeoisie in the Early Islamic Times," in *Journal of World History* vol. 3, 3 (1957), pp. 583–604. See in particular, however, Maxime Rodinson, *Islam und Kapitalismus,* pp. 56ff.; and my introduction to the second edition.

35. References to translations of Ibn Khaldun's *Prolegomena* into European languages, as well as secondary literature on this, may be found in Tibi, *Arab Nationalism,* pp. 112ff.

36. Freund, "Religionssoziologie," p. 116.

37. Ibid., p. 117.

38. Rodinson, *Islam und Kapitalismus,* p. 247.

39. Z. Chaabani, *Der Einfluss des Französischen auf das Arabische in Tunesien,* Frankfurt and Bern, 1984. The first authority was a Swiss colleague, the well-known Romance linguist and Arabist Gustav Ineichen. See ns. 1 and 4 to this chapter.

40. A. Abboud, *Deutsche Romane im arabischen Orient,* Frankfurt and Bern, 1984. The cosupervisor was a Frankfurt colleague, the well-known

Germanist Norbert Altenhofer. See my review of Abboud's book in *The Middle East Journal* vol. 39, 4 (1985), pp. 869–871.

41. On Tahtawi's life and works, see the highly informative dossier in the Cairo periodical *at-Tali'a* vol. 3, 6 (1967), pp. 152–186. See also Tibi, *Arab Nationalism,* pp. 58–62, which gives a complete list of literature on Tahtawi. Tahtawi's Paris diary is also available in German translation by Karl Stowasser, *Ein Muslim entdeckt Europa,* Munich, 1989. On Tahtawi's Paris diary, see also B. Tibi, "Akkulturationsprozesse im modernen Orient," in *Neue Politische Literatur* vol. 15, 1 (1971), pp. 77–84.

42. See James Heyworth-Dunne, "Arabic Literature in Egypt in the Eighteenth Century," in *Bulletin of the School of Oriental Studies* no. 9 (1937–1939), pp. 675–689. See also J. Heyworth-Dunne, *An Introduction to the History of Education in Modern Egypt,* 2d ed., London, 1968, especially pp. 1–95, which deal with education in the eighteenth century.

43. See the German translation of Tahtawi's *Takhlis al-Ibriz fi talkhis,* Paris, p. 148 (see n. 41 above).

44. Ibid., p. 150.

45. On these aspects, see Tibi, *Arab Nationalism,* pp. 58ff.

46. On the problem of translating into Arabic from European languages, see B. Tibi, "Hawl harakat tarjamat al-a'mal al-'ilmiyya wa al-adabiyya mina al-lughat al-urubiyya ila al-'arabiyya wa dauruha fi at-tarikh al-'arabi al-hadith" (On the Activities of Translating Scientific and Literary Works from European Languages into Arabic and Their Position in Recent Arab History), in *Shu'un 'Arabiyya/Journal of Arab Affairs,* published by the League of Arab States (Tunis), vol. 1, 7 (1981), pp. 116–129. See also James Heyworth-Dunne, "Printing and Translations Under Muhammad 'Ali of Egypt: The Foundation of Modern Arabic," in *Journal of the Royal Asiatic Society* (1940), pp. 325–349; and also R. F. Khoury, "Die Rolle der Übersetzungen in der modernen arabischen Renaissance, dargestellt am Beispiel Ägyptens," in *Die Welt des Islams* n.s. 13, nos. 1–2 (1971), pp. 1–10.

47. See Tibi, *Arab Nationalism,* pp. 70–79.

48. On S. 'Aql, see Theodor Hanf, *Erziehungswesen in Gesellschaft und Politik des Libanon,* Bielefeld, 1969, pp. 334ff.

49. S. Thanyan, "al-Majma' al-Laghawi al-'Arabi" (The Arab Philological Society), in *al-Shabab al-'Arabi,* no. 98 (21 October 1968), p. 6.

50. Ibid.

51. Ibid.

52. The two following sections are partly based on my earlier publication in Arabic. See B. Tibi, "Haul al-wad' al-hali lil-lugha al-'arabiyya" (On the Present State of the Arabic Language), *al-Ma'rifa* vol. 7, 84 (1969), pp. 128–148. This English version differs substantially from the Arabic one.

53. On Salama Musa, see B. Tibi (ed.), *Die arabische Linke,* Frankfurt/M, 1969, pp. 17–21; and the now remarkable monograph on Musa by Vernon Egger, *A Fabian in Egypt: Salamah Musa and the Rise of the Professional Classes in Egypt, 1909–1939,* Lanham, Md., and New York, 1986.

54. Salama Musa, *al-Ishtirakiyya* (Socialism), Cairo, 1913. English trans. in Sami Hanna and Georg Gardner (eds.), *Arab Socialism: A Documentary*

Survey, Leiden, 1969, summarized in Tibi, *Die arabische Linke,* pp. 18f. See also the informative dossier on Salama Musa in the Cairo periodical *at-Tali'a,* vol. 1, 8 (1965), pp. 126–152, where there is also a bibliography of Musa's writings (45 vols.).

55. Salama Musa, *Tarbiyat Salama Musa* (The Education of Salama Musa), 2d, extended ed., Cairo, 1958, p. 73. English trans. in L. O. Schuman (ed.), *The Education of Salama Musa,* Leiden, 1961. An early evaluation of Salama Musa's autobiography was published by Sylvia Haim, "Salama Musa: An Appreciation of His Autobiography," in *Welt des Islam* n.s., vol. 2 (1952–1953), pp. 237–250.

56. Salama Musa, *al-Mukhtarat* (Selected Writings), 2d ed., Beirut, 1963, p. 130.

57. Ibid., p. 130.

58. Salama Musa, *Ma hiya al-nahda?* (What Does Renaissance Mean?), Beirut, 1962, p. 124.

59. Ibid., p. 126.

60. Ibid., p. 127.

61. Salama Musa, quoted after Mahmud Sharqawi, *Salama Musa: al-Muffakir wa'l-insan* (Salama Musa, the Thinker and the Man), Beirut, 1965, p. 136. On Musa, see also the monograph by Ghali Shukri, *Salama Musa wa azmat ad-damir al-'arabi* (Salama Musa and the Crisis of Arab Consciousness), 2d ed., Beirut, 1965.

62. Salama Musa, *Ma hiya al-nahda?* pp. 98f. On the importance of language as a medium for communication among peoples, see W. Schmidt-Hidding, "Der Beitrag der Sprachwissenschaft zum Problem der internationalen Erziehung," in Dieter Danckwortt (ed.), *Internationale Beziehungen. Ein Gegenstand der Sozialwissenschaften,* Frankfurt/M, 1966, pp. 118–124.

63. Salama Musa, *Ma hiya al-nahda?* p. 106.

64. Musa quoted after Sharqawi, *al-Muffakir,* p. 163.

65. Tibi, *Arab Nationalism,* Part 3. A U.S. monograph on Husri is by William L. Cleveland, *The Making of an Arab Nationalist: Ottomanism and Arabism in the Life and Thought of Sati' al-Husri,* Princeton, N. J., 1971. On this, see my reprinted review article in the collection of articles, B. Tibi, *Internationale Politik und Entwicklungsländer-Forschung,* Frankfurt/M, 1979, pp. 142–150.

66. See in particular Sati' Husri, *Muhadarat fi nushu' al-fikra al-quamiyya* (Lectures on the Emergence of the Idea of a Nation), 5th printing, Beirut, 1964. For a detailed discussion of Husri's ideas on language and its importance for national education, see the published pedagogical dissertation of Yusif Khalil Yusif, *al-quamiyya al-'arabiyya wa dawr at-tarbiya fi tahqiqiha* (On the Role of Education in Realizing the Aims of Arab Nationalism), Cairo, 1967. See also Tibi, *Arab Nationalism,* pp. 117ff.

67. See W. L. Cleveland, *Making,* pp. 3ff.

68. Sati' Husri, *al-Lugha wa'l-adab wa 'alaqatuhuma bil-qaumiyya* (Language and Literature and their Relationship to Nationalism), Beirut, 1966, p. 112.

69. Ibid., p. 113.

70. On Faroukh, see T. Hanf, *Erziehungswesen,* pp. 209f. and 334f.

71. 'Umar Faroukh, *al-Qawmiyya al-fusha* (High Arab Nationalism), Beirut, 1961, especially pp. 77ff. and 151ff. Faroukh makes a sharp attack here against those who advocate the writing down of regional dialects, or the adoption of the Latin alphabet.

72. Husri, *al-Lugha,* p. 112.

73. Ibid., p. 115.

74. See George Makdisi, *The Rise of Colleges: Institutions of Learning in Islam and the West,* Edinburgh, 1981, pp. 75ff.

75. H. M. Azzam, *Der Islam. Plädoyer eines Moslem.* Stuttgart, 1981, p. 52.

76. Sadiq Jalal al-'Azm, "al-'ilm al-hadith wa al-naksa al-akhira" (Modern Science and the Recent Defeat), in *Dirasat 'Arabiyya* (Beirut), vol. 3, 10 (1967), pp. 34–53, particularly p. 39. For a structural and subsystemic analysis of the repercussions of the June War defeat on the Arab states, see B. Tibi, "Structural and Ideological Change in the Arab Subsystem Since the Six-Day War," in Y. Lukacs and A. Battah (eds.), *The Arab Israeli Conflict: Two Decades of Change,* Boulder, Colo., 1988, pp. 147–163.

77. al-Farabi quoted after de Boer, *Geschichte,* p. 206, translated from the Arabic.

78. al-Faisal in S. Husain and S. A. Ashraf (eds.), *Crisis in Islamic Education,* Jeddah, 1979, p. 120.

79. Ibid., p. 115.

80. Husri, *al-Lugha,* p. 114.

81. See de Boer, *Geschichte,* passim.

82. Bloch, *Avicenna,* p. 173.

83. de Boer, *Geschichte,* p. 173; see also Tayib Tisini, *Mashru' ru'ya jadida li'l-fikr al-'arabi fi al-'asr al-wasit* (Draft of a New Interpretation of Arab Thought in the Middle Ages), Damascus, 1971, pp. 355ff.

84. R. Boukraa, "al-Ma'na al-ideologi li tatbiq an-naziriyya al-alsuniyya 'ala al-lugha al-'Arabiyya" (The Ideological Implications of the Application of Linguistics to 'Arabiyya), in CERES, *al-Lisaniyyat,* pp. 403ff. particularly pp. 410f.

85. See Ben Salem Himmich, *De la formation idéologique en Islam,* Paris, 1980, pp. 193ff. (See also the foreword by M. Rodinson.)

86. See the conclusions on the secularization of Islam as a prospect for the future in B. Tibi, *The Crisis of Modern Islam: A Preindustrial Culture in the Scientific-Technological Age,* Salt Lake City, 1988, pp. 127–148.

Chapter 7: Institutions of Learning and Education in Islam: Their Historical Contribution to the Cultural Accommodation of Change and Their Current State of Crisis

1. For a detailed account, see T. Hanf, "Funktionswandel der Bildung zwischen Sozialisation und Allokation," in Hanf et al., *Funkkolleg, vol. 2, Sozialer Wandel,* Frankfurt/M, 1975, particularly pp. 100–119.

2. George Makdisi, *The Rise of Colleges: Institutions of Learning in Islam and the West,* Edinburgh, 1981. On the following, see pp. 12ff., 19ff. and 20ff.

3. W. M. Watt, *Der Islam I,* Stuttgart, 1980, pp. 226ff.

4. Makdisi, *The Rise of Colleges,* pp. 75ff.

5. On the Mu'tazilites, see the standard work on Islamic philosophy by T. J. de Boer, *Geschichte der Philosophie im Islam,* Stuttgart, 1901. On the historical context, see J. J. Saunders, *A History of Medieval Islam,* 4th printing, London, 1980; and G. Endress, *Einführung in die islamische Geschichte,* Munich, 1982.

6. Makdisi, *The Rise of Colleges,* pp. 75f (italics added).

7. On the Hellenization of Islam, see W. M. Watt, *Islamic Philosophy and Theology,* 5th printing, Edinburgh, 1979, pp. 37ff. and 91ff.

8. Makdisi, *The Rise of Colleges,* pp. 281ff.

9. Ernst Bloch, *Avicenna and die aristotelische Linke,* Frankfurt/M, 1963, p. 45.

10. Makdisi, *The Rise of Colleges,* p. 285.

11. Ibid., p. 282.

12. Ibid., p. 78.

13. Ibid., pp. 285 and 292.

14. See Norbert Elias, *Über den Prozess der Zivilisation,* 2 vols., 6th printing, Frankfurt/M, 1978.

15. Makdisi, *The Rise of Colleges,* pp. 80ff.

16. Ibid., pp. 99ff.

17. Ibid., p. 105.

18. This section contains a much-condensed version of the thesis I presented as a memorial lecture on the occasion of the 375th anniversary celebrations at the Justus Liebig University in Giessen in November 1982; B. Tibi, "Die Rolle der Universität als Intrument der Selbsthilfe in den Entwicklungsländern," in *Universität und Dritte Welt. Veranstaltungswoche aus Anlass der 375 Jahrfeier der Justus-Liebig-Universität Giessen,* Giessen, 1983, pp. 72–84.

19. See the German translation of this diary by Karl Stowasser (n. 41 to Chapter 6 above).

20. See n. 3 above and Chapter 3 of this book.

21. On the *ulema* and *faqihs,* see the appropriate contributions in the book by Nikki Keddie (ed.), *Scholars, Saints and Sufis: Muslim Religious Institutions in the Middle East Since 1500,* Berkeley and Los Angeles, 1972.

22. This comment refers to the distinction between nonliterate and advanced cultures. See the typology of Uwe Simson, *Auswärtige Kulturpolitik als Entwicklungspolitik,* Meisenheim/Glan 1975, pp. 25ff.

23. See the section on African Islam in B. Tibi, *The Crisis of Modern Islam: A Preindustrial Culture in the Scientific-Technological Age,* Salt Lake City, 1988, pp. 67–80.

24. Helmuth Plessner, *Die verspätete Nation,* Frankfurt/M, 1974 (reprint), pp. 23f.

25. See the chapter on the effects of modern education on Islam in Tibi, *Crisis of Modern Islam,* pp. 95–112.

26. For details on this, see the section "Modern Education and the Emergence of a Westernized Islamic Intelligentsia," in Tibi, *Crisis of Modern Islam.*

27. See Syed H. Alatas, *Intellectuals in Developing Societies,* London, 1977, passim.

28. T. Hanf, "Erziehung und politischer Wandel in Schwarzafrika," in René König (ed.), *Aspekte der Entwicklungssoziologie* (special issue of *Kölner Zeitschrift für Soziologie und Sozialpsychologie*), Cologne and Opladen, 1969, pp. 276–327, particularly 280ff.

29. Among other works, see T. Hanf, *Erziehungswesen in Gesellschaft und Politik des Libanon,* Bielefeld, 1969.

30. Sa'id Isma'il 'Ali, *Usul at-tarbiya al-islamiyya* (Foundations of Islamic Pedagogy), Cairo, 1978, p. 19.

31. Ibid., p. 27.

32. Sa'id Isma'il 'Ali, *Dirasat fi at-tarbiya al-islamiyya* (Studies on Islamic Pedagogy), Cairo, 1982, p. 256.

33. Ibid., p. 257.

34. On the dominance of Saudi Arabia in the Arab regional subsystem since the 1970s, see B. Tibi, "Vom 'Zentrum der Revolution' zum 'Zentrum des Petrodollars,' Ägypten und Saudi-Arabien in der neuen Arabischen Sozialordnung," in *Beiträge zur Konflikt-Forschung* vol. 14, 2 (1984), pp. 101–128; see also J. P. Piscatori, "Islamic Values and National Interest: The Foreign Policy of Saudi Arabia," in A. Dawisha (ed.), *Islam in Foreign Policy,* Cambridge, 1983, pp. 33–53; and, more recently, B. Tibi, *Konfliktregion Naher Osten* Munich, 1989, Chapters 4 and 7.

35. S. S. Husain and S. A. Ashraf (eds.), *Crisis in Muslim Education,* Jeddah and Kent, 1979.

36. Mohammad Wasiulla Khan (ed.), *Education and Society in the Muslim World,* Jeddah and Kent, 1981.

37. Husain and Ashraf, *Crisis,* pp. 2f.

38. Ibid., p. 4.

39. Ibid., p. 4.

40. Mahmud Sayyid Sultan, *Buhuth fi at-tarbiya al-islamiyya* (Research Work on Islamic Pedagogy), Cairo, 1979, p. 54.

41. Ibid., p. 45.

42. See Hanf, "Erziehung und politischer Wandel" and *Erziehungswesen;* as well as Hanf, "Arabismus und Islamismus. Der säkuläre Nationalismus im vorderen Orient vor der Herausforderung des islamischen Revivalismus," in H.A. Winckler (ed.), *Nationalismus in der Welt von heute,* Göttingen, 1982, pp. 157–176.

43. Mitchell is the author of a now classic study on the Muslim Brotherhood (see n. 10 on Chapter 9 below).

44. This lecture given by Mitchell was unfortunately not developed further, nor was it published in the proceedings of the conference. See Mourad Wahba (ed.), *Islam and Civilization: Proceedings of the First International Islamic Philosophy Conference,* Cairo, 1982 (my lecture on "Islam and Secularization"

is on pp. 65–80). Mitchell taught at Ann Arbor, Michigan and died in Cairo in September 1983.

45. B. Tibi, "Akkulturation und interkulturelle Kommunikation," in *Gegenwartskunde* vol. 29 (1980), pp. 173–190; and B. Tibi, "Kommunikationsstrukturen der Weltgesellschaft und der interkulturelle Konflikt. Das islamische Exempel," in *Beiträge zur Konflikt-Forschung* vol. 11, 3 (1981), pp. 57–77.

46. See n. 26 above; and B. Tibi, "Modern Education, Students and Social Change in Underdeveloped Societies—With Special Reference to the Islamic Middle East," in Mourad Wahba (ed.), *Youth, Intellectuals and Social Change: Proceedings of the Third Euro-Arab Social Research Group Conference,* Cairo, 1983, pp. 65–77.

Part Four

Introduction

1. See the chapter on "Modernization and Its Consequences" in M. C. Hudson, *Arab Politics: The Search for Legitimacy,* New Haven, 1977, pp. 126ff.

2. See G. H. Jansen, *Militant Islam,* New York, 1979; and the contributions to a conference on this subject held by the British Royal Institute for International Affairs, all of which are contained in James P. Piscatori (ed.), *Islam in the Political Process,* Cambridge, 1983.

3. Tilman Nagel, *Staat und Glaubensgemeinschaft im Islam,* 2 vols., Darmstadt, 1981. The author himself writes in his foreword: "I use the words [sic!] state and community only in the non-specific sense." Theoretical terms and methodological concepts are inaccessible, alien terminology to such German Orientalists.

4. Reinhard Bendix, *Kings or People,* Berkeley, 1978. The extent to which the comparative social historical method is enriching for research becomes impressively apparent here. On Bendix's book, see Charles Tilly, *Big Structures, Large Processes, Huge Comparisons,* New York, 1984, pp. 91–94.

5. B. Tibi, *The Crisis of Modern Islam: A Preindustrial Culture in the Scientific-Technological Age,* Salt Lake City, 1988, pp. 57ff.

6. Bendix, *Kings or People,* pp. 35 and 43.

7. See Ann S. Lambton, *State and Government in Medieval Islam. An Introduction to the Study of Islamic Political Theory: The Jurists,* Oxford, 1981. Here, too, there is, albeit a self-confessed, restriction to the interpretation of sources, although this Orientalist work is preferable to a comparable German one by Nagel mentioned in n. 3.

8. Bendix, *Kings or People.*

9. Abdalaziz Duri, "ad-demoqratiyya fi falsafat al-hukm al-'arabi," in Ali Hilal Dessouki et al., *ad-Demoqratiyya wa huquq al-insan fi al watan al-'arabi* (Democracy and Human Rights in the Arab Homeland), Beirut, 1983, pp. 191ff.

10. Muhsin Shishakli, *Dirasat fi al-mujtama' al-'arabi* (Studies on Arab Society), vol. 2, 2d printing, Aleppo, 1965, pp. 126ff.

11. See D. Khalid, F. Kandil, et al., *Re-Islamisierung und Entwicklungs-politik,* Munich, 1982, especially pp. 215ff, where it is shown how vague (the word used is "abstract") Islamists' concepts of the future are.

Chapter 8: A Religiosociological Interpretation of the Politicization of the Islamic Cultural System: Political Islam as a Defensive Cultural Reaction to Rapid Social Change

1. This text is based largely on an account I published in *Revue Suisse de Sociologie* vol. 9, 3 (1983), pp. 658–675, although it has been revised and rewritten so as to be integrated into this book as a whole.

2. This statement implies that the sociologist working on Islam should at the same time also be a scholar of Islam. The best example of this is the work of the French scholar Maxime Rodinson, who fulfills this criterion. See Maxime Rodinson, *Islam und Kapitalismus,* Frankfurt/M, 1971. On Rodinson's achievements, see my lengthy introduction ("Maxime Rodinson, der Islam und die westlichen Islam-Studien") to the second edition of Rodinson's book, *Islam und Kapitalismus,* Frankfurt/M, 1986, pp. ix–li. The work by the sociologist Bryan S. Turner, *Weber and Islam,* London, 1974, as well as of the Orientalist Tilman Nagel, *Staat und Glaubensgemeinschaft in Islam,* 2 vols., Darmstadt, 1981, leave something to be desired and may be cited as examples of the flawed work to which critique elaborated in the text applies.

3. A classic example of this is Muhammad Muslehuddin, *Philosophy of Islamic Law and the Orientalists: A Comparative Study of Islamic Legal System,* Lahore (Pakistan), undated.

4. See Bernard Lewis, "The State of Middle Eastern Studies," in *The American Scholar* vol. 48 (1979), pp. 365–381.

5. See Clifford Geertz, *Islam Observed: Religious Development in Morocco and Indonesia,* 2d printing, Chicago, 1971, which is a little masterpiece (136 pp.); see also n. 1 to Chapter 1 above.

6. As an example of this, see Turner, *Weber.*

7. B. Tibi, "Re-Islamization as Cultural Revival and Search for Identity in the Islamic Middle East: Recent Trends," in *Vierteljahresberichte,* no. 81, 1981, pp. 229–237. Self-correction here concerns merely the naming of the phenomenon; the analysis remains valid.

8. In contrast with the Arab East, the nationalist movement in the Maghreb was always markedly Islamic in character, as there is no Christian elite there. With the exception of Tunisia, *salafiyya* Islam was a part of nationalism. Taking Algeria as an example, this is illustrated by Ali Merad, *Le reformisme Musulman en Algerie,* Paris, 1967; see also the excellent article by Ibrahim Abu-Lughod, "Retreat from the Secular Path? Islamic Dilemmas of Arab Politics," in *Review of Politics* vol. 28 (1966), pp. 447–476. This analysis has lost hardly any of its validity.

9. This issue was the theme of a text I prepared at Harvard University, where I was working as visiting scholar at the Center for International Affairs in spring 1982 (see my report *Orient* vol. 2 [1982], pp. 183–192). A revised

version of this paper is published as B. Tibi, "The Renewed Role of Islam in the Political and Social Development of the Middle East," in *The Middle East Journal* vol. 37, 1 (1983), pp. 3–13.

10. A sample of the most important Islamic sources for those who do not know any Oriental languages is now available in English translation in John H. Donohue and John L. Esposito (eds.), *Islam in Transition: Muslim Perspectives,* Oxford, 1982; see also my review in *The Middle East Journal* vol. 36, 4 (1982), pp. 614–616.

11. See n. 2 above.

12. *The Koran,* trans. N. J. Dawood, Harmondsworth, Middlesex, 1974, here sura 33, verse 40.

13. Bouman writes on this, "The important thing here is the new idea '*Seal-Khatam,*' a word that appears only in this verse. The Arabic word originates from Aramaic and means ensealment (*obsignatio*), end and definitive conclusion (*conclusio*)." Johan Bouman, *Gott und Mensch im Koran, Eine Strukturform religiöser Anthropologie anhand des Beispiels Allah und Muhammad,* Darmstadt, 1977, p. 31.

14. Ibid., p. 69. On the importance of Bouman's work, see B. Tibi, "Der Islam als Gegenstand der Forschung," in *Neue politische Literatur* vol. 27, 1 (1982), pp. 70–83, particularly pp. 75ff.

15. See the comprehensive work by Marshall G. S. Hodgson, *The Venture of Islam,* 3 vols., Chicago, 1974.

16. B. Tibi, *The Crisis of Modern Islam: A Preindustrial Culture in the Scientific-Technological Age,* Salt Lake City, 1988.

17. Shakib Arslan, *Limadha ta'khara al-muslimun wa limadha taqaddama ghairahum,* Beirut, 1965 (first published in Cairo 1930). English trans.: *Our Decline and Its Causes,* 2d printing, London, 1952.

18. B. Tibi, *Crisis of Modern Islam,* Section 3.

19. R. Peters, *Islam and Colonialism: The Doctrine of Jihad in Modern History,* The Hague and Paris, 1979, especially pp. 105–121.

20. On both variants, see the appropriate section in B. Tibi, *Arab Nationalism,* London and New York, 1981 (or the new, enlarged ed., 1990).

21. In this connection, see the interesting article by Daniel Crecelius, "The Course of Secularization in Modern Egypt," in John L. Esposito (ed.), *Islam and Development: Religion and Sociopolitical Change,* Syracuse, 1980, pp. 49ff.; and B. Tibi, "Islam and Secularization, Religion and Functional Differentiation of the Social System," in *Archiv für Rechts- und Sozialphilosophie* vol. 66 (1980), pp. 207–222.

22. Ali Abdelraziq, *al-Islam wa usul al-hukm* (Islam and Forms of Government), Beirut, 1966 (first published in Cairo 1925). French trans. in *Revue des Etudes Islamiques,* vols. 7 and 8 (1933–1934).

23. Yusuf al-Qardawi, *Hatmiyat al-Hal al-Islami* (The Determination of the Islamic Solution), 2 vols., vol. 1, Beirut, 1974, especially pp. 88ff. Al-Qardawi has recently added to his influential two-volume series a third book, *Bayyinat al-Hall al-Islami* (The Salient Features of the Islamic Solution), Cairo, 1988.

24. Niklas Luhmann, "Die Weltgesellschaft," in Luhmann, *Soziologische Aufklärung,* vol. 2, Opladen, 1975, pp. 51–61.

25. In the Federal Republic of Germany, scholarly interest in the system of international relations has unfortunately not yet reached international standards; see Stanley Hoffmann (ed.), *Contemporary Theory in International Relations,* 2d printing, Westport, Conn., 1977. (See in particular the introduction "International Relations as a Discipline.") The authoritative, although outdated textbook of the respected and competent representative of this discipline in Germany, E.-O. Czempiel (ed.), *Die Lehre von den internationalen Beziehungen,* Darmstadt, 1969, hence understandably contains predominantly U.S. original contributions and not a single German piece.

26. See an analysis of Arabic literature on this subject, B. Tibi, "Von der Selbstverherrlichung zur Selbstkritik. Zur Kritik des politischen Schrifttums der zeitgenössischen arabischen Intelligenz," in *Die Dritte Welt* vol. 1, 2 (1972), pp. 158–184. This German article was published in an earlier version in Arabic. In the late 1960s it played a considerable role in the Arab intellectual debate in the aftermath of the June 1967 defeat. B. Tibi, "Fi al-Fikr al-'Arabi al-Mu'asir, Al-Kitabah al-Wasfiyah wa al-Kitabah al-Thawriyyah," in Adonis (ed.), *MAWAQIF* (Beirut), 3 (March/April 1969), pp. 93–117. Ajami refers to this article in his *Arab Predicament* (Cambridge, 1981), pp. 28–29.

27. See Michael C. Hudson, *Arab Politics: The Search for Legitimacy,* New Haven, 1977, in particular pp. 1–30. See also B. Tibi, "Structural and Ideological Change in the Arab Subsystem Since the Six-Day War," in Y. Lukacs and A. Battah (eds.), *The Arab-Israeli Conflict: Two Decades of Change,* Boulder, Colo., 1988, pp. 147–163.

28. This discussion is documented in Volker Matthies (ed.), *Süd-Süd-Beziehungen. Zur Kommunikation, Kooperation und Solidarität zwischen Entwicklungsländern,* Munich and Cologne, 1982; see also my article "Der Nord-Süd-Konflikt," in W. Mickel (ed.), *Handlexikon zur Politikwissenschaft,* Munich, 1983, pp. 313ff.

29. See John Waterbury and R. El-Mallakh, *The Middle East in the Coming Decade,* New York, 1980, particularly pp. 21ff and 41ff.

30. Roger Owen, *The Middle East in the World Economy, 1800–1914,* London and New York, 1981, especially pp. 4ff; and my review in *Neue Politische Literatur* vol. 27, 4 (1982), pp. 508–510; see also my article in Mickel, *Handlexikon.*

31. Philip Khoury, "Islamic Revivalism and the Crisis of the Secular State in the Arab World: A Historical Appraisal," in I. Ibrahim (ed.), *Arab Resources: The Transformation of a Society,* London, 1983, pp. 213ff., particularly p. 215 (proceedings of a symposium at Georgetown University). For a conceptual interpretation of this neo-Islamic variant of fundamentalism, see B. Tibi, "Neo-Islamic Fundamentalism," in *Development: Journal of the Society of International Development,* Rome, no. 1 (1987), pp. 62–66.

32. Michael C. Hudson, "Islam and Political Development," in Esposito, *Islam,* pp. 1–24.

33. More on this in Chapter 11 of this book.

34. See the now classic study on the Tunisian political system by C. H. Moore, *Tunisia Since Independence,* Berkeley and Los Angeles, 1965; and the

chapter on Tunisia in G. Grohs and B. Tibi, *Zur Soziologie der Dekolonisation in Afrika,* Frankfurt/M, 1973.

35. Norbert Elias, *The Civilizing Process,* 2 vols., New York, 1978 and 1982. On the relevance of Elias's categories for understanding modern Islam and its position in this global societal civilization process, see B. Tibi, "Kommunikationsstrukturen in der Weltgesellschaft und der interkulturelle Konflikt. Das islamische Beispiel," in *Beiträge zur Konflikt-Forschung* vol. 11, 3 (1981), pp. 57–77.

36. Franz Borkenau, *Der Übergang vom feudalen zum bürgerlichen Weltbild,* new ed., Darmstadt, 1980. Also relevant in this connection is the study by Ernst Topitsch, *Erkenntnis und Illusion, Grundstrukturen unserer Weltauffassung,* Hamburg, 1979, especially pp. 50ff.

37. On scholarly discussion about the sociological category of social change, see the still valuable anthology by Wolfgang Zapf (ed.), *Sozialer Wandel,* 2d printing, Cologne, 1970.

38. Niklas Luhmann, *Funktion der Religion,* Frankfurt/M, 1977, pp. 115ff, and 121ff.

39. Maxime Rodinson, *Mohammed,* Lucerne and Frankfurt, 1975, p. 281.

40. See the typology of these political systems in B. Tibi, "Die Verschiedenheit der politischen Systeme in der arabischen Region," in Karl Kaiser and Udo Steinbach (eds.), *Deutsch-Arabische Beziehungen,* Munich, 1981, pp. 13–26.

41. See also related articles in the two collected volumes by Esposito, *Islam;* and in Philip H. Stoddard et al. (eds.), *Change and the Muslim World,* Syracuse, 1981; as well as the book by Edward Mortimer, *Faith and Power: The Politics of Islam,* New York, 1982.

42. Wilfred C. Smith, *The Meaning and End of Religion,* paperback ed., New York, 1978, p. 117.

43. Thomas W. Arnold, *The Caliphate,* 2d printing, London, 1965.

44. S.H.M. Jafri, *The Origins and Early Development of Shi'a Islam,* London and Beirut, 1979, especially pp. 289ff.

45. Hamid Enayat, *Modern Islamic Political Thought,* Austin, 1982, p. 3; see also my review in *MESA Bulletin* vol. 17, 2 (1983), pp. 210–211.

46. Ali H. al-Kharbutli, *al-Islam wa al-Khilafa* (Islam and the Caliphate), Beirut, 1969.

47. See the new interpretation of Mawardi by Said Bensaid, *Daulat al-Khilafa, Dirasa fi at-tafkir as-siyasi 'and al-Mawardi* (The State of the Caliphate: A Study of the Political Thought of Mawardi), ad-Dar al-Baida' (Casablanca), undated.

48. Mustafa Abu-Zaid Fahmi, *Fan al-hikm fi al-Islam* (The Art of Government in Islam), Cairo, 1977.

49. Ali M. Jarisha and Mohammad S. Zaibaq, *Asalib al-ghazu al fikri li al-'alam al-Islami* (Methods of the Intellectual Invasion of the Muslim World), 2d printing, Medina, 1978.

50. Hausain Fawzi al-Najjar, *al-Islam wa as-siyasa* (Islam and Politics), Cairo, 1977, especially pp. 165ff. and 209ff. on the Islamic system of government.

51. Ahmad Abbas Salih, *al-Yamin wa al-yasar fi al-Islam* (The Right and the Left in Islam), Beirut, 1973.

52. Documentation in Abdelraziq, *al-Islam.*

53. See Rupert Emerson, *From Empire to Nation,* 3d printing, Boston, 1964.

54. See also Tibi, *Arab Nationalism.*

55. *Jihad* means not only "holy war" but also "effort," "endeavor," or "hard work." *Jihad* can therefore also be pursued in peace in order to overcome underdevelopment.

56. Leonard Binder, *The Ideological Revolution in the Middle East,* New York, 1964, p. 131.

57. See the case study by L. Creevey in Esposito (ed.), *Islam,* pp. 207ff.; and S. Gellar, *Senegal: An African Nation Between Islam and the West,* Boulder, Colo., 1982.

58. See the case study by von der Mehden in Esposito (ed.), *Islam,* pp. 163ff.

59. On this issue with regard to Saudi petrodollar aid, see Shireen Hunter, *OPEC and the Third World,* Bloomington, Ind., 1984, pp. 123–145. On Libyan policy, see René Lemarchand (ed.), *The Green and the Black: Qadhafi's Policies in Africa,* Bloomington, Ind., 1988, passim.

60. This is done, for example, by Daniel Pipes in a chapter titled "The Great Oil Boom," *In the Path of God: Islam and Political Power,* New York, 1983, pp. 281ff. Nuances with regard to the oil-focused interpretation of Afro-Arab relations are provided in my article on this, a subject that developed from fieldwork in West and Central Africa (in particular in Cameroon) and in Sudan. See B. Tibi, "Afro-arabische Beziehungen seit der Dekolonisation. Unter besonderer Berücksichtigung der Erdöl-Dimension," in *Afrika Spectrum* vol. 21, 3 (1986), pp. 315–335.

61. See B. Tibi, "Der amerikanische 'Area-Studies-Approach' in den 'International Studies,'" in *Orient* vol. 24 (1983), pp. 260–284.

62. For additional case studies on political Islam (although not along the line of inquiry pursued here, that is, cultural accommodation of social change), see the recent volume of Shireen T. Hunter (ed.), *The Politics of Islamic Revivalism: Diversity and Unity,* Bloomington, Ind., 1988.

Chapter 9: Oppositional Religiopolitical Underground Organizations and the Islam-legitimated Establishment in Egypt: The Roots of the Political Resurgence of Militant Islam

1. See the work on this mentioned above in n. 61 to Chapter 8.

2. Louis J. Cantori, "Religion and Politics in Egypt," in Michael Curtis (ed.), *Religion in the Middle East,* Boulder, Colo., 1981, pp. 77–90. On the history of Egypt and with regard to Islam there, see P. J. Vatikiotis, *The Modern History of Egypt,* 2d printing, London, 1976, especially pp. 13ff., 176ff., and 413ff.

3. On Muhammed Ali's period, see the seminal work of Afaf Lufti al-Sayyid-Marsot, *Egypt in the Reign of Muhammad Ali,* Cambridge, 1984; and also the older contributions of Henry Dodwell, *The Founder of Modern Egypt: A Study of Muhammad Ali,* Cambridge, 1931; on the cultural background to this era, see Ibrahim Abu-Lughod, *Arab Rediscovery of Europe: A Study in Cultural Encounters,* Princeton, N.J., 1963. See also the interpretation of B. Tibi, *Arab Nationalism: A Critical Inquiry,* New York, 1981, pp. 53–58.

4. F. Ajami, "In the Faraoh's Shadow: Religion and Authority in Egypt," in James Piscatori (ed.), *Islam in the Political Process,* Cambridge, 1983, pp. 12–35, particularly p. 13. See also Ajami's book, *The Arab Predicament,* Cambridge, 1981, which has enjoyed an unusually broad reception.

5. Ajami, "In the Faraoh's Shadow," pp. 30f.

6. See the chapter "Religious Organization: The Mosque and Governmental Policy," in Morroe Berger, *Islam in Egypt Today: Social and Political Aspects of Popular Religion,* Cambridge, 1970, pp. 9ff.

7. See the section on "Die Freien Offiziere," in B. Tibi, *Militär und Sozialismus in der Dritten Welt,* Frankfurt/M, 1973, pp. 195ff.

8. See the comprehensive interpretation of Islam by Mahmud Shaltut, *al-Islam aqida wa shari'a* (Islam, Faith and Law), 10th printing, Cairo and Beirut, 1980.

9. See the notes of Ajami, "In the Faraoh's Shadow," pp. 14ff. The Salafi views of 'Abdulhalim Mahmud are reflected in his book *al-Jihad wa al-nasr,* Cairo, 1968.

10. Richard Mitchell, *The Society of Muslim Brothers,* Oxford, 1969. I was fortunate enough to learn a great deal about the organization of the Muslim Brothers from the late Mitchell, who knew this group inside out.

11. On Shi'ite Islam, see n. 24 below; and M. Momen, *An Introduction to Shi'a Islam,* New Haven, 1985.

12. Berger, *Islam,* pp. 127ff. See also the section on this in Tibi, *Militär,* pp. 211ff.

13. John Waterbury, "Egypt: Islam and Social Change," in Philip Stoddard et al. (eds.), *Change and the Muslim World,* Syracuse, 1981, pp. 49–58. What is particularly impressive about Waterbury is his attempt to see Islam in the context of Egyptian society, which he knows from the inside and about whose most recent development he has written the best two books so far: J. Waterbury, *Egypt: Burdens of the Past/Options for the Future,* Bloomington, Ind., 1978; and *The Egypt of Nasser and Sadat,* Princeton, N.J., 1983.

14. Hamied N. Ansari, "The Islamic Militants in Egyptian Politics," in *International Journal of Middle East Studies* vol. 16 (1984), pp. 124–144, particularly pp. 127–129. See also Gilles Kepel, *Le Prophète et Pharaoh. Les Mouvements Islamistes dans L'Egypte Contemporaine,* Paris, 1984.

15. Ansari, "The Islamic Militants," p. 133; on classifying the role of fundamentalism in the Arab Middle East, see the attempt of John O. Voll, *Islam, Continuity and Change in the Modern World,* Boulder, Colo., 1982, pp. 171ff.

16. For a detailed account, see Chapter 12, "Nassers Erbe in Ägypten," in Tibi, *Militär,* pp. 319ff.

17. Anwar el-Sadat, *Geheimtagebuch der ägyptischen Revolution,* Düsseldorf and Cologne, 1957, pp. 44ff., in which he gives an account of his meeting with Hassan al-Banna, founder of the Muslim Brothers. During his reign in the aftermath of Nasser's death, Sadat "enjoyed good relations with much of the Islamic movement for at least the first half decade of his rule. . . . Sadat released many ikhwan leaders [Muslim brothers] from prison . . . , and allowed them to preach and organize." Raymond A. Hinnebusch, *Egyptian Politics Under Sadat,* 2d ed., Boulder, Colo., 1988, p. 206. There is now an English translation of some of Al-Banna's tracts in Charles Wendell (ed.), *Five Tracts of Hassan al-Banna (1906–1949),* Berkeley and Los Angeles, 1978; see also the work of Mitchell, *The Society.*

18. On the discussion of the claim of the Iranian revolution to exportability, see B. Tibi "The Iranian Revolution and the Arabs," in *Arab Studies Quarterly* vol. 8, 1 (1986), pp. 29–44.

19. See Yvonne Haddad, "The Arab-Israeli Wars, Nasserism and the Affirmation of Islamic Identity," in John L. Esposito (ed.), *Islam and Development: Religion and Sociopolitical Change,* Syracuse, 1980, pp. 107–121. Haddad has also written another interesting work, *Contemporary Islam and the Challenge of History,* Albany, 1982, in which she documents the various Islamic "responses" to the "challenges"; see pp. 83ff. On the specific effects of the 1967 June War, see B. Tibi, "Structural and Ideological Change in the Arab Subsystem Since the Six-Day War," in Y. Lukacs and A. Battah (eds.), *The Arab-Israeli Conflict: Two Decades of Change,* Boulder, Colo., 1988.

20. See Nikki R. Keddie, "Oil, Economic Power and Conflict in Iran," in *Race and Class,* vol. 21 (1979), pp. 13–29.

21. See Tibi, *Arab Nationalism,* pp. 53ff.

22. On Islamic modernism, see C. C. Adams, *Islam and Modernism in Egypt,* London, 1933; on the Muslim Brothers, see Mitchell, *The Society.*

23. See Afaf al-Sayyid-Marsot, *Egypt's Liberal Experiment, 1922–1936,* Berkeley, 1977.

24. S.H.M. Jafri, *The Origins and Early Development of Shi'a Islam,* London, 1979, is about Shi'a Islam; for the Shi'ite clerical viewpoint, see A.S.M.H. Tabataba'i, *Shi'ite Islam,* trans. from the Persian by S. H. Nasr, London, 1975.

25. See Daniel Crecelius, "al-Azhar in the Revolution," in *The Middle East Journal* vol. 20 (1966), pp. 31–49; see also n. 45 below.

26. Mitchell, *The Society,* pp. 105ff.

27. See Morroe Berger, *Islam in Egypt Today: Social and Political Aspects of Popular Religion,* Cambridge, 1970, pp. 128ff.; see also Michael Gilsenan, *Saint and Sufi in Modern Egypt: An Essay in the Sociology of Religion,* Oxford, 1973.

28. B. Tibi, "The Renewed Role of Islam in the Political and Social Development of the Middle East," in *The Middle East Journal* vol. 37 (1983), pp. 3–13.

29. Eric Rouleau, "Who Killed Sadat?" in *MERIP Reports* vol. 12, 103 (1982), pp. 3–5, particularly p. 5.

30. Saad Eddin Ibrahim, "Anatomy of Egypt's Militant Islamic Groups: Methodological Note and Preliminary Findings," in *International Journal of Middle East Studies* vol. 12 (1980), pp. 423–453. During several stays in Cairo in the period from 1982 to 1984, I had an opportunity to discuss this research in detail with Ibrahim and to speak at his seminar in Cairo. See also Nazih N. M. Ayubi, "The Political Revival of Islam: The Case of Egypt," in *International Journal of Middle East Studies* vol. 12 (1980), pp. 481–499.

31. For details on this issue, see the excellent analysis by Hudson, *Arab Politics: The Search for Legitimacy,* New Haven, 1979, pp. 126–162.

32. This according to 1976 statistics in Waterbury, *Egypt: Burdens of the Past,* p. 79. In 1966 the proportion of rural population was still 59.5 percent. Today the rural population may be slightly above 50 percent.

33. The best account of Cairo is to be found in Janet Abu-Lughod, *Cairo: One Thousand-One Years of the City Victorious,* Princeton, N.J., 1971; also worth reading is the chapter on Cairo in Waterbury, *Egypt: Burdens of the Past,* pp. 125ff., with maps and illustrations.

34. Ibrahim, "Anatomy," pp. 443ff.; and Ayubi, "The Political Revival," pp. 488ff.

35. On Durkheim's concept of "anomie" and its extension to include "cultural anomie," see B. Tibi, *The Crisis of Modern Islam: A Preindustrial Culture in the Scientific-Technological Age,* Salt Lake City, 1988, pp. 52ff.

36. Ibrahim, "Anatomy," p. 448.

37. Ansari, "The Islamic Militants," p. 133.

38. Some idea of the significance of the sheikh al-Azhar is conveyed authentically, ironically, and originally by Fouad Ajami: "His views . . . are not merely the views of an ordinary writer. Those could be right or wrong, sound or not; one could refute them, be moved by them, argue with them. The Shaykh's utterances are of a different order: they are *fetwa,* binding religious opinions. Behind them is the authority not only of the dominant traditions, but . . . of the state as well. What a reader encounters in this text, then, is the burden of an established tradition: religious interpretation in the service of the custodians of political power." Ajami, "In the Faraoh's Shadow," p. 14.

39. Tariq al-Bishri, *al-Muslimun wa al-aqbat fi itar al-jama'a al-watiniyya* (Muslims and Copts Within the National Community), Cairo, 1980, a comprehensive (761 pp.), source-based, but biased account.

40. A very differentiated and knowledgeable description of this is given in an article by Hamied Ansari, "Sectarian Conflict in Egypt and the Political Expediency of Religion," in *The Middle East Journal* vol. 38 (1984), pp. 397–418.

41. Raymond A. Hinnebusch "Children of the Elite: Political Attitudes of the Westernized Bourgeoisie in Contemporary Egypt," in *The Middle East Journal* vol. 36 (1982), pp. 535–561.

42. Recourse to Islamic values can take various forms and serve various purposes; modern Islam displays a diversity of forms. The most important Islamic tendencies are presented in an anthology by John J. Donohue and John. L. Esposito (eds.), *Islam in Transition,* Oxford, 1982. See also my review in *The Middle East Journal* vol. 4 (1982), pp. 614–616.

43. An analysis, also valid for Egypt, of fundamentalist Islam as a revolt of the rootless urban petite bourgeoisie and the *Lumpenproletariat* of rural origin is in Michael M. J. Fischer, "Islam and the Revolt of the Petite Bourgeoisie," in *Daedalus* vol. 3 (1982), pp. 101–125.

44. Al-Banna was murdered in 1949; Qutb was one of the Muslim Brothers who lived in internment camps for years under Nasser; he was executed in 1966. On al-Banna, see Sadat, *Geheimtagebuch;* and Wendell, *Five Tracts.* Texts by al-Banna and Qutb are in the Islam anthology by Donohue and Esposito, *Islam in Transition,* pp. 78ff. and 123ff.

45. Daniel Crecelius, "Non-Ideological Responses of the Egyptian Ulama to Modernization," in Nikki R. Keddie (ed.), *Scholars, Saints and Sufis: Muslim Religious Institutions in the Middle East Since 1500,* Berkeley and Los Angeles, 1972, pp. 167ff, particularly p. 185; see also Crecelius, "al-Azhar," and the contribution on this theme by Afaf L. S. Marsot in the volume by Keddie, pp. 149ff.

46. Crecelius, "Non-Ideological Responses," p. 208; and Crecelius, "The Course of Secularization in Modern Egypt," in John L. Esposito (ed.), *Islam and Development: Religion and Sociopolitical Change,* Syracuse, 1980, pp. 49ff.

47. *Bayan lil-Nas,* Cairo, 1984 and 1988, was edited by the al-Azhar sheikh Jad ul-Haq 'Ali Jad ul-Haq and includes statements on all important issues of life. On *bid'a,* see vol. 2, pp. 176ff., in particular p. 180, against the abuse of this notion of innovation in Islam.

Chapter 10: The Iranian Shi'ite Variant of Religiopolitical Revivalism: The Mullah Revolution in Iran

1. See B. Tibi, "Ein Zweiter Iran im Nahen Osten? Ägypten und die krisenhafte Entwicklung seiner Binnenstrukturen," in *Aus Politik und Zeitgeschichte,* supplement 49/83 (10 December 1983), pp. 49–62; and B. Tibi, "Die iranische Revolution und die Re-Islamisierung im Lichte des Nord-Süd-Konflikts," in the same journal, supplement 41/81 (4 April 1981), pp. 12–26.

2. For details on this, see Chapter 8 of this book.

3. See Chapter 4 in B. Tibi, *The Crisis of Modern Islam: A Preindustrial Culture in the Scientific-Technological Age,* Salt Lake City, 1988, pp. 57ff. and especially pp. 64ff.

4. Nikki Keddie, "The Roots of the Ulama's Power in Modern Iran," in Keddie (ed.), *Scholars, Saints and Sufis: Muslim Religious Institutions in the Middle East Since 1500,* Berkeley and Los Angeles, 1972, pp. 211ff., particularly pp. 217 and 220.

5. Michael M. J. Fischer, *Iran: From Religious Dispute to Revolution,* Cambridge, Mass., 1980, p. 104. On the major Iranian *madrasa,* Qum, see the illuminating book of Roy Mottahedeh, *The Mantle of the Prophet: Religion and Politics in Iran,* New York, 1985.

6. Keddie, "The Roots," pp. 216 and 225.

7. For a detailed account, see Peter Scholl-Latour, *Allah ist mit den Standhaften, Begegnungen mit der islamischen Revolution,* 3d printing, Stuttgart, 1983, pp. 93ff.; see also my review in *IRANZAMIN. Echo der Iranischen Kultur* vol. 2 (1983), pp. 171–173.

8. Nikki Keddie, *Religion and Rebellion in Iran: The Tobacco Protest of 1891–1892,* London, 1966.

9. Nikki Keddie, *Roots of Revolution: An Interpretive History of Modern Iran,* New Haven, 1981, pp. 132ff.

10. The Shi'ite title of *mujtahid* comes from the Islamic legal term *ijtihad,* which is elucidated in detail in Chapter 5 of this book.

11. Roger M. Savory, "The Problem of Sovereignty in an Ithna Ashari (Twelver) Shi'a State," in Michael Curtis (ed.), *Religion and Politics in the Middle East,* Boulder, Colo., 1981, pp. 129ff., particularly pp. 137ff.

12. Hamid Enayat, "Iran: Khumayni's Concept of the Guardianship of the Jurisconsult," in James Piscatori (ed.), *Islam in the Political Process,* Cambridge, 1983, pp. 160–180, particularly p. 161.

13. Enayat, "Iran," p. 176.

14. Reinhard Bendix, *Kings or People,* Berkeley, 1978, p. 43.

15. See Michael Fischer, "Imam Khomeini: Four Levels of Understanding," in John Esposito (ed.), *Voices of Resurgent Islam,* Oxford, 1983, pp. 150–174. See also Said Amir Arjomand, *The Turban for the Crown: The Islamic Revolution in Iran,* New York, 1988.

16. Robert Graham, *Iran: Illusion of Power,* London, 1978, p. 212.

17. See Bahman Nirumand, *Persien, Modell eines Entwicklungslandes,* Reinbek, 1967, p. 19.

18. Nikki Keddie, "Oil, Economic Policy and Social Conflict in Iran," in *Race and Class* vol. 21, 1 (1979), pp. 13–29.

19. On the first energy crisis (1973–1974), see B. Tibi, "Die Rohstoffe der Peripherie-Länder und der Reproduktionsprozess der Metropole: Das Beispiel Erdöl," in V. Brandes (ed.), *Perspektiven des Kapitalismus,* Frankfurt and Cologne, 1974, pp. 105–147. On the second energy crisis (1979), see H. Maull, "Die Zweite Öl-Krise, Probleme und Perspektiven," in *Europa-Archiv* vol. 35 (1980), pp. 579–588.

20. Graham, *Iran,* p. 86.

21. S. P. Huntington, *Political Order in Changing Societies,* New Haven, 1969; and B. Tibi, "Schwache Institutionalisierung als politische Dimension der Unterentwicklung," in *Verfassung und Recht in Übersee* vol. 13 (1980), pp. 3–26.

22. Fred Halliday, *Iran, Analyse einer Gesellschaft im Entwicklungskrieg,* Berlin, 1979, pp. 132ff., especially p. 140.

23. Graham, *Iran,* pp. 38ff., especially pp. 40 and 84.

24. Ibid., p. 79.

25. Ibid., p. 129.

26. Ibid., p. 142.

27. Karl A. Wittfogel, *Die orientalische Despotie. Eine vergleichende Untersuchung totaler Macht,* Cologne, 1962, p. 188.

28. Graham, *Iran,* pp. 49–50.

29. Relations between the Shi'ite clergy and the Pahlavis are examined by S. Akhavi, *Religion and Politics in Contemporary Iran: The Clergy-State Relations in the Pahlavi Period,* Albany, 1980. On the confrontation between the two, see especially pp. 91ff. and 117ff.

30. V. Petrossian, "Dilemmas of the Iranian Revolution," in *The World Today* vol. 36, 1 (1980), pp. 19–25, especially p. 19.

31. A German translation has been published by the Iranian Embassy in Bonn in the series *"Iran und die islamische Republik"*; see no. 6 (May 1980), especially Article 5 of this "constitution," p. 27.

32. Udo Steinbach, "Iran—Halbzeit der islamischen Revolution?" in *Aussenpolitik* vol. 31, 1 (1980), pp. 52–69, particularly p. 56.

32a. See B. Tibi, "Die Golfregion im globalen Kräftefeld," in Fred Scholz (ed.), *Wirtschaftsmacht im Krisenherd. Die Golfstaaten,* Braunschweig, 1985, pp. 17–35, particularly pp. 23ff. and 31ff.; and, more recently, Shahram Chubin and Charles Tripp, *Iran and Iraq at War,* Boulder, Colo., 1988, Chapters 8 and 9 (with a focus on the region) and Chapters 10 and 11 (on the superpowers).

33. For example, Fazlur Rahman, *Islam and Modernity,* Chicago, 1982; and Rahman, *Major Themes of the Qur'an,* Chicago, 1980.

34. For example, the Swiss publicist and writer Arnold Hottinger, "Islamische Revolution? Die Muslims im Konflikt mit der westlichen Moderne," in *Merkur* vol. 16, 3 (1979), pp. 204–216.

35. See Rodinson's views concerning the possibility of incorporating Islam into a strategy of transformation. Maxime Rodinson, *Islam und Kapitalismus,* Frankfurt, 1971, pp. 290ff.

36. Keddie, *Religion and Rebellion,* particularly p. 133.

37. Bani-Sadr's conception of Islam is contained in his piece, *The Fundamental Principles and Precepts of Islamic Government,* Lexington, Ky., 1981, especially the introduction on pp. 1–12. On Bani-Sadr see Arjomand, *The Turban for the Crown,* pp. 141–146.

38. See Ali Shariati, *On the Sociology of Islam,* Berkeley, 1979; as well as Shariati, *Marxism and Other Western Fallacies: An Islamic Critique,* Berkeley, 1980. On Shariati see Ervand Abrahamian, *The Iranian Mojahedin,* New Haven, 1989, pp. 105–125.

39. From Mangol Bayat, "Islam in Pahlavi and Post-Pahlavi Iran: A Cultural Revolution?" in J. Esposito (ed.), *Islam and Development,* Syracuse, 1980, p. 102.

40. Rouholla K. Ramazani, "Iran: The Islamic Cultural Revolution," in Philip H. Stoddard et al. (eds.), *Change and the Muslim World,* Syracuse, 1981, pp. 40–48. See also Ramazani's book *Revolutionary Iran: Challenge and Response in the Middle East,* Baltimore, Md., 1986.

41. See Shariati, *On the Sociology,* and *Marxism;* and Abrahamian, *The Iranian Mojahedin,* pp. 105–125.

42. Bayat, "Islam," p. 106.

43. Ibid., p. 105.

Chapter 11: Islam as Legitimation for "Royal Authority":
On the Relationship Between State, Religion, and Politics in the
Islam-legitimated Monarchies of Morocco and Saudi Arabia

1. A complementary reading to this chapter is the typology developed by B. Tibi, "A Typology of Arab Political Systems. With Special Reference to Islam and Government," in Samih Farsoun (ed.), *Arab Society: Continuity and Change,* Farsoun, London, 1985, pp. 48–64.

2. Reinhard Bendix, *Kings or People,* Berkeley, 1978.

3. Michael M. J. Fischer, "Islam and the Revolt of the Petite Bourgeoisie," in *Daedalus* vol. 3 (1982), pp. 101–125, particularly p. 119.

4. See Bernard Lewis, *The Emergence of Modern Turkey,* 2d ed., Oxford, 1979; and Kurt Steinhaus, *Soziologie der türkischen Revolution,* Frankfurt/M, 1969, especially pp. 94ff.

5. A full elaboration of this thesis is included in B. Tibi, *Crisis of Modern Islam: A Preindustrial Culture in the Scientific-Technological Age,* Salt Lake City, 1988, pp. 127–148.

6. This chapter is based on an evaluation of the following sources: Thomas W. Arnold, *The Caliphate,* 2d printing, London, 1965 (on the caliphate); on the imamate, see S.H.M. Jafri, *The Origins and Early Development of Shi'a Islam,* London and New York, 1979, pp. 289ff; on the first Islamic state, see W. Montgomery Watt, *Muhammad at Mecca,* London, 1953; and Watt, *Muhammad at Medina,* London, 1955. On the biography of the Prophet in the historical context, see Maxime Rodinson, *Muhammed,* Lucerne and Frankfurt, 1975. On the Umayyad and Abbasid dynasties, see the contributions by V. Vaglieri and D. Sourdel in P. M. Holt et al. (eds.), *Cambridge History of Islam,* Cambridge, 1970, vol. 1, pp. 57ff. and 104ff.

7. An account of the twelve imams and remarks on the expected *mahdi* can be found in the English translation of an introduction by an important Shi'ite cleric, A.S.M.H. Tabataba'i, *Shi'ite Islam,* trans. S. H. Nasr, London, 1975, pp. 173ff.

8. Information on the caliphate movement is given in the appendix by Sylvia Haim in Arnold, *The Caliphate,* pp. 205–244; and also by A. G. Chejne, "Panislamism and the Caliphate Controversy," in *The Islamic Literature* (1955), pp. 679–697.

9. See E.I.J. Rosenthal, *Islam in the Modern National State,* New York and Cambridge, 1965.

10. Fritz Steppat, "Der Muslim und die Obrigkeit," in *Zeitschrift für Politik* vol. 12 (1965), pp. 319–333, particularly pp. 326f.

11. See the treatment by Adib Nassur, "Mushkilat al-hukm fi dau' al-tarikh al-arabi" (The Government Question in Light of Arab History), in his collection of articles *Qabl fawat al-awan* (Before It Is Too Late!), Beirut, 1955, pp. 95–124.

12. See W. Montgomery Watt, *Islamic Political Thought,* Edinburgh, 1968; and Ann S. Lambton, *State and Government in Medieval Islam: An Introduction to the Study of Islamic Political Theory,* Oxford, 1981.

13. Nassur, "Mushkilat," pp. 122ff. The late Hamid Enayat, *Modern Islamic Political Thought,* Austin, 1982, shows that there was no tradition of Islamic political philosophy outside Islamic jurisprudence and theology prior to the modern intercultural confrontation with Europe.

14. See Nasser H. Aruri, *Jordan: A Study in Political Development (1921–1965),* The Hague, 1972.

15. Ruth First, *Libya: The Elusive Revolution,* New York, 1974, pp. 99ff.; see also Lisa Anderson, "Qaddafi's Islam," in John Esposito (ed.), *Voices of Resurgent Islam,* Oxford, 1983, pp. 134ff. On the typology of Arab political systems, see B. Tibi, "Die Verschiedenheit der politischen Systeme in der arabischen Region," in K. Kaiser and U. Steinbach (eds.), *Deutsch-Arabische Beziehungen,* Munich, 1981, pp. 13–26. See also the reference in n. 1 to this chapter.

16. Werner Ende, "Der Islam als politische Ideologie," expert seminar on Iran held at the Friedrich-Ebert-Stiftung, Bonn, 21–22 June 1979 (unpublished), p. 5.

17. On the critique of this Orientalization of the Orient, see Edward Said, *Orientalism,* London, 1978; on the debate, see B. Tibi, "Orient und Okzident, Feindschaft oder interkulturelle Kommunikation? Anmerkungen zur Orientalismus-Debatte," in *Neue Politische Literatur* vol. 29 (1984), pp. 267–286. Nevertheless, we must beware of becoming the intellectual victims of "Orientalism in reverse" (Sadiq al-Azm with regard to Edward Said), as Edward Said indeed ends up. To become a victim in this manner leaves no room for any criticism of anything in the Middle East, for this would be denounced as "Orientalism." This always happens when the—initially justified—reproach of Orientalism is taken to extremes. Ultimately, it becomes boring and *denkfaul* (to use the German term) on intellectual grounds.

18. See G. Noetzold, *Die arabischen Länder,* Gotha and Leipzig, 1970, especially pp. 94ff. On the critique of Soviet Marxist theory, see B. Tibi, "Zur Kritik der sowjetmarxistischen Entwicklungstheorie," in B. Tibi and V. Brandes (eds.), *Unterentwicklung,* Cologne, 1975, pp. 64ff.

19. Joseph Schacht, *An Introduction to Islamic Law,* 5th printing, Oxford, 1979, pp. 78ff. The question suggested by the framework of the inquiry of this book is: Why do people establish rules (the *shari'a* is indeed a historical product based on the human interpretation of the Koran) to which they do not submit but rather evade, at the same time believing that their actions are in line with "the letter of the law"? See also Maxime Rodinson, *Islam und Kapitalismus,* Frankfurt/M, 1971, pp. 64ff; N. J. Coulson, *A History of Islamic Law,* 2d printing, Edinburgh, 1971, pp. 139ff.

20. Rodinson, *Islam,* pp. 77ff; see also pp. 79f.

21. John Waterbury, *The Commander of the Faithful: The Moroccan Political Elite—A Study in Segmented Politics,* New York, 1970, p. 3.

22. Ibid., p. 5.

23. Ibid.

24. See R. Stephan Humphreys, "Islam and Political Values in Saudi Arabia, Egypt and Syria," in *The Middle East Journal* vol. 33, 1 (1979), pp.

1–19, which shows the varied extent to which Islamic values penetrate the countries mentioned.

25. See S. N. Eisenstadt, *Tradition, Wandel und Modernität,* Frankfurt/M, 1979, pp. 206ff., on Islam, pp. 221f.

26. See Bruce M. Borthwick, "Religion and Politics in Israel and Egypt," in *The Middle East Journal* vol. 33, 2, pp. 145–163, particularly pp. 154 and 155.

27. See B. Tibi, "Die Verschiedenheit der politischen Systeme."

28. Niklas Luhmann, *Funktion der Religion,* Frankfurt/M, 1977, pp. 227f.

29. Ibid., p. 228. An interpretation of modern Islam based, among other things, on Luhmann's sociology of religion is provided in the final part of B. Tibi, *Crisis.*

30. See S. P. Huntington, *Political Order in Changing Societies,* 2d printing, New Haven, 1969.

31. See B. Tibi, "Schwache Institutionalisierung als politische Dimension der Unterentwicklung. Huntingtons Praetorianismus-Theorie und eine Fallstudie über die Parteientwicklung in Ägypten," in *Verfassung und Recht in Übersee* vol. 13, 1 (1980), pp. 3–26.

32. See S. P. Huntington, "Political Development and Political Decay," in *World Politics* vol. 17, 3 (1965), pp. 386–430.

33. See Max Weber, "Die Drei reinen Typen der legitimen Herrschaft," in Weber, *Soziologie, Weltgeschichtliche Analysen, Politik,* ed. J. Winckelmann, 3d printing, Stuttgart, 1964, pp. 151ff.

34. See Georges Balandier, *Politische Anthropologie,* Munich, 1972, pp. 114ff., especially pp. 115ff. and 122.

35. Fritz Steppat, "Der Muslim und die Obrigkeit," p. 330. In contrast to Europe, Islam knows neither the division of power nor a traditional right to opposition; see B. Tibi, "Widerstandsrecht in rechtlosen Gesellschaften," in *Gegenwartskunde* vol. 28, 3 (1979), pp. 283–297, particularly pp. 291ff.

36. See Nikki Keddie (ed.), *Scholars, Saints and Sufis: Muslim Religious Institutions in the Middle East Since 1500,* Berkeley and Los Angeles, 1972.

37. See the case study by Arnold H. Green, *The Tunisan Ulama, 1873–1915,* Leiden, 1978.

38. On the importance of law as a medium of institutionalization, see Frank Rotter, *Verfassung und sozialer Wandel,* Hamburg, 1974, pp. 59ff.

39. See B. Tibi, *Militär und Sozialismus in der Dritten Welt,* Frankfurt/M, 1973.

40. Huntington, *Political Order,* p. 195; and Tibi, "Schwache Institutionalisierung."

41. Huntington, *Political Order,* p. 196.

42. See Anis Sayigh, *Fi Mafhum az-za'ama as-Siyasiyya. Min Faisal al-awal ila Gamal abd an-Nasir* (On the Concept of Political Leadership: From Faisal I to Nasser), Beirut and Saida, 1965; and Majid Khadduri, *Arab Contemporaries: The Role of Personalities in Politics,* Baltimore, Md., and London, 1973.

43. See Max Weber, "Der Beruf zur Politik," in Weber, *Soziologie,* pp. 167ff.

44. See Tibi, "Schwache Institutionalisierung."
45. Borthwick, "Religion and Politics," p. 158.
46. See Jerome B. Weiner, "The Green March in Historical Perspective," in *The Middle East Journal* vol. 33, 1 (1979), pp. 20–33, particularly pp. 23f.
47. On the first Moroccan constitution of 1962, see E. A. von Renesse et al., *Unvollendete Demokratie,* Cologne and Opladen, 1965, pp. 262ff. Information on the second constitution is given in G. Fulda, "Rückkehr zur absoluten Monarchie? Die zweite Verfassung des Königreichs Marokko," in *Verfassung und Recht in Übersee* vol. 24, 2 (1971), pp. 197–203. On the third constitution, see the *Neue Zürcher Zeitung* report "Ankündigung einer Neuen Verfassung in Marokko," in *Neue Zürcher Zeitung,* 19 February 1972, FA no. 49.
48. On the *bay'a* concept, see Weiner, "The Green March"; and the remarks made in the first part of Chapter 11.
49. See Waterbury, *Commander of the Faithful,* pp. 152ff; on scholarly discussion of the client relationship, see S. W. Schmidt, L. Guasti, et al. (eds.), *Friends, Followers and Factions: A Reader in Political Clientelism,* Berkeley and Los Angeles, 1977, especially Chapter 2, "Theories of Clientelism," pp. 75ff. On tribes as a counterforce to the Islamic *umma,* see B. Tibi, "The Simultaneity of the Unsimultaneous. Old Tribes and Imposed Nation-States in the Middle East," in Philip Khoury and Joseph Kostiner (eds.), *Tribes and State Formation in the Middle East,* Berkeley, 1990.
50. Joseph LaPalombara and Myron Weiner, "Parteien und Parteiensysteme in der Dritten Welt," in D. Berg-Schlosser (ed.), *Politische Probleme der Dritten Welt,* Hamburg, 1972, pp. 174–190, particularly p. 180.
51. Ibid.
52. Ibid., p. 179.
53. Waterbury, *Commander of the Faithful,* pp. 169ff.
54. Ibid., pp. 145f.
55. Ibid., pp. 17f.
56. Information on these two attempts at a *coup d'état* is given by Tibi, *Militär und Sozialismus,* pp. 138ff. and 156f.
57. J. B. Weiner, "The Green March," p. 25. This also concerns a specific feature of Moroccan Islam. See Dale Eickelman, *Moroccan Islam,* Austin, 1976.
58. Waterbury, *Commander of the Faithful,* p. 154.
59. See Richard Hartmann, "Die Wahhabiten," in *Zeitschrift der Deutschen Morgenländischen Gesellschaft* vol. 78, 2 (1924), pp. 176–213; and Tibi, *Arab Nationalism,* pp. 62ff.
60. The exploitation of the *ikhwan* in the foundation of the Saudi Arabian state is described in detail in John S. Habib, *Ibn Saud's Warriors of Islam: The Ikhwan of Najd and Their Role in the Creation of the Sa'udi Kingdom, 1910–1930,* Leiden, 1978; see also Christine Helms, *The Cohesion of Saudi Arabia,* London, 1981.
61. See details in Gary Troeller, *The Birth of Saudi Arabia: Britain and the Rise of the House of Sa'ud,* London, 1976, especially pp. 73ff. and 127ff.
62. Tribal segmentation on the Arabian peninsula before the founding of the Islamic religion is described by Maxime Rodinson in *Mohammed.* See

also the chapter on "The Unifying of the Arabs," in Montgomery Watt, *Muhammad at Medina,* 6th printing, Oxford, 1977, pp. 78–150. In his *Islamic Political Thought: The Basic Concepts,* Edinburgh, 1968, p. 14, Watt coins the term "super-tribe" to denote the new Islamic *umma.* For more details on this topic, see my contribution to the book cited in n. 49 above.

63. Hartmann, "Die Wahhabiten," p. 177.

64. Troeller, *The Birth of Saudi Arabia,* p. 169. For a more detailed account, see Habib, *Ibn Sa'ud's Warriors.*

65. See the monograph by Helen Lackner, *A House Built on Sand: A Political Economy of Saudi Arabia,* London, 1978, particularly pp. 14ff.

66. See Abdul H. Raoof, "The Kingdom of Saudi Arabia," in T. Y. Ismail (ed.), *Governments and Politics in the Contemporary Middle East,* Homewood, Ill., 1970, pp. 353ff., particularly pp. 364ff. and 366ff.

67. F. Al-Farsy, *Saudi Arabia: A Case Study in Development,* London, 1978, p. 69.

68. Ibid., p. 66.

69. Ibid., p. 169.

70. See the discussion in B. Tibi, "Islam and Secularization. Religion and Functional Differentiation of the Social System," in *Archiv für Rechts- und Sozialphilosophie* vol. 66 (1980), pp. 207–22.

71. Faruq Abdul-Salam, *al-Azhab as-siyasiyya wal-fasl bain ad-din wal-siyasa* (Political Parties and the Separation of Religion and Politics), Cairo, 1979, p. 4.

72. Ibid., p. 137.

73. Michael C. Hudson, *Arab Politics: The Search for Legitimacy,* 2d printing, New Haven and London, 1979, pp. 165–229.

74. Ibid., p. 167.

75. See Hedley Bull and Adam Watson, (eds.) *The Expansion of International Society,* 3d printing, Oxford, 1988.

76. Huntington, *Political Order,* p. 155.

77. S. P. Huntington, "The Political Modernization of Traditional Monarchies," in *Daedalus* vol. 95, 3 (1966), pp. 763–788, particularly p. 786.

78. Huntington's theses have also been tested in the case of Iran; see Tibi, *Crisis of Modern Islam,* pp. 103–112.

79. A similar line of argument is to be found in the contribution by T. G. Carroll, "Secularization and States of Modernity," in *World Politics* vol. 36 (1984), pp. 362–382.

80. On the Saudi Arabian petroleum sector and its importance for the world economy, Benjamin Shwadran, *The Middle East, Oil and Great Powers,* New York and Toronto, 1973, pp. 301ff.; and, more recently, William B. Quandt, *Saudi Arabia in the 1980s: Foreign Policy, Security and Oil,* Washington, D.C., 1981. For more details on the revival of Islam in Saudi Arabia, see the article by William Ochsenwald in Shireen T. Hunter (ed.), *Islamic Revivalism: Diversity and Unity,* Bloomington, Ind., 1988, pp. 103–115. On security, see the article on Saudi Arabia by A. Dawisha in S. F. Wells and M. Bruzonsky (eds.), *Security in the Middle East: Regional Change and Great Power Strategies,* Boulder, Colo., 1987, pp. 89–100.

81. Hudson, *Arab Politics,* p. 229.

82. This elite is also the subject of the excellent study by Waterbury, *Commander of the Faithful.*

83. William Rugh, "Emergence of a New Middle Class in Saudi Arabia," in *The Middle East Journal* vol. 27, 1 (1973), pp. 7–20, particularly p. 20.

84. John P. Entelis, "Oil Wealth and the Prospects for Democratization in the Arabian Peninsula. The Case of Saudi Arabia," in N. A. Sherbiny and M. A. Tessler (eds.), *Arab Oil: Impact on the Arab Countries and Global Implications,* New York, 1976, pp. 77–111, particularly p. 111.

85. Eric A. Nordlinger, *Conflict, Regulation in Divided Societies,* 2d printing (with a foreword by S. P. Huntington), Cambridge, Mass., 1977.

86. This weakly institutionalized form of government is also the subject of my account, "Schwache Institutionalisierung."

87. See B. Tibi, "Vom Zentrum der Revolution zum Zentrum des Petro-Dollars. Ägypten und Saudi-Arabien in der neuen Arabischen Sozialordnung," in *Beiträge zur Konflikt-Forschung* vol. 14, 2 (1984), pp. 101–128.

88. See Ragaei El-Mallakh, *Saudi Arabia: Rush to Development,* Baltimore, Md., 1982; and Quandt, *Saudi Arabia in the 1980s.*

Part Five

1. See B. Tibi, "Akkulturation, Modernisierung, Verwestlichung und auswärtige Kulturpolitik" (Göttingen inaugural lecture), in Tibi, *Internationale Politik und Entwicklungsländer-Forschung,* Frankfurt/M, 1979, pp. 176ff.

2. See the biography by Nikki Keddie, *Sayyid Jamal al-Din "al-Afghani,"* Berkeley and Los Angeles, 1972.

3. Al-Afghani, *al-A'mal al-kamilah* (Collected Works in One Volume), ed. M. 'Imara, Cairo, 1968, p. 328.

4. Rudolf Wendorff, *Dritte Welt und westliche Zivilisation,* Opladen, 1984, p. 65.

5. Ibid., p. 460.

6. See Helmuth Plessner, *Die verspätete Nation,* reprint, Frankfurt/M, 1974.

7. J. G. Herder, "Idee zur Philosophie der Geschichte der Menschheit," in Herder, *Werke in fünf Bänden,* ed. W. Dobbek, 3d printing, Berlin and Weimar, 1964, particularly vol. 4, p. 196.

8. See in this context the superb, extensive account by Reinhard Bendix, "Tradition and Modernity Reconsidered," in his collection of articles, *Nation-Building and Citizenship: Studies of Our Changing Social Order,* new and substantially revised ed., Berkeley and Los Angeles, 1977, pp. 361–434, especially pp. 411ff. Of particular significance is Bendix's thesis that the *modernization* of some spheres of life in non-European societies does not necessarily contribute to bringing about *modernity.*

9. See the standard work of the Frankfurt School on this subject by Franz Borkenau, *Der Übergang vom feudalen zum bürgerlichen Weltbild,* Darmstadt, 1980 (first published in German, although in Paris, in 1934, now reprinted).

10. Added to this preindustrial characteristic is the political dimension that permits the politicization of the sacred. In this context, see the chapter "Religion und Macht," in Georges Balandier, *Politische Anthropologie*, Munich, 1972, pp. 114ff.

11. Niklas Luhmann, "Die Weltgesellschaft," in Luhmann, *Soziologische Aufklärung*, vol. 2, Opladen, 1975, pp. 51–61. See also Theodore H. von Laue, *World Revolution of Westernization: The Twentieth Century in Global Perspective*, New York, 1987.

12. See the contributions on this in Luhmann, *Soziologische Aufklärung*.

13. See Chapter 3 in B. Tibi, *The Crisis of Modern Islam: A Preindustrial Culture in the Scientific-Technological Age*, Salt Lake City, 1988, pp. 43–56.

14. D. Nohlen and F. Nuscheler, "Was heisst Entwicklung?" in Nohlen and Nuscheler (eds.), *Handbuch der Dritten Welt*, vol. 1, 2d printing, Hamburg, 1982, pp. 48ff.

15. See the account "Romantische Entwicklungsideologien," in Tibi, *Internationale Politik*, pp. 32ff. For more details on these ideologies of decolonization and on their romantic glorification of the precolonial past, see B. Tibi, "Politische Ideen in der Dritten Welt während der Dekolonisation," in I. Fetscher and H. Münkler (eds.), *Pipers Handbuch der politischen Ideen*, 5 vols., vol. 5, Munich, 1987, pp. 361–402. Islamic ideas of decolonization are placed here in the context of the "Third World," although without the bias of "Third Worldism" (*Tiers-mondisme*).

16. Gérard Leclerc, *Anthropologie und Kolonialismus*, Munich, 1973, pp. 16ff.

17. See René König (ed.), *Aspekte der Entwicklungssoziologie*, Cologne and Opladen, 1969; and various essays in Tibi, *Internationale Politik*. A more recent survey of the contribution of German political science to dealing with the "Third World" (known as Third World research, or *Dritte Welt-Forschung*) is the volume by Franz Nuscheler (ed.), *Dritte Welt-Forschung. Entwicklungstheorie und Entwicklungspolitik*, Opladen, 1985. This volume shows how minor the place of area studies in German political science is, and how preponderant the normative German approach to this subject affected by Dieter Senghaas (see n. 29 below) is.

18. Daniel Lerner, *The Passing of Traditional Society*, Glencoe, Ill., 1958. Thinking on development has since gone far beyond Lerner's pathfinding work. See David E. Apter, *Rethinking Development*, Newbury Park, Calif., 1987; and David Harrison, *Sociology of Modernization and Development*, London, 1988.

19. See Roger Owen, *The Middle East in the World Economy, 1800–1914*, London and New York, 1981; as well as my review in *Neue Politische Literatur* vol. 4 (1982), pp. 508–510.

20. Norbert Elias, *The Civilizing Process*, vol. 2, New York, 1982.

21. Ibid., p. 247.

22. Ibid., p. 256.

23. Ibid., p. 255. On the groundbreaking work of Norbert Elias, see Stephen Mennell, *Norbert Elias: Civilization and the Human Self-Image*, Oxford, 1989.

24. See B. Tibi, "Akkulturation und interkulturelle Kommunikation," in *Gegenwartskunde,* vol. 29 (1980), pp. 173–190; and Tibi, "Kommunikationsstrukturen der Weltgesellschaft und der interkulturelle Konflikt," in *Beiträge zur Konflikt-Forschung* vol. 11, 3 (1981), pp. 57–77.

25. G. Höpp and M. Grzeskowiak, "Re-Islamisierung—Schreckgespenst oder Herausforderung? Bemerkungen zur Darstellung und Wertung eines aktuellen Prozesses durch die Islamwissenschaft der BRD und Westberlins," in *Asien, Afrika, Lateinamerika* (DDR), vol. 12, 3 (1984), pp. 477–490.

26. Bernard Lewis, "The Return of Islam," in Michael Curtis (ed.), *Religion and Politics in the Middle East,* Boulder, Colo., 1981, pp. 9–30.

27. B. Lewis, *The Muslim Discovery of Europe,* New York, 1982.

28. See G. M. Manousakis, *Der Islam und die NATO, Bedrohung an der Südflanke,* Munich, 1980.

29. Uwe Simson, "Wirtschaftliche und kulturelle Beziehungen zu Gesellschaften im Zeichen der Re-Islamisierung," in *Orient,* vol. 21 (1980), pp. 570–576, particularly p. 573. Dieter Senghaas is a left-wing German political scientist who has greatly contributed to disseminating the concept of decoupling from the world market as the sole solution to the problems arising from underdevelopment. See Dieter Senghaas, *Weltwirtschaftsordnung und Entwicklungspolitik. Plädoyer für Dissoziation,* Frankfurt/M, 1977.

30. Clifford Geertz, *Islam Observed,* 2d printing, Chicago, 1971, p. 56.

31. I. Mörth and F. Fürstenberg, "Religionssoziologie," in R. König (ed.), *Handbuch der empirischen Sozialforschung,* vol. 14, 2d printing, Stuttgart, 1979, pp. 1–84, particularly p. 46.

32. Ibid., p. 35.

33. Ibid., p. 49.

34. R. Bendix, "Modernisierung in internationaler Perspektive," in W. Zapf (ed.), *Theorien des sozialen Wandels,* 2d printing, Cologne and Berlin 1970, pp. 505ff., particularly p. 506.

35. Ibid., p. 507.

36. Ibid., p. 511.

37. R. Bendix, *Kings or People,* Berkeley, 1978, p. 582.

38. Ibid., p. 594.

39. Ibid.

40. Ibid., p. 603.

41. R. Bendix, *Freiheit und historisches Schicksal. Heidelberger Max-Weber-Vorlesungen,* Frankfurt/M, 1982, p. 132.

42. On this, see my accounts in *Orient,* vol. 23 (1982), pp. 366–369 (on Marrakech); and vol. 24 (1983), pp. 570–573 (on Cairo).

43. Jean-Paul Charnay, *Sociologie religieuse de L'Islam,* Paris, 1978.

44. Maxime Rodinson, *Islam und Kapitalismus,* Frankfurt/M, 1971; and my review in *Archiv für Rechts- und Sozialphilosophie,* vol. 59 (1973), pp. 155–158.

45. See Ernst Topitsch, *Erkenntnis und Illusion. Grundstrukturen unserer Weltauffassung,* Hamburg, 1979, pp. 97ff.

46. Ernest Gellner, *Muslim Society,* Cambridge and London, 1981 (collection of papers); see especially the first essay, "Flux and Reflux in the Faith of Men."

47. C. Seyfarth and W. Sprondel (eds.), *Seminar: Religion und gesellschaftliche Entwicklung. Studien zur Protestantismus-Kapitalismus-These Max Webers,* Frankfurt, 1973, p. 9.

48. Ibid., p. 15. See also the contribution in Wolfgang Schluchter (ed.), *Max Webers Sicht des Islams,* Frankfurt, 1987; also my review of this book in *Kölner Zeitschrift für Soziologie und Sozialpsychologie,* issue 4 (1988), pp. 808–810; and also my article "Gibt es einen Homo Islamicus?" in *Frankfurter Allgemeine Zeitung,* 20 September 1988.

49. Bendix, *Freiheit,* pp. 126ff.

50. Gellner, *Muslim Society,* p. 2.

51. See Muhammed 'Imara, *al-Islam wal-'uruba wal-'ilmaniyya* (Islam, Arabism, and Secularism), Beirut, 1981, particularly pp. 57ff.

52. T. G. Carroll, "Secularization and States of Modernity," in *World Politics* vol. 36, 3 (1984), pp. 362–382, particularly pp. 375 and 380.

53. Niklas Luhmann, *Funktion der Religion,* Frankfurt/M, 1977; and also my conclusions "The Secularization of Islam," in Tibi, *Crisis of Modern Islam,* which is conceptually based on Luhmann's sociology of religion.

54. This entire issue is well documented in the volume on this in the "Wege der Forschung" series by Heinz Horst Schrey (ed.), *Säkularisierung,* Darmstadt, 1981.

55. Daniel Bell, "The Return of the Sacred? The Argument on the Future of Religion," in Bell, *The Winding Passage: Essays and Sociological Journeys, 1960–1980,* New York, 1980, pp. 324ff., particularly p. 332.

56. Ibid., p. 333.

57. Ibid., p. 352.

58. See Gerrit W. Gong, *The Standard of "Civilization" in International Society,* Oxford, 1984, Chapters 1 and 2. Interesting in this context is the effort to establish the study of culture, which attempts to conduct its research in the light of the standardized differential in "communication" between members of various cultures. See Anton Hickman, *Die Wissenschaft von den Kulturen. Ihre Bedeutung und ihre Aufgaben,* Meisenheim/Glan 1967.

59. With regard to the Islamic views of the modern *nation state,* Piscatori reduces this issue to attitudes of "conformism" and "non-conformism." See James Piscatori, *Islam in a World of Nation States,* Cambridge, 1986, pp. 40–75. In the introductory chapter to the 2d ed. of B. Tibi, *Arab Nationalism: A Critical Inquiry,* London 1990, a critique of these views is elaborated on, showing that *conformism* is not tantamount to a cultural accommodation of change.

60. See the introduction to Tibi, *Crisis of Modern Islam,* pp. 1–8.

61. For such a reductionist economic view, see the influential work of Samir Amin, *Le Développement Inégal. Essai sur les formations sociales du capitalisme périphérique,* Paris, 1973. In addition to the monocausal reductionist drive of his book, Samir Amin derives economic underdevelopment from a

global structure of worldwide capitalism that leaves no room in his analysis for either local or regional uniqueness.

62. Samuel Huntington and the school of thought related to political development focus on the analysis of political structures, but unlike Amin never claim to cover the whole issue by reducing the overall structures to political factors. See the pathfinding work of Samuel Huntington, *Political Order in Changing Societies,* New Haven, 1968; and, more recently, Samuel Huntington and Myron Weiner (eds.), *Understanding Political Development,* Boston, 1987, in particular the introductory essay by Huntington, "The Goals of Development," pp. 3–32.

63. Cultural tradition is a recurring issue in Samuel Eisenstadt, *Tradition, Change and Modernity,* New York, 1973. See the critical discussion of these views in Chapter 4 of this book.

Selected Bibliography

The following bibliography contains a systematic selection of literature on the subject of this book and has been completely updated in line with the revisions in the original German version of this book. The bibliography is divided into four parts:

1. Social and Cultural Change in the Context of World Order: Theoretical and Conceptual Approaches
2. Modern Islam in the Context of Social and Cultural Change
3. Area and Country Studies Relevant to the Study of Modern Islam
4. Sources in Arabic: The Literature of Islamic Fundamentalism and Sunni Islamic Views on the Iranian Revolution

1. Social and Cultural Change in the Context of World Order: Theoretical and Conceptual Approaches

Abdel-Malek, Anouar. *Civilizations and Social Theory*. Albany: State University of New York Press, 1981.

Adorno, Theodor W. *Kritische Modelle,* vol. 2. Frankfurt/M.: Suhrkamp, 1970.

Alatas, Syed Hussein. *Intellectuals in Developing Societies*. London: Frank Cass Press, 1977.

Apter, David E. *Rethinking Development: Modernization, Dependency, and Postmodern Politics.* London: Sage Publications, 1987.

Archer, Margaret S. *Culture and Agency: The Place of Culture in Social Theory.* Cambridge: Cambridge University Press, 1988.

Balandier, Georges. *Anthropologie Politique*. Paris: Presses Universitaires, 1967.

Bell, Daniel. "The Return of the Sacred? Arguments on the Future of Religion." In *The Winding Passage: Essays and Sociological Journeys,* ed. Daniel Bell, 324–354. New York: Basic Books, 1980.

Bendix, Reinhard. *Freiheit und historisches Schicksal. Heidelberger Max-Weber-Vorlesungen.* Frankfurt/M.: Suhrkamp, 1982.

————. *Kings or People: Power and the Mandate to Rule.* Berkeley: University of California Press, 1978.

————. "Modernisierung in internationaler Perspektive." In *Theorien des sozialen Wandels,* ed. Wolfgang Zapf, 505–512. Cologne and Berlin: Kiepenheuer & Witsch, 1970.

Bloch, Ernst. *Thomas Münzer als Theologe der Revolution*. New edition. Frankfurt/M.: Suhrkamp, 1972.

――――. *Avicenna und die Aristotelische Linke*. Frankfurt/M.: Suhrkamp, 1963.

Borkenau, Franz. *Der Übergang vom feudalen zum bürgerlichen Weltbild*. New edition. Darmstadt: Wissenschaftliche Buchgesellschaft, 1980.

Bull, Hedley. *The Anarchical Society: A Study of Order in World Politics*. New York: Columbia University Press, 1977.

Bull, Hedley, and Watson, Adam, eds. *The Expansion of International Society*. 3d printing. Oxford: Clarendon, 1988.

Cantori, Louis, and Ziegler, Andrew, eds. *Comparative Politics in the Post-Behavioral Era*. Boulder, Colo.: Lynne Rienner Publishers, 1988.

Carroll, T. G. "Secularization and States of Modernity." *World Politics,* vol. 36 (1984), pp. 362–382.

Chilcote, Ronald H. *Theories of Comparative Politics: The Search for a Paradigm*. Boulder, Colo.: Westview Press, 1981 (Chapter 6: "Theories on Political Culture").

Dreier, Ralf. *Recht–Moral–Ideologie. Studien zur Rechtstheorie*. Frankfurt/M.: Suhrkamp, 1981.

Eisenstadt, S. N. *Tradition, Change, and Modernity*. New York: J. Wiley & Sons, 1973.

Elias, Norbert. *The Civilizing Process*. 2 vols. New York: Pantheon Books, 1978 and 1982.

Emerson, Rupert. *From Empire to Nation: The Rise to Self-Assertion of Asian and African Peoples*. Boston: Beacon Press, 1964.

Esser, Joseph. *Vorverständnis und Methodenwahl in der Rechtsfindung*. Frankfurt/M.: Athenäum, 1970.

Evans-Pritchard, E. E. *Theories of Primitive Religion*. Oxford: Clarendon, 1965.

Fürstenberg, Friedrich, ed. *Religionssoziologie*. Neuwied: Luchterhand, 1964.

Geertz, Clifford. *The Interpretation of Cultures*. New York: Basic Books, 1973.

――――. *Islam Observed*. Chicago: Chicago University Press, 1971.

Giddens, Anthony. *Social Theory and Modern Sociology*. Cambridge: Polity, 1987.

Gong, Gerrit W. *The Standard of "Civilization" in International Society*. Oxford: Clarendon, 1984.

Grohs, Gerhard. "Difficulties of Cultural Emancipation in Africa." *Journal of Modern African Studies,* vol. 14 (1976), pp. 65–78.

Haddad, Yvonne Yazbeck, and Findley, Ellison Banks, eds. *Women, Religion, and Social Change*. Albany: SUNY Press, 1985.

Hanf, Theodor. "Erziehung und politischer Wandel in Schwarzafrika." In *Aspekte der Entwicklungssoziologie,* ed. René König, 276–327. Cologne and Opladen: Westdeutscher Verlag, 1969.

Harrison, David. *The Sociology of Modernization and Development*. London: Unwin Hyman, 1988.

Hart, H.L.A. *The Concept of Law*. Oxford: Clarendon, 1970.

Henle, Paul et al. *Sprache, Denken, Kultur*. Frankfurt/M.: Suhrkamp, 1975.

Hickman, Anton. *Die Wissenschaft von den Kulturen. Ihre Bedeutung und ihre Aufgaben*. Meisenheim/Glan: Anton Hain, 1967.

Hoffmann, Stanley. *Janus and Minerva: Essays in the Theory and Practice of International Politics.* Boulder, Colo.: Westview Press, 1987.

Hoffmann, Stanley, ed. *Contemporary Theory in International Relations.* Westport, Conn.: Greenwood Press, 1977.

Hufnagel, Erwin. *Einführung in die Hermeneutik.* Stuttgart: Kohlhammer, 1976.

Huntington, Samuel P. *Political Order in Changing Societies.* New Haven, Conn.: Yale University Press, 1969.

Ineichen, Gustav. *Allgemeine Sprachtypologie. Ansätze und Methoden.* Darmstadt: Wissenschaftliche Buchgesellschaft, 1979.

Kandil, Fuad. *Nativismus in der Dritten Welt. Wiederentdeckung der Tradition als Modell für die Gegenwart.* St. Michael: Blaschke, 1983. (This book includes a chapter on "islamischen Nativismus.")

Klingenstein, Grete et al., eds. *Europäisierung der Erde? Studien zur Einwirkung Europas auf die aussereuropäische Welt.* Vienna: Verlag für Geschichte und Politik, 1980.

Kodjo, Samuel. *Probleme der Akkulturation in Afrika.* Meisenheim/Glan: Anton Hain, 1973.

Leclerc, Gérard. *Anthropologie et colonialisme.* Paris: Fayard, 1972.

Le Gassick, Trevor J. *Major Themes in Modern Arabic Thought: An Anthology.* Ann Arbor: University of Michigan Press, 1979.

Lerner, Daniel. *The Passing of Traditional Society.* Glencoe, Ill.: Free Press, 1958.

Loewenthal, Richard. *Social Change and Cultural Crisis.* New York: Columbia University Press, 1984.

Luhmann, Niklas. *Funktion der Religion.* Frankfurt/M.: Suhrkamp, 1977.

———. *Soziologische Aufklärung.* Vol. 1, *Aufsätze zur Theorie sozialer Systeme;* vol. 2. *Aufsätze zur Theorie der Gesellschaft.* Opladen: Westdeutscher Verlag, 1975.

McKinlay, R. D., and Little, R. *Global Problems and World Order.* Madison: University of Wisconsin Press, 1986.

Mansilla, H.C.F. *Die Trugbilder der Entwicklung in der Dritten Welt.* Paderborn: F. Schöningh, 1986.

May, Reinhard. *Frieden und die Aufgabe des Rechts.* Wiesbaden: Franz Steiner, 1979.

Mitchell, J. M. *International Cultural Relations.* London: Unwin Hyman, 1986.

Moore, Barrington, *Social Origins of Dictatorship and Democracy.* Boston: Beacon Press, 1969.

Mörth, Ingo. "Vom Pluralismus zum Integrismus. Aspekte religiösen Alltagsbewusstseins." *Schweizerische Zeitschrift für Soziologie,* vol. 9, (1983), pp. 559–578.

———. *Die gesellschaftliche Wirklichkeit von Religion. Grundlegung einer allgemeinen Religionstheorie.* Stuttgart: Kohlhammer, 1978.

Mörth, I., and Fürstenberg, Fr. "Religionssoziologie." In *Handbuch der empirischen Sozialforschung,* ed. René König, vol. 14, 1–84. Stuttgart: F. Enke, 1979.

Nuscheler, Franz, and Nohlen, D., eds. *Handbuch der Dritten Welt.* Vol. 1, *Theorien–Strategien–Indikatoren.* Hamburg: Hoffmann & Campe, 1982.

Plessner, Helmuth. *Die verspätete Nation*. New edition. Frankfurt/M.: Suhrkamp, 1974.

Pöggeler, Otto, ed. *Hermeneutische Philosophie*. Munich: Nymphenburger Verlagshandlung, 1972.

Pye, Lucian W. *Asian Power and Politics: The Cultural Dimensions of Authority*. Cambridge: Harvard University Press, 1985.

Riedel, James. *Myths and Reality of External Constraints on Development*. London: Gower for Trade Policy Research Centre, 1987.

Schrey, Heinz-Horst, ed. *Säkularisierung*. Darmstadt: Wissenschaftliche Buchgesellschaft, 1981.

Seiffert, Helmut. *Sprache heute*. Munich: C. H. Beck, 1977.

Seyfarth, Constans, and Sprondel, Walter, eds. *Seminar: Religion und gesellschaftliche Entwicklung. Studien zur Protestantismus-Kapitalismus-These Max Webers*. Frankfurt/M.: Suhrkamp, 1973.

Skocpol, Theda, ed. *Vision and Method in Historical Sociology*. Cambridge: Cambridge University Press, 1987.

Smith, Donald E., ed. *Religion and Political Modernization*. New Haven and London: Free Press, 1974.

Smith, Wilfred Cantwell, *The Meaning and End of Religion*. New York: Harper & Row, 1978.

Steinbacher, Franz. *Kultur. Begriff–Theorie–Funktion*. Stuttgart: Kohlhammer, 1976.

Tibi, Bassam. "Orient und Okzident. Feindschaft oder interkulturelle Kommunikation? Anmerkungen zur Orientalismus-Debatte." *Neue Politische Literatur,* vol. 29, no. 3 (1984), pp. 267–286.

―――――. "Der amerikanische Area-Studies-Approach in den International Studies." *Orient,* vol. 24 (1983), pp. 260–284.

―――――. "Der Nord-Süd-Konflikt." In *Handlexikon der Politikwissenschaft,* ed. Wolfgang Mickel, 313–318. Munich: Ehrenwirth, 1983.

―――――. *Arab Nationalism: A Critical Inquiry*. London and New York: Macmillan, 1981; 2d edition, 1990.

―――――. "Kommunikationsstrukturen in der Weltgesellschaft und der interkulturelle Konflikt." *Beitraege zur Konfliktforschung,* vol. 11, no. 3 (1981), pp. 57–77.

―――――. "Akkulturation und interkulturelle Kommunikation. Ist jede Verwestlichung Kulturimperialistisch?" *Gegenwartskunde,* vol. 29 (1980), pp. 173–190.

―――――. "Schwache Institutionalisierung als politische Dimension der Unterentwicklung." *Verfassung und Recht in Übersee,* vol. 13 (1980), pp. 3–26.

―――――. *Internationale Politik und Entwicklungsländer-Forschung. Materialien zu einer ideologiekritischen Entwicklungssoziologie*. Frankfurt/M.: Suhrkamp, 1979.

Tilly, Charles. *Big Structures, Large Processes, Huge Comparisons*. New York: Russell Sage Foundation, 1984.

Topitsch, Ernst. *Erkenntnis und Illusion. Grundstrukturen unserer Weltauffassung*. Hamburg: Hoffmann & Campe, 1979.

Turner, Bryan Stanley. *Marx and the End of Orientalism.* London: Allen & Unwin, 1978.

_____ . *Weber and Islam.* London: Routledge & Kegan Paul, 1974.

Viehweg, Theodor. *Topik und Jurisprudenz. Ein Beitrag zur rechtswissen-schaftlichen Grundlagenforschung.* 5th edition. Munich: C. H. Beck, 1974.

Walker, R.B.J., ed. *Culture, Ideology and World Order.* Boulder, Colo.: Westview Press, 1984.

Wallace, Anthony F. C. "Die Revitalisierungsbewegungen." In *Soziologie der Entwicklungsländer,* ed. P. Heintz, 431–454. Cologne: Kiepenheuer & Witsch, 1962.

Wendorff, Rudolf. *Dritte Welt und westliche Zivilisation. Grundprobleme der Entwicklungspolitik.* Opladen: Westdeutscher Verlag, 1984.

Wuthnow, Robert. *Meaning and Moral Order: Explorations in Cultural Analysis.* Berkeley: University of California Press, 1987.

_____ et al. *Cultural Analysis.* London: Routledge & Kegan Paul, 1986.

Yearley, Steven. *Science, Technology, and Social Change.* London: Unwin Hyman, 1988.

2. Modern Islam in the Context of Social and Cultural Change

Abboud, Abdo. *Deutsche Romane im arabischen Orient.* Frankfurt/M. and Bern: P. Lang, 1984. (This is a significant monograph on the Arabo-Islamic awareness of German literature as a variant of Western culture.)

Abu-Lughod, Ibrahim. "Studies on the Islamic Assertion." *Arab Studies Quarterly,* vol. 4 (1982), pp. 157–175.

_____ . "Retreat from the Secular Path? Islamic Dilemmas of Arab Politics." *Review of Politics,* vol. 28 (1966), pp. 447–476.

_____ . *Arab Rediscovery of Europe: A Study in Cultural Encounters.* Princeton, N.J.: Princeton University Press, 1963.

Ajami, Fouad. *The Arab Predicament: Arab Political Thought and Practice Since 1967.* Cambridge: Cambridge University Press, 1981.

Amin, Sayed Hassan. *Islamic Law in the Contemporary World: Introduction, Glossary and Bibliography.* Glasgow: Royston, 1985.

Anderson, Norman. *Law Reform in the Muslim World.* London: Athlone Press, 1976.

Antes, Peter. *Ethik und Politik im Islam.* Stuttgart: Kohlhammer, 1982.

Antoun, Richard T. *Muslim Preacher in the Modern World.* Princeton, N.J.: Princeton University Press, 1989.

Arjomand, Said Amir, ed. *From Nationalism to Revolutionary Islam.* Albany: SUNY Press, 1984.

Arkoun, Mohammed. "Logocentrisme et vérité religieuse dans la pensée is-lamique." *Studia Islamica,* vol. 35 (1972), pp. 5–52.

Arkoun, Mohammed, and Gardet, Louis. *L'Islam. Hier–Demain.* Paris: Buchet-Chastel, 1978.

Arnold, Thomas W. *The Caliphate*. 2d edition. London: Routledge & Kegan Paul, 1965.

Ayalon, Ami. *Language and Change in the Arab Middle East: The Evolution of Modern Political Discourse*. New York: Oxford University Press, 1987.

Al-Azmeh, Aziz. *Arabic Thought and Islamic Societies*. London: Croom Helm, 1986.

Baljon, J.M.S. *Modern Muslim Koran Interpretation*. Leiden: E. J. Brill, 1968.

Bazzaz, 'Abdurrahman. "Islam and Arab Nationalism." Trans. S. Haim. *Welt des Islams*, vol. 3 (1954), pp. 201–218.

Becker, Carl Heinrich. *Islamstudien. Vom Werden und Wesen der islamischen Welt*. 2d edition. 2 vols. Hildesheim: G. Olms, 1967 (first published 1924 and 1932).

Bell, Richard, and Watt, W. M. *Introduction to the Qur'an*. Edinburgh: Edinburgh University Press, 1977.

Bercher, L. "De la brochure intitulée 'sentence des grands Uléma' (d'al-Azhar) sur le livre 'L'Islam et les bases du pouvoir.'" *Revue des Etudes Islamiques*, vol. 9 (1935), pp. 75–86.

Berque, Jacques. *L'Islam au défi*. Paris: Gallimard, 1980.

Binder, Leonard. *Islamic Liberalism: A Critique of Development Ideologies*. Chicago: Chicago University Press, 1988.

————. *The Ideological Revolution in the Middle East*. New York: John Wiley & Sons, 1964.

————, ed. *The Study of the Middle East: Research and Scholarship in the Humanities and the Social Sciences*. New York: John Wiley & Sons, 1976.

Bosworth, C. E., and Schacht, J., eds. *Legacy of Islam*. 2d edition. Oxford: Clarendon, 1974.

Bouman, Johan. *Gott und Mensch im Koran*. Darmstadt: Wissenschaftliche Buchgesellschaft, 1977.

Braune, Walther. *Der islamische Orient zwischen Vergangenheit und Zukunft*. Bern and Munich: Francke, 1960.

Bravmann, Mei'r Max. *The Spiritual Background of Early Islam*. Leiden: E. J. Brill, 1972.

Carré, Olivier, ed. *L'Islam et l'Etat dans le Monde aujourd'hui*. Paris: Presse Universitaire de France, 1982.

Chamie, Joseph. *Religion and Fertility: Arab Christian-Muslim Differentials*. Cambridge: Cambridge University Press, 1981.

Charnay, Jean-Paul. *Sociologie Religieuse de L'Islam*. Paris: Sindbad, 1977.

Clément, Jean François. "Problèmes de l'Islamisme." *Esprit* (October 1980), pp. 11–38.

————. "Pour une compréhension des mouvements islamistes." *Esprit* (January 1980), pp. 38–51.

Cole, Juan R. I., and Keddie, Nikki R., eds. *Shi'ism and Social Protest*. New Haven, Conn.: Yale University Press, 1986.

Corbin, Henry. *Creative Imagination in the Sufism of Ibn 'Arabi*. Trans. Rolf Mannheim. Princeton, N.J.: Princeton University Press, 1969.

Coulon, Christian. "Islam africain et Islam arabe: autonomie ou dépendance?" *Année africaine* (1976), pp. 250–275.

Coulson, Noel J. *A History of Islamic Law.* Edinburgh: University Press, 1978.
_____ . *Conflicts and Tensions in Islamic Jurisprudence.* Chicago: Chicago University Press, 1969.
_____ . "The Concept of Progress and Islamic Law." In *Religion and Progress in Modern Asia,* ed. R. N. Bellah, 74–92. New York: Free Press, 1965.
Crone, P. *Slaves on Horses: The Evolution of the Islamic Polity.* Cambridge: Cambridge University Press, 1980.
Cudsi, A. S., and Dessouki, A.E.H., eds. *Islam and Power in the Contemporary Muslim World.* Baltimore, Md.: Johns Hopkins University Press, 1981.
Curtis, Michael, ed. *Religion and Politics in the Middle East.* Boulder, Colo.: Westview Press, 1981.
Dawisha, Adeed, ed. *Islam in Foreign Policy.* Cambridge: Cambridge University Press, 1983.
Dekmejian, R. Hrair. *Islam in Revolution: Fundamentalism in the Arab World.* New York: Syracuse University Press, 1985.
Dessouki, Ali E. Hillal. *Islamic Resurgence in the Arab World.* New York: Praeger, 1982.
Djait, Hichem. *Europe and Islam: Cultures and Modernity.* Trans. Peter Heinegg. Berkeley: University of California Press, 1985.
_____ . "Renaissance, réformismes, révolutions dans l'Islam depuis un siècle: 1880–1980 (Resurrection)." *Annales d'Etudes Internationales,* vol. 11 (1980–1981), pp. 13–30.
_____ . *La Personnalité et le Devenir Arabo-Islamique.* Paris: Editions du Seuil, 1974.
Donohue, J. J., and Esposito, J. L., eds. *Islam in Transition.* New York and Oxford: Oxford University Press, 1982.
Eickelman, Dale F. *The Middle East: An Anthropological Approach.* Englewood Cliffs, N.J.: Prentice-Hall, 1981.
Enayat, Hamid. *Modern Islamic Political Thought.* Austin: University of Texas Press, 1982.
Esposito, John L. *Islam and Politics.* 2d revised edition. Syracuse, N.Y.: Syracuse University Press, 1987.
_____ . *Women in Muslim Family Law.* Syracuse, N.Y.: Syracuse University Press, 1982.
_____ , ed. *Voices of Resurgent Islam.* New York and Oxford: Oxford University Press, 1983.
_____ , ed. *Islam and Development: Religion and Sociopolitical Change.* Syracuse, N.Y.: Syracuse University Press, 1980.
Al-Farnqi, I. R. "Science and Traditional Values in Islamic Society." *Zygon,* vol. 2 (1969), pp. 231–246.
Farsoun, Samih K., ed. *Arab Society: Continuity and Change.* London: Croom Helm, 1985.
Fernea, Elizabeth W., and Bezirgan, B. Q., eds. *Middle Eastern Muslim Women Speak.* Austin: University of Texas Press, 1977.
Freund, W. S. "Religionssoziologische und sprachkulturelle Aspekte des Entwicklungsproblems in der islamischen Welt." *Intern. Jahrbuch für Religionssoziologie,* vol. 7 (1971), pp. 105–126.

Gellner, Ernest. *Islamic Dilemmas: Reformers, Nationalists, and Industrialization.* Berlin and New York: Mouton, 1985.

——— . *Muslim Society.* Cambridge: Cambridge University Press, 1981.

——— . "A Pendulum Swing Theory of Islam." *Annales Marocaines de Sociologie* (1968), pp. 4–14.

Ghaussy, A. Ghanie. *Das Wirtschaftsdenken im Islam. Von der orthodoxen Lehre bis zu den heutigen Ordnungsvorstellungen.* Bern and Stuttgart: Kohlhammer, 1986.

Gibb, H.A.R. *Islam: A Historical Survey.* 3d edition. Oxford: Oxford University Press, 1978.

——— . *Modern Trends in Islam.* Chicago: Chicago University Press, 1947.

Gibb, H., and Bowen, H. *Islamic Society and the West: A Study of the Impact of Western Civilization on Moslem Culture in the Near East.* 2 vols. London: Oxford University Press, 1950 and 1957.

Gilsenan, Michael. *Recognizing Islam: Religion and Society in the Modern Arab World.* New York: Pantheon Books, 1982.

Girdhari, L. Tikku. *Islam and Its Cultural Divergence.* Chicago: University of Chicago Press, 1971.

Goitein, S. D. *Studies in Islamic History and Institutions.* Leiden: E. J. Brill, 1966.

Grunebaum, G. E. von. *Modern Islam.* New York: Vintage Books, 1964.

Haddad, Yvonne. *Contemporary Islam and the Challenge of History.* Albany: SUNY Press, 1982.

Hanafi, Hassan. "Des idéologies modernistes à l'Islam révolutionnaire: une analyse théoretique des changements sociaux." *Peuples méditerranéens,* vol. 21 (1982), pp. 3–13.

Hartmann, R. "Die Wahhabiten." *Zeitschrift der Deutschen Morgenländischen Gesellschaft,* vol. 78 (1924), pp. 176–213.

Hassan, Farooq. *The Concept of State and Law in Islam.* Washington, D.C.: University Press of America, 1981.

Himmich, Ben Salem. *De la formation idéologique en Islam.* With a preface by Maxime Rodinson. Paris: Anthropos, 1980.

Hodgkin, Thomas. "The Revolutionary Tradition in Islam." *Race and Class,* vol. 21, no. 3 (1980), pp. 221–237.

Hodgson, M.G.S. *The Venture of Islam.* 3 vols. Chicago: University of Chicago Press, 1974.

Holt, P. M., Lambton, A.K.S., and Lewis, B., eds. *Cambridge History of Islam.* 2 vols. Cambridge: Cambridge University Press, 1970.

Höpp, G., and Grzeskowiak, M. "Re-Islamisierung—Schreckgespenst oder Herausforderung?—Bemerkungen zur Darstellung und Wertung eines aktuellen Prozesses durch die Islamwissenschaft der BRD und Westberlins." *Asien, Afrika, Lateinamerika,* vol. 12 (1984), pp. 477–490.

Hourani, Albert. *Arabic Thought in the Liberal Age, 1798–1939.* 2d edition. Cambridge: Cambridge University Press, 1983 (first printed by Oxford University Press, 1962).

Hudson, Michael C. *Arab Politics: The Search for Legitimacy.* New Haven, Conn.: Yale University Press, 1979.

Hunter, Shireen T., ed. *The Politics of Islamic Revivalism: Diversity and Unity.* Bloomington: Indiana University Press, 1988.

Ismael, Tareq Y., and Ismael, J. S. *Government and Politics in Islam.* London: Frances Pinter, 1985

Itzkowitz, Norman. *Ottoman Empire and Islamic Tradition.* Chicago: University of Chicago Press, 1980.

Jafri, Syed Husain M. *Origins and Early Development of Shi'a Islam.* London: Longman, 1979.

Jansen, Godfrey H. *Militant Islam.* New York: Harper & Row, 1979.

Johansen, Baber. *The Islamic Law on Land Tax and Rent.* London: Croom Helm, 1988.

Karpat, Kemal, ed. *The Political and Social Thought in the Contemporary Middle East.* 2d edition. New York: Praeger, 1982.

Keddie, Nikki. *An Islamic Response to Imperialism.* 2d edition. Berkeley and Los Angeles: University of California Press, 1983.

———, ed. *Scholars, Saints and Sufis.* Berkeley and Los Angeles: University of California Press, 1972.

Kedouri, Elie. *Afghani and 'Abduh: An Essay on Religious Unbelief and Political Activism in Modern Islam.* London: Frank Cass, 1966.

Kerr, Malcolm, *Islamic Reform.* Berkeley and Los Angeles: University of California Press, 1966.

Khoury, Philip. "Islamic Revivalism and the Crisis of the Secular State in the Arab World." In *Arab Resources: The Transformation of a Society,* ed. I. Ibrahim, 231–236. London: Croom Helm, 1983.

Kramer, Martin. *Islam Assembled.* New York: Columbia University Press, 1986.

———. "The Ideals of an Islamic Order." *Washington Quarterly,* vol. 3 (Winter 1980), pp. 3–13.

———. *Political Islam.* Beverly Hills: Sage Publications, 1980.

———, ed. *Shi'ism, Resistance and Revolution.* Boulder, Colo.: Westview Press, 1987.

Lambton, Ann S. *State and Government in Medieval Islam: An Introduction to the Study of Islamic Political Theory.* Oxford: Oxford University Press, 1981.

Laoust, Henri. *Les Schismes dans Islam: Introduction à une étude de la Religion musulmane.* Paris: Payot, 1965.

Lazarus, Yafeh Hava. *Some Religious Aspects of Islam.* Leiden: E. J. Brill, 1981.

Lewis, Bernard. *The Political Language of Islam.* Chicago: University of Chicago Press, 1988.

———. *The Muslim Discovery of Europe.* New York: W. Norton, 1982.

Makdisi, George. *The Rise of Colleges: Institutions of Learning in Islam and the West.* Edinburgh: Edinburgh University Press, 1981.

Manousakis, Gregor M. *Der Islam und die Nato.* Munich: Bernard und Graefe, 1980.

Martin, Richard C. *Islam in Local Contexts.* Leiden: E. J. Brill, 1982.

Mérad, Ali. *Le reformisme Musulman en Algérie.* Paris and The Hague: Mouton, 1967.

Mitchell, Richard P. *The Society of the Muslim Brothers.* Oxford: Oxford University Press, 1969.

Momen, Moojan. *An Introduction to Shi'i Islam: The History and Doctrines of Twelver Shi'ism.* New Haven, Conn.: Yale University Press, 1985.

Mortimer, Edward. *Faith and Power: The Politics of Islam.* New York: Random House, 1982.

Mottahedeh, Roy P. *Loyalty and Leadership in Early Islamic Society.* Princeton, N.J.: Princeton University Press, 1980.

Musallam, Basim F. *Sex and Society in Islam: Birth Control Before the Nineteenth Century.* Cambridge: Cambridge University Press, 1983.

Nadolski, Dora Glidewell. "Ottoman and Secular Civil Law." *International Journal of Middle East Studies,* vol. 4 (1977), pp. 517–543.

Nicholson, R. A. *Studies in Islamic Mysticism.* New edition. Cambridge: Cambridge University Press, 1980.

Noeldeke, Theodor. *Geschichte des Qur'ans.* Reprint edition. Hildesheim: G. Olms, 1981 (originally Leipzig: T. Weicher, 1909).

Paret, Rudi. *Mohammed und der Koran.* Stuttgart: Kohlhammer, 1976.

Parvin, Manoucher, and Sommer, Maurie. "Al-Islam. The Evolution of Muslim Territoriality and its Implications for Conflict Resolution in the Middle East." *International Journal of Middle East Studies,* vol. 12 (1980), pp. 1–21.

Peters, R. *Islam and Colonialism: The Doctrine of Jihad in Modern History.* The Hague and Paris: Mouton, 1979.

Piamenta, M. *Islam in Everyday Arabic Speech.* Leiden: E. J. Brill, 1979.

Pipes, Daniel. *In the Path of God: Islam and Political Power.* New York: Basic Books, 1983.

Piscatori, James P. *Islam in a World of Nation-States.* Cambridge and New York: New York University Press, 1986.

———, ed. *Islam in the Political Process.* Cambridge: Cambridge University Press, 1983.

Rabbath, Edmond. *Les Chrétiens dans l'Islam des premiers temps.* 2 vols. Beirut: Librairie Orientale, 1980 and 1981.

Rahman, Fazlur. *Islam and Modernity: Transformation of an Intellectual Tradition.* Chicago: University of Chicago Press, 1982.

———. *Major Themes of the Qur'an.* Minneapolis and Chicago: Bibliotheca Islamica, 1980.

———. *Islam.* Chicago: University of Chicago Press, 1979.

Rodinson, Maxime. *Islam und Kapitalismus.* With an introduction by B. Tibi. Frankfurt/M.: Suhrkamp, 1986.

———. *Europe and the Mystique of Islam.* Trans. Roger Veinus. London: Tauris, 1988 (originally published in French in 1980).

———. *Mohammed.* Lucerne and Frankfurt/M.: Bucher, 1975.

———. *Marxisme et Monde Musulman.* Paris: Editions du Seuil, 1972.

Rondot, Pierre. "Reformisme Musulman et 'Islam Révolutionaire.'" *L'Afrique et L'Asie Modernes* (1976), pp. 26–38.

———. *L'Islam et les Musulmans d'aujourd'hui.* Paris: Editions de L'Orante, 1958.

Rosenthal, E.I.J. *Islam in the Modern National State.* Cambridge: Cambridge University Press, 1965.

Royster, J. E. "The Study of Muhammad: A Survey of Approaches from the Perspective of the History and Phenomenology of Religion." *Muslim World,* vol. 62 (1972), pp. 49–70.

Said, Edward W. *Covering Islam.* New York: Pantheon Books, 1981.

_____. *Orientalism.* New York: Vintage Books, 1979.

Salamé, Ghassane. "L'Islam en Politique." *Politique Etrangère,* vol. 47 (1982), pp. 365–379.

Schacht, Joseph. *An Introduction to Islamic Law.* Oxford: Oxford University Press, 1964.

Shepard, William E. "Islam and Ideology: Towards a Typology." *International Journal of Middle East Studies,* vol. 19 (1987), pp. 307–336.

Sivan, Emmanuel. *Interpretations of Islam: Past and Present.* Princeton, N.J.: Darwin Press, 1986.

_____. *Radical Islam: Medieval Theology and Modern Politics.* New Haven, Conn.: Yale University Press, 1985.

Stoddard, P. H. et al., eds. *Change and the Muslim World.* Syracuse: Syracuse University Press, 1981.

Stowasser, Barbara Freyer, ed. *The Islamic Impulse.* London: Croom Helm, 1987.

Stowasser, Karl, trans. and ed. *Al-Tahtawi. Ein Muslim entdeckt Europa. Die Reise eines Ägypters im frühen 19. Jahrhundert nach Paris.* Munich: C. H. Beck, 1989.

Tapiero, Norbert. *Les idées réformistes d'al-Kawakibi 1849–1902. Contributions à l'étude de l'Islam modern.* Paris: Les éditions arabes, 1956.

Tibi, Bassam. *Arab Nationalism: A Critical Inquiry.* 2d, enlarged edition. London: Macmillan Press, 1990.

_____. *The Crisis of Modern Islam.* Salt Lake City: University of Utah Press, 1988.

_____. "The Interplay Between Social and Cultural Change. The Case of Germany and the Middle East." In *Arab Civilization: Challenges and Responses,* eds. George Atiyeh and Ibrahim Oweiss, 166–182. Albany: SUNY Press, 1988.

_____. "Islam and Arab Nationalism." In *The Islamic Impulse,* ed. Barbara Stowasser, 59–74. London: Croom Helm, 1987.

_____. "Islam and Modern European Ideologies." *International Journal of Middle East Studies,* vol. 18, no. 1 (1986), pp. 15–29.

_____. "Die gegenwärtige politische Revitalisierung des Islam: eine religions-soziologische Deutung." *Revue Suisse de Sociologie,* vol. 9, no. 3 (1983), pp. 657–675.

_____. "Islam and Secularization. Religion and the Functional Differentiation of the Social System." In *Youth, Violence, Religion: Secularization and De-secularization: Proceedings of the Fourth EASRG-Conference,* ed. M. Wahba, 69–85. Cairo: Anglo-Egyptian Bookshop, 1983.

_____. "Modern Education, Students and Social Change in Underdeveloped Societies—with Special Reference to the Islamic Middle East." In *Youth,*

Intellectuals and Social Change: Proceedings of the Third EASRG-Conference, ed. M. Wahba, 65–77. Cairo: Anglo-Egyptian Bookshop, 1983.

―――― . "The Renewed Role of Islam in the Political and Social Development of the Middle East." *Middle East Journal,* vol. 37 (1983), pp. 3–13.

―――― . "Cultural Innovation in the Developmental Process of the Islamic Middle East as a Future Perspective." *Archiv für Rechts- und Sozialphilosophie,* vol. 67 (1981), pp. 545–550.

―――― . "Islam and Social Change in the Modern Middle East." *Law and State,* vol. 22 (1980), pp. 91–106.

―――― . "Re-Islamization as Cultural Revival and Search for Identity in the Islamic Middle East." *Vierteljahresberichte. Probleme der Entwicklungsländer,* no. 81 (September 1980), pp. 229–237.

―――― . "The Social Background of Ideologies in the Arab Middle East." In *The Contemporary Middle Eastern Scene: Basic Issues and Major Trends,* eds. G. Stein and U. Steinbach, 84–93. Opladen: Leske, 1979.

―――― . "The Genesis of the Arab Left. A Critical Viewpoint." In *The Arabs Today: Alternatives for Tomorrow,* eds. Edward Said and Fuad Suleiman, 31–42. Columbus, Ohio: Forum Associates, 1973.

Trimmingham, J. Spencer. *The Sufi Orders in Islam.* Oxford: Clarendon Press, 1971.

Voll, John Obert. *Islam: Continuity and Change in the Modern World.* Boulder, Colo.: Westview Press, 1982.

Waardenburg, Jacques. "The Puritan Pattern in Islamic Revival Movements." *Revue Suisse de Sociologie,* vol. 9, no. 3 (1983), pp. 687–701.

―――― . "Official and Popular Religion in Islam." *Social Change* (1978), pp. 315–341.

Wahba, Mourad, ed. *Islam and Civilization: Proceedings of the First International Islamic Philosophy Conference.* Cairo: Ain Shams University Press, 1982.

Watt, W. Montgomery. *Islamic Fundamentalism and the Modern World.* New York: Routledge, Chapman & Hall, 1989.

―――― . *Islamic Philosophy and Theology.* Edinburgh: Edinburgh University Press, 1979.

―――― . *Muhammad: Prophet and Statesman.* 4th printing. Oxford: Oxford University Press, 1978.

―――― . *Muhammad at Medina.* 6th printing. Oxford: Clarendon Press, 1977.

―――― . *The Formative Period of Islamic Thought.* Edinburgh: Edinburgh University Press, 1973.

―――― . *Islamic Revelation in the Modern World.* Edinburgh: Edinburgh University Press, 1969.

―――― . *Islamic Political Thought.* Edinburgh: Edinburgh University Press, 1968.

―――― . *What Is Islam?* London and Beirut: Longman, 1968.

―――― . *Islam and Integration of Society.* London: Routledge, 1961.

Welch, A. T., and Cachia, P., eds. *Islam: Past Influence and Present Challenge.* New York: SUNY Press, 1979.

3. Area and Country Studies Relevant to the Study of Modern Islam

Abd-Allah, Umar F. *The Islamic Struggle in Syria.* Berkeley: Mizan Press, 1983.

Abrahamian, Ervand. *The Iranian Mojahedin.* New Haven, Conn.: Yale University Press, 1989.

Adams, Charles C. *Islam and Modernism in Egypt: A Study of the Modern Reform Movement Inaugurated by Muhammad 'Abduh.* New York: Russell & Russell, 1968.

Ahmed, Aziz. *Religion and Society in Pakistan.* Leiden: E. J. Brill, 1971.

Ahmed, Manzooruddin. *Pakistan: The Emerging Islamic State.* Karachi: Allies Book Corporation, 1966.

Ajami, Fouad. *The Vanished Imam: Musa al Sadr and the Shia of Lebanon.* Ithaca: Cornell University Press, 1986.

––––––. "In the Faraoh's Shadow: Religion and Authority in Egypt." In *Islam in the Political Process,* ed. James Piscatori, 12–35. Cambridge: Cambridge University Press, 1983.

Akhavi, Sharough. *Religion and Politics in Contemporary Iran.* New York: SUNY Press, 1980.

Ali, Mukti. "Islam and Indonesian Culture." In *Proceedings of the First International Islamic Conference* (19–22 November 1979), ed. M. Wahba, 15–33. Cairo: Ain Shams University Press, 1982.

Ansari, Hamied. "The Islamic Militants in Egyptian Politics." *International Journal of Middle East Studies,* vol. 16 (1984), pp. 124–144.

––––––. "Sectarian Conflict in Egypt and the Political Expediency of Religion." *The Middle East Journal,* vol. 38 (1984), pp. 397–418.

Antoun, Richard T. "The Islamic Court, the Islamic Judge and the Accommodation of Traditions. A Jordanian Case Study." *International Journal of Middle East Studies,* vol. 12 (1980), pp. 455–467.

Arjomand, Said Amir. *The Turban for the Crown: The Islamic Revolution in Iran.* New York: Oxford University Press, 1988.

Ayubi, Nazih N. M. "The Political Revival of Islam. The Case of Egypt." *International Journal of Middle East Studies,* vol. 12 (1980), pp. 481–499.

Badr, Siham. *Frauenbildung und Frauenbewegung in Ägypten. Ihre Geschichte und Probleme.* Wuppertal and Düsseldorf: Henn, 1968.

Baer, Gabriel. *Studies in the Social History of Modern Egypt.* Chicago: University of Chicago Press, 1969.

Baroody, G. M. "The Practice of Law in Saudi Arabia." In *King Faisal and the Modernization of Saudi Arabia,* ed. W. A. Beling, 113–124. London: Croom Helm, 1980.

Behrmann, Lucy C. *Muslim Brotherhoods and Politics in Senegal.* Cambridge: Harvard University Press, 1970.

Bennigsen, A., and Lanercier-Quelquejay, *Islam in the Soviet Union.* New York: Praeger, 1967.

Bennigsen, A., and Wimbush, S. Enders. *Muslim National Communism in the Soviet Union.* Chicago: University of Chicago Press, 1979.

Berger, Morroe. *Islam in Egypt Today; Social and Political Aspects of Popular Religion.* Cambridge: Cambridge University Press, 1970.

Bianchi, Robert. "Islam and Democracy in Egypt." *Current History,* vol. 88, no. 535 (1989), pp. 93–95 and 104.

Binder, Leonard. *In a Moment of Enthusiasm: Political Power and the 2nd Stratum in Egypt.* Chicago: University of Chicago Press, 1978.

Bligh, Alexander. "The Saudi Religious Elite (Ulama) as Participant in the Political System of the Kingdom." *International Journal of Middle East Studies,* vol. 17 (1985), pp. 37–50.

Boland, B. J. *The Struggle of Islam in Modern Indonesia.* The Hague: Nijhoff, 1971.

Borthwick, B. M. "Religion and Politics in Israel and Egypt." *The Middle East Journal,* vol. 33 (1979), pp. 145 –163.

Bromberger, Christian. "Islam et Révolution en Iran." *Revue de l'Occident Musulman et de la Méditerranée* (1980), pp. 109–130.

Carré, Olivier. "L'Islam Politique dans l'Orient Arabe." *Futuribles,* vol. 18 (1978), pp. 747–773.

Crecelius, Daniel. "Non-Ideological Responses of the Egyptian Ulama to Modernization." In *Scholars, Saints and Sufis,* ed. N. Keddie, 167ff. Berkeley: University of California Press, 1972.

———. "al-Azhar in the Revolution." *The Middle East Journal,* vol. 20 (1966), pp. 31–49.

Dekmejian, R. Hrair. *Egypt Under Nasir: A Study in Political Dynamics.* Albany: SUNY Press, 1972.

Divine, Donna Robinson. "Islamic Culture and Political Practice in British Mandated Palestine 1918–48." *Review of Politics,* vol. 45 (1983), pp. 71–93.

Dyk, Cornelius. *Rebellion Under the Banner of Islam: The Darul Islam in Indonesia.* The Hague: Nijhoff, 1981.

Eccel, A. Chris. *Egypt, Islam and Social Change: Al-Azhar in Conflict and Accommodation.* West Berlin: Klaus Schwarz, 1984.

Eickelman, Dale F. *Moroccan Islam: Tradition and Society in a Pilgrimage Center.* Austin: University of Texas Press, 1976.

Esposito, John, ed. *Islam in Asia: Religion, Politics, and Society.* New York: Oxford University Press, 1987.

al-Farsy, Fouad. *Saudi Arabia: A Case Study in Development.* London: Stacy International, 1978.

Fischer, Michael. *Iran: From Religious Dispute to Revolution.* Cambridge: Harvard University Press, 1980.

Fleuhr-Lobban, Carolyn. *Islamic Law and Society in the Sudan.* Totowa, N.J.: Biblio Distribution Center, 1987.

Gellar, Sheldon. *Senegal: An African Nation Between Islam and the West.* Boulder, Colo.: Westview Press, 1982.

Gellner, Ernest, and Vatin, Jean-Claude, eds. *Islam et Politique au Maghreb.* Paris: Editions du CNRS, 1981.

Green, Arnold H. *The Tunisian Ulama, 1873–1915.* Leiden: E. J. Brill, 1978.

Habib, J. S. *Ibn Sa'ud's Warriors of Islam.* Leiden: E. J. Brill, 1978.

Haddad, Yvonne Yazbeck. "Islamic Awakening in Egypt." *Arab Studies Quarterly,* vol. 9, no. 3 (1987), pp. 234–259.

Halliday, Fred. "'Islam' and Soviet Foreign Policy." *Arab Studies Quarterly,* vol. 9, no. 3 (1987), pp. 217–233.

Hanafi, Hassan. "The Relevance of the Islamic Alternative in Egypt." *Arab Studies Quarterly,* vol. 4 (1982), pp. 54–74.

Hanf, Theodor. *Erziehungswesen in Gesellschaft und Politik des Libanon.* Bielefeld: Bertelsmann, 1969.

Hanna, J. "The Roots of Islam in Modern Tunisia." *Islamic Culture,* vol. 46 (1972), pp. 93–100.

Harris, Christina Phelps. *Nationalism and Revolution in Egypt: The Role of the Muslim Brotherhood.* The Hague: Mouton, 1964.

Heper, Metin. "Islam, Polity and Society in Turkey." *Middle East Journal,* vol. 35 (1981), pp. 345–363.

Hooker, M. B., ed. *Islam in South-East Asia.* Leiden: E. J. Brill, 1983.

Humphreys, S. "Islam and Political Values in Saudi Arabia, Egypt and Syria." *The Middle East Journal,* vol. 33 (1979), pp. 1–19.

Ibrahim, Saad Eddin, "An Islamic Alternative in Egypt." *Arab Studies Quarterly,* vol. 4 (1982), pp. 75–93.

Islam, Nasir. "Islam and National Identity. The Case of Pakistan and Bangla Desh." *International Journal of Middle East Studies,* vol. 13 (1981), pp. 55–72.

Jansen, Johannes J. G. *The Neglected Duty: The Creed of Sadat's Assassins and Islamic Resurgence in the Middle East.* New York and London: Macmillan, 1986.

———. *The Interpretation of the Koran in Modern Egypt.* Leiden: E. J. Brill, 1974.

Jawed, N. "Islamic Secularism: An Ideological Trend in Pakistan in the 1960's." *Muslim World,* vol. 65 (1975), pp. 196–215.

Johnson, Michael. *Class and Client in Beirut: The Sunni Muslim Community and the Lebanese State, 1840–1985.* London: Ithaca Press, 1986.

Jones, Sidney R. "It Can't Happen Here: A Post-Khomeini Look at Indonesian Islam." *Asian Survey,* vol. 20 (1980), pp. 311–323.

Kalidar, A. R. "Religion and State in Syria." *Asian Affairs* (1974), pp. 16–22.

Karson, J. Henry. "Islamization and Social Policy in Pakistan." *Journal of South Asia and Middle East Studies* (1982), pp. 71–90.

Kayali, Nabil M. "Politics and Religion in Uman." *International Journal of Middle East Studies,* vol. 11 (1979), pp. 567–579.

Kechichian, Joseph A. "The Role of the Ulama in the Politics of an Islamic State: The Case of Saudi Arabia." *International Journal of Middle East Studies,* vol. 18 (1986), pp. 53–71.

Keddie, Nikki R. *Religion and Politics in Iran: Shi'ism from Quietism to Revolution.* New Haven, Conn.: Yale University Press, 1983.

———. *Roots of Revolution: An Interpretative History of Modern Iran.* New Haven, Conn.: Yale University Press, 1981.

————. *Religion and Rebellion in Iran: The Tobacco Protest of 1891–1892.* London: Frank Cass, 1966.

Kepel, Gillis. *Muslim Extremism in Egypt: The Prophet and Pharaoh.* Berkeley: University of California Press, 1985.

al-Khalik, Samir. *Republic of Fear: The Politics of Modern Iraq.* Berkeley: University of California Press, 1989.

Klein, Martin A. *Islam and Imperialism in Senegal.* Palo Alto: Hoover Institution, Stanford University, 1968.

Krämer, Gudrun. *Ägypten unter Mubarak.* Baden Baden: Nomos, 1986.

Kritzek, James, and Lewis, W. H., eds. *Islam in Africa.* New York: Van Nostrand-Reinhold, 1969.

Laban, Abdel Moneim. *Einige Aspekte der Akkulturation und des sozialen Wandels in Ägypten von 1900 bis 1952.* Frankfurt/M.: Haag & Herchen, 1977.

Labaune, P., and Brizard, S. "Les Problèmes Politico-Religieux dans la République Arabe du Yémen (1962–1972)." *L'Afrique et l'Asie,* (1974), pp. 41–47.

Lackner, Helen. *A House Built on Sand: A Political Economy of Saudi Arabia.* London: Ithaca Press, 1978.

Lemarchand, René, ed. *The Green and the Black: Qadhafi's Policies in Africa.* Bloomington: Indiana University Press, 1988 (in particular the essay of E. Joffe, "The Role of Islam").

Niblock, Tim. *Class and Power in Sudan: The Dynamics of Sudanese Politics, 1898–1985.* London and Albany: SUNY Press, 1987.

Ochsenwald, William. "Saudi Arabia and the Islamic Revival." *International Journal of Middle East Studies,* vol. 13 (1981), pp. 271–286.

O'Kane, J. "Islam in the New Egyptian Constitution: Some Discussions in al-Ahram." *Middle East Journal,* vol. 26 (1981), pp. 137–148.

Pawelka, Peter. *Herrschaft und Entwicklung im Nahen Osten: Ägypten.* Heidelberg: UTB, 1985.

Picard, Elisabeth. *Liban. Etat de Discorde. Des Fondations aux Guerres Fratricides.* Paris: Flammarion, 1988.

Quandt, William B. *Saudi Arabia in the 1980s.* Washington, D.C.: Brookings Institution, 1981.

Ramazani, R. K. *Revolutionary Iran: Challenge and Response in the Middle East.* Baltimore, Md.: Johns Hopkins University Press, 1986.

Roy, Oliver. *Islam and Resistance in Afghanistan.* New York: Cambridge University Press, 1986.

Sahliyeh, Emile. *In Search of Leadership: West Bank Politics Since 1967.* Washington, D.C.: Brookings Institution, 1988 (in particular Chapter 7, "Islam as an Alternative").

Said, Aly A., and Wenner, M. F. "Modern Islamic Reform Movements: The Muslim Brotherhood in Contemporary Egypt." *Middle East Journal,* vol. 36 (1982), pp. 336–361.

Salamé, Ghassan. "Islam and Politics in Saudi Arabia." *Arab Studies Quarterly,* vol. 9, no. 3 (1987), pp. 306–326.

Salem, Norma. *Habib Bourguiba; Islam and the Creation of Tunisia.* London: Croom Helm, 1984.

al-Sayyid-Marsot, Afaf. *Egypt's Liberal Experiment.* Berkeley: University of California Press, 1977.

Schimmel, Annemarie. *Islam in the Indian Subcontinent.* Leiden: E. J. Brill, 1980.

Sivan, Emmanuel. "Sunni Radicalism in the Middle East and the Iranian Revolution." *International Journal of Middle East Studies,* vol. 21, no. 1 (1989), pp. 1–30.

Tibi, Bassam. "Structural and Ideological Change in the Arab Subsystem Since the Six-Day War." In *The Arab-Israeli Conflict: Two Decades of Change,* eds. Y. Lukacs and A. Battah, 147–163. Boulder, Colo.: Westview Press, 1988.

――― . "The Iranian Revolution and the Arabs." *Arab Studies Quarterly,* vol. 8, no. 1 (1986), pp. 29–44.

――― . "A Typology of Arab Political Systems. With Special Reference to Islam and Government as Exemplified in Arab Monarchies." In *Arab Society: Continuity and Change,* ed. S. Farsoun, 48–64. London: Croom Helm, 1985.

――― . "Political Freedom in Arab Societies." *Arab Studies Quarterly,* vol. 6 (1984), pp. 222–227.

――― . "Vom Zentrum der Revolution zum Zentrum des Petro-Dollars. Ägypten und Saudi-Arabien in der Neuen Arabischen Sozialordnung." *Beiträge zur Konfliktforschung,* vol. 14, no. 2 (1984), pp. 101–128.

Toprak, Binaz. *Islam and Political Development in Turkey.* Leiden: E. J. Brill, 1981.

Triaud, Jean-Louis. *Islam et Sociétés Soudanaises au Moyen-âge.* Paris: Collège de France Laboratoire d'anthropologie sociale, 1973.

Trimingham, J. Spencer. *The Influence of Islam Upon Africa.* 2d edition. London: Longman. 1980.

――― . *A History of Islam in West Africa.* Oxford: Oxford University Press, 1962.

Warburg, Gabriel. "Islam and Politics in Egypt." *Middle East Studies* (1982), pp. 131–157.

――― . *Islam, Nationalism and Communism in a Traditional Society: The Case of Sudan.* London: F. Cass, 1978.

――― . "Religious Policy in the Northern Sudan. Ulama and Sufism 1899–1919." *Asian and African Studies* (1971), pp. 89–119.

Warburg, Gabriel R., and Kupferschmidt, Uri M., eds. *Islam, Nationalism and Radicalism in Egypt and the Sudan.* New York: Praeger, 1983.

Waterbury, John. *The Egpyt of Nasser and Sadat.* Princeton, N.J.: Princeton University Press, 1983.

――― . *The Commander of the Faithful: The Moroccan Political Elite.* New York: Columbia University Press, 1970.

Wheeler, G. "Islam and the Soviet Union." *Middle East Studies,* vol. 13 (1977), pp. 40–49.

al-Yassini, Ayman. *Religion and State in the Kingdom of Saudi Arabia.* Boulder, Colo.: Westview Press, 1987.

4. Sources in Arabic

The Literature of Islamic Fundamentalism

'Abdulfattah, Nabil. *al-Mishaf wa al-saif. Sira' al-din wa al-dawla fi Misr.* Cairo: Madbuli Press, 1984.

'Abdulmawla, Mahmud. *Anzimat al-mujtama' wa ad-dawla fi al-Islam.* Tunis: al-Sharika al-Tunisiyya li al-Tawzi', 1973.

'Abdulsalam, Faruq. *al-Ahzab as-siyasiyya was al-fasl bain al-din wa as-siyasa.* Cairo: Maktab Qalyub, 1979.

Abu-Alfattuh, Abu-Almu'ati. *Hatmiyat al-hall al-Islami.* 2d edition. Cairo: al-Andalus, 1987.

Ahmad, Rif'at Sayyid. *al-Islambuli. Ru'yah jadidah li tanzim al-Jihad.* Cairo: Maktabat Madbuli, 1988.

'Ali, Said Ismail. *Disarat fi at-taribya al-islamiyya.* Cairo: 'Alam al-Kutub, 1982.

———. *Usul at-taribya al-islamiyya.* Cairo: Dar al-Thaqafah, 1978.

al-'Awwa, Muhammad Salim. *Fi an-nizam as-siyasi lil-dawla al-Islamiyya.* 6th printing. Cairo: al-Maktab al-Misri al-Hadith, 1983.

Ben-Aschur, Muhammad T. *Maqasid al-Schari'a al-islamiyya.* Tunis: al-Sharika al-Tunisiyya, 1978.

Ben-Khuja, Muhammad al-Habib. *Mawaqif al-Islam.* Tunis: Dar al-Kutub al-Sharqiyya, 1972.

Bensa'id, Sa'id. *Dawlat al-Khilafa.* Casablanca: Dar al-Nashr al-Maghribiyya, no date.

Darwaza, Muhammad 'Izzat. *al-Mar'a fi al-Qur'an wa al-Sunna.* 2d edition. Beirut: al-Maktabah al-'Asriyya, 1980.

Fahmi, Mustafa Abu-Zaid. *Fan al-hukm fi al-Islam.* Cairo: al-Maktab al-Misri al-Hadith, 1981.

Hanafi, Hassan. *al-Din wa al-thawrah fi Misr 1952–1981.* 8 vols. Cairo: Madbuli Press. Most important are vol. 5, *al-harakat al-diniyyah al-mu'asirah,* 1988; and vol. 6: *al-Usuliyya al-Islamiyya,* 1989.

———. *al-Turath wa al-tajdid.* Beirut: Dar al-Tanwir, 1981.

'Imara, Muhammed. *al-Islam wal-'uruba wal-'ilmaniyya.* Beirut: Dar al-Wihda, 1981.

———. *Muslimun thuwwar.* 2d edition. Cairo: al-Mu'assasah al-'Arabiyya, 1979.

Jamal, Ahmad Muhammad. *Muhadarat fi al-thaqafa al-Islamiyya.* 3d edition. Cairo: Dar al-Sha'b, 1975.

al-Jamali, Muhammad Fadil. *Nahwa tawhid al fikr at-tarbawi fi al-'alam al-Islami.* 2d edition. Tunis: al-Dar al-Tunisiyya, 1978.

Jarischa, 'Ali, M. and Zaibaq M. S. *Asalib al-ghazu al-fikri li al 'alam al-islami.* 2d edition. Medina and Cairo: Dar al-'Tisam, 1978.

Karkar, 'Ismataddin. *al-Mar'a min khilal al-ayat al-Qur'aniyya.* Tunis: al-Sharika al-Tunisiyya, 1979.

Khalafallah, Muhammad Ahmad. *al-Qur'an wa al-Dawla.* 2d printing. Cairo: al-Mu'assasa al-'Arabiyya, 1981.

al-Khalidi, Mahmud. *Ma'alim al-khilafah fi al-fikr al-siyasi al-Islami.* Beirut: Darl al-Jil, 1984.

Khalil, 'Imadulddin. *Tahafut al-'ilmaniyya.* Beirut: Mu'assasat al-Risala, 1979.

al-Khartabuli, 'Ali Husni. *al-Islam wa al-Khilafa.* Beirut: Dar Beirut, 1969.

Kishk, Muhammad Jalal. *al-Sa'udiyyun wa al-hall al-Islami.* 4th printing. Cairo: al-Matba'a al-Fanniyya, 1984.

Mahmud, 'Abdulhalim. *al-Qur'an wa al-nabi.* Cairo: Dar al-Ma'arif, 1979.

————. *Urobba wa al-Islam.* Cairo: Dar al-Ma'arif, 1979.

Markaz Dirasat al-Wihda al-Arabiyya, ed. *al-Harakat al-islamiyya al-mu'asira fi al-watan al-'arabi.* Beirut: Markaz Dirasat Press, 1987.

————. *al-Qawmiyya al-'arabiyya wa al-Islam.* 2d edition. Beirut: Markaz Dirasat al-Wihda al-Arabiyya Press, 1982.

al-Najjar, Husain Fawzi. *al-Islam wa al-siyasa.* Cairo: Dar al-Sha'b, 1977.

Qardawi, Yusuf. *Hatmiyat al-hal al-Islami.* 2 vols. Vol. 1: *al-hulul al-mustwrada;* Vol. 2: *al-hal la-Islami farida wa darura.* Beirut: Mu'assat al-Risala, 1980 (first printing 1974).

Sa'b, Hassan. *Islam al-hurriya la islam al-'ubudiyya.* 2d edition. Beirut: Dar al-'Ilm al-Malayin, 1979.

Sadiq, Hassan. *Judhur al-fitna fi al-firaq al-Islamiyya.* Cairo: Madbuli Press, 1988.

al-Sa'id, Rif'at. *Hasan al-Banna, mata? Kaif? wa Limadha?* Cairo: Maktabat Madbuli, 1977.

Salih, Ahmad 'Abbas. *al-Yamin wa al-yasar fi al-Islam.* 2d edition. Beirut: al-Mu'assasah al-'Arabiyya, 1973.

al-Salih, Subhi. *Ma'alim al-Shari'a al-islamiyya.* Beirut: Dar al-'Ilm al-Malayin, 1975.

al-Sayyid, Ridwan. *al-Islam al-mu'asir.* Beirut: al-'Ulum, 1986.

————. *al-Umma wa al-jama'a wa al-sulta. Dirasat fi al-fikr al-'arabi al-Islami.* Beirut: Dar 'qra', 1984.

Shaltut, Mahmud. *al-Islam aqidah wa Schari'a.* 10th printing. Cairo: Dar al-Shuruq, 1980.

al-Sharbasi, Ahmad. *Shakib Arslan da'iyat al-'uruba wa al-Islam.* Beirut: Dar al-Jil, 1978.

Taffaha, Ahmad Zaki. *al-Mar'a, wa al-Islam.* Beirut and Cairo: Dar al-Kitab al-Lubnani, 1979.

Tu'aima, Sabir. *al-Shari'a al-Islamiyya fi'asr al-'ilm.* Beirut: Dar al-Jil, 1979.

al-'Ushmawi, Muhammad Said. *usul al-Shari'a.* 2d edition. Cairo and Beirut: Maktabat Madbuli, 1983.

al-Yasin, Muhammad Hassan. *Hawamish 'ala kitab naqd al-fikr ad-dini,* 6th edition. Beirut: Dar al-Nafa'is, 1980.

Sunni Islamic Views on the Iranian Revolution

(See also my article "The Iranian Revolution and the Arabs" and the article of E. Sivan, "Sunni Radicalism in the Middle East and the Iranian Revolution," both cited in section 3 of this bibliography.)

'Abdulmu'min, Muhammad al-Sa'id. *Masa'lat al-thawrah al-Iraniyya*. Cairo, 1981. (Abdulmu'min is professor for Iranian Studies at Ain Shams University, Cairo. This book, published by the author, is available in Cairo bookshops.)

Desuqi-Sheta, Ibrahim. *al-Thawrah al-Iraniyya al-Judhur-al-'ideologiyya*. Beirut: al-Watan al-'Arabi, 1979.

Fahs, Hani. *Mashru'at as'ilah qabl Iran kanat kha'ifa*. Beirut: Dar al-Tawjih al-Islami, 1980.

Hilmi, Mustafa. *Nizam al-khilafah bain ahl al-Sunna wa al-Shi'a*. Cairo: Dar al-Da'wa, 1988.

Huwaidi, Fahmi. *Iran min al-dakhil*. 3d edition. Cairo: al-Ahram Press, 1988.

Mardini, Zuhair. *al-Thawrah al-Iraniyya bain al-waqi' wa al-sturah*. Beirut: Iqra', 1986.

al-Nu'mani, Muhammad Manzur. *al-thawrah al-Iraniyya fi mizan al-Islam*. Cairo: Matu'at 'Abir lil-Kitab, 1986.

al-Sabruti, 'Abdulfattah 'Abdulmun'im. *al-Haqa'iq al-khafiya fi al-harb al-iraqiyya al-iraniyya wa al-harb al-qadhirah*. Cairo, 1986. (Al-Sabruti is a lawyer in Cairo and, like 'Abdulmu'min, published his book himself.)

al-Shabi, 'Ali. *al-Shi'a fi Iran*. Tunis: Presse Universitaire de Tunis, 1980.

Name Index

Abdelraziq, Ali, 73, 125, 132
Abduh, Muhammed, 21
Afghani, Jemaladdin, 21, 180
Ajami, Fouad, on *ulema,* 136
Alatas, Syed Hussein, on
    intellectuals in developing
    countries, 111
Ali, Muhammed, 107, 136
    reforms of, 139, 145
'Ali, Sa'id Isma'il, on the Koran, 114
Ansari, Hamied, on Egyptian
    fundamentalists, 138, 141–143
'Aqqad, 'Abbas Mahmud, 94
Arslan, Shakib, 124
Ashur, Ben, 67
Averroës (Ibn Rushd), 39, 69, 105
    and doctrine of dual nature of
    truth, 26–27
Avicenna (Ibn Sina), 69, 105
Ayubi, Nazih N. M., on Egyptian
    fundamentalist groups, 141–143
Azzam, Hamdy Mahmoud, 97–98

Balandier, Georges, on
    "correspondence between sacred
    and political," 123
Bani Sadr, Hassan, and Rajawi, 158
Bayat, Mangol, on Shariati's writings,
    159
Bell, Daniel, on restriction of
    secularization concept, 195
Bendix, Reinhard
    comparative social historical
        approach, 189
    on concept of modernization, 189–
        193

on critique of international
    society, 182
Heidelberg Max Weber lectures by,
    190
on legitimation of "royal
    authority," 120, 136, 160
Bloch, Ernst
    on "the Aristotelian Left" in
        Islam, 99, 105
    on the Islamic philosopher, 99
    on modernization of Islam, 69,
        83–84
de Boer, T. J.
    on Averroës, 100
    on basic structures of Arabic, 82
Bonaparte, Napoleon, Egyptian
    campaign of (1798), 20, 42–43,
    107–108, 135–136, 139
Borkenau, Franz, on "transition from
    feudal to bourgeois worldview,"
    129
Bouman, Johan, and Koranic text
    analysis, 27–28, 35, 124

Carroll, T. G., on relationship
    between Islam and
    modernization, 193
Coulson, Noël J., on Islamic legal
    system, 40, 64–65, 74
Crecelius, Daniel, on modernization
    of Islam, 145

Dreier, Ralf
    on theory of law, 60
    on topics discussion, 63, 71
Duri, Abdalaziz, 121

263

Durkheim, Emile
on *fait social,* 11, 122
on anomie thesis, 53

Eisenstadt, Shmuel N., 48, 51–52,
184
Elias, Norbert
on civilizing process, 2–3, 18, 120,
185, 193–194
theory of civilization, 62, 129, 147
Enayat, Hamid
on Khomeini, 150
on political thought in Islam, 132
Entelis, John, on petrodollar wealth
and its effects, 176
Esser, Joseph, 69(n46), 74

al-Farabi, Abu Nasr Muhammed, 163
on poetry in High Islam, 98
Fischer, Michael
on Khomeini, 161
on Qum, 149

Gadamer, Hans Georg, 74
Geertz, Clifford, 5–15, 47, 54, 78,
179, 187–188
anthropology of religion, 1, 4, 8
on cultural diversity in Islam, 133
line of argument, 14
Graham, Robert, 151, 154
Green, Arnold H., on *ulema,* 167

al-Hallaj, Ibn Mansur, 24
Halliday, Fred, on Iranian
industrialization policy, 153
Hanf, Theodor
on socialization process, 113
on self-perception of Muslims,
80(n13)
Hart, H.L.A., 59, 62–63
on "open texture," 63, 70
Henle, Paul, on connection between
language, thought, and culture,
77, 79
Herder, Johann Gottfried von
on nation as a cultural
community, 94

unified community concept, 181–
182, 194
Hudson, Michael
on Islam, 129
on "modernizing monarchies," 174
Huntington, Samuel P.
theory of institutionalization, 152,
166
on modernization of traditional
monarchies, 175
Husri, Sati', 80, 90, 99
and renaissance of *'arabiyya,* 94–
97

Ibn Abd al-Wahhab, Muhammed
(founder of Wahhabi
movement), 20, 172
Ibn Bultan, on classification of
sciences in Islam, 104, 107
Ibn Khaldun, 163
prolegomena of, 84–85
Ibn Saud (founder of Saudi Arabia),
169–171
Ibrahim, Saad Eddin, on Egyptian
fundamentalists, 141–143
'Imara, Muhammed, on
modernization of Islamic
societies, 193
Ineichen, Gustav, on language and
change, 77–78

Keddie, Nikki R.
on the Tobacco Uprising in Iran,
158
on *ulema* and legitimation of rule,
148–149, 160, 167
Khadduri, Majid, on contemporary
history of the Orient, 168
Khomeini, 46
Khoury, Philip, on politicization of
Islam, 128

Lahbabi, Mohammad 'Aziz, on
language and Islam in change,
77
LaPalombara, Joseph, on political
parties and social change, 170

Lerner, Daniel, 46, 184
Lewis, Bernard, on the "return of Islam," 186
Luhmann, Niklas, 10, 13, 125, 130, 166, 183
Luther, Martin, 50

Makdisi, George, on Islamic education, 103–104
May, Reinhard
  on comparison of laws, 68
  on world peace through law, 60–61
Mitchell, Richard, on Islam and modern technology, 117
Mörth, Ingo, on everyday religious awareness, 54
Mosaddeq, Mohammed (Iran), 149
Mubarak, Hosni, 143
  and Egyptian fundamentalists, 144
Muhammed, 9, 17–18, 27–37, 40, 124, 162, 188–189
  and Arabic, 81–82
  charismatic prophecy of, 120
  recognition as Prophet of God, 35
Musa, Salama, 80
  on modernization of Arabic, 90–94
Muslehuddin, Muhammad, 73–74

Nasser, Jamal Abdel, 136–140
  as charismatic leader, 168
  neutralization of Islam in Egypt by, 140
  reform of al-Azhar by, 145
Nassur, Adib (Syrian constitutional lawyer), on Islamic constitutional law, 163

Otte, G., on topics discussion, 63
Owen, Roger, on comparison between Orient and Occident, 127–128

Plessner, Helmuth, 60
  on conquest of the world by Europeanism, 110

Rajawi, Masud (commander of "holy people's fighters" in Iran), 158. *See also* Bani Sadr
Rodinson, Maxime, 50–51, 124, 164–165
  on critique of Orientalism, 15
  on Islamic language, 78, 86
  on Muhammed, 162
  presentation of pre-Islamic culture, 64–65

Sadat, Anwar el-
  murder of (1981), 138, 143
  as successor to Nasser, 138
Said, Edward, on critique of Orientalism, 15
Savory, Roger, on Twelver Shi'ite theological doctrine, 150
Schacht, Joseph, on the Islamic legal system, 40, 64
Seiffert, Helmut, as critic of modern linguists, 78
Senghaas, Dieter, dissociative development strategy, 187
Seyfarth, Constans, and Walter Sprondel, on Weber's protestantism/capitalism thesis, 192
Shah, Reza (Iran), 155
  modernization experiment, 151–154
  and the oil crisis (1950), 149
  regime, 19, 139, 151, 154
  Sadat on, 141
Shariati, Ali, 158–159
Simson, Uwe, on "re-Islamization," 187
Smith, Wilfred C., on the *nizam* (system) concept in the Koran, 131
Sprondel, Walter. *See* Seyfarth, Constans, and Walter Sprondel
Steppat, Fritz, on Islam, 167

Tahtawi, Rifa'a, in Europe, 86–87, 100, 107–108, 144

Viehweg, Theodor, topics approach, 61–63, 67–68, 70–73

Wahba, Mourad (Egyptian philosopher), 69, 191–192
Waterbury, John
  on Arab political systems, 126, 165
  on Morocco, 65–66, 170–171
Watt, W. Montgomery, 34–35, 39, 133–134

Weber, Max
  on the legitimacy of rule, 167
  protestantism/capitalism thesis, 192
Weiner, Myron, on political parties and social change, 170
Wittfogel, Karl A., on the concept of Oriental despotism, 153–154

Subject Index

Abbasids
  empire, 19, 84–85, 162
  epoch, 84
Acculturation, processes of, 53, 108, 183
Africa
  and Islam, 24–25, 183
  nonliterate, 60
Alawi dynasty, 168–171
al-Azhar, 108
  authorities, 143–146
  reform under Nasser, 140
  scholars, 125, 132
  university, 72, 102, 135–136, 139–140, 145–146, 148
Algeria, Islam in, 17
Alliance, *bazaari-ulema,* 149, 158
Anthropology, 8–12. *See also in Name Index* Geertz, Clifford
Anticolonialism, Islam as, 125
Apostasy, Islamic penal law on, 36
Asia, 3

Bay'a (oath of loyalty), 162, 170

Caliph, 18, 162. *See also* Caliphate
Caliphate, 132, 136, 162. *See also* Caliph
Change
  accommodation of, 4, 13, 45–46, 55, 75–76, 97–102, 106, 155–159, 174–175, 179–180
  of Arabic language, 76–86
  basic patterns for the perception of, 32–34
  cultural and social, 45, 49, 52–58

cultural processing of, 8–9, 32, 53–54, 193
  and the Islamic cultural and legal system, 68–75
  and Koranic exegesis, 37–39
  social, 49, 55, 57–58, 74, 127–129, 141, 152–153, 156–157, 174–177
Christianity
  and Islam, 35–36, 66, 180
  and secularization, 194
Civilization, 21, 24, 181, 190
  golden age of Islamic, 105–106
  process of, 2, 120–121, 129–130, 185, 196
  stagnation of Islamic, 106–108
Clergy
  dictatorship in Iran of, 150, 159, 176
  Shi'ite, 147–150
Colonialism, 86
  hegemony of, 91
  power of, 47, 171
Colonization, 107, 185
Communication
  globalized, intercultural, 179–186, 195
  in international society, 68
  processes, 182–183
Community concept, unified, German, 181–182
Conflict, sociocultural and intercultural, 183–186
Crisis
  of legitimacy, 126, 131
  modern Islam in, 124–125, 188

Culture, 2, 7, 10, 17, 21, 32, 43, 47,
    52–53, 68, 88, 145–146, 164–165,
    179–180, 184–185
  African and Asian, 108
  Arab Islamic, 26, 32, 46, 107
  and *culture universelle,* 179–180
  defensive, 53–54
  definition, 54
  fostering by elites of, 53
  indigenous, 26, 125, 131
  innovations in, 45–46, 52
  language and, 78, 81–101
  plurality of, 117, 180, 185, 194
  religious, 195
  sociology of, 10, 45–46, 49, 64
  Western industrial, 52, 115, 194

Dar al-Harb and Dar al-Islam, 1, 33
Decolonization, 183–184
Democracy, 162, 195
Desacralization, of Islamic society,
    194
Despotism, oriental, 151–154
Development, 38–39, 46–52, 182–184
  concept, 183
  Islamic doctrine on, 35
  Islamic law and, 39–42
  relationship between Islam and,
    33–34, 39–44
  salafiyya on, 39
  sociology of, 48, 193

Education and learning
  imported form, 114
  in Islam, 102–112, 118–119
  in Islamic law, 42
Elite
  as instigators of change, 55, 189–
    190
  Islamic, 55, 190–191
  modern, 53
  Westernized, 128, 144
England, 185, 189
Enlightenment
  and Islam, 168
  in the Occident, 181

Ethic, protestant, 49, 192. *See also
    in Name Index* Weber, Max
Euro-Arab Social Research Group,
    191
Europe
  civilization in, 3, 97
  colonization from, 107–112, 189–
    190, 193
  education in the sense of, 107–
    109, 111–112
  and Islam, 33, 68
  Islamic history in, 20
  language development in, 97
  as a model of over-Westernized
    elite, 55
  and oriental culture, 87
  Sati' Husri in, 95
  secular ideologies from, 125
  Tahtawi in, 100, 108
Evolutionism, 3, 48
  rejection, 193
  tradition, 183–184

Fiqh (Islamic sacred jurisprudence),
    27, 40, 66–69, 108, 140
  scholar(s), 64, 66–67, 69, 72–73
  sources, 74
France, 43, 108, 185, 189
Fundamentalism
  Catholic, 193
  Islamic, 157. *See also*
    Fundamentalists, Islamic
Fundamentalists, Islamic, 27, 122,
    137–138, 140–143. *See also*
    Muslim Brotherhood;
    Neofundamentalists

Greater Syria, literary renaissance in,
    88

Hadith (tradition of the prophet),
    114–115
  exegesis, 97, 104–105
  learning of sacral knowledge from,
    114
  science, 140

as a source of Islamic law, 58
tradition, 64
writing, 12
Hashemites, 163, 171
Hellenization
of Islam, 39, 68, 76, 86, 104–105
Heresy, 69, 117, 187
Hermeneutics, juristic, 63, 70, 74.
    See also in Name Index
    Gadamer, Hans Georg

Identity
and authenticity, 191
in elites, 52–53
preservation of, 130
Ideology, 5, 10, 17, 128
critic of, 1
Islam as an, 137, 142
political, 2, 123
secular, 123, 126, 128, 139
Ikhtiyar (choice of Muhammed's
    successor), 162
Ikhwan, 171–172
Imam
principle, 18
of Sunni religion, 137
Imamate, tradition, 131–132
Indonesia, Islam in, 122, 187
Innovation
cultural, 45–55
from Europe, 108
of Islam, 145
of the *shari'a,* 60
Institution, 154
of education and learning, 102–
    112
Institutionalization
of the political system, 166–168
of social change, 167–168
theory of, 152
See also in Name Index
    Huntington, Samuel P.
Iran, 4, 147–159, 161
hostages affair in, 61–62
Islam in, 17
Khomeini in, 46
mullah revolution in, 147–159

ulema in, 147–151
Iraq
political system, 166
Shi'ites in, 19
Islam
in Africa, 22, 24–26, 183
as anticolonialism, 125
and Arabic, 82–83
cultural accommodation to change
    in, 4–5, 7–14
and development, 34–44
in Egypt, 135–146
hellenization of, 68, 77, 86, 104–
    105, 107
in international society, 186–187
in Iran, 147–159
and law, 59–75
learning and education in, 102–
    112
legitimation for "royal authority"
    by, 160–164
Maliki (Africa), 25
meaning of, 16–31
as mobilizing ideology, 155–157
as model for reality, 32–44
in Morocco and Saudi Arabia,
    168–173
as political culture and simple
    social system, 164–168
politicization of, 119–123, 144–145
popular form of, 22, 26
Shari'a, 23, 26
Shi'a, 17–19, 22, 120–121, 131–132,
    136, 139, 147–151, 155
Sufi, 23–24, 64
Sunni, 18–19, 120–121, 131–132,
    135–137, 139, 161

Judaism, and Islam, 27, 35

Kalam (Islamic theology), 27, 40, 64
Koran, 9, 64, 71, 74, 96, 114–116,
    124, 130, 164
acceptance of, 35
exegesis of, 37–39, 97, 104
language of, 16–17, 81–82, 85–89

and learning, 103–107, 114
on management, 21
on the position of Muhammed, 27
rituals in, 58
text of, 12, 27, 35, 85

Language
Arabic, 16–17, 26, 40, 57–58, 63,
66, 69, 76–80, 82–83, 87–88, 90,
94–97
causal relationship of thought and
culture to, 78–79, 85–86
and change, 76–78, 81–86
and culture, 78, 92
and Islamic cultural system, 119
as lexicon and syntax, 77
modernization of, 97
scientific and scholarly form of,
26–27
Law
awareness of, 59
European, 59, 61–62
and Islamic cultural system, 39–
44, 65–66, 71, 119
Islamic language of, 66
notion of, 59–63
sacred, 60
as a social regulative, 39–44
tradition, 68
See also Fiqh
Legitimacy, 137, 144, 160–164
crisis, 126, 131, 171
and illegitimacy of rule, 162
Legitimation, 2, 148
oppositional groups using Islam
as, 160
Legitimators, 144

Madrasa (Mosque as place of
education), 103–104, 107, 112–
113
Makhzan (state in Morocco), 170–
171, 176
Maktab (Koranic school), 103
Malaysia
call to unified Islamic *umma* in,
134

Islam in, 17
minority conflicts in, 144
Meaning, 121
production of, 10, 13–14
See also in Name Index Geertz,
Clifford
Messianic movements. *See* Salvation
movements
Models
for reality, 32–34
"for/of something," 8, 11
Modernism, 21
and archaic fundamentalism, 22
and Islam, 21–22, 50, 87
total, 195
Modernity, 48
and identity/authenticity, 191–192
as a West European phenomenon,
52
Modernization, 180–182, 189–190
of elites, 52–53
forcible, 156
of Islamic law, 70
process of, 88, 91, 94, 99, 164
Shah's experiment in Iran of, 151–
154, 156, 190
theory, 13, 47, 189
Monarchy, 5
Islamically legitimated form, 160–
164
Morocco, 5, 19, 47, 51, 121, 160–164
Islam in, 17, 122–123, 187
John Waterbury on, 65
political culture in, 170–171
Mosque, 103, 136–137
number of (in Egypt), 137
occupation (Mecca, 1979), 129
as place of political activities,
137–138
Mullah Revolution, 147–151
Muslim Brotherhood (Egypt), 22,
139–140
Mysticism, Islamic, 23

Nationalism, 1, 123
Arabian, 88, 94–95
pan-Arab, 89, 95

secular, 125
Neofundamentalists, 127, 131–132, 142. *See also* Fundamentalism
Norms
  social and cultural, 46, 53
  systems of, 46
North-South
  conflict, 127
  gap, 127–128, 158, 182, 184, 195

Opposition, Islam as ideology of, 128
Orientalism, critics of, 15
Ottomans, 19–20, 88, 162

Pahlavi dynasty (Iran), 151
Philosophy
  concept of science in lay Arab form of, 100
  Islamic, 84
Politicization, 4
  of the cultural system, 119–123
  of Islam, 119–121, 135, 144, 147
  of religiocultural symbols, 119, 155–157
Profanation (*Entzauberung*), of the concept of secularization, 195. *See also in Name Index* Bell, Daniel, on restriction of secularization concept; Weber, Max

Qajarites, 151
Question formulation (macrosociological), 48
Qum (university), 5, 148

Rationalism, Arabic Islamic, 26–27, 107
Reception. *See* Change, accommodation of
Reformation, 9, 50
Religion(s), 7–15, 17, 137
  functional differentiation of the system of, 193–194
  Geertz's anthropology of, 1, 4–5

meaning producing symbols of, 10
  monotheistic, 51–52
  relationship to development and social change, 43–44, 180
  Shi'a Islam, 22
  sociology of, 15, 193
  system of, 4–5, 33, 41, 57, 66, 122
  and traditionality, 51
Repoliticization, 4, 7
  of Islam, 121, 124, 140, 186–187
  of the sacred, 123, 126, 147, 180–183, 186
Revitalization, 88
  of Islam, 125, 130–131, 134, 147
  religious movements of, 50
Revivalism
  Islamic, 21, 55, 119–121, 132, 147–154
  utopia of retro-oriented political, 131–134
Rule, 5, 121
  and Islam, 148, 160–177
  legal (Max Weber), 167
  legitimacy and illegitimacy of, 162
  of minority parasitic social strata, 131
  religiously legitimized, 148–149
  traditional form of, 173

Safavids, 148, 160
Salaf, 100
Salafism, retro-oriented ideology of, 100, 163
Salafiyya, as definition of development, 39, 120
Salvation movements, 188
Saudi Arabia, 4–5, 51, 121, 160–177
  and Islam, 17
  Islamically legitimated monarchy in, 155
  Saudi dynasty in, 171–172
Senegal, 16, 134
Shari'a (divine law), 23–27, 36, 58–60, 63, 65–66, 68–71, 113, 121, 132, 166–168, 174
  and charging of interest in, 65
  development of, 39–42

as a form of worship and religious
legal system, 64–68
jurists of, 73
principles of, 66
Shi'a, 18, 22, 143, 147–151
Shi'ites, 19, 120–121
clergy, 147–151
difference from Sunnis, 147
in Lebanon and Iraq, 19
Shura (consultation), 162
as Islamic principle, 163
structures of global dominance in,
180–181
Sufi
Islam, 23, 64
tradition, 24
Sunna, 18, 22, 35, 37, 39, 120–121,
143, 164
difference from Shi'a, 147
Symbol, 3, 10–15
cultural, 3, 126
and dimensions of social behavior,
54–55
politicization, 119
religiocultural, 10–13, 54
sociocultural, 8
and systems, 8–13, 32–33, 119–120
System, 1–2, 119, 131
cultural, 1–5, 8–15, 43, 57–58,
119–121, 179–183
institutionalized political, 166–167
Islamic, 4, 131–132, 141, 143–144,
167
of law, 105
religious symbolic, 13, 57
social, 57–58, 75, 164–166, 183

Tariqa, 23
as a form of Islam, 26

Theology
hellenized, 105
Islamic, 9, 38, 84
and science in Europe, 100
Topics, 63, 68–69, 72
as a form of thought, 71, 73–75
Tradition, 51, 55, 61
Traditionality, 48–49, 51, 184

Ulema, 26, 40–41, 64, 71, 97, 108,
135–137, 139, 144–146, 155, 163,
166–170, 172–173
alliance with *bazaari,* 149, 158
in Iran, 147–150
Umayyads, 18, 37, 147–148, 162
Umma, 1–2, 11, 32–33, 40, 67, 118,
126, 133–134, 159, 180
arabiyya, 2, 80
islamiyya, 2
symbol of, 14
Underdevelopment, 46–47, 51–52
as cultural traditionality, 45–55
feature, 127
overcoming, 46, 54, 191, 194
perception, 183–184
structures, 62
Universalism, Islamic, 1
University, 103, 112
European notion, 107–112
outside Europe, 109–112

Wahhabism, 172
movement of, 20
World
concept of, 1–2, 27, 57
culture, 2, 117, 180–186
as international society, 2, 12–13,
52, 61, 109–110, 125, 163, 179,
182, 184–187
Islam as civilization of, 37
Muslim view of, 3, 27